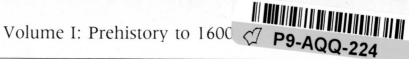

Reflections on Western Civilization: A Reader

Ronald H. Fritze
Lamar University

■

James S. Olson
Sam Houston State University

■

Randy Roberts
Purdue University

HarperCollins*Publishers*

Sponsoring Editor: Bruce Borland
Development Editor: Brown Editorial Service
Project Coordination, Text and Cover Design: Brown Editorial Service
Photo Research: Sandy Schneider
Production: Michael Weinstein
Compositor: Pam Frye Typesetting, Inc.
Printer and Binder: R. R. Donnelley & Sons Company
Cover Printer: The Lehigh Press, Inc.

Reflections on Western Civilization: A Reader
Copyright © 1991 by HarperCollins Publishers Inc.

Library of Congress Cataloging-in-Publication Data
Fritze, Ronald H., 1951–
    Reflections on Western civilization: a reader / Ronald H. Fritze,
James S. Olson, Randy Roberts.
        p.   cm.
    Includes bibliographical references.
    Contents: v. 1. Prehistory to 1600 — v. 2. 1600 to the present.
    ISBN 0–673–38403–9 (v. 1). — ISBN 0–673–38404–7 (v. 2)
    1. Civilization, Occidental—History.   I. Olson, James Stuart,
1946.   II. Roberts, Randy, 1951–   .   III. Title.
CB245.F75   1991
909'.09821—dc20   90-5162
                                                          CIP

90 91 92 93 9 8 7 6 5 4 3 2 1

Contents

BOOK

HISTORY TODAY

HORIZON

HT

BK

Preface

College students frequently complain that history is boring. Their instructors, in turn, are saddened and mystified when they hear such talk. A history teacher might feel, to borrow from Samuel Johnson, that the person bored by history must be bored by life. History is concerned with the lives of human beings and how human life has changed or remained the same over the course of time.

All human beings and all places on earth come within the scope of history in its infinite variety. Practical considerations, however, of the limited amount of time available for instruction and study in history in any college curriculum limit what can be taught and what can be included in any introductory textbook. Many fascinating and important subjects are glossed over or ignored by textbooks struggling to cover the basic events in the history of Western civilization. The purpose of this reader is to cover some of those topics that survey textbooks are often forced to neglect or ignore.

People are the focus of this reader—how they worked, how they played, how they lived, what they thought, what they ate, the good and the bad they did. We present this material through a mixture of excerpts from books, articles, and primary sources. In this way, students are introduced both to some interesting secondary scholarship and to some original documents. They can learn about the nature and types of historical writing along with the history itself.

In selecting the books, articles, and documents appearing in this work, we have tried to create a balance between popular culture and elite culture. Women are the focus of some articles; men are the focus of others. Many selections are general, encompassing both men and women and elite and popular cultures. Sometimes the focus of a piece is on social history; in other cases it is intellectual, religious, military, or a combination. But at all times, human beings remain at the center of the presentation.

We have selected these excerpts and documents for their immediate ability to interest students. From these selections, students can gain insights into the course of human existence. What was it like to grow old in Classical Greece? What were the nomadic invaders of late antiquity really like? Why did modern manners and etiquette develop? How did people deal with terminal diseases before the rise of modern medicine? What were the place of drinking and sports in the working class culture of the industrial revolution? How has the nature of warfare changed from the ancient Greeks to the Vietnam conflict?

The two volumes of *Reflections on Western Civilization* are divided into standard chronological and topical sections. At the beginning of each part, a brief introduction discusses the major themes of the period or topic. Each individual reading also begins with a short discussion placing that topic in its historical context. The purpose of these introductions is to provide students with some guidance on how to understand what is sometimes complex and unfamiliar material. Therefore, the introductions to documents are sometimes more in the form of short articles rather than brief introductory statements. Every selection concludes with some study questions and a bibliographic essay. The study questions are to assist students in comprehending the reading, whereas the bibliographic essays supply the authors and titles of additional publications for those who wish to pursue a topic further.

We would like to thank our reviewers, who read the manuscript carefully and provided many invaluable suggestions: Carol Bresnahan Manning, University of Toledo; Laura Gellott, University of Wisconsin—Parkside; Marion W. Gray, Kansas State University; and Philip B. Crow, North Harris County College.

And we especially thank Lynn Brown and Pat Schorr for all the attention and effort they devoted to this project.

Ron Fritze
James S. Olson
Randy Roberts

Reflections on Western Civilization: A Reader

Part One

ANCIENT BEGINNINGS

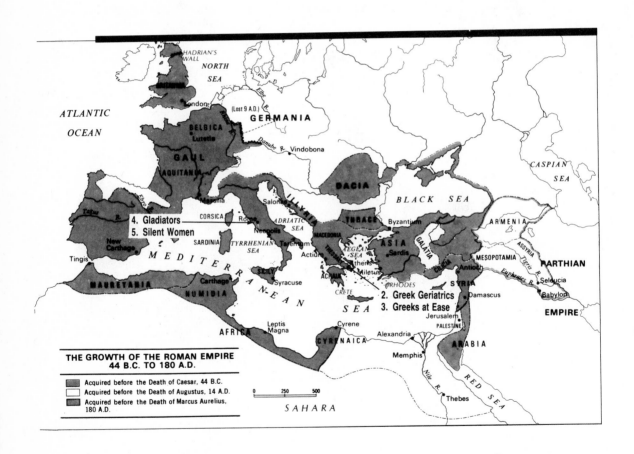

THE GROWTH OF THE ROMAN EMPIRE
44 B.C. TO 180 A.D.

Acquired before the Death of Caesar, 44 B.C.
Acquired before the Death of Augustus, 14 A.D.
Acquired before the Death of Marcus Aurelius, 180 A.D.

The search for human origins has become one of the most intense of any scientific endeavor. Legions of archaeologists in the field uncover the remains of long ago animal and human societies or classify and analyze them in university laboratories. Molecular anthropologists and geneticists hover over electron microscopes and computer printouts trying to link one generation to another through chromosomal evidence. Scholarly journals, the popular press, *National Geographic*, and public television regularly inform us about the latest discoveries. The debate over evolution—at least among some religious groups and their patrons in public school districts—still elicits visceral feelings and affects textbook and curriculum decisions. The question of where human beings came from remains a matter of great concern to most people.

The beginning of humanity is shrouded in the prehistoric past, although most scholars today look to Africa for the first men and women. Evolution was a "hit-and-miss" process until perhaps 50,000 years ago, when Cro-Magnon people appeared and spread around the world. Modern society emerged from those Cro-Magnon settlements, which James S. Olson explores in his reading. What we call *civilization*—communities characterized by complex social structures, agriculture, and a sense of time and the future—appeared in the Middle East and Egypt, India, China, and the Americas 8,000 to 15,000 years ago. But what we call *Western civilization* first appeared perhaps 2,500 years ago in the eastern Mediterranean. Greece, Judea, and Rome gave birth to the cultural values that became Western civilization.

The Greeks' legacy to the modern world revolved around their notions of skepticism, democracy, and individualism. An ancient Greek proverb states that "Wonder is the mother of thought," and Xenophon wrote that "Education is questioning." All of the Greek philosophers—including Socrates, Plato, and Aristotle—questioned the nature of reality, arguing that human perception might be flawed, that things were not always what they appear to be, that there were differences between the real and the ideal, and that the discovery of the true nature of the universe was an obligation of civilized people.

The Greeks were not troubled by doubt, uncertainty, and intellectual debate; they believed that truth would ultimately emerge from speculative dialogue. Greek historians like Herodotus and Thucydides applied that skepticism to the past, arguing and debating about how and why events had occurred. When the citizens of Athens developed their democratic notions, in which all political decisions were made by majority vote at mass meetings, Western civilization created a political philosophy that is still at the heart of political debate in the 1990s. Greek culture also created a cult of the individual that reflected itself in the artistic glorification of the human form. In this culture medical science was advanced even to studies of aging, as Robert Garland's article notes.

If Greek civilization bequeathed the ideas of skepticism, democracy, and individualism to the modern world, it was the religion of Judea that eventually became the tradition of Western society. The Jewish pilgrims following Moses out of the Sinai and into the promised land brought their god—Jehovah—with them and the commandment that "Thou shalt have no other gods before me." In a world of polytheism and animism, of tribal deities unique to individual ethnic groups, the Jews insisted that there was only one god, that their god *was* God. Jesus gave that same idea to Christians, and the Prophet Mohammed gave it to Moslems, and those two groups then spread the message of one god to much of the rest of the world.

It was the Roman empire that eventually carried Greek philosophy and Judean religion beyond their original borders to a wider world. The Romans were more of a political than a cultural group. By subjecting the regions conquered by the imperial army to Roman law but also giving them Roman privileges, Rome built an empire that extended from the Caspian Sea and the Persian Gulf in the east to the Atlantic Ocean in the west, and from Britannia in the north to the southern shores of the Mediterranean. However, more than philosophy and religion were carried on the tide of the Romans' conquests; their forms of relaxation, including gladiatorial contests and sporting events, dominated the leisure time of the people. Gilbert Highet and Keith Hopkins describe these contests in detail.

Although the Graeco-Roman cultures helped found democracy, women were nonetheless second-class citizens at best. Eva Cantarella explores the subjugation of women in Roman society.

Although the Roman Empire eventually disintegrated, the values and institutions it exported to the rest of Europe became the cultural foundations of Western civilization.

1. FROM THE TWENTY-FIRST CENTURY TO THE GARDEN OF EDEN: THE SEARCH FOR HUMAN ORIGINS

James S. Olson

When Charles Darwin wrote his book *The Origin of Species* in 1859, he made an extraordinary contribution to biological science but also sparked a cultural and religious debate that still rages in many parts of the world. Moslems condemn Darwin's ideas as direct contradictions of the Holy Koran, a blasphemy against Allah. Many Orthodox Jews feel the same, as do fundamentalist Protestants in the United States, Europe, and South Africa. The idea of apes being their direct ancestors remains repugnant to large numbers of churchgoers. But in the scientific community the theory of evolution has become the central theoretical premise of modern biology, as secure in its intellectual hegemony as the law of gravity is to physics and molecular bonding is to chemistry. Biologists may debate the pace, timing, stages, and results of evolution, but they do not debate whether it occurs. All life on the planet was, and is, subject to processes of change and adaptation or change and extinction. In this reading, James S. Olson surveys the history of the search for the beginnings of the human race.

Genesis, Chapter 2

1. Thus the heavens and the earth were finished, and all the host of them.
2. And on the seventh day God ended his work which he had made; and he rested on the seventh day from all his work which he had made. . . .
6. But there went up a mist from the earth, and watered the whole face of the ground.
7. And the Lord God formed man of the dust of the ground, and breathed into his nostrils the breath of life; and man became a living soul.
8. And the Lord planted a garden eastward in Eden; and there he put the man whom he had created. . . .
18. And the Lord God said, It is not good that the man should be alone; I will make him a help meet for him. . . .
21. And the Lord God caused a deep sleep to fall upon Adam, and he slept; and he took one of his ribs, and closed up the flesh instead thereof;
22. And the rib, which the Lord God had taken from man, made he a woman, and brought her unto the man.
23. And Adam said, This is now bone of my bones, and flesh of my flesh: she shall be called Woman, because she was taken out of Man.

■■■

For nearly two thousand years the Biblical account of the creation satisfied most people in the western world. God created the earth in six days and on the seventh day he rested. He formed Adam out of the dust of the ground, breathed life into him, and then shaped Eve from Adam's rib. Placed in the luxurious Garden of Eden, they eventually surrendered their birthright by partaking of the forbidden fruit

at the seductive suggestion of Satan. As punishment, God expelled them from the Garden of Eden. Barred forever from the garden, Adam and Eve went forth into the world, where they were commanded to "multiply and replenish the earth." Soon after, Adam "knew" Eve and she gave birth to Cain, her first child. From that original family descended the human race.

Darwin's Impact

Although geologists had already questioned the Biblical concept of time and German historians had raised doubts about the Bible's reliability, Charles Darwin's book *The Origin of Species* in 1859 launched the modern controversy over evolution. After studying plant and animal life around the world, but particularly in the Galapagos Islands, Darwin decided that the creation had consumed millions of years, not seven days, and that all life on earth had evolved from a common beginning according to the theory of natural selection. Organisms capable of adapting to environmental change survived; those that could not adapt became extinct. Human beings happened to be the most complex of those organisms, but they were organisms nonetheless, with a natural history rooted somewhere in the primate family of apes, baboons, chimpanzees, gibbons, and orangutans. Adam and Eve had not appeared from nothing by an act of God; they too evolved according to the natural selection. Darwin's "survival of the fittest" theory did not deny the hand of God in the creative act; it simply ignored Him.

Ever since the publication of *The Origin of Species,* biologists have labored to figure out the jigsaw puzzle of life. It was obvious to even the most casual observers that human behavior resembled the individual habits and social life of other primates. When the first European explorers went into the interior of Africa and encountered the great apes and chimpanzees, they noticed physical and social similarities with themselves, even speculating that black Africans had evolved from the apes. Beyond idle speculation and racist notions, scientists drew no firm connections between the various primate species until the late nineteenth and twentieth centuries.

Although religious leaders roundly condemned Darwin, biologists and geologists saw his theory as a meaningful explanation for the diversity and interdependence of beings in the natural world. Anthropologists began a search for the "missing link," an animal caught in the evolutionary line somewhere between men and monkeys. Rumors of large, half-man, half-ape creatures have circulated for years, holding out some faint hope of a living "missing link," but the consistent lack of physical confirmation has relegated those claims to "Ripley's Believe It or Not" columns and the headlines of *The Enquirer.* "Big Foot," "Sasquatch," or "Yeti" may be out there in the Himalayas or the Pacific Northwest of the United States, but the only sightings of any consequence were in Steven Spielberg's 1987 film, *Harry and the Hendersons.*

Lacking a living, breathing "missing link," scientists turned to the prehistoric world buried in geologic formations. Skeletons and skulls were the only data available in the search for human origins. For thousands of years, in the process of moving or digging or farming, people have accidentally come upon animal and human skulls. Surely they speculated about where those bones had come from, but until Charles Darwin suggested that human beings evolved from lower species, nobody was really inclined to even wonder how old the skulls were, what type of animal they actually represented, or how they came to rest at a particular location. The idea of comparing the skulls of various creatures, especially those skulls coming from older geological structures, developed in the wake of *The Origin of Species.* Locating skeletons and skulls that were neither monkey nor human became the obsession of modern anthropologists.

Viewing the Evidence

When researchers viewed skulls it was easy to differentiate between the skull of a lemur, a chimpanzee, a mountain gorilla, and a human being. But in the late nineteenth and twentieth centuries, anthropologists began digging up skulls that were very old and very different from the skulls of any living primates. Eventually, scientists focused on several physiological characteristics of skulls and bones to distinguish between those that were from humans or near-humans and those from lower primates. In a skull they examine the foramen magnum—the hole in the bottom of the skull through which the spinal cord passes into the brain. Scientists are intrigued with whether the angle of entry is upright. If the hole is upright, it indicates that the creature walked standing up on two legs, rather than hunched over on all fours. If the angle of entry is not upright, then the head of the animal had hung forward from the spine, more like a monkey or great ape than a human. Walking upright is a critical ability of a human-like creature, because it indicates that use of the hands had become more important in the life of the animal than the feet. Walking frees the hands for making tools.

Next, the anthropologists examine the teeth. The presence of large canine teeth instead of small, square teeth indicates that the animal was a hunter, the teeth used to tear tough, raw flesh rather than preparing it before consumption. The mouth, not the hands, is the primary tool in securing a hunter's food. On the other hand, smaller canines and an abundance of short, square teeth reveals that the animal is a forager rather than a hunter. In the evolutionary process the canine teeth became less important as the animal learned how to soften food through cooking. Hands and tools had become more critical than the mouth, at least in terms of securing and preparing food. Pitted marks on the teeth also revealed whether the animal had consumed plants. Animals who pulled plants out of the ground and ate them often had pits and marks made on their teeth by the grit and sand on the roots and leaves.

Anthropologists also look at the size of and shape of the cranium, trying to deduce the structure of the animal's brain. Paleontologists know that dinosaurs were probably dim-witted creatures, with body weights in the hundreds of tons and brains the size of wal-nuts. In primates scientists are convinced that the larger the cranium compared with the weight of the body, the more intelligent the an-imal. Skulls with large cranial capacities prob-ably come from animals who were close to modern human beings. If humans actually evolved from lower species, there should be a fossil record of progressively larger cranial capacities over time, with cranial sizes getting gradually larger, approaching the human brain, which is approximately 1,350 milliliters.

The shape of the skull is also important. A sloping forehead, like those of apes and mon-keys, probably indicates an underdeveloped frontal lobe, at least when compared with the perpendicular forehead of human beings. Creatures with large frontal lobes were prob-ably capable of abstract, analytical thought rather than simple, instinctive reactions, mak-ing them more like modern humans. Scientists could also tell from the shape of the skull whether the animal's brain possessed what is known as "Broca's region," the area respon-sible for speech. In order to speak, however, the animal must also have a larynx, which is located close to the throat. That requires a skull base that is bent. Modern humans are the only species with such a larynx. The animal who left behind a skull with a flexed base and a high forehead probably possessed the capac-ity for speech.

Anthropologists also look at the relationship between the nose and the eyes of skulls they discover. A prominent nose sitting on the end of a bony snout indicates that the animal selected food primarily using its sense of smell rather than vision. The location of the eyes in-dicates the degree of depth perception and stereoscopic vision. Eyes set to the sides of the skull indicate a lack of depth perception, whereas eyes set close together in the front of the skull provide for it.

In summary, twentieth-century anthropol-ogists searching for the "missing link" are af-ter the skulls of creatures that walked upright supporting heads with extensive cranial capac-ity, prominent frontal lobes, small teeth, a weak sense of smell, a strong sense of vision, and a rudimentary ability to speak.

When they locate bones, anthropologists carefully examine markings and indentations, especially on thigh and pelvic bones. All bones are attached to muscles. In human beings the muscle attachments on the large bones of the leg and pelvis permit bipedal movement, walking upright on both legs, whereas the other primates have muscle attachments for walking on all fours. In fossil bones scientists can locate where the muscles were once at-tached and then conclude whether the animal moved about on two legs or four.

Finally, the paleoanthropologists are in-terested in what else they find amidst bones. Are there hand tools scattered among the bones? Are the tools simply objects they have picked up in the natural environment, or did the animals collect raw materials and then reshape them? How skillful were the creatures in manipulating their environment? Are there charcoal deposits in the ancient campsites, showing that they were familiar with fire? What about their dead? Are there any burial grounds or skeletons adorned with ceremonial objects? Did they bury their dead? Did they bury artifacts with the body? If so they prob-ably believed in a life after death and had an embryonic religious faith. What other animal bones are present at the campsite? What did these people eat? How long did they live?

Early Discoveries

In the nineteenth century scientists could dis-tinguish between the fossil remains of other primates and human beings, but they could

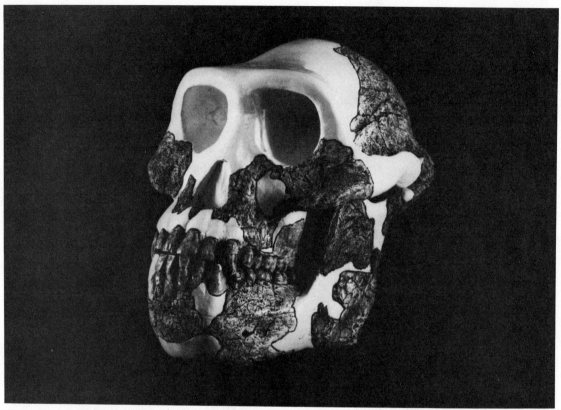

■■ *Anthropologists and archaeologists have been slowly piecing together the course of human evolution from scattered remains. This afarensis skull was reconstructed in 1979 from the remains of several individuals.*

not do much with obviously ancient skulls falling somewhere in between the two groups. Limestone miners in the Neander Valley near Dusseldorf, Germany, found a skull in 1856 that did not resemble a modern human. Eventually, university scientists carefully examined it. The skull caught them off guard. It was certainly not a human, at least not in the sense that they were human.

It was not a monkey either. The bones of the "Neanderthal" skull were thick and heavy, the brow pronounced, the forehead sloping somewhat to the back. Its cranial capacity was too large. At 1,400 milliliters, it was even a bit larger than those of modern human beings. Scientists argued about the skull's origins, claiming it was either an individual with a birth defect, some long-forgotten animal that

had come off Noah's ark, or a stupid Russian soldier from the Napoleonic campaigns. Fifty-two years later, near La Chapelle-aux-Saints in southwestern France, a nearly complete skeleton of a similar animals was uncovered. The creature was obviously more human than ape, used tools, walked upright, cooked its food, and buried its dead with ceremonial artifacts. At the time most anthropologists could not make much of the animal, but later experts called it "Neanderthal Man," a human ancestor that had lived approximately 100,000 to 50,000 years ago.

In 1868 railroad workers laying track in southwestern France uncovered several human skeletons and a variety of tools, plus the bones of reindeer, bison, and mammoths. The human skulls had high foreheads, small browridges, and large brain capacity—1,350 milliliters. These were certainly human skulls, but the presence of the extinct mammoth' bones proved the skeleton was very old. As hunters, the animals had manipulated fire and made a wide variety of tools. To survive in the cold northern climates, the animals made clothing from animal skins. The caves in which they lived often had paintings on the walls—the earliest known human art. The wall paintings at Altamira in Spain are still admired for their elegance and sensitivity. Dubbed "Cro-Magnon Man," these creatures were human, direct ancestors of modern people, who lived in Europe, Africa, and Asia around 25,000 years ago.

Neanderthal Man and Cro-Magnon Man were the first of many fossil finds. In 1891 Eugene Dubois, a French anthropologist obsessed with finding the missing link, headed off to Java in the Dutch East Indies. Dubois hired fifty convict laborers, who must have thought he was crazy, and set them to work examining and digging up the ground near the Solo River. After several years they discovered the remains of a prehistoric human-like creature. Dubois publicized his find and anthropologists dubbed the creature "Java Man," an animal that walked upright, fashioned its own tools (especially a variety of hand axes), and made use of fire. Although the skull had a heavy brow and a sloping forehead, its brain size was 1,000 milliliters. Dubois called the remains *Pithecanthropus erectus*—the "upright ape-man." Eventually this specimen's species became known as *Homo erectus*.

For a generation scientists considered Java Man the missing link, until in 1929 a similar skull was uncovered in a limestone cave near Beijing, China. The skull found its way to the Peking Union Medical College, where Davidson Black, a Canadian physician, worked. He carefully examined it and brought in trained anthropologists to look at it. They named the skull *Sinanthropus pekinensis*, popularly known as "Peking Man." Peking Man was remarkably like Java Man, and when radiometric dat-

ing techniques became available after World War II, both creatures were identified as existing up to 1.6 million years ago. They had scattered widely throughout Asia and had become the dominant hominid species of their time.

Modern Paleoanthropology

But even while Java Man and Peking Man were coming to the forefront, new discoveries were already changing the consensus. That became the premier problem in the search for the first human being. What one anthropologist claimed lasted only until the next anthropologist found an older fossil. South African workers digging out a lime quarry near Tuang in 1924 came across a small fossil skull. They delivered the bones to Professor Raymond Dart just before he was to head off to be the best man at a friend's wedding. It was all Dart could do to keep the appointment. He fondled the bones like a child opening Christmas gifts until his wife insisted they leave. Dart fumbled his way through the wedding ceremony, irritating the bride and groom with his distracted clumsiness. All Dart could think about was that little skull. Within an hour of returning home Dart was convinced the skull was "one of the most important finds in the history of anthropology," a human-life creature much older than either Java Man or Peking Man. Dart named the creature *Australopithecus africanus*.

Subsequent research proved him correct. Subsequently developed dating techniques confirmed that *Australopithecus africanus* had wandered southern Africa more than 2.5 million years ago. Baboon skulls had been found again and again at the Tuang site, but Dart knew this was no baboon. The animal had died as a child. The skull was small, perhaps 440 milliliters, and the forehead low, but the canine teeth were also small and the foramen magnum's angle such that the Tuang child had walked upright. For Professor Dart, *Australopithecus africanus* was a *hominid* (of the family of humans), not an ape, monkey, or baboon.

Dart's "Tuang child" accelerated the search for human-like fossils. In 1938 Robert Barlow, another South African paleoanthropologist, purchased a fossil jawbone from the foreman of a limestone quarry in Sterkfontein. When Barlow found out that the quarryman had borrowed the bone from a schoolboy, he immediately searched out the boy. The child was shy and reticent, suspicious of Barlow, but after receiving a few reassurances, the boy pulled a piece of bone out of his pocket that took Barlow's breath away. Later in his life Barlow could still remember his hands trembling and his heart pounding when he saw the fossil—two small teeth in a jawbone. The boy showed Barlow where he found the fossils. Barlow called the animal *Paranthropus robustus.*

Anthropologists eventually settled on the name *Australopithecus robustus.* With a brain capacity of 525 milliliters, this creature had a greater intellectual capacity than *Austropithecus africanus,* even though this species lacked a forehead, possessed a heavy lower jaw, and small teeth. *Robustus* walked upright and used bone tools, lived around 1.5 to 2 million years ago, and was much farther along the evolutionary trek toward human beings than its *Africanus* predecessor.

But *A. robustus* was not alone in the world. A contemporary, a different hominid, also walked the earth. Louis Leakey brought the other creature to light. Leakey, the son of British missionaries in Africa, went to northern Tanzania in 1931 to hunt for fossils. Leakey and his wife Mary worked in the dust of Olduvai Gorge for twenty-eight years. One day in 1959, while Louis was in their tent recuperating from a high fever, Mary was walking slowly down a dry creek bed that fed the gorge. Carefully examining the ground with each step, she noticed two teeth exposed along with another piece of bone. In the next few days the Leakeys found more than 400 other bone fragments, enough to reconstruct the skull of an animal they called *Zinjanthropus*—

"East African Man." Physicists dated the skull, concluding that *Zinjanthropus* died in the Olduvai Gorge about 1.8 million years ago. Anthropologists settled on the name of *Australopithecus boisei.* Its brain capacity was 530 milliliters, and it made use of primitive tools, but it was a different creature from *robustus.* Exactly 100 years after the publication of *The Origin of Species,* the Leakeys found human-like creatures who lived in East Africa nearly two million years ago.

New discoveries soon proved that *robustus* and *boisei* were not alone. In 1968 Richard Leakey, the son of Louis and Mary, discovered the bones of a 1.8-million-year-old creature near Lake Turkana in Kenya. Although a contemporary of *robustus* and *boisei, Homo habilus,* or "Handy Man," had a much larger brain, at 680 milliliters, and a small frontal lobe and the Broca's region, indicating a primitive speaking ability. Handy Man walked upright. Members of this species also maintained a large collection of diverse tools, perhaps because they had developed a sense of place and a more complex group social structure. *Robustus* and *boisei* lived at the same time as *H. habilus,* but it was the Handy Man who made the leap forward toward humanity.

Then, in 1974, a new discovery pushed human origins back another million years. Donald C. Johanson, a member of an international research team in central Ethiopia, reconstructed a nearly complete skeleton of a small, female human ancestor. The team members stayed up all night drinking beer and celebrating their discovery. Because the Beatles' song "Lucy in the Sky with Diamonds" had been playing again and again on a portable record player the day of the discovery, they named the skeleton "Lucy," although her scientific designation became *Australopithecus afarensis.*

Lucy was a diminutive adult woman standing three feet six inches tall and weighing about sixty-five pounds. She had a small brain of 375 milliliters and lacked the ability to speak, and her skull had only the smallest forehead and a pronounced brow—an ape-like appearance. Lucy's ability to fashion tools was quite limited. But the shape of her pelvis and angle of the foramen magnum made it clear that she walked upright, unlike the baboons who lived nearby. Lucy had made a quantum leap beyond the world of the apes, leaving behind their knuckle-walk for the upright gait of a creature using its hands. She lived in northern Africa nearly 3.5 million years ago.

Paleoanthropology made great strides in the 1960s and 1970s. The fossil record became even more complicated with a variety of new finds. A year after Mary Leakey found bones in Olduvai Gorge, a group of shepherds stumbled upon a cave near Thessaloniki, Greece. They found bones and brought some professors to the cave to look at what they had found. Inside were the bones of "Petralona Man," or *Homo sapiens* (Archaic), a human ancestor from 500,000 years ago. Although bigbrowed, with a sloping forehead, the creature's cranial capacity exceeded 1,000 milliliters and it had a capacity for making tools that was quite sophisticated. Members of *H. sapiens* (Archaic) had scattered widely throughout Europe, Africa, and Asia.

The Evolutionary Sequence We Know Today

By the 1980s anthropologists had constructed a complicated record of human evolution. More than 3.5 million years ago, *Australopithecus afarensis* emerged in East Africa as the earliest hominid separate from the apes. *Afarensis* remained the dominant hominid for nearly a million years, disappearing and giving way to *Australopithecus africanus* about 2.7 million years ago. For another million years *africanus* played the role of human ancestor until three new creatures appeared: *Australopithecus robustus*, *Australopithecus boisei*, and *Homo habilus*. *Robustus* and *boisei* were evolutionary dead ends, but *habilus* dominated the landscape for more than a million years until Java Man and Peking

Man appeared and spread throughout Africa and Asia. Sometime between 500,000 and 100,000 years ago *Homo erectus* disappeared, only to be replaced by *Homo sapiens* (Archaic). Neanderthal Man succeeded this species about 100,000 years ago and dispersed widely until Cro-Magnon, or modern *Homo sapiens*, rose to dominance. Cro-Magnon Man evolved into modern human beings.

Outstanding scientists have spent more than a century putting together the fossil record, but for all of the work and speculation there remain many unanswered questions. Although fossil finds confirmed the existence of early human predecessors and allowed scientists to locate human origins in Africa, each new skull raises two new questions for every one it answers. Cro-Magnon, Neanderthal, Petralonal, Java Man, Peking Man, *Australopithecus africanus*, *Australopithecus afarensis*, *Zinjanthropus*—are any of these creatures the so-called missing link for which anthropologists have been searching since 1859? When and where did human beings first split off from the ape line and become people? Could paleoanthropologists precisely map the genealogy of the human race? Was there some more exact way of locating "the Garden of Eden" than sifting through ancient campsites, reconstructing skeletons from bone fragments, dating the finds with radiometric analysis, and then speculating on the life of each particular species?

Impact of Molecular Anthropology

There was no other way of finding the missing link, at least until the development of molecular biology. In 1944 scientists at Rockefeller University discovered that genes are composed of DNA—deoxyribonucleic acid, the building blocks of life on earth. Nine years later physicist Francis H. C. Crick and biochemist James D. Watson made their Nobel Prize-winning discovery of the "double helix," the molecular structure of DNA. A long, chainlike molecule composed of three billion nucleo-tides, DNA constitutes the genes inside all liv-ing cells. Those genes govern the behavior of all protein reactions in the body; each protein has a particular function in the life of an or-ganism. The genes are chemical messengers communicating from one generation to the next, telling the new organism how to grow, react, survive, reproduce, and—eventually—how to die.

In human beings the DNA in genes is lo-cated on 46 chromosomes, 23 of which come from the sperm of the father and 23 from the ovum of the mother. Every human being has a unique genetic imprint in each of its trillion cells, a kind of fingerprint different from the print of every other person. Each cell contains the same chromosomes and the same genes. Each time a cell divides, certain enzymes pass along the entire length of the DNA molecule, cutting it lengthwise in half, creating two iden-tical cells where there was one before.

With the assistance of electron microscopes, biochemists began mapping genetic structures. In 1967 two scientists at the University of California at Berkeley, Allan Wilson and Vin-cent Sarich, compared the molecular compo-sition of blood proteins in baboons, chimpanzees, apes, and humans. Some of those proteins change and evolve at predict-able rates, permitting measurements of the timing of changes to be made from differences among various species. There were enormous differences between chimpanzees and ba-boons, indicating an early evolutionary split between the two species. Less substantial differences dividing chimps from apes indi-cated a more recent division. What startled Wilson and Sarich, however, were the similar-ities between chimpanzees and human beings. Chimpanzees and human beings are 99 per-cent genetically identical. Humans and gorillas are about 97 percent identical. In fact, the chimpanzees are more closely related geneti-cally to humans than to gorillas. Scientists con-sider those genetic differences to be a

molecular clock telling ancient time. Baboons split off genetically from human about 30 mil-lion years ago, gibbons 20 million years ago, orangutans 16 million years ago, gorillas 10 million years ago, and chimpanzees perhaps 5 million years ago.

But what about the missing link? Where did that first person live and when was he or she born? Molecular biologists don't know much about Adam, but they are finding out more about Eve, not in the fossil skulls of long-dead women but in the chromosomes of living women. What all human beings share—those living today and those living anciently—is a common genetic heritage that separates them from all other animals. Sometime, somewhere, that first man and woman appeared who car-ried all the genes we now possess. They were not chimpanzees or apes, or some "Big Foot" in between, but human beings. If scientists could compare the genetic structures of Java Man and *Australopithecus afarensis* and all the others with the genes of human beings, they could tell definitively exactly how human-like those creatures were. The problem is that it is impossible to locate intact soft-tissues from pre-historic animals and extract their chromo-somes. Skeletal remains do not yield the necessary genetic information.

However, there appears to be another way, an indirect approach to genetic comparisons, a computer-driven technique for constructing a genealogy chart of the human back 10,000 generations. For 150 years biologists have known that all life is composed of cells: a thin membrane surrounding liquid cytoplasm, with a nucleus floating in the middle and chro-mosomes inside. Located all along those chro-mosomes are DNA-based genes that biochemically regulate life. Outside the nucleus but inside the cell membrane is another small structure—the mitochondrion—that serves as the energy center for the cell.

Molecular biologists learned in the 1960s that the mitochondrion was full of DNA, but in the 1970s they made another startling discovery: mitochondrial DNA is inherited only from the mother, unlike the mixture of paternal and maternal DNA located inside the nucleus. Although the DNA of the nucleus is mixed and scrambled with each generation, the mitochondrial DNA is far more stable and less likely to change, except for random mutations. The same mitochondrial DNA is handed down from mother to daughter in each generation, and has been for tens of thousands of years. Indeed, the mitochondrial DNA inside each woman on earth today is the same DNA as that of the very first woman. There was one woman whose DNA became the DNA of all women who have ever lived.

But how could biologists reach back across thousands of generations and find that first woman? Rebecca Cann of the University of Hawaii had a way. She compared the tissues of women from around the world, looking at the composition of their mitochondrial DNA. One problem she faced was getting enough tissue from each woman to be able to perform her experiments. A lot of people would give a little blood sample, but very few would be willing to donate a large chunk of their body for Professor Cann to dissect. The solution was to collect the placentas of women who had just given birth. Cann started her search in the United States, eventually extending it to the Australian bush to get some tissue samples from Aborigines. The request for placentas no doubt raised the eyebrows of more than a few prospective donors, but when the unique "scavenger hunt" was over, Cann had frozen placentas from 147 women in North America, South America, Europe, the Middle East, Africa, and Australia.

In her laboratory she took the tissue samples and after treating them chemically, she centrifuged them, which eventually separated the mitochondrial DNA from the rest of the cellular components. She then cut the DNA into pieces and began to compare them. Although the total chromosomal imprint for all human beings is overwhelmingly similar, separating people from all other animals, there are tiny,

almost infinitesimal differences among individuals. Those differences are caused by random mutations occurring over the course of tens of thousands of years. No two people are exactly alike because the chances of random mutations affecting more than one person are infinite.

By comparing the DNA mutations, Cann placed the 147 people into groups based on their genetic similarities. She postulated that mutations in the genes had occurred randomly over time at a fairly constant rate. Moving back through time, she assumed there would be fewer and fewer mutations, a closer and closer genetic relationship among ancestors, a reverse family tree. Cann found that the 147 original donors could be separated into two groups. One of the groups was exclusively African, whereas the other included all other Africans and everyone else. Among the small African group, there were a greater number of mutations and they were widely distributed, a sign that the group had existed for a long time. The second group had fewer, less widely distributed mutations, indicating more recent origins.

Cann concluded that human beings originated with the small African group, and that the other group split off at a later date. Other molecular biologists compared the DNA in blood cells among various human populations and concluded that the splinter group then divided again into Caucasoid and Mongoloid groups. Cann brought statisticians, mathematicians, and computer scientists into the picture, asking them to use her 147 people to construct a family tree, which would trace back to one woman. With her data they eliminated the most recent genetic mutations. Each elimination brought the 147 people closer together genetically, collapsing the branches of the family tree, compressing the number of ancestors into a progressively smaller and smaller group of people. Using a mathematical model based on the number of mutations at the outset and the approximate timing of each random mutation, they projected the family tree back through more than 10,000 generations, back to one woman who lived somewhere in Africa between 150,000 and 200,000 years ago. During her lifetime, no doubt, there were other hominid creatures wandering the globe. *Homo sapiens* (Archaic) were probably around, some of the *erectus* subspecies might still have lived, and perhaps a few Neanderthals had launched their struggle for survival. But they all died out, succumbing to a changing habitat or maybe even disappearing through interbreeding into modern *Homo sapiens*. Whatever the reason, all they left behind were the bones and skulls that anthropologists began pulling out of the ground in the 1800s. But a woman survived. She walked upright. Her head had a high forehead and inconsequential brow ridges, with a cranial capacity of 1,350 milliliters. She spoke, fashioned tools, and buried her dead. Her cells carried 46 chromosomes, millions of genes, and billions of nucleotides. She gave birth to the human race. She was, in the words of Genesis 3:20, "Eve, . . . the mother of all living."

■■■

STUDY QUESTIONS

1. What is the Biblical description of the origins of human beings?

2. According to Charles Darwin, how did human beings evolve? What are the basic differences between Darwin's explanation and the Biblical description of the origins of human beings?

3. Describe the primary biological characteristics of Java Man, Peking Man, Lucy, and Neanderthal Man.

4. What are the scientific methods of traditional archaeologists and anthropologists? In what ways can they determine the biological and social characteristics of early human beings using bones and artifacts?

5. What is molecular anthropology? What techniques do molecular anthropologists use to determine the origins and evolution of human beings?

6. Have scientists yet discovered a specific "missing link" that conclusively shows the evolutionary connection between human beings and the higher primates? Is there a fossil and molecular record that demonstrates such a connection?

BIBLIOGRAPHY

For two highly readable accounts of the evolutionary history of human beings, see John J. Putman, "The Search for Modern Humans," *National Geographic*, 174 (October 1988), 438–477, and Kenneth F. Weaver, "The Search for Our Ancestors," *National Geographic*, 168 (November 1985), 560–629. Mahmoud Y. El-Najjar and K. Richard McWilliams, in *Forensic Anthropology* (1978), describe the scientific methods of archaeologists and anthropologists who deal with ancient human artifacts. Richard E. Leakey and Roger Lewin have written two excellent, highly readable accounts of recent anthropological discoveries: *Origins* (1977) and *People of the Lake: Mankind and Its Beginning* (1978). Jeffrey H. Schwartz's *The Red Ape: Orang-utans and Human Origins* (1987) argues for a close connection between those primates and people. Donald Johanson and Maitland Edey's book *Lucy: The Beginnings of Humankind* (1981) is an excellent account of recent opinion concerning human origins. Finally, Roger Lewin's *Bones of Contention. Controversies in the Search for Human Origins* (1987) surveys the current debate among scientists about human evolution.

2. "GREEK GERIATRICS"

Robert Garland

Until fairly recently, when industrialization and the rise of modern medicine combined to dramatically extend the average lifespan, there were relatively few people who lived to advanced ages. Consequently, the status of the elderly in the society was not much of a social issue. In more primitive societies, where marginal economies made it difficult to support nonproductive people, euthanasia evolved as a way of disposing of the elderly as well as the chronically sick and the retarded. But in more economically prosperous societies capable of supporting a few senior citizens, the status of the elderly and the quality of care they receive becomes a social issue of some importance. Ancient Greece was one of those societies. Older people were relatively few in number, but they exerted some influence in political life. The problems of aging—failing health, dementia, and sexuality—were debated and discussed. Some of their concerns are becoming increasingly relevant in modern society, where people over the age of sixty-five now compose the most rapidly increasing segment of the population. In this selection Robert Garland deals with the way one ancient society felt about its elderly citizens.

The status of the elderly and the care and attention that they receive from their relatives differ markedly from one human society to the next. How geriatrics are treated has implications not only for other age-groups, but also for the rigidity or progressiveness of political and social institutions.

It would be natural to suppose that in ancient Greece, where the majority of those who survived infancy did not live to be fifty, individuals who attained the age of sixty or seventy would have wielded considerable influence in the community. Although this may have been true of conservative Greek states such as Sparta, in Classical Athens, by contrast, an extreme and radical democracy the like of which has never existed since, the reverse may actually have been the case. The degree of regard accorded to old age by these same societies was not unrelated to the political systems which they individually espoused.

We do not have much evidence with which to estimate the age structure of the population of ancient Greece. Greek funerary monuments, unlike Roman ones, rarely record age at death except in the case of extreme youth and extreme longevity. Only recently have archaeologists begun to collect data from skeletal remains, and as yet no clear picture has emerged from their researches for the Classical period. In his study of Roman sepulchral inscriptions, Keith Hopkins claims that the median age of wives at death was 34 and of husbands 46.5. Very similar results have emerged from the American anthropologist Lawrence Angel's study of skeletal remains found in Greece dating to the period of Roman occupation: in this case adult longevity is estimated to have been 34.3 for women and 40.2 for men. In Greek as in Jewish belief, however, "three score years and ten" were regarded as the "natural" span of life.

The Athenian lawgiver Solon, who flourished in the early sixth century B.C., declared that this was the age "when a man could receive the apportionment of death, not dying prematurely." Though only a small minority of Greeks can have attained seventy, it is instructive to note that *total life span*, as opposed to *mean longevity*, was no different in antiquity than it is today. One of the strongest indications that only a minute fraction of the population attained the age of eighty is provided by the fact that a short treatise falsely attributed to the satirist Lucian entitled *Makrobioi* or "The Long Lived" treats *makrobios* as "octogenarian or over." The gravestone of an otherwise unknown Athenian called Littias proudly records that the deceased lived to be 100.

Average age at death in modern nonindustrial societies is reckoned at thirty-five years, and there is no reason to suppose that it would have been any higher in preindustrial societies such as Greece or Rome. But average age at death is not the same as the age at which most people die. The so-called mortality curve has peaks at birth, early childhood, and the early twenties. In ancient Greece a woman's chances of surviving to old age were greatly reduced by the fact that she was expected to begin producing children soon after puberty, which seems generally to have occurred in the fourteenth year. For adult males the greatest hazard apart from disease was, of course, warfare, which in the case of an Athenian male, rendered him liable to annual military service between the ages of eighteen and fifty-nine.

Ancient explanations of longevity conform remarkably closely to those currently in vogue. The treatise on "The Long Lived" cites climate, diet, occupation, physical fitness, and mental alertness as factors in the promotion of long life. The longevity of philosophers and men of learning was ascribed to the simple fact that they "took good care of their bodies." Three of the so-called Seven Wise Men—Solon, Thales and Pittacus—are said to have lived to 100, a circumstance which, whatever its ver-

"Greek Geriatrics" by Robert Garland, *History Today*, Vol. 37, September 1987, pp. 12–19. Reprinted by permission.

acity, implies that true wisdom was perceived to be a function of age and, conversely, that the attainment of age was a function of wisdom.

The secret of a long and healthy life was no less eagerly sought in antiquity than it is today. Gorgias, a famous rhetorician and sophist of the fifth century B.C. who came from Leontini in Sicily and who lived to the grand old age of 108, when asked about the secret of his longevity, replied that he had never accepted a dinner invitation from anyone. In mythology, the belief that a person could stave off death by supplying the gods of the underworld with a substitute-sacrifice provided the basis for Euripides' play the *Alcestis*, which treats the theme of a young wife who agrees to die in order that her husband can remain alive. The same belief is reflected in an anecdote reported by Herodotus concerning Amestris, wife of the Persian king Xerxes, who buried fourteen Persian boys of illustrious family "by way of a present [to the god of death] instead of her own life."

As today, so in antiquity certain races had a reputation for longevity. Of these the most famous were the Ethiopians, whose life expectancy is put by Herodotus at 120. They allegedly fed on a restricted diet of boiled meat and milk and bathed in fragrant spring water that was so lacking in density that even wood sank to its bottom. A more extreme regimen is reported for a people called the Seres, probably the Chinese: thanks to a diet of nothing but water, they were said to live to 300.

Greek geriatrics were no doubt active and vigorous until their final illness which, in the overwhelming majority of cases, would have been brief and relatively painless. Even in the case of the well-to-do, there is unlikely to have been the time or the economic resources necessary to pay much attention to the plight of the aged. It was a matter of pride as well as economic necessity for an elderly person to be able to demonstrate his or her usefulness to the family in however humble a capacity: in Homer's *Odyssey* Laertes, the father of Odysseus and "retired" king of Ithaca, though possessing servants to look after his farm, nonetheless continues to labour in his vineyard.

Gerontology as a specific branch of medical inquiry had no ancient equivalent. The Hippocratic corpus does nonetheless contain a scattering of observations concerning the physical condition of the elderly that evince an incipient interest in the study of the process of aging. Thus in the *Aphorisms* it is stated that old age is subject to

difficulty in breathing, catarrh accompanied by coughing, strangury [a disease of the urinary tract], difficult micturition, arthritis, nephritis, dizzy spells, apoplexy, cachexia, itching of the whole body, sleeplessness, watery discharge from bowels, eyes and nostrils, dullness of vision, glaucopia and hardness of hearing.

The most memorable portrait of old age in Greek literature is undoubtedly that of Nestor in Homer's *Iliad*, senior adviser to the Greek overlord Agamemnon in the Trojan War. Because the old man claims that he has "seen two generations pass away and is now ruling over the third," we should probably think of him as being at least in his mid-sixties or early seventies. Like many geriatrics, Nestor is garrulous, long-winded, prone to lapsing into lengthy recollections of the past, by no means averse to singing his own praises, and highly critical of the younger generation.

Despite these quirks, his portrait would have aroused both affection and respect in the Greek audience. In Book I of the *Iliad* Nestor is introduced as "a man from whose tongue flowed speech sweeter than honey," and it is wholly due to his powers of oratory that the war of words that erupts at the beginnings of the poem between Achilles and Agamemnon ends without bloodshed. Later, when Nestor offers advice to Agamemnon as how best to deploy his troops in battle, he chides the Greek chieftains for arguing "like silly little boys who have no practical experience of war." His commander, far from taking this as an insult to his

■■ *Old age was not necessarily a golden time in ancient Greece, as this statue of a drunken old woman shows.*

youth, pleasant alike for men and women. But when painful old age overtakes a man and makes him ugly outside and foul-minded within, then wretched cares eat away at his heart and no longer does he rejoice to gaze upon the sun, being hateful to children and despicable to women. Such a grievous affliction has the gods made old age.

It would, however, be unwise to conclude that Greeks of the Archaic period habitually regarded old age as a fate worse than death. Lyric poetry addressed itself first and foremost to the theme of love and love-making. The poet tended to adopt the persona of the experienced yet still vulnerable lover who is in a sense "genre-bound" to rail loudly against the ravages of time. Admetus in the *Alcestis* of Euripides surely utters a universal truth when he complainingly observes:

It is meaningless the way old men pray for death and complain of age and the long time they have to live. Let death only come close, not one of them still wants to die. Their age is not a burden any more.   [trans. R. Lattimore]

An opinion expressly claimed to represent the universal aspiration of all Greeks is found in Plato's dialogue *Hippias Major*, where it is alleged that the highest condition attainable by a human being was "to be rich, healthy, honoured by the Greeks, live to old age, and, after burying one's parents decently, to be decently laid out by one's own children and buried in magnificent style." The same sentiment occurs on an Athenian gravestone, where a deceased woman declares herself to have been "blessed" in having set eyes upon her grandchildren before passing to the world below.

For moral philosophers, the commonly perceived drawbacks of old age were in fact positive advantages since in their opinion these tended to promote virtue and reason. At the beginning of Plato's *Republic*, the elderly Cephalus, on being questioned by Socrates as to how he coped with old age, answered with an anecdote about the poet Sophocles. The latter,

own powers of leadership, pays the old man the handsome compliment of declaring that if he had ten men like Nestor to advise him, Troy would soon be captured. Though Nestor's speeches are rambling and repetitive, he performs an important function within the *Iliad* as the touchstone of commonsense—and is not merely a tedious old windbag.

In Greek poetry of the seventh and sixth centuries B.C., old age is stigmatised as a condition that arouses distaste and loathing in oneself and others. Mimnermus, who lived in Asia Minor in the second half of the sixth century, has the following bleak comments to make on the subject:

What kind of life, what kind of joy is there without golden Aphrodite? May I die when I no longer take any interest in secret love affairs, in sweet exchanges and in sex. These are the flowers of when asked by a friend whether his sexual drive had abated now that he had reached advanced years, replied, "Don't even mention the subject—I'm delighted to have escaped the thing you talk of, as if I had escaped from a savage and raging beast that was my master." The theory that the waning of the sexual appetite is compensated for by increased spirituality set the model for a philosophical "type" and greatly influenced later, Stoic thinking.

The Platonic ideal of cheerful resignation and philosophical detachment in the face of old age finds fullest expression in Cicero's dialogue *On Old Age*, the inspiration for which derives directly from Plato's portrait of Cephalus. Cicero, who puts his remarks into the mouth of the elderly Roman Cato, claims that moroseness, querulousness, and tetchiness are in fact states of mind to which persons of any age are subject and by no means confined to the elderly. Cato goes so far as to eulogise old age as the consummation of all life's travails, stating, "The nearer I get to death, the more I feel like someone eventually sighting land who is about to anchor in harbour after a long voyage"—a thoroughly non-Greek sentiment, it may be noted. However, his further assertion that death comes to the elderly with less violence and pain was a widely held belief in the ancient world, symbolised in mythology by the image of the silver arrows of Apollo that the god was believed to shoot at the elderly in order to put them painlessly asleep.

Aristotle in the *Rhetoric* (2.12.13) delivers what is surely one of the most savage and devastating assaults upon the mental condition of the elderly ever made, perhaps an intentional corrective to Plato's eulogising upon the joys and rewards of waning sexual desire:

Older men and those who have passed their prime have in most cases characters opposite to those of the young. For, owing to their having lived many years and having been more often deceived by others or made more mistakes themselves, and since most human things turn out badly, they are positive about nothing, and in everything they show an excessive lack of energy. They always "think," but "know" nothing; and in their hesitation they always add "perhaps," or "maybe"; all their statements are of this kind, never unqualified. They are malicious; for malice consists in looking upon the worse side of everything. Further, they are always suspicious owing to mistrust, and mistrustful owing to experience. And neither their love nor their hatred is strong for the same reasons; but, according to the precept of Bias [one of the Seven Wise Men of Greece], they love as if they would one day hate, and hate as if they would one day love. And they are little-minded, because they have been humbled by life; for they desire nothing great or uncommon, but only the necessaries of life. . . . They live not for the noble, but for the useful, more than they ought, because they are selfish; for the useful is a good for the individual, whereas the noble is good absolutely.
[trans. J. H. Freese]

It is the highest degree unlikely that the Greek medical profession condoned euthanasia, a coined word of Greek etymology that has no ancient equivalent. The famous Hippocratic Oath, which was no doubt widely disseminated in the ancient world, required those who took it "not to administer a poison to anybody when asked to do so and not propose such a course." In certain philosophical circles, contrastingly, it was a point of honour for the very aged to terminate their existence before entering upon their dotage. When at the age of ninety-eight Zeno, the founder of the Stoic school of philosophy, stumbled and fell upon entering the Athenian assembly, he barked back at Pluto, the god of the underworld, "I'm on my way. Why are you shouting?"—and subsequently went home and starved himself to death, evidently seeing in this trivial incident evidence of an irreversible and unacceptable physical decline. In the *Suppliants*, Euripides makes a plea for what is today technically called patho-euthanasia, the withdrawal of life support systems and drugs from the terminally ill, when he puts into the mouth of one of his characters the statement:

I can't stand people who drag out their life with food and drink and magic spells, trying to keep death out of the way.

Compulsory euthanasia is recorded by Herodotus in the case of a nomadic people called the Massegetai who lived to the east of the Caspian Sea in a region known today as Turkman. A fixed lifespan or "fair term of years" was instituted for all members of the community. When one of their number reached advanced years, all his relatives assembled and sacrificed him alongside numbers of cattle. Then they boiled his flesh and ate it. Such a death, comments Herodotus, was regarded among the tribe as the most felicitous.

In antiquity, no less than today, the tensions produced by the existence of three and sometimes even four generations living under one roof must have been quite unbearable. That is surely why Plato recommended in the *Republic* that newlyweds should not live with elderly relatives. Though Greek lexicographers refer cryptically to the existence of an institution known as a *gêroboskeion*, a word that may roughly be translated as "old people's home," it is possible that it is merely an invention of comic writers. It is most unlikely that Greek states would have provided the elderly with financial or other assistance, though in Athens for example they would have been included in the periodic distributions of corn in times of crisis.

Athenian law was somewhat ambivalent in the safeguards that it afforded to the elderly. In the first place, sons were not just morally bound to look after and maintain their parents in old age—they were legally compelled to do so as well. Those who failed in this essential duty underwent punishment and were debarred from ever holding public office. The requirement laid down by the law extended to the care and protection of grandparents and great-grandparents as well, if these happened

to be alive. The only parents not protected by it were those who had farmed their sons out as prostitutes or those who had failed to teach them a basic skill.

This legal safeguard indicates that distressing cases of neglect and mistreatment were not unheard of in ancient Athens.

In the second place, the Athenian lawcode, like its Roman counterpart, contained a provision restraining heads of families from wasting their estates if it could be proved by their heirs that they had lapsed into senility, a condition referred to as *paranoia*. The story is told that when Sophocles' sons dragged their father into court in order to declare him incapable of managing his business affairs, the old poet, who was then ninety, replied to the charge by reading out to the jury the play that he was currently working on, the *Oedipus at Colonus*, and then disingenuously innocently inquiring, "Does that play seem to be the work of an idiot?" The Athenians had no hesitation in dismissing the charge. In some cases, however, the headship of a family was voluntarily ceded to the son by the father, who thus in effect retired. In Homer's *Odyssey*, Odysseus occupies both the headship of the household and the kingship of the island, though his father Laertes is still alive.

The structure of Athenian society was such that elderly parents were extremely dependent upon their offspring. Though fathers could charge their sons with criminal neglect, the latter in turn could accuse their fathers of senility. Moreover, because fathers were legally bound to leave their entire estate to their sons, they were not in a position to exert moral blackmail by threatening to disinherit them.

Recourse to adoption was a common occurrence in Athens on the part of elderly men who had no son to take care of them. As for elderly women, widows as well as wives enjoyed a certain degree of security, because the dowry that a new bride took with her to her new home remained in the possession of that home only as long as she herself resided in it. If she was divorced, or if upon the death of her husband there was a move to eject her, a not un-usual occurrence in the case of a woman who had produced no male offspring, then the dowry had to be returned.

The elderly poor, the men who had no for-tune to bequeath and the women who had no dowries to reclaim, were immeasurably worse off. For men a source of income was jury ser-vice, which paid enough at least to enable them to purchase the bare necessities of life. However, this occupation was not reserved for the elderly but available to any Athenian male over the age of thirty. Even more distressing must have been the condition of old women who had no families to support them. Solon humanely enacted that women above the age of sixty were permitted to act as mourners at the funerals of those to whom they were not closely related, a service for which they prob-ably earned at least a pittance. Other women served as midwives, a cheerless profession in a society with high infant mortality where the exposure of newborn infants was practised routinely in the name of economic necessity. Old women were frequently compelled to go out and work, while younger ones were con-strained to remain inside the home.

The common fantasy of agelessness or even rejuvenation of the elderly is presented by the figure of Iolaus in Euripides' *Children of Hera-kles*. Iolaus is Herakles' nephew and companion-in-arms. When Eurystheus arrives at Marathon in order to kidnap the children of Herakles, the old man is resolutely bent on facing him in battle. The dramatist invests the scene in which he arms for the coming strug-gle with pathos and humour:

Iolaus: Hurry, I can't afford to miss the fight.
Attendant: You are the dawdler, not me.
Iolaus: But don't you see how very fast I'm walking?
Attendant: I see the speed is largely in your mind.
Iolaus: You'll change your tune as soon as I'll get there.

Attendant: What will you do? I want to see you win.
Iolaus: You'll see me smash clean through somebody's shield.
Attendant: If ever we arrive there, which I doubt.
[lines 733–40, trans. R. Gladstone]

However, Iolaus is miraculously rejuvenated when he reaches the field of battle and is per-sonally responsible for the capture of Eurystheus.

In Attic tragedy the elderly tend to play only a minor, supporting role, except in cases where the dominant theme of the drama is unrelieved suffering. Geriatrics are generally characterised either by irascibility, as in the case of Oedipus in Sophocles' *Oedipus at Colonus*, or feebleness, as in the case of the chorus of old men in Aes-chylus' *Agamemnon* who dither about help-lessly while their king is murdered offstage. For Euripides in particular, the aged Hecuba, Queen of Troy, was a haunting symbol of the kind of suffering and degradation inflicted upon the elderly in time of war. In the *Hecuba* and *Trojan Women* she is forced to witness the sacrifice of her daughter Polyxena and the bloody and brutal slaughter of her infant grandson Astyanax—events that follow swiftly upon the killing of her son Hector and husband Priam.

In Attic comedy, the elderly are generally caricatured as either helpless or irascible. The most memorable comic portrait of age is that of Philocleon in Aristophanes' *Wasps*. The poet's fantasy is to depict the elderly Philocleon as a suitable case for borstal, a su-perannuated delinquent who looks back wist-fully upon his youth as a time when he was able to run riot with impunity. His sole remain-ing pleasure in life is to serve on the jury and pass waspish verdicts on those who break the law as a way of revenging himself on society for his physical decline. Though Aristophanes' caricature of Philocleon as a hyperactive teenager is on one level merely a comic inver-sion of real life, it nonetheless contains more than a grain of psychological aptness as a stereotypical portrait of the frustrations of old age. In the *Ekklesiazousai* or "Women in Assembly," Aristophanes exploits the notion that old women retain a large appetite for sex and are frequently frustrated of any outlet.

Not before the fifth century was any serious attempt made by artists to portray the infirmity and pathos of old age. The earliest example in sculpture is that of the Seer on the east pediment of the Temple of Zeus at Olympia (470–456 B.C.) who is depicted with a sagging belly and deeply furrowed brow. Foreseeing that the chariot race between Pelops and Oinomaus that is about to take place will have a tragic outcome, the Seer stands as an epitome of the curse of old age, which is to have understanding in painful abundance but not the strength to act upon it.

Many indications suggest that in Athenian society the elderly were not venerated and that their counsels were not esteemed particularly highly. When an elderly Athenian was looking for a place to sit in the theatre of Dionysus, the only members of the audience who stood up and offered him theirs were some Spartan ambassadors sitting in the front row who were official guests of the Athenian state. On witnessing this act of courtesy, the audience broke out into applause, whereupon one of the Spartans turned and remarked to his companions, "These Athenians know how to recognise good manners, but they don't know how to practice them."

As already noted, military service for an Athenian lasted until the age of fifty-nine, after which the only position to which an "elder" could aspire was the relatively humdrum one of judicial arbitrator in cases where both prosecution and defence preferred to settle out of court. Even then, the period of incumbency only lasted one year. Though Aristotle in the *Politics* recommended that old men should serve as priests, there is no actual evidence to indicate that this suggestion was adhered to. Plato in *The Laws*, written when he himself was over seventy, has one of his interlocutors inquire, "Would it not be universally recognised that older men have an obligation to rule and younger men to submit?" Whatever the answer on the domestic level, certainly on the public level and most notably in the sphere of Athenian democracy, no such obligation existed.

In certain forms of debate in the ancient world, such as the College of Augurs at Rome, precedence in debate was granted to speakers in descending order of age. The orator Aeschines reports that Solon had passed a law at Athens at the beginning of the sixth century B.C. imposing the same rule upon both the Council and the Assembly. The practice had, however, lapsed before the middle of the fourth century. As Aeschines further informs us, it nonetheless seems to have been customary for the herald in the Assembly to open each debate by asking, "Who of those aged above fifty wishes to address the meeting?" In Sparta, in contrast to Athens, the chief decision-making body was the Gerusia; council of *elders* in the strict sense of the word. The Gerusia comprised the two kings (Sparta had a dual kingship) plus twenty-eight citizens all of whom had to be over sixty.

The only occasion in Athenian history when geriatrics are similarly known to have been assigned powers by virtue of their advanced years was in 413 B.C., immediately after the calamitous defeat of the expedition that had been sent out to Sicily two years previously. On this occasion the democratic constitution was suspended and a ten-man committee (later increased to thirty) was temporarily appointed to tide Athens through the critical period. The minimum age requirement for service on this committee is not known, but at least one member of it, the poet Sophocles, is known to have been over eighty.

The prominence of thiry Athenian geriatrics at a time of almost unprecedented national emergency only serves to underline, however, how little their counsels counted for under normal conditions. The vote in the Assembly that originally approved the expedition to Sicily had, as Thucydides reports, been divided along age lines. Alcibiades, the principal speaker in favour of the expedition, pitched his appeal directly at the young, while Nicias, who was bitterly opposed to it, sought his natural allies among the elderly.

That the caution of the elderly failed to carry the day not only has implications for the decision-making processes and political tendency of Athenian democracy in general, but may even contain as well a part of the reason why Athens became a democracy in the first place. Had the average citizen been innately respectful towards his or her elders, it would probably not have been necessary to pass laws requiring children to look after their parents. It was precisely because Athenian culture enabled and indeed encouraged him to be flexible and adaptable that he was in fact able to rise to the challenge of full, participatory democracy. Political systems largely reflect, and are to some measure the product of the underlying social structures out of which they have grown. As in the modern world, so in antiquity, gerontocracies are not noted for radical solutions.

■ ■ ■

STUDY QUESTIONS

1. What was the average life span in ancient Greece? Why did women die at younger ages than men? How did total life span in ancient Greece compare with total life span in contemporary Western Europe and the United States?

2. Did Greeks worry about growing older? How did they explain longevity and what did they do to extend their life spans?

3. To what extent did the Greeks associate old age with wisdom?

4. Did the Greeks routinely associate any advantages with old age? What, if anything, was good about growing old?

5. How did the Greeks deal with the problem of senility?

6. Compare the views of Plato, Aristotle, and the Stoics about old age. In what ways were they different?

BIBLIOGRAPHY

For primary sources on the Greek attitude toward old age, see Aristophanes, *The Frogs and Other Plays* (Penguin Books, 1964); Cicero, *On Old Age* (Loeb Classical Library, 1950); Homer, *Iliad* (Penguin Books, 1950); and Plato, *The Republic* (Penguin Books, 1955). The only really detailed discussion of the whole problem of aging in Greek society is B. E. Richardson, *Old Age Among the Ancient Greeks* (1933). W. K. Lacey's *The Family in Classical Greece* (1968) deals with the advantages and disadvantages of having several generations living in one home, and Robert Garland's *The Greek Way of Life: From Conception to Old Age* (1990) deals with the whole range of social life in Ancient Greece.

3. GREEKS AND ROMANS AT THEIR EASE

Gilbert Highet

The amount of leisure time a society enjoys is a product of the sophistication of its economy, its ability to produce a surplus of goods sufficient to free increasingly large numbers of people from the constant grind of locating food and shelter. Once a society can produce more food than it needs, some people are released from that production process to engage in other endeavors. In primitive hunting and foraging societies, most people have no choice but to spend nearly all of their time working. More complex economies produce more complex social structures, with people pursuing a variety of religious, social, political, and economic tasks. One of those pursuits is leisure—ritualized methods of relaxing, laughing, playing, and talking. Traditionally, when we think of the rise of Western civilization, we usually focus on political centralization; the separation of church and state; the rise of agriculture, commerce, towns, cities, and universities; scientific progress and intellectual achievement; and the development of individual rights. But the availability of leisure time for most people is also an accomplishment of Western civilization. In this essay, Gilbert Highet looks at how the Greeks and Romans developed social institutions to ritualize their enjoyment of leisure time.

Rich people have always had leisure, and most of them have always used it for the same occupations: killing animals and birds, collecting beautiful women and other works of art, building large houses and filling them with useless but decorative equipment, eating and drinking, and working out systems of social differentiation almost as elaborate as the intestines of a computer. Ordinary people have always had festivals: a time to relax after getting in the harvest, a dance and a few drinks after making the new wine, a big blast to kick out the old year and welcome in the new—all usually tied up with religion, so that a holy day is a holiday.

As far as I know, the Jews were the first people to introduce, not simply seasonal festivals, but regular periods of leisure for everybody, rich and poor alike. Once every seven days, on the Sabbath, "thou shalt not do any work, thou, nor thy son, nor thy daughter," and the commandment goes on through the servants and the livestock and even the visitors from outside. This is real leisure: a blessed day of rest. Later the rule was extended, and the Jews were commanded not only to do no work on the Sabbath, but to enjoy it: wear their best clothes, eat three meals, and rejoice. It is a great gift, the Sabbath.

However, it was the classical Greeks who took the idea of general free-floating leisure and improved it by thinking of something to do that was quite different from work. They invented the gymnasium. The word and the idea *athlete* are both Greek. Nowadays we are apt to think of the Greeks as brilliant thinkers and agile conversationalists, but many of them were handsome bodies with much spirit and grace and not a great deal of brain. Everyone who goes to Delphi and sees the bronze charioteer is charmed by the skill of the sculptor and

"Greeks and Romans at their Ease" by Gilbert Highet, *Horizon*, Spring 1969, Vol. XI, No. 2, pp. 9–10. Copyright © 1969 Horizon, a division of the American Heritage Publishing Co., Inc. Reprinted by permission.

disappointed by the expressionless face of the young man whose victory he commemorated. But this is correct. The Greeks founded the Olympic games in 776 B.C., long before a single philosopher opened his mouth.

"Health is best," begins one of their drinking songs, which does not even mention intelligence. Healthiest and stupidest of all were the Spartans. They did no work at all, ever. They hunted in the rugged mountains and exercised and drilled for the next war and sat around talking laconically, while the Helots whom they had conquered worked on the farms.

The gymnasium was a Greek solution to the problem of leisure. But it became something more than a training school for young athletes and an exercise area for the middle-aged. A Greek who did not have to work all day on his farm or sell goods in a shop gravitated to the gymnasium. The Greeks loved talking, and some Greeks were highly intelligent; so, as they sat in the gymnasium, resting between bouts of physical training or watching the youngsters leap and wrestle, they exchanged ideas. In time the gymnasium became a club, in which serious matters were discussed. It came to embody that fine balance between body and mind that was the best product of Greece. Socrates would often sit in a sunny corner questioning the young men in order to make their minds as supple as their muscles. Greek education kept growing more elaborate. A library was added to the gymnasium, teachers of literature joined the staff, classes were systematized, and what had at one time been a place in which men of leisure could run and jump and take sunbaths grew into a school.

School is a Greek word, *scholé*. If a Greek was really poor, he had to help his father on the farm, grubbing up roots and watching the goats. If he had a little extra cash, he went to the place of leisure.

The Romans were originally not much for leisure. They were too busy conquering the world. This was not primarily an imperialistic plan. It was the expression of their driving restlessness and their built-in love of challenge

■ ■ *Wrestling was one of the common forms of physical activities found in a Greek gymnasium.*

and difficulty and effort. Work, fight, serve, work, save, plan, work. Old Cato objected bitterly to the time people spent standing around yakking in the Forum: he wanted it paved with sharp-edged shells. Like other Romans he despised the Greeks for wasting hours every day oiling their bodies and wrestling, and oiling their tongues and arguing. Why didn't they get together and build a few decent roads and bridges and aqueducts? They are still there, the great Roman highways, and they symbolize the republican Romans' belief that wasting time and avoiding hard work was a sin.

Rome started out poor and had to work. Rome became rich—so rich that for many of its people work was a waste of time. As the conquest of the world was completed, the small subsistence farmers had their land swallowed up by big landholders; the long-term soldiers were discharged with nothing to do; floating populations from all over the empire drifted into the big cities with no real trade or skill to guarantee them a steady livelihood. Under the republic the city-dwelling Romans worked hard. Under the emperors they worked less and less. Not only Rome but the other big centers, Alexandria and Antioch and many more, were full of surplus people who had to be fed and amused. The government was forced to provide free food and amusement for this mass leisure. Juvenal called the solution "bread and circuses."

Food was a problem of agriculture, transport, and economics, and it would take a large book to describe how the Roman officials tried to solve it. (Food tickets, extra handouts of oil and wine and sometimes cash, but no guaranteed income.) Once the Romans had adopted the idea of leisure, they arranged it with efficient vulgarity through three large-scale institutions. These institutions satisfied basic human impulses: physical exercise and comfort, competition, and hunting.

Much leisure was spent in the huge public baths: exercising, being massaged, showering, playing handball, swimming, and sunbathing—and also gambling, chatting, strolling, looking at the exhibitions of paintings and statues, and occasionally listening to poets reciting their own works. The Roman baths were projections of the Greek gymnasiums into a more affluent era: they were superclubs. Admission was a few cents only. Did it matter if you slept in a six-story walkup if you could spend most of the day in an establishment that would have made a Hilton hotel look like a slum?

■ ■ ■

The Romans also loved to watch men kill animals and one another. The same impulse that makes Arab sheiks in air-conditioned Cadillacs run down gazelles and butcher them with machine guns made the Romans enjoy seeing men grapple with wild beasts in the arena. The modern descendant of the Roman beast hunt is the Spanish bullfight, in which there can be no satisfaction without a killing. *Arena* is the Latin word for sand; and the sand, like the eyes of the spectators, will soak up blood of beast or man without discrimination.

One of the great spectacles was a hunt. Strange imported animals were driven into the circus (sometimes prepared as a jungle with exotic trees and bushes), and trained hunters tried to capture or kill them. A single man would face a lion. A woman alone would tackle a wild boar. The emperor Commodus personally killed five hippopotamuses and two elephants in two days; one of his stunts was beheading ostriches from the imperial box with a broad-bladed arrow. (The disgusting trick of tying up criminals and setting animals to devour them was a late invention, based on

Gresham's law that bad shows drive out good.)

Gladiators—the word means "swordsmen," and a gladiolus is a little sword—were originally war prisoners sacrificed at the funeral of the general who captured them. They fought one another to the death—a more honorable fate than being passively butchered—and their blood fed his spirit. This was the one practice, among the many cruelties and vulgarities of the Romans, that other nations despised most bitterly. But the Romans were rich and powerful, and subject peoples wished to please them, and so the habit spread. Even in the theatre of Dionysus at Athens, where men had once staged noble tragedies to honor the god, trained fighters killed each other, so that the blood splashed the front seats and the distinguished spectators who sat in them. After the emperor Trajan conquered what is now Rumania, he brought back many millions of dollars' worth of gold and booty. He gave Rome public shows that lasted for 117 days of honorific leisure. Nearly five thousand pairs of gladiators were pitted against each other, while the crowds roared.

Horse races were seldom run as they are now, with single horses ridden by jockeys. Each entry was a group of four horses yoked to a light chariot and driven by a skilled charioteer. This was the only spectator sport in antiquity organized by teams. Each team had special horses, stables, drivers, supporters, and colors: red, white, green, blue. The sillier Roman emperors would wear the colors of their favorite team and even sleep in the stables with the drivers. After Christian Rome was founded in Constantinople, the horse races continued there amid wild enthusiasm. Disputes between fan clubs grew into large-scale disorders. During the WIN WIN WIN riots in A.D. 532 the powerful emperor Justinian was besieged in his palace, the cathedral of the Holy Wisdom was burned down, and for five days the mob ruled the city.

Magnificent public baths, savage animals killed by hunters for show; the Colosseum filled with water so that sea battles could be staged to amuse the public; expert swordsmen fighting duels, and in the lunch interval criminals sent in with swords but without armor, to kill each other off as quickly and bloodily as possible; chariot races; and always the yelling mobs. These were the occupations of mass leisure in the Roman Empire.

▪▪▪

Where did Roman culture come from, then? It came from the gymnasium and not from the arena. The Greeks founded Western civilization and taught the Romans how to use it. In mind, the greatest Romans were half-Greek.

They exercised their bodies, but they developed their minds in leisure. They had nothing but loathing, or at most patient contempt, for the races and the beast hunts and the blood on the sand. The Greeks created an almost complete civilization of the spirit. The Romans have left us a tradition of law and politics, some splendid public architecture, and several hundred fine books written by men in quiet rooms from which they could scarcely hear the voice of the many-headed beast in the circus roaring WIN WIN WIN! Leisure, for the mass, is a narcotic or an intoxicant. For the thoughtful man leisure is the Sabbath in which he can have a conversation with his soul.

▪▪▪

STUDY QUESTIONS

1. What is the difference between the festivals "ordinary people have always had" and the leisure pursuits of the Greeks and Romans?

2. In what ways did the Jewish people institutionalize the notion of leisure time?

3. The Greeks invented the gymnasium to ritualize their leisure time. What was the function of the gymnasium, and how did it evolve?

4. How did the Romans view the way Greeks pursued leisure time?

5. Some historians have argued that Roman society had too many people with too much leisure time on their hands. What do they mean by this?

6. How did the Romans spend their leisure time?

BIBLIOGRAPHY

For general surveys of Greek and Roman social history, see Geza Alfoldy, *The Social History of Rome* (1985); Tenney Frank, *Aspects of Social Behavior in Ancient Rome* (1932); Mikhail Rostovtzeff, *Social and Economic History of the Roman Empire* (1987); Ian Jenkins, *Greek and Roman Life* (1986); and C. E. Robinson, *Everyday Life in Ancient Greece* (1933). For more specific discussions of the use of leisure time in Greece and Rome, see J. C. Gosling and C. C. Taylor, *The Greeks on Pleasure* (1982); Kenneth McLeish, *Food and Drink* (1978); W. C. Firebaugh, *The Inns of Greece & Rome* (1928); and Harriet Preston and Louise Dodge, *The Private Life of the Romans* (1919).

4. MURDEROUS GAMES: GLADIATORIAL CONTESTS IN ANCIENT ROME

Keith Hopkins

In the late summer of 1988, billions of people around the world excitedly watched and read about the games of the twenty-fourth Olympiad in Seoul, Korea. Short of war, few events have been as powerful as the Olympic Games in demonstrating and inspiring nationalism and patriotism. But this was hardly a new phenomenon. Europeans follow the World Cup soccer matches with a fervor once confined to religious fanatics. Canadians are equally intense in their devotion to the Stanley Cup hockey play-offs, and Americans have created a cult that follows the Super Bowl. Rome was not much different, except in the level of ritual violence their sporting events promoted. Boxing, rugby, American football, auto racing, ice hockey, and bullfighting tolerate their own violence thresholds, but they pale when compared with the gladiator spectacles of ancient Rome. The Romans were a militaristic people whose civilization rose to greatness through conquest. Along with farming, soldiering was the major occupation in the Roman economy, and Roman citizens worshipped the principals of loyalty, bravery, and self-discipline. Rome was a society that raised controlled violence to the level of a social grace. In the following essay Keith Hopkins describes those gladiator contests and their significance in Roman history.

Rome was a warrior state. After the defeat of Carthage in 201 B.C., Rome embarked on two centuries of almost continuous imperial expansion. By the end of this period, Rome controlled the whole of the Mediterranean basin and much of northwestern Europe. The population of her empire, at between 50 and 60 million people, constituted perhaps one-fifth or one-sixth of the world's population. Victorious conquest had been bought at a huge price, measured in human suffering, carnage, and money. The costs were borne by tens of thousands of conquered peoples, who paid taxes to the Roman state, by slaves captured in war and transported to Italy, and by Roman soldiers who served long years fighting overseas.

The discipline of the Roman army was notorious. Decimation is one index of its severity. If an army unit was judged disobedient or cowardly in battle, one soldier in ten was selected by lot and cudgelled to death by his former comrades. It should be stressed that decimation was not just a myth told to terrify fresh recruits; it actually happened in the period of imperial expansion, and frequently enough not to arouse particular comment. Roman soldiers killed each other for their common good.

When Romans were so unmerciful to each other, what mercy could prisoners of war expect? Small wonder then that they were sometimes forced to fight in gladiatorial contests or were thrown to wild beasts for popular entertainment. Public executions helped inculcate valour and fear in the men, women, and children left at home. Children learnt the lesson of what happened to soldiers who were defeated. Public executions were rituals that helped maintain an atmosphere of violence, even in times of peace. Bloodshed and slaugh-

ter joined military glory and conquest as central elements in Roman culture.

With the accession of the first emperor Augustus (31 B.C.–A.D. 14), the Roman state embarked on a period of long-term peace (*pax romana*). For more than two centuries, thanks to its effective defence by frontier armies, the inner core of the Roman empire was virtually insulated from the direct experience of war. Then in memory of their warrior traditions, the Romans set up artificial battlefields in cities and towns for public amusement. The custom spread from Italy to the provinces.

Nowadays, we admire the Colosseum in Rome and other great Roman amphitheatres such as those at Verona, Arles, Nîmes, and El Djem as architectural monuments. We choose to forget, I suspect, that this was where Romans regularly organised fights to the death between hundreds of gladiators, the mass execution of unarmed criminals, and the indiscriminate slaughter of domestic and wild animals.

The enormous size of the amphitheatres indicates how popular these exhibitions were. The Colosseum was dedicated in A.D. 80 with 100 days of games. One day 3,000 men fought; on another 9,000 animals were killed. It seated 50,000 people. It is still one of Rome's most impressive buildings, a magnificent feat of engineering and design. In ancient times, amphitheatres must have towered over cities, much as cathedrals towered over medieval towns. Public killings of men and animals were a Roman rite, with overtones of religious sacrifice, legitimated by the myth that gladiatorial shows inspired the populace with "a glory in wounds and a contempt of death."

Philosophers, and later Christians, disapproved strongly. To little effect; gladiatorial games persisted at least until the early fifth century A.D., wild-beast killings until the sixth century. St. Augustine in his *Confessions* tells the story of a Christian who was reluctantly forced along to the amphitheatre by a party of friends; at first, he kept his eyes shut, but when he heard the crowd roar, he opened them, and

"Murderous Games; Gladiatorial Contests in Ancient Rome" by K. Hopkins, *History Today*, Vol. 33, June 1983, pp. 16–23. Reprinted by permission.

became converted by the sight of blood into an eager devotee of gladiatorial shows. Even the biting criticism quoted below reveals a certain excitement beneath its moral outrage.

Seneca, Roman senator and philosopher, tells of a visit he once paid to the arena. He arrived in the middle of the day, during the mass execution of criminals, staged as an entertainment in the interval between the wild-beast show in the morning and the gladiatorial show of the afternoon:

All the previous fighting had been merciful by comparison. Now finesse is set aside, and we have pure unadulterated murder. The combatants have no protective covering; their entire bodies are exposed to the blows. No blow falls in vain. This is what lots of people prefer to the regular contests, and even to those which are put on by popular request. And it is obvious why. There is no helmet, no shield to repel the blade. Why have armour? Why bother with skill? All that just delays death.

In the morning, men are thrown to lions and bears. At mid-day they are thrown to the spectators themselves. No sooner has a man killed, than they shout for him to kill another, or to be killed. The final victor is kept for some other slaughter. In the end, every fighter dies. And all this goes on while the arena is half empty.

You may object that the victims committed robbery or were murderers. So what? Even if they deserved to suffer, what's your compulsion to watch their sufferings? "Kill him," they shout, "Beat him, burn him." Why is he too timid to fight? Why is he so frightened to kill? Why so reluctant to die? They have to whip him to make him accept his wounds.

Much of our evidence suggests that gladiatorial contests were, by origin, closely connected with funerals. "Once upon a time," wrote the Christian critic Tertullian at the end of the second century A.D., "men believed that the souls of the dead were propitiated by human blood, and so at funerals they sacrificed prisoners of war or slaves of poor quality

bought for the purpose." The first recorded gladiatorial show took place in 264 B.C.: it was presented by two nobles in honour of their dead father; only three pairs of gladiators took part. Over the next two centuries, the scale and frequency of gladiatorial shows increased steadily. In 65 B.C.., for example, Julius Cæsar gave elaborate funeral games for his father involving 640 gladiators and condemned criminals who were forced to fight with wild beasts. At his next games in 46 B.C., in memory of his dead daughter and, let it be said, in celebration of his recent triumphs in Gaul and Egypt, Cæsar presented not only the customary fights between individual gladiators, but also fights between whole detachments of infantry and between squadrons of cavalry, some mounted on horses, others on elephants. Large-scale gladiatorial shows had arrived. Some of the contestants were professional gladiators, others prisoners of war, and others criminals condemned to death.

Up to this time, gladiatorial shows had always been put on by individual aristocrats at their own initiative and expense, in honour of dead relatives. The religious component in gladiatorial ceremonies continued to be important. For example, attendants in the arena were dressed up as gods. Slaves who tested whether fallen gladiators were really dead or just pretending, by applying a red-hot cauterising iron, were dressed as the god Mercury. Those who dragged away the dead bodies were dressed as Pluto, the god of the underworld. During the persecutions of Christians, the victims were sometimes led around the arena in a procession dressed up as priests and priestesses of pagan cults, before being stripped naked and thrown to the wild beasts. The welter of blood in gladiatorial and wild-beast shows, the squeals and smell of the human victims and of slaughtered animals are completely alien to us and almost unimaginable. For some Romans they must have been reminiscent of battlefields, and, more immediately for everyone, associated with religious sacrifice. At one remove, Romans, even at the height of their

■■ *This detail from a Roman mosaic in Libya shows two swordsmen engaged in a gladiatorial combat.*

civilisation, performed human sacrifice, purportedly in commemoration of their dead.

By the end of the last century B.C.., the religious and commemorative elements in gladiatorial shows were eclipsed by the political and the spectacular. Gladiatorial shows were public performances held mostly, before the amphitheatre was built, in the ritual and social centre of the city, the Forum. Public participation, attracted by the splendour of the show and by distributions of meat, and by betting, magnified the respect paid to the dead and the honour of the whole family. Aristocratic funerals in the Republic (before 31 B.C.) were political acts. And funeral games had political implications, because of their popularity with citizen electors. Indeed, the growth in the splendour of gladiatorial shows was largely fuelled by competition between ambitious aristocrats, who wished to please,

excite, and increase the number of their supporters.

In 42 B.C., for the first time, gladiatorial fights were substituted for chariot-races in official games. After that in the city of Rome, regular gladiatorial shows, like theatrical shows and chariot-races, were given by officers of state, as part of their official careers, as an official obligation and as a tax on status. The Emperor Augustus, as part of a general policy of limiting aristocrats' opportunities to court favour with the Roman populace, severely restricted the number of regular gladiatorial shows to two each year. He also restricted their splendour and size. Each official was forbidden to spend more on them than his colleagues, and an upper limit was fixed at 120 gladiators a show.

These regulations were gradually evaded. The pressure for evasion was simply that, even under the emperors, aristocrats were still competing with each other, in prestige and political success. The splendour of a senator's public exhibition could make or break his social and political reputation. One aristocrat, Symmachus, wrote to a friend: "I must now outdo the reputation earned by my own shows; our family's recent generosity during my consulship and the official games given for my son allow us to present nothing mediocre." So he set about enlisting the help of various powerful friends in the provinces. In the end, he managed to procure antelopes, gazelles, leopards, lions, bears, bear-cubs, and even some crocodiles, which only just survived to the beginning of the games, because for the previous fifty days they had refused to eat. Moreover, twenty-nine Saxon prisoners of war strangled each other in their cells on the night before their final scheduled appearance. Symmachus was heart-broken. Like every donor of the games, he knew that his political standing was at stake. Every presentation was in Goffman's strikingly apposite phrase "a status bloodbath."

The most spectacular gladiatorial shows were given by the emperors themselves at

Rome. For example, the Emperor Trajan, to celebrate his conquest of Dacia (roughly modern Roumania), gave games in A.D. 108–9 lasting 123 days in which 9,138 gladiators fought and eleven thousand animals were slain. The Emperor Claudius in A.D. 52 presided in full military regalia over a battle on a lake near Rome between two naval squadrons, manned for the occasion by 19,000 forced combatants. The palace guard, stationed behind stout barricades, which also prevented the combatants from escaping, bombarded the ships with missiles from catapults. After a faltering start, because the men refused to fight, the battle according to Tacitus "was fought with the spirit of free men, although between criminals. After much bloodshed, those who survived were spared extermination."

The quality of Roman justice was often tempered by the need to satisfy the demand for the condemned. Christians, burnt to death as scapegoats after the great fire at Rome in A.D. 64, were not alone in being sacrificed for public entertainment. Slaves and bystanders, even the spectators themselves, ran the risk of becoming victims of emperors' truculent whims. The Emperor Claudius, for example, dissatisfied with how the stage machinery worked, ordered the stage mechanics responsible to fight in the arena. One day when there was a shortage of condemned criminals, the Emperor Caligula commanded that a whole section of the crowd be seized and thrown to the wild beasts instead. Isolated incidents, but enough to intensify the excitement of those who attended. Imperial legitimacy was reinforced by terror.

As for animals, their sheer variety symbolised the extent of Roman power and left vivid traces in Roman art. In 169 B.C., sixty-three African lions and leopards, forty bears, and several elephants were hunted down in a single show. New species were gradually introduced to Roman spectators (tigers, crocodiles, giraffes, lynxes, rhinoceros, ostriches, hippopotami) and killed for their pleasure. Not for Romans the tame viewing of caged animals in a zoo. Wild beasts were set to tear criminals to pieces as public lessons in pain and death. Sometimes, elaborate sets and theatrical backdrops were prepared in which, as a climax, a criminal was devoured limb by limb. Such spectacular punishments, common enough in preindustrial states, helped reconstitute sovereign power. The deviant criminal was punished; law and order were reestablished.

The labour and organisation required to capture so many animals and to deliver them alive to Rome must have been enormous. Even if wild animals were more plentiful then than now, single shows with 100, 400, or 600 lions, plus other animals, seem amazing. By contrast, after Roman times, no hippopotamus was seen in Europe until one was brought to London by steamship in 1850. It took a whole regiment of Egyptian soldiers to capture it, and involved a five-month journey to bring it from the White Nile to Cairo. And yet the Emperor Commodus, a dead-shot with spear and bow, himself killed five hippos, two elephants, a rhinoceros, and a giraffe in one show lasting two days. On another occasion he killed 100 lions and bears in a single morning show, from safe walkways specially constructed across the arena. It was, a contemporary remarked, "a better demonstration of accuracy than of courage." The slaughter of exotic animals in the emperor's presence, and exceptionally by the emperor himself or by his palace guards, was a spectacular dramatisation of the emperor's formidable power: immediate, bloody, and symbolic.

Gladiatorial shows also provided an arena for popular participation in politics. Cicero explicitly recognised this towards the end of the Republic: "the judgement and wishes of the Roman people about public affairs can be most clearly expressed in three places: public assemblies, elections, and at plays or gladiatorial shows." He challenged a political opponent: "Give yourself to the people. Entrust yourself to the Games. Are you terrified of not being applauded?" His comments underline the fact that the crowd had the important option of giving or of withholding applause, of hissing or of being silent.

Under the emperors, as citizens' rights to engage in politics diminished, gladiatorial shows and games provided repeated opportunities for the dramatic confrontation of rulers and ruled. Rome was unique among large historical empires in allowing, indeed in expecting, these regular meetings between emperors and the massed populace of the capital, collected together in a single crowd. To be sure, emperors could mostly stage-manage their own appearance and reception. They gave extravagant shows. They threw gifts to the crowd—small marked wooden balls (called *missilia*) which could be exchanged for various luxuries. They occasionally planted their own claques in the crowd.

Mostly, emperors received standing ovations and ritual acclamations. The Games at Rome provided a stage for the emperor to display his majesty—luxurious ostentation in procession, accessibility to humble petitioners, generosity to the crowd, human involvement in the contests themselves, graciousness or arrogance towards the assembled aristocrats, clemency or cruelty to the vanquished. When a gladiator fell, the crowd would shout for mercy or dispatch. The emperor might be swayed by their shouts or gestures, but he alone, the final arbiter, decided who was to live or die. When the emperor entered the amphitheatre, or decided the fate of a fallen gladiator by the movement of his thumb, at that moment he had 50,000 courtiers. He knew that he was *Cæsar Imperator*, Foremost of Men.

Things did not always go the way the emperor wanted. Sometimes, the crowd objected, for example to the high price of wheat, or demanded the execution of an unpopular official or a reduction in taxes. Caligula once reacted angrily and sent soldiers into the crowd with orders to execute summarily anyone seen shouting. Understandably, the crowd grew silent, though sullen. But the emperor's increased unpopularity encouraged his assassins

to act. Dio, senator and historian, was present at another popular demonstration in the Circus in A.D. 195. He was amazed that the huge crowd (the Circus held up to 200,000 people) strung out along the track, shouted for an end to civil war "like a well-trained choir."

Dio also recounted how with his own eyes he saw the Emperor Commodus cut off the head of an ostrich as a sacrifice in the arena, then walk towards the congregated senators whom he hated, with the sacrificial knife in one hand and the severed head of the bird in the other, clearly indicating, so Dio thought, that it was the senators' necks that he really wanted. Years later, Dio recalled how he had kept himself from laughing (out of anxiety, presumably) by chewing desperately on a laurel leaf which he plucked from the garland on his head.

Consider how the spectators in the amphitheatre sat: The emperor in his gilded box, surrounded by his family; senators and knights each had special seats and came properly dressed in their distinctive purple-bordered togas. Soldiers were separated from civilians. Even ordinary citizens had to wear the heavy white woolen toga, the formal dress of a Roman citizen, and sandals, if they wanted to sit in the bottom two main tiers of seats. Married men sat separately from bachelors, boys sat in a separate block, with their teachers in the next block. Women, and the very poorest men dressed in the drab grey cloth associated with mourning, could sit or stand only in the top tier of the amphitheatre. Priests and Vestal Virgins (honorary people) had reserved seats at the front. The correct dress and segregation of ranks underlined the formal ritual elements in the occasion, just as the steeply banked seats reflected the steep stratification of Roman society. It mattered where you sat, and where you were seen to be sitting.

Gladiatorial shows were political theatre. The dramatic performance took place, not only in the arena, but between different sections of the audience. Their interaction should be included in any thorough account of the Roman constitution. The amphitheatre was the Roman crowd's parliament. Games are usually omitted from political histories, simply because in our society, mass spectator sports count as leisure. But the Romans themselves realised that metropolitan control involved "bread and circuses." "The Roman people," wrote Marcus Aurelius' tutor Fronto, "is held together by two forces: wheat doles and public shows."

Enthusiastic interest in gladiatorial shows occasionally spilled over into a desire to perform in the arena. Two emperors were not content to be spectators-in-chief. They wanted to be prize performers as well. Nero's histrionic ambitions and success as musician and actor were notorious. He also prided himself on his abilities as a charioteer. Commodus performed as a gladiator in the amphitheatre, though admittedly only in preliminary bouts with blunted weapons. He won all his fights and charged the imperial treasury a million sesterces for each appearance (enough to feed a thousand families for a year). Eventually, he was assassinated when he was planning to be inaugurated as consul (in A.D. 193), dressed as a gladiator.

Commodus' gladiatorial exploits were an idiosyncratic expression of a culture obsessed with fighting, bloodshed, ostentation, and competition. But at least seven other emperors practised as gladiators and fought in gladiatorial contests. And so did Roman senators and knights. Attempts were made to stop them by law; but the laws were evaded.

Roman writers tried to explain away these senators' and knights' outrageous behaviour by calling them morally degenerate, forced into the arena by wicked emperors or their own profligacy. This explanation is clearly inadequate, even though it is difficult to find one that is much better. A significant part of the Roman aristocracy, even under the emperors, was still dedicated to military prowess: all generals were senators; all senior officers were senators or knights. Combat in the arena gave aristocrats a chance to display their fighting skill and courage. In spite of the opprobrium and at the risk of death, it was their last chance to play soldiers in front of a large audience.

Gladiators were glamour figures, culture heroes. The probable life-span of each gladiator was short. Each successive victory brought further risk of defeat and death. But for the moment, we are more concerned with image than with reality. Modern pop-stars and athletes have only a short exposure to full-glare publicity. Most of them fade rapidly from being household names into obscurity, fossilised in the memory of each generation of adolescent enthusiasts. The transience of the fame of each does not diminish their collective importance.

So too with Roman gladiators. Their portraits were often painted. Whole walls in public porticos were sometimes covered with life-size portraits of all the gladiators in a particular show. The actual events were magnified beforehand by expectation and afterwards by memory. Street advertisements stimulated excitement and anticipation. Hundreds of Roman artefacts—sculptures, figurines, lamps, glasses—picture gladiatorial fights and wild-beast shows. In conversation and in daily life, chariot-races and gladiatorial fights were all the rage. "When you enter the lecture halls," wrote Tacitus, "what else do you hear the young men talking about?" Even a baby's nursing bottle, made of clay and found at Pompeii, was stamped with the figure of a gladiator. It symbolised the hope that the baby would imbibe a gladiator's strength and courage.

The victorious gladiator, or at least his image, was sexually attractive. Graffiti from the plastered walls of Pompeii carry the message:

Celadus [a stage name, meaning Crowd's Roar], thrice victor and thrice crowned, the young girls' heart-throb, and Crescens the Netter of young girls by night.

The ephemera of A.D. 79 have been preserved by volcanic ash. Even the defeated gladiator had something sexually portentous about him. It was customary, so it is reported, for a new Roman bride to have her hair parted with a spear, at best one that had been dipped in the body of a defeated and killed gladiator.

The Latin word for sword—*gladius*—was vulgarly used to mean penis. Several artefacts also suggest this association. A small bronze figurine from Pompeii depicts a cruel-looking gladiator fighting off with his sword a dog-like wild-beast that grows out of his erect and elongated penis. Five bells hang down from various parts of his body and a hook is attached to the gladiator's head, so that the whole ensemble could hang as a bell in a doorway. Interpretation must be speculative. But this evidence suggests that there was a close link, in some Roman minds, between gladiatorial fighting and sexuality. And it seems as though gladiatorial bravery for some Roman men represented an attractive yet dangerous, almost threatening, macho masculinity.

Gladiators attracted women, even though most of them were slaves. Even if they were free or noble by origin, they were in some sense contaminated by their close contact with death. Like suicides, gladiators were in some places excluded from normal burial grounds. Perhaps their dangerous ambiguity was part of their sexual attraction. They were, according to the Christian Tertullian, both loved and despised: "men give them their souls, women their bodies too." Gladiators were "both glorified and degraded."

In a vicious satire, the poet Juvenal ridiculed a senator's wife, Eppia, who had eloped to Egypt with her favourite swordsman:

What was the youthful charm that so fired Eppia? What hooked her? What did she see in him to make her put up with being called "The Gladiator's Moll"? Her poppet, her Sergius, was no chicken, with a dud arm that prompted hope of early retirement. Besides, his face looked a proper mess, helmet scarred, a great wart on his nose, an unpleasant discharge always trickling from one eye. But he was a Gladiator. That word makes the whole breed seem handsome, and made her prefer him to her children and country, her

sister and husband. Steel is what they fall in love with.

Satire certainly, and exaggerated, but pointless unless it was also based to some extent in reality. Modern excavators, working in the armoury of the gladiatorial barracks in Pompeii found eighteen skeletons in two rooms, presumably of gladiators caught there in an ash storm; they included only one woman, who was wearing rich gold jewellery, and a necklace set with emeralds. Occasionally, women's attachment to gladiatorial combat went further. They fought in the arena themselves. In the storeroom of the British Museum, for example, there is a small stone relief, depicting two female gladiators, one with breast bare, called Amazon and Achillia. Some of these female gladiators were free women of high status.

Behind the brave facade and the hope of glory, there lurked the fear of death. "Those about to die salute you, Emperor." Only one account survives of what it was like from the gladiator's point of view. It is from a rhetorical exercise. The story is told by a rich young man who had been captured by pirates and was then sold on as a slave to a gladiatorial trainer:

And so the day arrived. Already the populace had gathered for the spectacle of our punishment, and the bodies of those about to die had their own death-parade across the arena. The presenter of the shows, who hoped to gain favour with our blood, took his seat. . . . Although no one knew my birth, my fortune, my family, one fact made some people pity me; I seemed unfairly matched. I was destined to be a certain victim in the sand. . . . All around I could hear the instruments of death: a sword being sharpened, iron plates being heated in a fire [to stop fighters retreating and to prove that they were not faking death], birch-rods and whips were prepared. One would have imagined that these were the pirates. The trumpets sounded their foreboding notes; stretchers for the dead were brought on, a funeral

parade before death. Everywhere I could see
wounds, groans, blood, danger . . .

He went on to describe his thoughts, his
memories in the moments when he faced
death, before he was dramatically and conveniently rescued by a friend. That was fiction.
In real life gladiators died.

Why did Romans popularise fights to the
death between armed gladiators? Why did
they encourage the public slaughter of unarmed criminals? What was it which transformed men who were timid and peaceable
enough in private, as Tertullian put it, and
made them shout gleefully for the merciless destruction of their fellow men? Part of the answer may lie in the simple development of a
tradition, which fed on itself and its own success. Men liked blood and cried out for more.
Part of the answer may also lie in the social
psychology of the crowd, which relieved individuals of responsibility for their actions, and
in the psychological mechanisms by which
some spectators identified more easily with the
victory of the aggressor than with the sufferings of the vanquished. Slavery and the steep
stratification of society must also have contributed. Slaves were at the mercy of their
owners. Those who were destroyed for public edification and entertainment were considered worthless, as nonpersons; or, like
Christian martyrs, they were considered social
outcasts, and tortured as one Christian martyr
put it "as if we no longer existed." The brutali-
sation of the spectators fed on the dehumani-
sation of the victims.

Rome was a cruel society. Brutality was
built into its culture in private life, as well as
in public shows. The tone was set by military
discipline and by slavery. The state had no legal monopoly of capital punishment until the
second century A.D. Before then, a master
could crucify his slaves publicly if he wished.
Seneca recorded from his own observations
the various ways in which crucifixions were
carried out, in order to increase pain. At private dinner-parties, rich Romans regularly

presented two or three pairs of gladiators:
"when they have finished dining and are filled
with drink," wrote a critic in the time of Augustus, "they call in the gladiators. As soon as
one has his throat cut, the diners applaud with
delight." It is worth stressing that we are dealing here not with individual sadistic psycho-
pathology, but with a deep cultural difference.
Roman commitment to cruelty presents us
with a cultural gap that it is difficult to cross.

Popular gladiatorial shows were a by-
product of war, discipline, and death. For centuries, Rome had been devoted to war and to
the mass participation of citizens in battle.
They won their huge empire by discipline and
control. Public executions were a gruesome
reminder to noncombatants, citizens, subjects,
and slaves that vengeance would be exacted
if they rebelled or betrayed their country. The
arena provided a living enactment of the hell
portrayed by Christian preachers. Public
punishment ritually reestablished the moral
and political order. The power of the state was
dramatically reconfirmed.

When long-term peace came to the heart-
lands of the empire, after 31 B.C., militaristic
traditions were preserved at Rome in the
domesticated battlefield of the amphitheatre.
War had been converted into a game, a drama
repeatedly replayed, of cruelty, violence,
blood, and death. But order still needed to be
preserved. The fear of death still had to be as-
suaged by ritual. In a city as large as Rome,
with a population of close on a million by the
end of the last century B.C., without an adequate police force, disorder always threatened.

Gladiatorial shows and public executions
reaffirmed the moral order, by the sacrifice of
human victims—slaves, gladiators, condemned criminals, or impious Christians. Enthusiastic participation, by spectators rich and
poor, raised and then released collective tensions, in a society that traditionally idealised
impassivity. Gladiatorial shows provided a
psychic and political safety valve for the
metropolitan population. Politically, emperors
risked occasional conflict, but the populace

could usually be diverted or fobbed off. The crowd lacked the coherence of a rebellious political ideology. By and large, it found its satisfaction in cheering its support of established order. At the psychological level, gladiatorial shows provided a stage for shared violence and tragedy. Each show reassured spectators that they had yet again survived disaster. Whatever happened in the arena, the spectators were on the winning side. "They found comfort for death" wrote Tertullian with typical insight, "in murder."

■■■

STUDY QUESTIONS

1. What was "cudgelling"? Why did Roman soldiers do it to their own comrades?

2. What was the origin of gladiatorial combat?

3. Why did the Romans conduct the gladiator fights?

4. What was Seneca's opinion of gladiator combat?

5. Describe the religious content of the gladiator spectacles. When did the religious element give way to political symbolism? Why did the change occur?

6. What was the element of capricious terror in the gladiator spectacles?

7. Who sponsored the spectacular events? Why?

8. What was the significance of gladiator shows as places for Roman rulers and Roman citizens to confront one another?

9. How did seating arrangements reflect the stratification of Roman society?

BIBLIOGRAPHY

For general histories of Roman civilization, see Theodor Mommsen, *The History of Rome* (1957), and William Sinnigen and A. E. R. Boak, *A History of Rome to A.D. 565* (1977). The best social histories of Rome are J. P. Balston, *Life and Leisure in Ancient Rome* (1969); Jerome Carcopino, *Daily Life in Ancient Rome* (1971); and W. L. Westermann, *The Slave Systems of Greek and Roman Antiquity* (1955). For descriptions of gladiator life in Rome, see Keith Hopkins, *Death and Renewal. Sociological Studies in Roman History* (1983), and Michael Grant, *Gladiators* (1976).

5. THE SOCIAL STATUS OF WOMEN IN REPUBLICAN ROME

Eva Cantarella

Few patterns in human existence are as consistent, across time and across cultures, as the subjugation of women. Except in the rarest societies, men have controlled political and economic life, whereas women have occupied subservient positions in the social and legal structure. Most anthropologists believe this social arrangement had its origins in the mix between reproductive biology and premodern economics. In premodern societies, where most women were destined to a dozen pregnancies over the course of their reproductive lives, the basic reality of pregnancy, childbirth, and nursing infants kept women confined in the presence of small children and, inevitably, the home. Social, economic, and political responsibilities outside the home tended to become the domain of men. The institutions of male control and female subjugation eventually became woven into the social fabric of most societies, even when economic reality no longer dictated it. Because women enjoyed so little political and economic power, they left behind few records describing the nature of their existence, especially in ancient society. In the following selection, Eva Cantarella looks at the status of women, or lack thereof, in Roman society.

System of Nomenclature

Roman citizens had three names: a first name, *praenomen*, which was the individual's name; a second, *nomen*, which was the name of the *gens*[1]; and a third, *cognomen*, which indicated the particular family group. Women, however, had only the gentile name and the family name. They had no individual names.

Cornelia, Caecilia, Tullia—these are gentile, not personal names. When there was more than one woman in a group and confusion might arise, designations such as Maior and Minor (elder and younger) or Prima, Seconda, and Tertia were added. This peculiarity of the naming system prompts us to ask whether Roman women really did not have names or whether they had names that were never used.

In the opinion of some, the absence of names was not original. Female *praenomina* once existed but disappeared before the historical era. According to others, they never existed at all. Still others maintain that they existed but, as among other peoples (such as the Sabines), they were never said aloud for reasons of good manners. In an attempt to resolve the problem R. I. Menager has reexamined the sources and identified three types of female naming.

The first type, the majority, is a single name: Anicia, Aptronia, Aulia, Plautia, Roscia, Saufeia are some examples documented in the inscriptions from the cemetery of Praeneste. Examples from literary sources are Ocrisia and Pinaria. These are single names and merely the feminine form of the name of the father or of the *gens*. The second type is *gentilicium* plus the father's *praenomen* followed by *filia*.[2] As has been justly observed, this system "expresses in its turn the negation of the identity, and a legal relationship identical with that which emerges from the primitive designation of the slave as Gaipor (slave of Gaius), Marcipor (slave of Marcus), Quintipor," and so on.

The third type, which is quite rare, included the *praenomen*. This means that some female *praenomina* existed. . . . Among "ancient" women the names Rutilia, Caesella, Rodacilla, Murrula, and Burra were common. These derive from color terms (evidently from the hair or skin of the woman so called). We also find Gaia, Lucia, Publia, Numeria, all deriving from male names. . . .

Evidently, although the use of *praenomina* for women is attested, it was extraneous to Roman culture and an absolutely exceptional practice, which seems according to all the indicators to have been adopted from another culture. Again the Etruscans enter the picture, because they, unlike other peoples, regularly called women by their first names.

If, for Pericles, great was "the glory of the woman who is talked about the least, whether in praise or blame," for the Romans the glory of women required that their names never be pronounced. It was said of the Bona Dea[3] that no man (except her husband) ever heard her name as long as she lived. In the fifth century, Macrobius[4] praises the modesty of a woman whose name nobody knew. It is difficult not to share the observation made by Moses Finley. By not indicating women with *praenomina*, he writes, "it is as if the Romans wished to suggest that women were not, and ought not be genuine individuals, but only fractions of a family. Anonymous and passive fractions at that. . . ."

---

[1]Clan or tribe.

Form *Pandora's Daughters* by Eva Cantarella, translated by Maureen B. Fant. Copyright © 1987 by The Johns Hopkins University Press.

---

[2]Female child.

[3]Roman goddess worshipped exclusively by women.

[4]Roman philosopher, circa 400 A.D.

Female Discontent and Bacchic Cults

By our standards at least, the conditions of Roman women's lives were ample reason for discontent. A unique and difficult-to-interpret episode narrated by Livy[5] reveals a certain tension in relations between the sexes.

A trial for poisoning was held in 331 B.C. at Rome. During the consulship of M. Claudius Marcellus and C. Valerius Potitus, many illustrious persons died mysteriously. Reported by a female slave, certain *matronae*[6] were accused of having poisoned them. *Venena*, poisons, were found in their houses but the women said they were medicines. Challenged to drink them, the *matronae* did so and died. At the end of the trial, 160 women had been condemned. However one interprets this disturbing episode, it and other signs indicate the definite existence of a problem.

Around the second century B.C., the status of women deteriorated. Women who lived in the country deeply resented the loss of privileges involved in the female role in the peasant family. Women of the better-off classes had seen their chances to enjoy the privileges of wealth diminish. A series of sumptuary laws *(leges sumptuariae)* had established rigorous limitations on female luxury.

The *lex Oppia*[7] in 215 B.C. had forbidden women to wear excessive quantities of jewelry or colored clothing. Twenty years later, in 195, demonstrations of discontent brought about the repeal of this law. But in 169 a new provision, the *lex Voconia* . . . established that women (with the exceptions of Vestal Virgins[8] and the Flaminica Dialis[9]) could not inherit more than 200,000 asses, which greatly irritated the women of the wealthier classes. Fur-

thermore, women of all social classes had to endure the inconvenience caused by the absence of the men, who were occupied in continual wars.

It is no wonder that in this context Bacchic cults asserted themselves increasingly. Our best information comes from Livy. At first limited to women, these cults spread thanks to the intervention and innovations of the Campanian priestess Paculla Annia and were opened to men as well. After orgiastic dances in the woods of Stimula (the goddess of madness in whose woods, *lucus Stimulae*, at the foot of the Aventine the Maenads[10] had taken refuge), the participants in the rite ran toward the Tiber, into which they threw lit torches.

Should this ritual be interpreted as an expression of freedom or sexual dissoluteness? "Licentious" behavior did take place. The rituals were accompanied not only by the drinking of wine (which, of course, was forbidden to women) but by both heterosexual and homosexual relations. To deduce from this, however, that the Roman woman enjoyed the slightest bit of this freedom in her daily life would certainly be a mistake.

In the first place, the ritual that allowed otherwise forbidden sexual couplings was justified by the pretext of "possession." Second, as we have already seen with reference to the Greek world, the ritual represented a world turned upside down, an inversion of everyday life, a reversal of roles clearly revealed by the fact that the male participants dressed as women.

The Bacchic rites[11] indicate a social reality that was the exact opposite of what one might think at first sight. They actually reveal the sexual repression of the Roman woman. Such repression was, of course, perfectly functional for the purpose of procreation, where there was no room for eroticism and love. Every dis-

---

[5]Roman historian 59 B.C.–17 A.D.

[6]Married women.

[7]Law of Oppius.

[8]Keepers of the flame of Vesta, goddess of the hearth.

[9]Priestesses of Jupiter, the chief Roman god.

[10]Female companions of Bacchus, god of wine.

[11]Orgiastic religious rites devoted to the god Bacchus.

Romans glorified the institution of marriage, which in this picture is shown in the company of the gods of valor, success, and good fortune.

play of emotion, in the context of family life in general and conjugal life in particular, was vigorously reproved. Very significant in this regard is the story (it does not matter whether it is real or imaginary—what is important is that it was retold for didactic purposes) that the senator Manilius risked being expelled from the Senate for kissing his wife in public.

The enormous spread of the Bacchic cults—celebrated primarily by women and at first only by them—must be placed in this context. The ritual was the only moment in which women could express a part of themselves that had been suppressed—only then could they experience eroticism. It was a moment in which they found compensation for the dissatisfaction of an ungratifying emotional and erotic life.

Altogether understandable, then, are the reasons for the enormous spread of the Bacchanalia. Just as understandable are the reasons for the fierce repression with which they were stopped, in the course of which the accusations were again brought against women for using poisons. In the wake of the Bacchanalian scandal, another trial for poisoning was held that made the trial of 331 B.C. appear negligible. Again there were mysterious deaths and a special investigation. The subsequent trial concluded with more than 2,000 women condemned. One of these was the widow of a consul who wanted to get rid of her husband, so went the accusation, so that her son by her first marriage might have access to the consulship. But despite these, let us say, pathological episodes, new and troubling social phenomena pointed to a crisis at hand.

The Population Crisis

The birth rate began to fall during the Republic. It fell in massive proportions in the centuries to follow. One hypothesis posits mass lead poisoning. The conduits of the aqueducts that brought water to Rome were made of lead; Roman women used cosmetics that contained large amounts of lead; vessels for food and drink were often made of lead. The theory is not unreasonable; indeed traces of lead have been found in Roman skeletons. But lead poisoning alone, no matter how widespread, cannot account for all the circumstances that contributed to making a declining birth rate a serious social problem.

Contraception was in use by this time. Apart from utterly ineffective measures (spells and amulets, such as a cat's liver tied to the left foot or a spider bound in the skin of a stag and held in contact with the body), some methods, although rudimentary, were certainly more effective, such as a piece of soft wool saturated with substances that prevented fertilization. Furthermore, abortion was widely practiced.

Decline in the birth rate was due in part to external causes, but it was certainly also partly due to women's life-choices. For women of the lower classes the motivation to use contraception was economic; for the privileged, it was the desire to enjoy the advantages that their new status allowed. They hoped to find an identity that was not exclusively tied to motherhood.

But this could not be allowed, because it conflicted with the need to reproduce a social body and transmit a family and political ideology. Actions against the worrisome phenomenon were taken as soon as it appeared. The provisions of the *lex Iulia . . .* can be interpreted as such a response. The legislative provisions, moreover, were accompanied by a massive "ideological campaign" intended to forestall transgression in whatever form it took, and to reconfirm the traditional models yet again. We can see this in anecdotes about certain female figures and in funerary inscriptions about women who, having passed their lives in anonymity, were remembered after death for their "exemplary qualities."

Models and
Transgressions

So far what has interested us are the general conditions of Roman women's life. Now we will look at some female figures who managed to emerge from anonymity to become celebrated models and exemplars of behavior. The first observation to make about these women is that, other than their "heroic" moment, usually linked to some political event,

we know almost nothing of their lives. Apart from the exemplary deed to which they owe their immortality, all is shadow and silence.

Of the women chosen to be remembered in the history of Rome written by men (again, it is not important whether their recorded actions are real or legendary), we begin with Lucretia and Virginia.

Wife of Collatinus, Lucretia killed herself after being raped by Sextus, son of Tarquinius Superbus. The people reacted by rising against the foreign kings and throwing them out of the city. Virginia, object of the desires of the decemvir Appius Claudius, did not kill herself but was killed by her father. In her case too, the popular reaction led to the ouster of the decemvir.

The syntactic structure of the two legends is almost identical. Object of illicit desire, a woman dies to affirm the supreme value of conjugal fidelity (Lucretia) and virginity (Virginia). The people find in the outrage the strength to react against power and reconfirm this value, sanctioning the fundamental importance of a law of family morality, evidently one of the pillars on which the social and political organization was based.

Equally predictable and instructive are the stories of Veturia, Volumnia, and Cornelia. Veturia and Volumnia, respectively mother and wife of Coriolanus,[12] went to his camp as he was leading the Volscians against Rome and obtained from him what ambassadors, magistrates, and priests had been unable to obtain. They convinced Coriolanus to abandon arms.

The hagiography of Cornelia, second daughter of Scipio Africanus and mother of the tribunes Tiberius and Gaius Gracchus, is well known. She had twelve children (only three of whom lived to adulthood); her daughter Sempronia married Scipio Aemilianus. After the death of her husband, Cornelia would not

---

[12]Legendary Roman general who after 491 A.D. joined Rome's enemies the Volscians after failing to gain election as consul.

remarry and refused even the proposal of Ptolemy VII Physcon. She was the exemplary image of the *univira*,[13] a woman who had only one man in her entire life. Cornelia remained the ideal model of womanly behavior, despite the evident contradiction with a strong population policy. What is more, Cornelia was educated and intellectually polished: Even Cicero admired the style of her letters. But Cornelia owes her fame to her reply when asked why she did not wear jewels. "These," she said, pointing to her children, "are my jewels." And on the statue erected in her honor she was remembered with the inscription "Cornelia, mother of the Gracchi."

We come finally to Marcia, who became the wife of Cato after he repudiated Atilia for her moral conduct. Marcia was a perfect wife. The orator Hortensius, by now old and alone, asked Cato to let him have Marcia in order to have children by her. Cato agreed and Marcia, although she loved her husband, accepted his decision without protest. The traditions diverge at this point. According to one version, Cato divorced Marcia, who married Hortensius. In the other version, Cato simply lent her to his friend. In either case, Marcia accepted her husband's decision and returned to Cato when Hortensius died.

The popular reaction to this episode was conflicting. Some accused Cato of greediness. Others invoked ethnological precedents to justify his action. In the schools, rhetoricians used to exercise their skills by debating "an Cato recte Marciam Hortensio tradiderit," whether Cato was right to give Marcia to Hortensius, or more generically, "conveniate res talis bono viro," whether such behavior was seemly for a good man.

Perhaps the Stoic Cato "lent" his wife, following without reservation the precepts of the Stoic school, namely, that one should not claim to possess a woman because, being created for procreation, women ought to be common to

all. What is interesting to us, however, is Marcia's reaction. What made her accept what was probably contrary to her desires and also in contrast with the model of the *univira?*

There were also women who refused the role of the model woman. Among these, Clodia is famous. She was loved by Catullus[14] and celebrated by him with the name Lesbia. Clodia was a free woman: we are in the first century B.C., when a new type of woman appears on the scene in Rome. Some Roman women were inspired by actresses or Greek hetaerae, and tried to imitate them. In 61 B.C., at age thirty-three, Clodia met Catullus, then twenty-seven. In 59, at the death of her husband, she left Catullus for the even younger Caelius. Few facts are recorded, but they are more than sufficient to understand that Clodia was far from the example propagandized by the women discussed previously; she was a woman who chose and left her lovers, who refused to be an object of possession. When, later abandoned by Caelius, she accuses him of not having returned money she lent him, of having stolen her jewelry, and, finally, of having tried to poison her, the oration written by Cicero in defense of Caelius does not spare her image: "Clytemnestra,"[15] he calls her, and worse, *quandrantaria*—a two-bit Clytemnestra. He dwells not so much on the facts contested by Caelius as on Clodia herself, a woman whose conduct alone makes her accusations unreliable.

As soon as she was widowed, said Cicero (not missing the chance to insinuate that Clodia had poisoned her husband), she gave herself to a dissolute life of orgiastic parties both in Rome and at her villa in Baiae on the Bay of Naples. The slaves who testified in her favor had no credibility: they too participated in their mistress's debauchery, and she had not

---

[13]One-man woman.

[14]Roman poet circa 84–54 B.C.

[15]Wife of Agamemnon, King of Mycenae. She committed adultery with Aegisthus and together they murdered her husband.

hesitated to free them in order to obtain their complicity. As if that were not enough, Clodia was the incestuous lover of Clodius, her brother, the bitter enemy of Cicero.

That was essentially Caelius' defense, and he was acquitted. The case is symptomatic; Clodia's accusations could not have any grounds. She was "different," and as such could not possibly be telling the truth.

Despite the clear signs of malcontent and rebellion that spread in the second century, despite the attempt at "liberation" sought in the Bacchanalia, despite the "Lesbias" (there must have been others, not loved by Catullus and thus not known), the average Roman woman, the anonymous woman, the woman not talked about, was probably not very different from Lucretia or Cornelia. . . .

■ ■ ■

STUDY QUESTIONS

1. What does the system of women's names indicate about their social status in ancient Rome?

2. In what ways did Roman women show their discontent with their social status?

3. What effects did the population crisis of Roman society have on the social status of women?

4. What were the characteristics of an ideal Roman woman as indicated by the stories of various Roman heroines?

5. Compare and contrast the status of Roman women with that of women in modern America. Why do the various similarities and differences exist?

BIBLIOGRAPHY

For general surveys of Roman history, see Thomas W. Africa, *The Immense Majesty: A History of Rome and the Roman Empire* (1974), and Karl Christ, *The Romans: An Introduction to Their History and Civilization* (1984). Students interested in the social history of Rome should consult Geza Alfoldy, *The Social History of Rome* (1985), or Harriet Preston and Louise Dodge, *The Private Life of the Romans* (1919). For specific histories of the Roman family, see Beryl Rawson, ed., *The Family in Ancient Rome* (1986), and Peter Hodge, *Roman Family Life* (1974). Two important books on the life and status of women in Roman society are J. P. Balsdon, *Roman Women* (1983), and Jane Gardner, *Women in Roman Law and Society* (1986).

Part Two

DARKNESS AND LIGHT: THE WORLD AFTER ROME, 400–1000

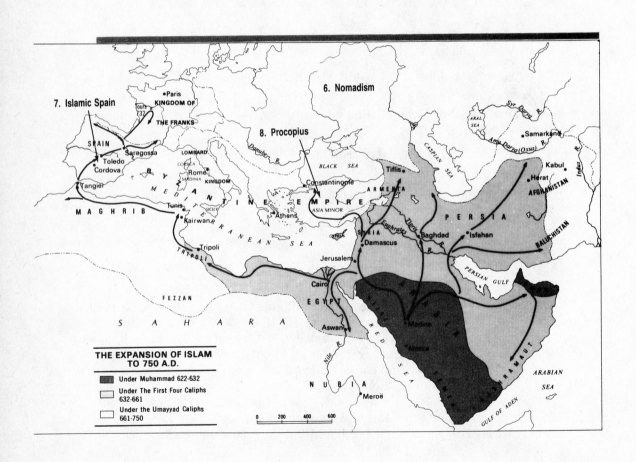

7. Islamic Spain

6. Nomadism

8. Procopius

THE EXPANSION OF ISLAM
TO 750 A.D.

Under Muhammad 622-632

Under The First Four Caliphs
632-661

Under the Umayyad Caliphs
661-750

0   200   400   600

In the popular mind, the fall of Rome was a seemingly brief event. Barbarian hordes are believed to have increased in numbers until one day they burst through Rome's defenses with the suddenness of flood waters breaking through a failing dike. After a flurry of senseless violence and destruction, the survivors existed in the midst of grim devastation. These latter days are commonly referred to as the ''Dark Ages'' and supposedly lasted until medieval civilization started to recover, about 1000 A.D. This historical image has so strongly impressed the popular mind that it has even influenced the presentation of the various recent post-apocalyptic science fiction movies such as *The Road Warrior.*

Popular conceptions of many historical eras and events, however, are often quite inaccurate. Barbarians are always shown as traveling around swiftly on horses in overwhelming numbers, invincible. In fact, most of the real barbarians moved about in family groups of fairly small numbers and did not rely heavily on horses. Furthermore, they were often defeated and were far from invincible. The best known of the Barbarian leaders, Attila the Hun, is now remembered for his most famous battle: his defeat at Châlons in 451. The warring style of the Huns is the topic J. Otto Maenchen-Heflen explores.

Rome's fall was neither sudden nor complete. Edward Gibbon, its most famous historian, ended his *Decline and Fall of the Roman Empire* with the capture of Constantinople in 1453. Rome was sacked by the Visigoths in 410 and the Vandals in 455, but Constantinople and the Eastern Empire survived and largely thrived for another thousand years after those events. Justinian and Theodora, who ruled the Byzantine or Eastern Roman Empire from 527–567, may have been cruel and depraved, but they ruled over one of the world's most powerful and advanced civilizations. The selection from Procopius explores the Byzantine culture of Justinian. It could never be called a dark age. It preserved and improved much of the classical learning and eventually passed some of that knowledge on to a reviving Western Europe during the latter Middle Ages.

Byzantium was not the only great state to follow Rome. The Islamic Empire of the Arabs also appeared at this time. Bursting out of the Arabian peninsula after Mohammed's death in 632, by 740 the Islamic Empire covered the territory from Spain to Afghanistan. That society, contrary to the popular picture given in the *Arabian Nights*, was no fairy tale. At its height, the Islamic Empire led the world. Some of its splendor was as close to Western Europe as Spain.

The impact of the Moslems on Spanish society is Gerald Brenan's topic. This close proximity was yet another way that classical learning was restored to the Europeans after the fall of Rome, because the Arabs were great students and preservers of classical learning.

In the world of the early Middle Ages, it was the Western Europeans who lived a backwater existence, both politically and culturally. Apart from a brief recovery under the great Frankish king, Charlemagne (768–814), a relatively stable medieval European civilization would not appear until around the year 1000 and with it the end of the "Dark Ages." Even then, Europe would continue to lag behind the other great civilizations for centuries to come.

6. HORSES AND BOWS: THE MILITARY FOUNDATIONS OF THE HUNS

J. Otto Maenchen-Heflen

Nomadism is now simply an exotic, distant, and increasingly rare life-style to the citizens of industrial western societies. For people whose ideal of home is a fixed residence, preferably a single-family house, living in a tent on a permanent basis is hard to imagine. To a society whose fundamental form of property is land, measuring wealth solely in terms of herds of domestic animals is completely alien. This inability of settled industrial and agricultural societies to understand the nomadic herder is a constant of history. The conflict of these two life-styles is as old as Cain's (the farmer) murder of Abel (the herder). What the Cain and Abel story distorts, however, is the fact that up until quite recently, the nomads have been the aggressors.

History is full of the fire and sword of invasions by wandering tribes of so-called barbarians. The vast but transitory empires of Genghiz Khan (1167?–1227) and Tamerlane (c. 1336–1405) were the wonders and the terrors of their ages. Their military power was based on lightning strikes by vast swarms of mounted archers. Neither of these great nomadic leaders ever campaigned in Europe west of the Carpathian Mountains. Instead, the earlier tribes of Huns, Avars, and Hungarians (Magyars) actually invaded Western Europe. In the historical imagination, the greatest and most infamous of these invaders were Attila and his Huns. Known as the "Scourge of God," Attila (406?–453) and his tribesmen preyed on the crumbling remnants of the Western Roman Empire. In this excerpt, J. Otto Maenchen-Heflen discusses the importance of the horse and the bow and arrow to the Huns' ability to wage war.

In the seventy years between the first clash of the marauders with Roman frontier troops and the battle at the *locus Mauriacus*,[1] the warfare of the Huns remained essentially the same. Attila's horsemen were still the same mounted archers who in the 380s had ridden down the Vardar Valley and followed the standards of Theodosius.[2] Their tactics were determined by the weapons they carried, and as these did not change, the Huns fought at Metz and Orléans as they had fought at Pollentia. It is true that in Attila's army there were men who could build and serve siege engines, clearly not Huns but Roman prisoners or deserters. Unlike Alaric,[3] who boasted that Thrace forged him spears, swords, and helmets, Attila had no Roman *fabricae*[4] work for him. But at least some Huns, like the Goths in 376, must have "plundered the dead bodies and armed themselves in Roman equipment," and others may have fought with Persian weapons. But all this has little significance. Had Priscus[5] in the 470s described the weapons and tactics of the Huns, he would have written more or less as Ammianus Marcellinus[6] wrote in 392:

When provoked they sometimes fight singly, but they enter the battle in tactical formation, while their medley of voices makes a savage noise. And as they are lightly equipped for swift motion, and unexpected in action, they purposely divide suddenly in scattered bands and attack, rushing about in disorder here and there, dealing terrific slaughter; and because of their extraordinary rapidity of movement, they cannot be discerned when they break into a rampart or pillage an enemy's camp. And on this account you would not hesitate to call them the most terrible of all warriors, because they fight from a distance with missiles having sharp bone, instead of their usual points, joined to the shafts with wonderful skill; then they gallop over the intervening spaces and fight hand to hand with swords regardless of their own lives; and while the enemy are guarding against wounds from sword-thrusts, they throw strips of cloth plaited into nooses over their opponents and so entangle them that they fetter their limbs and take from them the power of riding or walking.

The Goths from whom Ammianus gathered his information were even after so many years still deafened by the wild howls of the Huns and dazed by the incredible speed of their attacks. About the social and political structure of the Huns the Goths knew next to nothing. They could not fail to notice that the Huns formed *cunei*[7] but whether these consisted of the members of one clan or tribe, or were formed *ad hoc,* they could not tell Ammianus. From a passage in Procopius it appears that in the initial phase of a battle hereditary privileges played some role with the later Huns. The same may well have been true for their predecessors; the *čur*[8] probably handed down their rank for generations. Strangely, Ammianus did not mention the feigned flight, a stratagem of the Huns as of all steppe warriors. Still, incomplete as his description is, it shows that the tactics of the Huns were not markedly

[1] Another name for the battle of Châlons-sur-Marne in 451 A.D.

[2] Roman emperor who reigned 379-395.

[3] King of the Visigoths, reigned 395-410.

[4] Craftspeople.

[5] Roman philosopher (c. 305-396).

[6] Roman historian (c. 330-395).

[7] A wedge-shaped formation.

[8] A mark of nobility.

From *The World of the Huns: Studies in Their History and Culture* by Otto Maenchen-Helfen, translated and edited by Max Knight. Copyright © 1973 The Regents of the University of California. Reprinted by permission.

■ ■ *This nineteenth-century illustration is a traditional but historically inaccurate representation of Attila and his Huns during their invasion of Italy.*

different from those of the other mounted bowmen of northern Eurasia. The volleys of arrows with which the enemy was showered were followed by hand-to-hand fighting.

I pass over the "war crimes" of which the Huns were so often accused. In an apocalypsis of the seventh century, a Syriac cleric let his fancy run a little too wild: the Huns (he probably meant the Hephthalites[9]) roast pregnant women, cut out the fetus, put it in a dish, pour water over it, and dip their weapons into the brew; they eat the flesh of children and drink the blood of women. Most Germans of the Folkwandering[10] period behaved in no way more humanely than the Huns. In 406, the Germanic invaders of Gaul killed the hermits, burned the priests alive, raped the nuns, devastated the vineyards, and cut down the olive trees.

Horses

The Huns "are almost glued to their horses, which are hardy, it is true, but ugly, and sometimes they sit on them woman-fashion, and thus perform their ordinary tasks. And when deliberations are called for about weighty matters, they all consult for a common object in that fashion."

The Huns, indeed, carried on their negotiations with the Roman diplomats on horseback. The Sarmatians in South Russia and the Lazi in the Caucasus often rode side saddle also.

The characterization of the Hun horses as *deformes*[11] is too vague to draw conclusions from it. To a Roman most steppe horses must have looked as misshapen as the horses of the

Scythians, with their short legs and big heads, or those of the Sigynnae, shaggy and snubnosed, allegedly too small to ride upon.

The only author to give a good description of the Hun horse is Vegetius.[12] For a long time, he complains in the prologue to the second book of his *Mulomedicina*, veterinary medicine has been steadily declining. Horse doctors are so poorly paid that no one devotes himself any longer to a proper study of veterinary medicine. Of late, however, following the example set by the Huns and other barbarians, people have altogether ceased to consult veterinarians. They leave the horses on the pasture the year round and give them no care whatever, not realizing what incalculable harm they thereby do themselves. These people overlook that the horses of the barbarians are quite different from Roman horses. Hardy creatures, accustomed to cold and frost, the horses of the barbarians need neither stables nor medical care. The Roman horse is of a much more delicate constitution; unless it has good shelter and a warm stable, it will catch one illness after another. Although Vegetius stresses the superiority of the Roman horse, its intelligence, docility, and noble character, he concedes that the Hun horse has its good points. Like the Persian, Epirotic, and Sicilian horses it lives long. In the classification of various breeds according to their fitness for war, Vegetius gives the Hun horse the first place because of its patience, perseverance, and its capacity to endure cold and hunger. As his description shows, Vegetius, who probably kept a few Hun horses himself, had ample opportunity to observe them. They have, he says, great hooked heads, protruding eyes, narrow nostrils, broad jaws, strong and stiff necks, manes hanging below the knees, overlarge ribs, curved backs, bushy tails, cannon bones of

---

[9]Another Asiatic tribe similar to the Huns.

[10]Another term for the migrations of the Germanic tribes.

[11]Misshapen.

[12]A Roman military writer c. 390.

great strength, small pasterns, wide-spreading hooves, hollow loins; their bodies are angular, with no fat on the rump or the muscles of the back, their stature inclining to length rather than to height, the belly drawn, the bones huge. The very thinness of these horses is pleasing, and there is beauty even in their ugliness. Vegetius adds that they are quiet and sensible and bear wounds well. . . .

The Huns were superior horsemen. Sidonius[13] compared them with centaurs: "Scarce had the infant learnt to stand without his mother's aid when a horse takes him on his back. You would think that the limbs of man and horse were born together, so firmly does the rider always stick to the horse; any other folk is carried on horseback, this folk lives there." The horsemanship of the Huns and Alans was unsurpassed.

As the Huns had no spurs, they had to urge the horses to a faster pace by using whips, handles of which were found in many graves. So far no stirrups have been found that could be assigned to the Huns. If the Huns had them, they must have been of perishable material, wood or leather. A potent argument against the assumption that the Huns had stirrups is the fact that the Germanic horsemen rode without them for centuries after the fall of Attila's kingdom. Unlike the composite bow, leather or wooden stirrups could have been easily copied. But the specific factor that gave the Hun archers an advantage even over the best troops in the Roman armies *may* have been the stirrup, . . . which [gave stability] to the mounted bowmen.

"The soldiers of Rome," wrote Jerome[14] in the summer of 396, "conquerors and lords of the world, now are conquered by those, tremble and shrink in fear at the sight of those who cannot walk on foot and think themselves as good as dead if once they reach the ground." Jerome's odd description of the Huns was not based on observation; he never had seen a Hun. Like Eunapius[15] who too maintained that the Huns could not "stand firmly on the ground," Jerome copied Ammianus, who wrote: "Their shoes are formed upon no last, and so prevent their walking with free steps. For this reason they are not adapted to battles on foot."

Ammianus' explanation of the peculiar gait of the Hun horsemen when they dismounted and walked is naive. All equestrian nomads who spend a great part of their lives on horseback walk clumsily. And yet the Hun shoes must have struck Ammianus' Gothic informants as strange, very different from their own. Apparently these shoes were fitted to the specific needs of the horsemen. So were those of the Magyars[16] in the tenth century. Their soles were soft and pliable, so that the shoes could be slipped into the nearly round wooden and iron stirrups and be held firmly on them. . . .

Bows and Arrows

"A wondrous thing," wrote Jordanes,[17] "took place in connection with Attila's death. For in a dream some god stood at the side of Marcian, emperor of the East, while he was disquieted about his fierce foe, and showed him the bow of Attila broken in the same night, as if to intimate that this race owed much to that weapon. . . .

The bow was *the* weapon of the Huns. In Ammianus' description of their armament, bow and arrow take the first place. Olympiodorus[18] praised the skill of the Hun-

[13]Roman poet and letter writer (432–480/90).

[14]Early church father (c. 345–420).

[15]Greek historian (345/6–c. 414).

[16]A later tribe of nomads.

[17]A fifth-century historian.

[18]Another fifth-century historian.

nic leaders in shooting with the bow. Aetius,[19] who got his military education with the Huns, was "a very practiced horseman and skillful archer." Shapely bows and arrows, said Sidonius Apollinaris, were the delight of the Huns; they were the best archers. He found no higher praise for Avitus' bowmanship than by saying that he even surpassed the Huns. In the battle on the Nedao the Huns fought with bows and arrows.

A century later, after the East Romans had taken over so many of the weapons and tactics of the barbarians, they were "expert horsemen, and able without difficulty to direct their bows to either side while riding at full speed, and to shoot at opponents whether in pursuit or in flight." And yet Belisars' Massagets, that is, Huns, were still the best bowmen. Even dismounted and running at great speed, they "knew how to shoot with the greatest accuracy."

Although Ammianus had the highest respect for the Hunnic bow, he was not well informed about it. The Huns could, he said, easily be called the fiercest of all warriors, because they fight from a distance with missiles having sharp bone points instead of the ordinary points, joined to shafts with wonderful skill. Why the bone points should have turned the Huns into such superior archers is by no means clear. . . .

The Skill Required

Composite war bows technically as perfect as those of the Huns could only be made by professional bowyers. They must have had workshops like those in the Roman fort at Carleon and Parthian Merv. The making of even such a simple bow as the English longbow required a good deal of craftsmanship. It had to be tapered correctly, with patience and care, from the middle toward each end to bring it to an even curve when full drawn; all knots and irregularities in the grain had to be carefully watched and "raised" or followed skillfully to eliminate weak spots. For a detailed description, the chapter on "Making the Bow" in Pope's classical *Hunting with Bow and Arrow* should be read. "While the actual work of making bows," he wrote, "takes about eight days, it requires months to get one adjusted so that it is good." Turkish manuals on archery contain the names of outstanding bowyers, and there exist long lists of Japanese bowyers, who wrote their names and the date on their bows. . . . The idea that each Hunnic archer could make his own bow could have been conceived only by cabinet scholars who never held a composite bow in their hands.

---

[19]Roman general who defeated Attila at Châlons.

■ ■ ■

STUDY QUESTIONS

1. According to Roman historians like Ammianus Marcellinus, how did the Huns wage war?

2. In what ways did the horses of the Huns differ from those used by the Romans?

3. What type of skills and technologies were involved in the production and use of bows and arrows by the Huns?

4. Traditionally, the Huns have been considered to be the worst of the barbarian tribes. Which aspects of the Hun's culture can be considered crude and which can be considered sophisticated and complex? What are the traits that make one people "barbarians" and others "civilized"?

BIBLIOGRAPHY

A classic and well-written overview of the various nomadic empires is René Grousset, *Empire of the Steppes: A History of Central Asia* (1970). Two interesting works specifically on the Huns are J. Otto Maenchen-Helfen, *The World of the Huns: Studies in Their History and Culture* (1973), and the older but still useful E. A. Thompson, *A History of Attila and the Huns* (1948). A debunking and realistic study of the true effects of the various barbarian invasions is provided by Walter A. Groffart, *Barbarians and Romans, A.D. 418–584: The Techniques of Accommodation* (1980). For a detailed look at a significant battle between settled Europeans and barbarian invaders, see K. Leyser, "The Battle at the Lech, 955: A Study in Tenth-Century Warfare," *History* 50 (1965).

7. WHEN ISLAM RULED IBERIA

Gerald Brenan

Somewhere between the towns of Tours and Poitiers in western France two armies, each numbering about 50,000 soldiers, met in battle during October 732 A.D. One force was composed largely of infantry, the Franks led by Charles Martel. The other consisted of light cavalry, the Moslems under the leadership of Abd er-Rahman, the Islamic governor of Spain. Because he was aware of the danger posed by the highly maneuverable Moslem horse-soldiers, Charles Martel had placed his troops in a solid phalanx on some high ground and awaited attack. Abd er-Rahman and his cavalry did not make him wait long. They charged the Frankish position with great ferocity but met unbreakable resistance and were repulsed. Undaunted, the Moslems charged again and again until sundown brought an end to the fighting for that day. At that point the Moslems discovered that their leader Abd er-Rahman had been killed. Panic set in and the hitherto invincible warriors of Islam abandoned their camp and fled. The next morning the weary and cautious Franks discovered that they had actually won the battle of Tours or Poitiers.

According to the famous eighteenth-century historian Edward Gibbon in his *Decline and Fall of the Roman Empire,* if the Moslems had won the battle, ''Perhaps the interpretation of the Koran would now be taught in the schools of Oxford.'' Instead, Europe and Christendom were saved by Charles Martel and his troops. But what were they saved from? This essay by Gerald Brenan surveys the history of Spain and Portugal from 711 to 1238 under Islamic rule. During those years the interpretation of the Koran was taught in the schools of Córdoba, the Islamic capital of Spain. It was a time of stability and high culture, especially in comparison with the rest of Western Europe at that same time.

One morning in July 711, a battle took place that decided the fate of Spain for more than five centuries. All the country south of the Pyrenees was then ruled by Visigoths, who had occupied it during the last years of the Roman Empire. But far away in the East a new power had arisen which, under the inspiration of a prophet called Mohammed, had overrun Syria, Mesopotamia, Persia, and Egypt. Exhilarated by their easy conquests, the armies of this militant new religion had marched on along the African coast till they reached Morocco. Here they had orders to stop, but the attraction of slaves and booty was too strong: Tarik, the military governor of Tangier, sent 400 men across the Straits of Gibraltar to see what could be picked up. They returned with a cargo of beautiful women who so impressed Musa ibn Nusair, the caliph's governor in North Africa, that he ordered Tarik to take across a stronger contingent the following year.

Tarik landed with a small force, while Rodrigo, the Visigothic king, marched to encounter him with a much larger one. They met on the banks of the shallow lagoon of La Janda, close to Tarifa, and Rodrigo was defeated. Musa himself landed the next summer with another army, and within a couple of years most of the Iberian Peninsula had been occupied by the invaders.

The ramshackle but oppressive Visigothic regime had fallen, and a much more vital one had taken its place. Over the course of years the Moslems were to introduce into Spain the culture of the Alexandrian Greeks and the refinement of the Persians, creating a brilliant civilization that could compare with anything in the East. Yet their long occupation of the

Peninsula was largely an interruption of Spanish history. The Christian state that emerged after centuries of fighting was, as one might expect, a militant state fortified by a militant church. The Spaniards acquired the special character they have had since the Middle Ages not so much by learning from the Moors as by crusading against them, and the culture they eventually adopted was borrowed in all but a few details from France and Italy.

At first, however, the Moslem invaders had it entirely their own way. In every city of Spain they found people who welcomed them. This was partly the result of their tolerant and easygoing policy: everyone who submitted was allowed to keep his estates; the privileges of the great feudal lords were confirmed by special treaties; and there was complete religious toleration, except that the Christians had to pay a poll tax from which the Moslems were exempted. So many Spaniards went over to the new faith in order to escape taxation that within a hundred years of the Arab conquest most of the population professed the creed of Mohammed.

Yet the Moslems did not at first bring settled government. For forty years the country was torn by civil strife. The old feuds of the desert broke out again on Spanish soil, with the men of northern Arabia lined up against those of Yemen. A raid into France to loot the tomb of Saint Martin of Tours was repelled by Charles Martel in 732 at Poitiers, the farthest limit of the Moslem advance. More important for Spain, a center of Christian resistance appeared in the mountains of Asturias: the Visigoth chieftain Pelayo, hiding in a cave with his thirty followers, marks the beginning of the *Reconquista*. Soon his successor, Alfonso, was carving out a kingdom in the northwest, where the wet, forested country held no appeal for the Moslems. From now on there were to be two Spains, perpetually at war with each other.

Meanwhile, great changes were taking place in the East: the Umayyad caliphate of

From ''When Islam Ruled Iberia'' by Gerald Brenan, *Horizon*, September 1962, Vol. V, No. 1, pp. 73–92. Copyright © 1962 Horizon, a division of the American Heritage Publishing Co., Inc. Reprinted by permission.

Damascus had been undermined by the rise of the Shi'ite and Kharijite heresies, and in 750 it fell and was succeeded by that of the Abbasids at Baghdad. The new caliph caught and beheaded every male member of the Umayyad family except one. This was Abd al-Rahman, who, after a series of hairbreadth adventures, escaped to Morocco. From here, on the invitation of one of the factions, he crossed to Spain in 755 and the next year was proclaimed emir of al-Andalus, as the Moslems called their Spanish kingdom. He was twenty-five and his real difficulties were only beginning.

Abd al-Rahman reigned for thirty-two years. Every one of those years was filled with risings and insurrections, made not by the conquered Spaniards but by his ungovernable compatriots. Even his own family conspired against him, and he needed all his energy and ruthlessness to maintain his position. He was a sad man who always dressed in white, the color of his house, and his private tastes lay in gardens and plants that, with the nostalgia of the exile, he imported from his native Syria. But we owe him a debt of gratitude for building the Great Mosque at Córdoba. . . .

Abd al-Rahman was succeeded by his son, Hisham I. His short reign (788–796) is notable for the introduction of the Malikite school of theology. This is the most conservative of the four orthodox Islamic schools, and in Spain it became more conservative than anywhere else. Under the direction of the *fakihs*, or men of religion, it led to a speculative paralysis that down to the end of the caliphate (in 1027) prevented any discussion on philosophic or scientific questions. Every work on these subjects was regarded as heretical. Because the Moslem world elsewhere was being racked at this time by religious controversies, the Malikite orthodoxy helped to keep Spain quiet and so was supported by the emirs in spite of their being themselves inclined to tolerance. One is reminded of the rigid doctrinal control

exercised later by the Spanish Inquisition in order to keep out Protestantism.

The next two emirs had very different reigns. The first, al-Hakam I, was a pleasure-loving man who enjoyed hunting cranes by the river, playing ball, and listening to recitations of poetry; but he incurred the enmity of the *fakihs* because he drank wine, and they stirred up against him riots and rebellions that he put down with great severity. This allowed a long and peaceful reign (822–852) to his successor, Abd al-Rahman II. The work of consolidation now seemed to be over and the emirate of Córdoba took its place among the leading states of the world. It had at least no rivals, for the Abbasid caliphate in Baghdad was in rapid decay, North Africa had split up into independent states, and Europe was sunk in the lowest depths of the Dark Ages. In contrast to this, the life of the court and aristocracy at Córdoba was one of refinement and luxury. Exquisite brocades, gold and ivory caskets, rare books, and accomplished singing girls were imported from the East, while the emir's agents had bought up most of Harun al-Rashid's jewelry.

The person who taught the Córdoban court and aristocracy how to display wealth with elegance was the Iraqi musician Ziryab. He was the best singer of his day and is said to have known more than a thousand songs by heart, each with its appropriate tune. He invented a lute that had five strings instead of four and set up a conservatory in which the ''Andalusian'' music that may be heard today in the gardens of Fez—it is really Persian—acquired its form. But he was more than a musician; he was a man of wide culture and discriminating taste. Finding the customs of the Córdobans crude and provincial, he decided to reform them. With the encouragement of the emir, he laid down rules as to what clothes should be worn in each season, changed hair styles, and taught new ways of cooking and serving food. Thus we find him introducing asparagus and substituting drinking glasses for gold or silver goblets and replacing tableclothes of stamped leather with damask ones.

The history of Moslem states has a peculiar rhythm of its own: a generation or two of stable government is regularly followed by a period of chaos. Autocratic rule is commonly subject to these explosions, which break out when the discontent due to bad trade or to a failure of crops is fanned by local disaffection or by religious fanaticism. So now, after Abd al-Rahman II's death in 852, thirty years of utter anarchy set in. The mountainous region of the south rose under a guerrilla leader from Ronda, and all the great cities rebelled and declared themselves independent. The emirate of Córdoba seemed about to disappear when, in 912, a young man of twenty-one succeeded to the throne. This was Abd al-Rahman III, who was perhaps the greatest ruler Spain was ever to know.

It took him twenty years of hard fighting to reimpose his will on the country. After that he had to contain the Christian states of the north and to assert himself in Morocco, which had been conquered by the Fatimid dynasty that ruled in North Africa and Egypt. It was not till 929 that he felt himself strong enough to take the next step and to assume the title of caliph, Commander of the Faithful. This was possible because the caliphate at Baghdad had by now sunk to a shadow.

Córdoba at this time was a city of well over half a million inhabitants. That is to say, it was a little larger than Fez in Morocco is today. The general appearance of its streets must have been very similar, but it was a place of far greater wealth, and its Moslem aristocracy, hidden away in their palaces and gardens, lived in ease and luxury. In addition to the Great Mosque, which had now been enlarged, there were 700 smaller mosques and oratories and 900 public baths. But the court was the center of everything, and to get an idea of what it was like one must look at the new palace that Abd al-Rahman III put up a few miles outside the city.

Madinat al-Zahra he called it, after a harem favorite. It took thirteen years to build because it was not only a palace but an administrative center that had to house a considerable population. The palace apartments contained 14,000 male domestics, all of them Franks, and 6,000 women, including slaves, living in the harem. As an indication of the cost of supplying this establishment, we are told that 12,000 loaves of bread were brought in every day merely to feed the fish in the ponds. The style of decoration was as lavish as anything to be seen at that time in Constantinople or Baghdad. Four thousand marble columns were employed for the mosque and for the various arcades, whereas the walls of the principal apartments were lined with green and rose marble that had been imported from Tunisia. The ceilings were gilded and the doors inlaid with silver, ivory, and precious stones. But the room known as the Hall of the Caliphs surpassed all the rest. Its vaulted ceiling was encrusted with mosaics, its windows were of translucent alabaster, and it was entered by eight doors paneled with glass. In the center there was a huge marble basin filled with quicksilver. A mechanical device enabled a slave to agitate it; when that happened the whole room seemed to be turning in circles and throwing out spokes of light.

It was in this hall that Abd al-Rahman received the embassies of foreign nations. One came from Emperor Otto of Germany and another from the Byzantine emperor, Constantine Porphyrogenitus. To reach the Caliph they had to ride for four miles between rows of armed and mounted soldiers and then to pass on foot through room after room spread with rare Oriental carpets and hung with silk brocades. At the end they saw the Caliph seated on his throne, with his eight sons and his viziers and chamberlains standing on either

■■ *The chapel of Villaviciosa in the Great Mosque of Córdova.*

side of him, and looking, as Otto's ambassador wrote, like an inaccessible divinity. On another occasion old Queen Tota, her son King Garcia of Navarre, and her grandson Sancho the Fat, deposed king of León, arrived and prostrated themselves before him. The Caliph had sent Sancho a Jewish doctor to cure him of his fatness, and now that he was thin again he had come to beg for an army to restore him to his throne.

It can be imagined what an effect these receptions had on the poor monarchs and ambassadors from the north. Europe was now touching its lowest level of misery and squalor, so that to a German or a Basque the court of Córdoba must have seemed as dazzling as Paris would have been fifty years ago to a Mongol from the Asiatic steppes. Yet it should be remembered that everything the caliphate could show—ceremonies, institutions, objects of luxury and display, palaces, libraries—had been borrowed from Damascus or Baghdad. There had been a complete break with the Roman and Visigothic world and, if we except the architecture of the Great Mosque, nothing new in the arts and refinements of life had made its appearance. A cultivated Iraqi or Egyptian would have found Córdoba dull and provincial.

However, there was one exception to the Oriental color of al-Andalus, and that lay in the language. The upper classes spoke most readily the debased Latin, mixed with Arabic words, that was growing into Spanish. The emirs and caliphs learned it in the nursery, for their mothers, like most of the women in the harem, were Galicians or Basques. For this reason the caliphs had blue eyes and fair hair.

Abd al-Rahman III died in 961 after a forty-nine year reign. He was a man of great presence and majesty who surrounded himself with Byzantine ceremony yet was frank and easy with his friends. His generosity and benevolence made him well-liked, and he had achieved all that he had set himself to do. Yet it seems that he did not regard himself as happy. After his death a paper was found on which he had noted those days of his reign on which he had been completely happy and free from care: they numbered only fourteen.

His son al-Hakam II was forty-six when he succeeded to the throne. He was a bookish man with a loud voice, a beaked nose, and short legs, who suffered from poor health. For this reason he had spent the years before his succession in assembling and reading a library of 400,000 volumes. Few libraries in Europe at this time contained more than 500, but the manufacture of paper had recently been introduced from China to Iraq and paper books cost only a fraction of vellum ones. Arabic script, too, is a sort of shorthand, so that a vast spate of literary, theological, and philosophical works, among them translations from Greek, had begun to appear in the Near East. Many private persons in Córdoba also acquired large libraries; the standard of education in the city was so high that almost everyone could read and write at a time when, in northern Europe, few princes or emperors could read a line.

Al-Hakam II's reign showed a steady advance both in literary culture and in the crafts that minister to luxury. Córdoba ceased to depend on the East for its gold- and silverwork, its carved ivory, its fine cottons and silk brocades, and began to excel in the curing and tooling of leather. The old English word "cordwain," now replaced by "cordovan," preserves a memory of this. In agriculture, too, new plants were introduced—rice, sugar cane, cotton, the date palm, and the pomegranate. (Sweet oranges and lemons came in later.) Mulberry trees were planted in great numbers to feed the silkworms, and the area of land under artificial irrigation was greatly extended. Thus the plains of Valencia, Granada, and Málaga were being transformed into the rich oases one sees today, while in the cities, gardens were laid out with roses, Madonna lilies, and sweet-smelling herbs, edged with borders of rosemary or box. In northern Europe there were as yet no gardens.

After a reign of fifteen years al-Hakam II

died, in 976, leaving a child of twelve, Hisham II, to succeed him. The real ruler, however, was not to be Hisham but an ambitious court official, Ibn Abi Amir, who is best known by the title he later took of al-Mansur, "the Victorious," which in Spanish became Almanzor. By seducing Hisham's Basque mother, he was able to raise himself to the position of chief minister. Then, to conciliate the *fakihs*, he ordered all the books in al-Hakam II's library that treated of science or philosophy to be destroyed; after which, to secure the army, he married the daughter of the powerful frontier general Ghalib. But the critical moment of Hisham's coming of age was approaching. Fortunately for Almanzor, the young Caliph was a weak creature who had been brought up in the harem and was alleged to be prematurely enfeebled by sexual indulgence. He was therefore easily persuaded to delegate the management of public affairs to his chief minister on the grounds that he wished to give himself up to religious exercises. So after suppressing an uprising by his father-in-law, Ghalib, Almanzor became the sole power in the country.

■■■

His first act was to give orders that his name should be mentioned immediately after the Caliph's in the mosques. This gave him the treatment of emir. He then married a daughter of the Christian king of Navarre, who paid him a visit in Córdoba, prostrated himself humbly, and kissed his feet. Ten years later Almanzor took a third wife, a daughter of the king of León. Meanwhile he had built himself a new palace and chancellery just outside Córdoba. Paraphrasing the name of Abd al-Rahman III's palace, he called it Madinat al-Zahira, "the brilliant city," and all the offices of the government were housed there. The older palace-city then became almost deserted, for Hisham had been removed to a fortress next to the Great Mosque in Córdoba.

But it is as a military commander, "the Scourge of the Christians," that Almanzor ac-

quired his reputation. He began by reorganizing the army, increasing the number of the Berber and Frankish mercenaries, and reducing the strength of the native Andalusian levies. Then he pacified Morocco, extending his influence as far as Fez. He was now free to give all his attention to the Christian states in the north of Spain. Twice every year he led an army of from 30,000 to 60,000 men across the frontier, capturing and sacking cities, cutting down trees, and bringing back as slaves the inhabitants he caught. Barcelona, León, Coimbra, Zamora, and Burgos were all taken by him and then burned and destroyed. But Almanzor's crowning exploit was his raid on the shrine of Saint James at Santiago de Compostela. After Rome it was the most famous pilgrimage place in Europe, and he knew that its destruction would send a wave of terror and anger through the Christian world. Marching northward, therefore, along the Portuguese coast, so that his fleet could provision him, he reached the city without opposition and found it abandoned by its inhabitants. He demolished it thoroughly, but spared the tomb of Saint James and the solitary monk who guarded it. Then, carrying with him the doors and the bells of the basilica, he returned to Córdoba. Five years later he was dead. A monk of Burgos recorded it tersely in his chronicle: "In 1002 Almanzor died and was buried in Hell."

These enormously expensive expeditions that the caliphs and Almanzor led across the Christian frontier were not aimed at conquest. No attempt was ever made to gain and occupy fresh territory. They were simply razzias, or raids, made in fulfillment of the command of the Prophet to carry on a holy war against the infidel. They had also the secondary purposes of raising the prestige of the ruler and of capturing slaves. The great prosperity of al-Andalus in Almanzor's time was partly due to the low price of slaves. Yet although these raids were so ruthlessly conducted—all prisoners taken on the battlefield were put to the sword, all cities were sacked, all men, women, and children who could be gathered in were carried off into slavery—there were at the same time close and often friendly relations between the people of the two religions. In al-Andalus itself there was complete religious toleration, and Moslems and Christians intermarried freely. There was some trade across the frontiers, conducted by Jews, and the people of the north imitated the manners and dress of the Moslems. Most surprising of all to our minds, the kings of León and Navarre sometimes enlisted the help of Moslem armies in their civil wars, while in Almanzor's raid on Santiago we read of a number of Leónese counts flocking to his standard and helping him in his assault on the holy shrine. Religion to the men of that day was one thing; war with the profit and honor it brought was another.

Almanzor was succeeded in power by his eldest son, who died after a reign of six years, and then pandemonium broke out. During this period the feeble caliph-in-name-only, Hisham II, was forced to abdicate; a great-grandson of Abd al-Rahman III was made caliph in his place; and contending factions sacked and demolished, within a few months of each other, first the Madinat al-Zahira (so completely that no trace of it remains) and then the Madinat al-Zahra. The latter was the work of rebellious Berber mercenaries who marched back from the frontier and, after destroying al-Zahra, laid siege to the city. At the end of a year and a half it was starved into submission and the Berber troops poured in, looting the palaces and putting the inhabitants to the sword. But the Berbers had no wish to remain in Córdoba. The caliphate was finished, so they obliged the puppet whom they had put on the throne to make over to them the provinces of Granada and Jaén. Other Berbers from Africa occupied Málaga and the hill country around; the Slavs, as the Frankish mercenaries were called, took the east coast from Almería to Valencia; and the Moslem governors of Seville, Badajoz, Toledo, and Saragossa each proclaimed their

independence. Córdoba settled down to be a republic, ruled by its Arab aristocracy, and the twenty years of anarchy known as the *fitna* were over.

Moslem Spain had now broken up into some thirty independent states, and one would have expected that the high standard of culture and learning that had developed during the caliphate would decline. In fact, the opposite happened. The Taifa kingdoms, as they were called, saw a flowering of literature and science that makes it possible to compare them to the Italian cities of the Renaissance. For the rulers of these new states, always in competition with one another, culture was an article of prestige; and so they lavished their money on libraries and *objets d'art* and on salaries to poets, philosophers, and mathematicians. The *fakihs*, who had lost much of their influence, had to bow to this. Thus, while the states where the Berbers had settled remained backward, Seville, Córdoba, Almería, Toledo, Badajoz, and Saragossa became centers where the arts and sciences were enthusiastically cultivated.

Poetry had always been the chief art form of the Arabs: there were great poets in Arabia before Mohammed's day. The caliphs of Córdoba had not only written poems themselves but had maintained a body of professional poets at their court (Almanzor is said never to have gone on a campaign without taking at least forty with him). But this poetry had been of poor quality. Now, however, a number of eminent poets appeared whose work could compare with anything that was being written in the East. Among them we may mention Ibn Hazm, a Córdoban of Spanish descent who also wrote a remarkable prose work on the psychology of love, as well as a comparative history of religion. And there was King al-Mutamid of Seville, whose tragic story has been related by Reinhart Dozy in his *Spanish Islam*. Now this, it will be remembered, is the period in which Provençal poetry was springing up in the south of France. Although there can be no question of any direct influence, it seems likely that the idea that writing love poetry was a proper occupation for courts emanated from al-Andalus, and with it, perhaps, came a certain new attitude toward women. One of the causes of the ending of the Dark Ages was the discovery that the Moslem countries possessed a more refined and luxurious style of living than northern Europe and the desire to the feudal lords to raise more money so as to emulate it.

Philosophy developed for the most part a little later, in the twelfth century. Here the famous names are Avempace, Averroës, Ibn Tufail, and Ibn al-Arabi, to which must be added the Jewish philosophers Avicebrón and Maimonides. It was not a very original philosophy, for it considered mainly of adaptations and combinations of Aristotelian and Neoplatonist ideas; but when it reached the Schoolmen of the north, it made a strong impact. Astronomy and medicine were also much practiced, but again with little advance on the work of the Alexandrian Greeks. Arithmetic, on the other hand, was more or less a creation of the Arabs—although they made little progress with it until they imported the notation we use today, including the sign for zero, from India.

The Taifa kingdoms lasted a bare sixty years. They were too weak to hold back the advancing Christians. Unwillingly, therefore, they called in the new power that had arisen in Morocco. Known as the Almoravids, these camel-riding Berbers from the Sahara lived on dates and veiled their faces (as their descendants, the Tuaregs, still do): they were recent converts to Islam and therefore full of zeal and fanaticism. Their emir, Yusuf, landed in Spain, cut to pieces the Castilian army that had marched to meet him, and then mopped up the Taifa kingdoms. The poets had to stop writing because there was no one to pay them their pensions, and the philosophers had to go into exile because the *fakihs* hated them. After the death of Yusuf there was a little more latitude, but Spanish Moslem culture had now to live on the impetus it drew from the past rather than on any new stimulus. And when Ferdinand III of Castile captured Córdoba in 1236 and Seville in 1248, Moslem rule in al-Andalus was over. Only the small kingdom of Granada remained.

But before this happened a very important thing for European culture had taken place. In 1084, just before the Almoravids crossed over to Spain, Alfonso VI of León and Castile had occupied Toledo. To bring the Spanish church into line with the Roman, he had given the most important posts in it to monks of the Benedictine order of Cluny. They, being Frenchmen, were deeply interested in Scholastic philosophy, and so the next archbishop of Toledo, Raymond, set up an institution for translating the Arab and Jewish philosophers into Latin. This was done by Spanish Jews, who were often trilingual; and in this way a large number of books, including Arab translations of Aristotle, became available about 1150 to Western Europe. They arrived just when the need for them was greatest, and Avicebrón's *Well of Life* and Averroës's commentaries on Aristotle, to name only two, set off the great movement in Western philosophy that culminated in Albertus Magnus, Thomas Aquinas, and Duns Scotus. Other and more accurate translations followed, under the supervision of the Scottish alchemist and Arabic scholar Michael Scot, and works on medicine, astronomy, and mathematics were among them.

Here again it was mainly Greek science that the Arabs passed on. Their great physicians, Avicenna and Avenzoar, whose names were household words in the Middle Ages, introduced the system of Hippocrates, Dioscorides, and Galen. It was not a very useful system, for it was based on the false theory of the four humors; the Arabs, though they had brought in from India some new and valuable drugs, had neglected to pursue the Alexandrian practice of dissection, which might have led them to a better understanding of the functions of the bodily organs. The skill of their doctors was really founded on clinical experience, little of which found its way into their learned treatises. In the same way, Arab astronomy was based almost entirely on Ptolemy's *Almagest*, which Gerard of Cremona translated from Arabic into Latin about 1170. But Indian advances in trigonometry, as well as the more exact observations of their own astronomers, had enabled the Arabs to plot the movements of the stars and planets with greater accuracy; and for this reason the Tables of Arzachel of Toledo became the classic work on astronomy for the peoples of northern Europe and so prepared the way for Copernicus and Tycho Brahe.

Thus we see Spanish Islam passing on its acquisitions to a more creative and energetic world just as it was coming to an end itself (though the Berber kingdom of Granada lingered on till 1492, it had nothing to offer to other peoples). Then in 1610 the Moriscos, as the Moors who had now been forcibly converted to Christianity were called, were expelled from the country. After that scarcely a trace of Arab or Moorish blood remained in the Iberian Peninsula. And very little of their culture either; for apart from the words they had long before brought into the language, the plants and fruit trees they had introduced, a few skills in pottery and in making *artesonado* ceilings that they passed on to their successors, and a few noble buildings, they left nothing behind them. Even the art of flamenco singing and dancing, which is often thought to be Moorish, owes nothing to them. Their great gift to Europe had been the philosophy and science they had passed on, not to the Spaniards, but to the nations of the north. Even this had not been very original, for the talent of the Arabs in these matters lay in assimilation rather than in original creation, which was reserved for poetry and architecture and for their exquisite materials and handicrafts. But races must be judged for themselves, not for what they convey to others; and so we may be glad that during the darkest age of Western history the Arabs gave to a little corner of Europe a brilliant civilization.

■ ■ ■

STUDY QUESTIONS

1. Describe the Moslem conquest of Spain from the Visigoths. How did the native population react to the Moslem conquest?

2. What was the Malikite school of Islamic theology, and what influence did its leaders, the *fakihs*, have on the intellectual life of Moslem Spain?

3. Córdoba was the capital of Islamic Spain. Describe this city and the culture that reached its height under the rule of Caliph Abd al-Rahman III.

4. Who was Almanzor and how did he come to control the Caliphate of Córdoba? What was the long-term effect of his rule on Islamic Spain?

5. What did Islamic Spain contribute to medieval Europe? What was Islam's impact on the development of Spanish culture?

BIBLIOGRAPHY

A good overview of Spanish history during the period covered by the Brenan article and after is Joseph F. O'Callaghan, *A History of Medieval Spain* (1975). More specialized is Roger Collins, *The Arab Conquest of Spain, 710–797* (1989), in the new multivolume history of Spain being edited by John Lynch. Two useful surveys of Islamic Iberia are Anwar G. Chejne, *Muslim Spain: Its History and Culture* (1974), and Jan Read, *The Moors in Spain and Portugal* (1975). W. Montgomery Watt, *The Influence of Islam on Medieval Europe* (1972), is brief and readable. The history of Western Europe's reactions to Islam is provided by Norman Daniels, *Islam and the West: The Making of an Image* (1960), and R. W. Southern, *Western Views of Islam in the Middle Ages* (1962).

8. THE SECRET HISTORY

Procopius

The Emperor Justinian was in many ways like the great architectural structures built during his reign. Take, for example, the Basilica of San Vitale in Ravenna, Italy, built between 526 and 547. The outside of this domed church is plain and unattractive. Its interior, however, is beautifully decorated with a variety of marbles and detailed mosaics. It is fitting that San Vitale houses the famous mosaic of Justinian and his wife Theodora. For like the architectural style of San Vitale, the stately calm of Justinian's reign—the exterior of achievements and progress—opens to an interior world of intrigue, scandal, and complex personalities that form the backdrop of the Justinian Age.

From his Byzantine capital of Constantinople, Justinian attempted to recapture the glory of Rome. He sent his armies west, and they conquered North Africa, Spain, and eventually Italy, defeating along the way the Vandals, the Visigoths, and the Ostrogoths. And he prayed ''that God will grant us the remainder of the empire that the Romans lost through indolence.'' In addition, Justinian codified Roman law. Issued in 533, his *Code* became the foundation for most European law. The arts also flourished under Justinian—religious arts, architecture, and literature of great quality marked his reign. Although criticized for being overly conservative, Justinian's rule enriched the early Middle Ages.

Basic sources for Justinian's reign are the writings of Procopius. Little is known of Procopius' early life. In 527 he became the legal secretary—*consiliarius*—for Belisarius, an ambitious young general. Devoted to the general, Procopius followed Belisarius on the foreign campaigns against the Vandals in North Africa, the Ostrogoths in Italy, and the Goths in Italy. Out of his experiences, Procopius wrote his *History in Eight Books*, also known as the *Wars*, which detail Justinian's wars against the Persians, Vandals, and Goths between 527 and 554. The hero of these books in Belisarius, not Justinian, and they cover events in the capital as well as the actions on the battlefield. Procopius details the insurrection of 532 and terrible plague that ravaged Constantinople ten years later. In addition to the *Wars*, Procopius wrote a six-volume work entitled *Buildings*, an examination of Justinian's architectural achievements. This work was clearly written to advance Procopius' position. Written in a ponderous, pompous style, it is brimming with flattery for the emperor.

Procopius' third work is *The Secret History*, a short volume written between his two longer works, probably in 550. It was not written for public consumption and it was not published until long after its completion. The reason is obvious: *The Secret History* is scandalous. Far from flattering Justinian, *The Secret History* savages him and his wife Theodora. Probably penned for a small, select group of friends, the book recounts the malicious stories and gossip that were whispered about the emperor and empress. The modern reader can well understand why *The Secret History* was not published during Justinian's life. A more difficult question is why it was written at all. Was it because Procopius was slighted or felt slighted? Did it have something to do with Belisarius, who was constantly falling in and out of favor with Justinian? Or did Procopius simply want to leave a complete record of the truth as he saw it, as he heard it, as he believed it? This we do not know. Whether *The Secret History* is the work of a disgruntled bureaucrat, a promotion-seeking official, or an objective historian is unknown.

For the modern historian, *The Secret History* offers an unusually candid insight into Byzantine society and presents a complex maze of problems. Put most simply, the historian must decide what is true and what is not. It is difficult, if not impossible, to verify many of the stories Procopius tells. To be sure, Procopius asserts facts that today we would consider impossible. For example, we would not contend that the wickedness of an emperor could cause the Deity to send floods, earthquakes, and other natural disasters to Constantinople. Nor do we believe the magic that seemed only too real to Procopius. But what of the other wild charges against Justinian and Theodora? Undoubtedly many of his stories are false or at least exaggerated; Procopius was apt to accept and repeat hearsay and rumor. But as the distinguished historian J. B. Bury noted, "in no instance can we convict him [Procopius] of a statement which has no basis in fact." It should be noted, however, that the lack of evidence to prove guilt does not necessarily indicate innocence, for much of the detail in *The Secret History* is found only here. Nowhere is this more true than in Procopius' treatment of Theodora. As one authority asks, "Was she really the daughter of a bearkeeper in the circus? Was she an actress in the theater and a prostitute with an alarming sexual appetite before she married Justinian? Did she really instigate the Gothic king Theodatus to put Amalasuntha to death?" We simply do not know, because *The Secret History* is our only source.

Procopius' attitude toward Theodora in particular and women in general is interesting to the historian and the psychoanalyst alike. He seems to regard women as creatures who use sex to control men. They lie, cheat, scheme, and employ every form of moral and ethical depravity to achieve their ends. Surely this attitude tells us more about Procopius than about the women of Byzantium. On other points, where Procopius had no particular axe to grind, *The Secret History* is enlightening. Historian G. A. Williamson observed that the reader of *The Secret History* will confront a world that is both strange and familiar. Along with tales of demon-lovers and demon-empresses, the reader will learn "of social services, with state-employed doctors and teachers and subsidized entertainment; of elaborately organized postal services; of espionage and counter-espionage; of rates and taxes, custom-offices, import duties, and prohibited imports; of defective street lighting and inadequate water supplies; of monopolies, price-fixing, rake-offs, under-the-counter sales, and the cornering of supplies; of the rising cost of living and depreciation of the currency; of smaller loaves and adulterated flour; of a statute of limitations; of a mad passion for sport and the frantic and aggressive partisanship of its devotees." The reader will, in brief, enter a world peopled by men and women who live with many of the same problems that we live with today.

Justin's nephew, Justinian, ran the whole government and was responsible for evils to the Romans of a kind and magnitude such as no man before ever heard of. He readily advanced to the wicked slaughter of men and to the seizure of property to which he had no right, and it was nothing to him if many tens of thousands of men perished, even though they had done nothing to deserve it. He would not maintain the existing order and was all for continual change; to sum up, this man did more destruction than anything or anyone else. At least, though the plague (which I described in my earlier work) fell on the entire earth, as many men escaped as perished from it, either through never having caught the disease or else having survived it after they had contracted it. But no Roman whatever succeeded in escaping from this man—he fell like a disaster from heaven over the whole race and left no one whatever untouched. Some he killed without cause, others he left contending with poverty, more wretched than the dead, praying to him to release them from their present troubles, even by a cruel death. From some, however, he took their lives *and* their money. Since it was nothing to him to destroy only the Roman state, he succeeded in gaining the mastery over Africa and Italy as well, simply in order to destroy the people there, together with those under his sway already. Before he had been ten years in power, he put to death among others Amantius, the chief of the palace eunuchs, for no reason, the only charge against the man being that he had spoken hastily to John, the archbishop of the city. After this, he was the most feared of all men. He even recalled the usurper Vitalian forthwith, first giving him guarantees of safety and allowing him to participate in the Christian mysteries. And shortly afterwards when he had crossed him, he murdered him—on suspicion, without justification—in the palace with his followers, without a thought for these solemn pledges.

■■■

The people had long been split into two factions, as I have related in my earlier work, and by espousing one himself—that of the Blues—which he had been supporting already, he succeeded in throwing everything into confusion and disorder. As a result of this, he brought the Roman state to its knees.[1]

Not all the Blues were ready to follow his wishes, however—only the factious among them. Even these gave the appearance, as the evil wore on, of being the soberest of men, for the magnitude of their crimes did not match up to that of their opportunities. Not that the factious ones among the Greens remained inactive—they, too, were always committing crimes, so far as they were able, though they were constantly being punished individually. This incited them all the time to still greater boldness. For when men are wronged they usually turn to folly. So then while he was fanning and openly stirring up the Blues, the entire Roman Empire was shaken to the core, as if an earthquake or a flood had fallen upon it, or as if every city had been captured by the enemy. There was total confusion in them; nothing was the same any longer. The laws and order in the state were completely controverted in the confusion which befell them.

First the factious elements changed their hair style to a new fashion. They had it cut quite differently from the other Romans. They did not touch the moustache or beard, wanting them to grow very long, like the Persians. They cut off the front of their hair as far as the

[1]The Blues and the Greens were factions originating in athletic competitions at the circus or stadium.

temples and allowed the back hair to hang down very long, in a disorderly way, like the Massagetai. Hence they called this the "Hunnic style."

Then they all developed a passion for clothes and adopted a costume more splendid than their rank warranted. They could get these things from stolen funds. The part of the tunic which came to their hands was gathered in very closely around the wrist, while the rest of the sleeve, as far as the shoulder, billowed out in great width. When their hand was waved about while they applauded at the theater and at the Hippodrome, or while they urged on their favorites in the usual way, this part actually ballooned out, so that unsophisticated people thought that their physique was so fine and strong that they needed garments like this to cover them. For they did not realize that the scrawniness of their bodies was actually accentuated by the fineness and looseness of their clothing. Their cloaks and trousers and most of all their shoes were classed as "Hunnic," both in name and style.

At first nearly all of them carried arms—openly at night, but during the day they hid two-edged swords at their thighs, under their clothing. When it grew dark, they would gather together in groups and rob rich men, both in the open market place and in the narrow streets, taking from those who fell in with them their clothing and their girdle and their gold pins and anything else they had in their hands. Some they saw fit to kill as well as rob in order to stop them from telling anyone what had happened. Everyone, including the more sober of the Blues, was very upset by this behavior—for not even the other Blues remained unscathed. As a result many took to wearing bronze girdles and pins, and clothing far inferior to their standing, so as not to perish thanks to their love of display, and went back home before sunset and hid there. As the evil dragged on and there was no check to the miscreants from the city authorities their boldness kept increasing all the time. Given license,

wrongdoing usually increases beyond all bounds, for even crimes which are punished are not completely checked. For the majority turn easily to wrongdoing by nature.

So this was how the Blues went on. Of their opposing faction, some went over to their party, wanting to share in their crimes without being punished, while others secretly fled to other countries. Many also were caught there and killed by their enemies, or else punished by the government. Many other young men flooded into this society, though they had never before cared for such things, driven there by the chance of power and lawlessness. There is no pollution named by men which was not committed at that time and left unpunished. First they destroyed their opponents, but then they went further and killed even those who had had no quarrel with them. Many actually bribed them and pointed out their own enemies to them; these they killed at once, accusing them of being Greens, even when they were quite unknown to them. And this no longer occurred in darkness or in concealment, but at every time of day and in every place in the city; the deeds were at times even done under the eyes of eminent persons. They no longer needed to conceal their crimes, for no fear of punishment lay upon them; instead, they actually conceived a desire for competition and held displays of strength and bravery, killing an unarmed passerby with one blow, and no man had any hope any longer of survival in this perilous situation. Everyone thought in his terror that death was upon him; no place seemed safe, no time secure for safety. Men were killed even in the holiest churches and at public assemblies without the slightest pretext, and no trust remained any longer in friends or relatives. Many died after actually being attacked by their closest associates.

But no inquiry was held into these events. Disaster came to all unexpectedly, and no one helped those who had fallen. In no law or contract was there left any power resting on the security of the established order—everything turned to violence and confusion, and the state resembled a tyranny. Not, however, an established one—one that was changing every day and still in the process of being constituted. The minds of the magistrates seemed as if they were stunned, for their spirit was enslaved through fear of one man, and the judges giving decisions on disputed points did not vote as they held to be just and lawful, but according to the goodwill or hostility of the rioters to the disputants. Death was the punishment for the judge who disregarded their instructions.

Many money-lenders under great duress had to hand back their notes to their debtors, without receiving any of the money owing; and many freed their household slaves, much against their will. It is said that some women were actually forced by their own slaves to acts without their consent. The sons of prominent men now joined these youths also and forced their fathers to do many things, including giving up their property to them. Many boys were compelled to submit against their will to impious unions with the rioters in the full knowledge of their fathers. Women, too, who were living with their husbands had to suffer the same fate. It is said that one woman dressed in great luxury was sailing with her husband to a suburb on the opposite shore. Some of the rioters came upon them on this journey, took her from her husband with threats, and put her on their own boat. She entered the boat with the youths, whispering to her husband to have courage and fear no disgrace on her behalf, for her person would not be outraged. And while her husband was still looking at her in great distress she threw herself into the sea and perished at once.

This, then, was the extreme to which these rioters resorted in Byzantium. But this caused less grief to those who encountered it than the wrongs committed against the state by Justinian. This is because those who have suffered terrible things from villains are greatly comforted in their indignation at the disorder which has befallen them by the continual expectation of vengeance from the government. When there is hope for the future, men bear their present situation more easily and with less distress. But when they are oppressed by the government of the state, their distress is naturally increased; they will always fall into despair because they have no hope of vengeance. Justinian did wrong not only because he would not support the wronged, but also because he was actually willing to take a public stand as the champion of these rioters. He supplied these youths with large sums of money and kept many of them with him and saw fit to summon some of them to offices and to other honors.

■ ■ ■

So this was what was going on in Byzantium and in all the cities. Like any other disease, the evil started there and spread all over the Roman Empire. But the Emperor, who had no perception, paid no attention to what was happening, even though he was a continual spectator of the events in the hippodromes. He was extremely stupid, like a lazy donkey that follows the man, dragging the bridle with much shaking of the ears. Not only did Justinian do this—he stirred up everything else, too. As soon as he took over his uncle's throne, he was eager to spend all the public money at once without caring, now that he was master of it. He kept lavishing great sums destined for the state on any Huns he came into contact with; as a result it came about that the land of the Romans was exposed to constant attacks. Once these barbarians had tasted Roman gold they would not any longer keep off the road which led to it.

He also saw fit to squander large sums on building on the seacoast, trying to force back the continual swell of the waves. He was always trying to advance out from the shore with piles of stones, vying with the onslaughts of the ocean, as if setting his immense wealth in competition with the power of the sea. He gathered to himself the private property of Romans from every land, bringing a random and undeserved charge against some, and in other cases making up fairy tales about them, saying that they had given it to him. Many who were charged with murder and other similar charges escaped from paying the penalty for their crimes by giving him all their property. Others, who were for instance disputing with their neighbors over some land to which they had no right, and could not get a decision against their rivals by arbitration since the law was against them, got free by bestowing the disputed property on him. In this way they gained an advantage without strings—they had become known to him, and they had managed in this disgraceful fashion to get the better of their opponents.

I do not consider it inappropriate to give some idea of his appearance also. In figure, then, he was neither too tall nor too short, but of medium height. Nor was he thin, but a little stout, and his face was round and not unhandsome. He had a high color, even when he had not drunk for two days. . . .

So this was his physical appearance. As for his character, I cannot describe it in full. This man was both wicked and gullible, the sort they call "both knave and fool." He was not truthful with those whom he met, but dissembling in all his words and actions, and at the same time a ready victim for deceivers. In him there was a strange mixture of folly and vice. Perhaps this was what one of the Peripatetic philosophers meant in ancient times when he said that men's characters are formed of a mixture of the most extreme opposites, like the mixing of colors. Nevertheless, I am setting down what I have been able to achieve.

This Emperor, then, was dissembling, treacherous, false, secret in his anger, two-faced; a clever man, well able to feign an opinion; one who wept not from joy or from sorrow but on purpose, at the right moment to suit the present need. He was always deceiving—yet not without purpose, even after laying things down in writing and swearing the most solemn oaths to ratify his agreements; all this to his own subjects. He would retreat at once from his agreements and his oaths, like the lowest of slaves brought to agree on oath through terror of threats of torture. He was an unreliable friend; an enemy who would not keep a truce; a passionate lover of murder and of money. He always stirred up trouble and change; he was easily led to evil, but never for any reason did he turn to good. Quick to devise and to carry out vice, he thought the very hearing of virtue distasteful. How could anyone set down Justinian's character in writing? He could be seen to have these and many still worse superhuman vices; nature seemed to have taken away wickedness from all other men and put it all in his heart. Besides this, he was too susceptible to slander and too quick to punish. He never made an investigation before he gave his decision—immediately on hearing the testimony of slander, he would make his decision and order its publication. He would make decrees without any hesitation— the capture of strongholds and the burning of cities and the enslavement of whole populations for no reason. If, then, anyone were to estimate all that has happened to the Romans from ancient times and to counterbalance it with this, I think greater slaughter would be found to have taken place under this man than has happened in the whole of the rest of history. He never hesitated to acquire other men's money in secret, never even seeing fit to assume some pretext as a cover of justification before laying his hands on what did not belong to him. And once it was his own, he was very ready to squander it in senseless ostentation and pour it out at random upon the barbarians. In sum, he neither had any money himself, nor allowed anyone else to have any—as if he were a victim of a grudge against

■ ■ *Mosaic of the Empress Theodora and her attendants.*

those who had it, rather than greedy for money. So by depriving all the Roman Empire of its wealth, with the greatest of ease, he became responsible for general poverty.

■■■

So this was Justinian's character, so far as I am able to describe it. I will now reveal the birth and upbringing of the woman he married, and how after being united to this man in marriage, she ruined the whole Roman state from top to bottom.

There was in Byzantium a certain Acacius, an animal keeper who tended the wild beasts owned by the Green faction and used in the Hippodrome. This office is called Bearkeeper. This man died of disease in the reign of the Emperor Anastasius, leaving three female children, Comito, Theodora, and Anastasia, the eldest of whom had not yet reached the age of seven years. His widow married another man, who meant to look after the household and the office of Bearkeeper in future, together with her. But the Dancing Master of the Greens, whose name was Asterius, ejected them from the post in return for a bribe from someone else, and substituted for them, without opposition, the man who had paid him. The Dancing Masters had the power of arranging this freely as they liked. When the woman saw all the people gathered at the beast hunt, she put garlands on the heads of her children and in their hands and sent them down as suppliants. The Greens, however, would not accept their plea. But the Blues appointed them to the same post, for their animal keeper had just died.

When these children grew up, their mother put them on the stage at once, for they were beautiful. Not all at the same time, however, but as each in turn seemed old enough. The first, Comito, had already become famous among the prostitutes at her age. Theodora, the next, used to wear a sleeved frock fit for a slave girl and follow her around, attending her and carrying on her shoulders the stool on which she used to sit at assemblies. At this time Theodora was immature and could not sleep with men, nor have intercourse with them as a woman. But she did allow the wretches to make love to her as if she were a boy—slaves, who came with their masters to the theater and indulged in this filthiness as a sideline to their existing easy life—and she spent much time in the brothel in this unnatural act. As soon as she grew and matured, her mother put her on the stage and she became a prostitute at once—what used to be called a "whore." She could not play the flute or the harp, and she had not even trained her in dancing; she simply sold her beauty to all comers, putting her whole body to work. Then she joined with the actors in all the productions of the theater and took part in their performances, helping out their comedy and clowning. She was very witty and full of jokes and became famous for it at once. The girl had no shame, and no one ever saw her embarrassed. She would undertake shameless services without hesitation, and she was the sort of girl who would joke and laugh out loud when she was being beaten or struck about the head. She would bare herself front and back to whomever she met, showing them what men ought not to see or to catch a glimpse of.

As she played with her lovers, she would keep bantering them, and she always managed to win over the hearts of the licentious by the coyness with which she suggested new positions. She never even expected that any of the men she was with would make the approach; instead she approached them herself, with laughter and clowning, shimmying her hips at everyone who came near, especially if they were young boys. There was never such a slave to pleasure of every kind. She even went on picnic parties on many occasions with ten or more young men, all very strong, ones who had made a job of lovemaking, during which she would lie with all her fellow diners all night long, and when they had all tired, she would go to their attendants, thirty of them perhaps, and pair off with each one in turn, and even so she could not get enough of this lewdness. . . .

She would often actually take off her clothes in the theatre, before an audience of the whole population, and stand naked in their midst, except for a girdle around her private parts—not because she was ashamed to show them to her audience, but because it is forbidden for anyone to be completely naked there, without a girdle around the loins. In this outfit she would lie down flat on her back on the ground. Some attendants posted for the job would scatter barley over her private parts, and geese at hand for the purpose would peck it from there with their beaks and eat it. She would stand up without a blush—she even seemed to take pride in this act. Not only was she without shame herself—she was also better than anyone else at thinking up shameless deeds. . . . To those who saw her, especially at dawn, she was a bird of ill-omen. And toward her fellow actresses she was always very bitchy, for she was a spiteful woman.

Some time later she was in attendance on Hecebolus, a Tyrian who had taken over the government of Pentapolis, performing all sorts of disgusting services for him. She quarreled with him, however, and was at once thrown out. So she was in need of food, which she supplied from then on by prostitution in her usual manner. So she came first to Alexandria. Later after going all over the East, she returned to Byzantium, plying in every city the trade which, I believe, no man can name and keep the mercy of God—as if God could not endure that there should be any place unaware of the wantonness of Theodora.

In this way, then, the woman was born and reared and became notorious in the eyes of many prostitutes as well as of all mankind. When she came to Byzantium for the second time, Justinian fell passionately in love with her and at first associated with her as his mistress, though raising her to the rank of patrician. So Theodora managed to acquire enormous power at once and also a considerable amount of money. As happens with all who are passionately in love, Justinian thought nothing sweeter than to give every kind of present and money to his mistress. The state served as fuel for this love affair. So with her he set about still further destruction of the people, not only in Byzantium but throughout the Roman Empire. They had both long belonged to the Blue faction and gave these rioters full reign over the affairs of state. But long afterwards most of the evil was relieved, in the following way.

It so happened that Justinian was ill for many days, so dangerously ill that he was even reported to have died. But the factionists still went on committing the crimes which I have described, and in broad daylight they killed a certain Hypatius, a man of some eminence, in the church of Sophia. After this crime, the disturbance created by the action reached the Emperor, and his attendants all took advantage of his absence from the scene to magnify the extraordinary nature of what had happened, recounting all that had taken place right from the beginning. At this, the Emperor gave orders to the City Prefect to exact punishment for all this. This man was called Theodotus, surnamed Colocynthius. He made full-scale investigations and managed to arrest many of the criminals and deal with them by the

processes of the law, but many went undetected and saved themselves. For it was fated that they should destroy the affairs of Rome in the meantime. But Justinian was suddenly cured, making an unexpected recovery, and at once set about putting Theodotus to death as a wizard and magician. When he could not do away with him on any pretext, he tried by terrible torture to force some of his friends to give false information against him. Everyone kept out of the way, lamenting in silence for his plots against Theodotus, and only Proclus, who held the office called the "quaestor," said openly that the man was innocent of the charge and did not deserve to be put to death. For this reason Theodotus was sent by order of the Emperor to Jerusalem. But he heard that some men had come to kill him, so he stayed permanently in the temple and lived in this way for the rest of his life.

This then was what happened in the case of Theodotus. After this the factionists became the most sober of men. They no longer went on committing the same crimes, even though they had the opportunity of exploiting still more freely their lawless way of life. This is clear, for when a few of them pursued the same outrageous behavior later, no punishment followed. Whoever was in charge of punishing them kept allowing these criminals freedom to escape, in this way by his complicity inducing them to trample on the laws.

So while the Empress was still alive, it was quite impossible for Justinian to make Theodora his legal wife. In this matter alone, though she opposed him in nothing else, she stood in his way. For she was wholly virtuous, a countrywoman, a barbarian by birth, as I have narrated. She never managed to acquire any polish at all and remained to the end of her life quite ignorant of politics—a woman who did not even come to the palace under her own name because it sounded ridiculous, but with the new name of Euphemia. But later it came about that the Empress died. The Emperor was now senile and very old and was laughed at by his subjects, who all despised him for not understanding what was going on. They paid no attention to him, but paid court to Justinian in great fear. For he kept on stirring everything up by causing continual confusion and disturbance. At this time, he set about marrying Theodora. Because it was impossible for a man of senatorial rank to marry a prostitute (it had been forbidden long ago by very ancient laws), he forced the Emperor to revoke the laws by another law, and after this he lived with Theodora as his wife and made marriage to prostitutes possible for all the others. He immediately set about usurping and acquiring the place of the Emperor, hiding force under a dissembling pretext for his action. All the leading citizens proclaimed him Emperor of Rome, his uncle being induced to vote for this in great terror. So Justinian and Theodora took over the Imperial power three days before the Easter festival [A.D. 527], at a time when it is not permitted to greet a friend or to say "Peace be with you." And not many days later, Justin died of sickness after a reign of nine years, and Justinian, together with Theodora, got the Imperial power for himself.

■ ■ ■

So then after being born, reared, and brought up in this kind of way, as I have said, Theodora attained the rank of Empress without any hindrance being put in her way. No consciousness of wrong came to her husband, that though it was possible for him to choose a bride from the entire Roman Empire and make his wife the highest born and most discreetly reared of all women, one who was not unversed in modesty and who lived with sobriety, and furthermore, one of remarkable beauty, a virgin, and as the saying goes, firm breasted, instead he saw fit to make his own the curse of all men, without being cast down by any of what I have described, and to join himself to a woman who was responsible, among many great pollutions, even for the slaying of many children by voluntary abortion. I do not think I need say more about this man's character. This marriage will be enough to indicate the whole state of his soul. It will serve as interpreter, witness, and recorder of his ways. A man who pays no heed to the disgrace incurred by past actions and does not shrink from appearing despicable to those he meets will tread any path to crime, and he will advance to the wickedest of actions without thought or hesitation, with shamelessness on his face. Yet no member of the Senate, on perceiving that the state was taking upon itself this disgrace, raised a voice in protest or objected to this action, even though they would all have to do obeisance to her as to a god. There was not even a priest to be seen objecting, and this, too, though they were going to have to call her their sovereign. The populace which had formerly watched her perform, at once, with upturned hands, disgracefully demanded the position of her slave. No soldier made any difficulties at the prospect of undergoing the dangers of campaign on behalf of Theodora's interests, nor did anyone whatsoever oppose her. Everyone, I suppose, yielded and gave way to the idea that this was ordained, thus allowing Fortune to give a display of her power—Fortune, which directs all human affairs and cares neither that what happens should be reasonable nor that it should seem to men to be happening rationally. At any rate, she will suddenly raise a man by some irrational power to a great height, and though many obstacles seem to encompass him, she opposes him in nothing whatever, and he is carried along by every possible means in whatever direction she has laid down, while everything readily stands aside and gives way to the advance of Fortune. But let this be as God wishes and be recorded thus.

Theodora had a lovely face and was generally beautiful, but she was short and pale—not completely, but enough to seem pallid—and her expression was always serious and frowning. All time would not be enough for anyone who tried to record most of her past life on the stage. I have selected a little in what I said before, and I may perhaps have succeeded in indicating for posterity the general scope of the woman's character. Now I must speak briefly of what she and her husband did, for they never acted separately in their life together. For a long time they gave everyone the impression that they were constantly at odds in opinions and mode of life. But later it was realized that this was deliberately cultivated by them so that their subjects, far from joining together and rebelling against them, would all have different views about them.

First, then, they divided the Christians and created divisions among them all by feigning to differ from each other in their disputes, as I shall shortly record. Later they divided the factionists also. Theodora pretended to be supporting the Blues with all her might and allowed them freedom against their opponents, giving them the chance of committing terrible and violent crimes with complete lawlessness. Justinian gave the impression of being secretly angry and enraged, but unable to withstand his wife's orders. They often reversed their roles and adopted the opposite course. Then Justinian punished the Blues as criminals, while Theodora claimed that she was angry and complained that she was being overridden by her husband.

But the members of the Blue faction, as I have said, gave the impression of being very sober. They would not harm their neighbors as much as they could have done, and in the quarrels about lawsuits each side seemed to support one of the parties, though it was inevitable that the one which had allied with the unjust cause would win; in this way they got unjust possession of most of the property of the disputants. This Emperor enabled many of those whom he counted among his friends to do violence and to commit what crimes they liked against the state. But when they were seen to have acquired a large amount of wealth, they immediately fell foul of his wife and were found to have done her some offense. At first Justinian would favor them with great enthusiasm, but later he would change his mind toward them and suddenly begin to waver in his support. At once she would set about ruining them, while he, as if knowing nothing of what was happening, shamelessly grabbed all their property. With these devices they were always in agreement with each other, though on the surface they pretended to be at odds, and thus they were able to divide their subjects and strengthen their rule.

■■■

STUDY QUESTIONS

1. What distinguished the Blues from the Greens in the political power struggle during Justinian's reign?

2. Describe the background and character of Justinian and Theodora. By what means did they acquire power?

3. Describe Procopius' attitude toward women.

4. Why do you think Procopius wrote *The Secret History?* Whom did he hope to please?

BIBLIOGRAPHY

The age of Justinian is known for its many achievements as well as for its excesses. Four standard overviews are Steven Runciman, *Byzantine Civilization* (1970); A. A. Vasiliev, *History of the Byzantine Empire, 324–1453* (1952); M. Grant, *The Dawn of the Middle Ages* (1981); and P. Brown, *The World of Late Antiquity, A.D. 150–750* (1971). J. Hussey, *The Byzantine World* (1961), treats Justinian in the context of his times. An interesting look at Theodora is A. Bridge, *Theodora: Portrait in a Byzantine Landscape* (1984). J. A. S. Evans, *Procopius* (1972), and G. A. Williamson's introduction to Procopius, *The Secret History* (1966 Penguin Books edition), place the writings in a proper perspective. On Justinian and the politics of his reign, see J. W. Baker, *Justinian and the Later Roman Empire* (1966); R. Browning, *Justinian and Theodora* (1971); G. Downey, *Constantinople in the Age of Justinian* (1966); and P. N. Ure, *Justinian and His Age* (1951).

Part Three

FAITH AND ORDER: CHURCH AND STATE IN FEUDAL EUROPE, 1000–1350

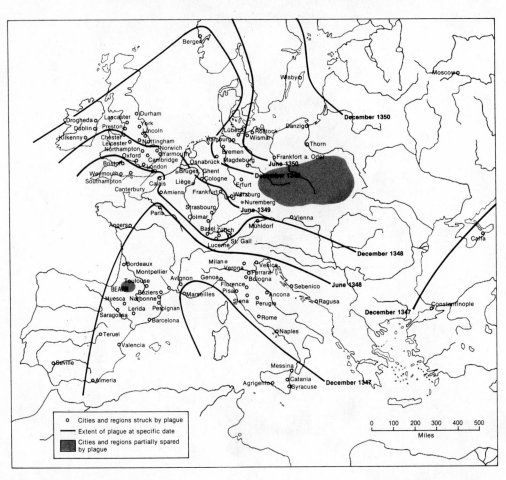

Cities and regions struck by plague
— Extent of plague at specific date
▓ Cities and regions partially spared by plague

Although historians used to describe medieval Europe as the "Dark Ages" when social and political life was static and unchanging, those centuries were actually times of dynamic change, particularly in terms of religious life. From its humble beginnings in Judea, Christianity spread throughout Europe, imposing a similar cultural tradition on widely diverse peoples. Within Roman Catholicism, a revolution occurred that led to the creation of what we recognize as the modern church. During the eleventh and twelfth centuries, medieval Catholicism institutionalized the practices of individual confession and priestly celibacy, the belief in transubstantiation—the actual conversion of the sacramental bread and wine into the body and blood of Christ—and the image of Christ on the cross as a dying man-God who deserved worship and compassion.

But during those years the Church also became the preeminent political institution in Europe, a separate sovereign entity in its own right, independent of the other monarchs and princes of the time. The great western tradition of separation of church and state was established in the triumphant independence of Roman Catholicism. In Eastern Europe, the orthodox Christian groups never achieved that separation, always remaining an extension of and subordinate to the state. In Rome, the "papal revolution" of the eleventh and twelfth centuries liberated the church from lay control; set the clergy up as a distinct group separate from the rest of society; established new monastic orders, like the Hospitallers and Cistercians, which spread throughout Europe but which were centrally controlled by Church officials; and gave to the pope, as head of the Church, a political status equal to that of the other heads of state in Europe. The independence of the Church was not won without a struggle; the ruling prelates of Europe were loath to surrender any of their prerogatives, but the church prevailed in that struggle and basked in its independence.

The political power of the Church was nothing compared to the cultural power it wielded. It is difficult for people living in the late twentieth century to appreciate the influence of the Church on the daily life of individual people. Medieval Europeans did not just believe in God or attend mass; they saw the Roman Catholic Church as *the* earthly manifestation of the majesty of God, *the* way in which the will of God was expressed to human beings. Religious belief permeated daily life, shaping the way people interpreted their past, governed their present, and anticipated their future. Such complete permeation of religion in daily life is shown by Rudolph Bell in describing how Margaret of Cortona became anorexic as a religious gesture.

There were, of course, heretical movements during the twelfth century, as the first reading in this part reveals. Like any other institution enjoying wealth, political power, and cultural influence, the Church began to seem too worldly and materialistic to more ascetic Christians. At the same time, the Church's drive to assign miraculous powers to priests introduced a new distance between the clergy and laypeople. At times common people felt spiritually inferior to the clergy. In the latter part of the twelfth century, these two trends inspired a series of protest movements, such as those by the Albigensians and the Waldensians. A later rebellion is described here by Malcolm Barber. In response the Church emphasized the omnipotence of the Papacy and crushed dissent. The instrument the Church used to achieve this control was the Inquisition, which inquired after heretical ideas and rooted them out.

But for the vast majority of people, the rule of behavior was obedience and loyalty. All truth, they believed, was circumscribed in the teachings and rulings of Roman Catholicism. All medieval art and literature reflected that reality. From the great crusades to liberate the Holy Land from the "infidels," described here by Jonathan Riley-Smith, to the daily devotions of tens of millions of people, the "Church triumphant" was the central theme of religious life in medieval Europe. With that conviction, that passion, Roman Catholicism dominated the private lives of individual people and conducted public campaigns against dissenters and unbelievers.

9. DREADFUL SYMMETRY: HERESY'S THREAT TO MEDIEVAL CHRISTENDOM

For the people of the Middle Ages there was one true religion and Church. It was impossible for there to be more. Little room existed for differences of opinion, because truth was an absolute and eternal thing. It was not often relative and changeable, as it tends to be for modern people. To oppose accepted religious truth was to be a heretic. As Robert Grosseteste (c.1170–1253), the great English scholar and churchman, put it, heresy was "an opinion chosen by human faculties, contrary to holy Scripture, openly taught and obstinately defended." It was the Inquisition's job to find heretics, to teach them the error of their ways, or to see that they were removed as a threat to Christian society.

Furthermore, medieval society accepted the belief that a true faith in the tenets of Christianity was the one sure way to eternal joy in heaven. Any unauthorized variation in belief would result in damnation and endless torment in hell. So when heretics converted some innocent to belief in their errors, they had potentially killed their victim's soul for eternity. Murderers only killed their victim's body in its temporary, earthly existence. Given these assumptions, a heretic was obviously much more dangerous than a murderer. But such soul-murder was not the only danger that heretics posed to Christian society.

By challenging the authority of the medieval Church, heretics threatened an institution that had brought stability and order to the people of Europe. Without the Church, true civilization was impossible. This belief was based on concrete fact. Medieval civilization, like most past societies, teetered much closer to the abyss of breakdown and anarchy than do modern societies. Even a monarch whose true loyalties to Christianity were as widely suspect as those of Emperor Frederick II (1194–1250) did his part to aid in the suppression of heresy (see documents 1 and 2).

Furthermore, the threat of heresy was very real. Medieval people imagined that heretics would turn into loathsome toads (see document 6) or that they were in league with the devil (see document 3). These sorts of stories were both superstitious fantasy and a way of dehumanizing the enemy. Heretics—even those as numerous as the Albigensians of the late twelfth and early thirteenth centuries—did not leave any surviving records that tell their side of the story. But even the hostile accounts of the orthodox provide occasional glimpses of the real human beings behind the heresies. The Albigensians (also variously and imprecisely called Patarins, Cathars, or Manicheans) prided themselves on their holy and simple lives according to the description of their persecutor Bernard of Gui (fl. early 1300s) (see document 4). They claimed to be creating a purer church that could replace what they saw as the corrupt Church of Rome that had control over medieval society. Caesar of Heisterbach (c.1180–1240) may have thought that the two heretics received all their power from the devil (see document 3) but even he admitted that they achieved their initial success by the example of their generosity and self-sacrifice. Certainly the wife of the heretic who saved himself by confessing his errors to the Church's officers thought that their faith was worth dying for and quickly reminded her husband of that fact (see document 5). In other words, beneath all the superstition and paranoia connected with heresy there were real human beings, not bogeymen. These heretics were sincere in their beliefs, but they were ultimately the losers. Furthermore, they did represent a genuine danger to the fragile order of medieval Europe. Religious differences have always been a major source of conflict in human history. Society after society has been torn apart by religious conflict. Therefore, the savage suppression of the various heretics of the Middle Ages is understandable, despite the fact that it was an ugly chapter in human history.

Document 1: Laws Concerning Heresy in the Kingdom of Sicily

The Emperor Frederick II (1194–1250) was the ruler of Sicily in addition to being the Holy Roman Emperor of Germany. His contemporaries generally considered him to be a libertine, a wizard, and a heretic in spite of his provision of the stern laws against heresy.

The heretics endeavor to rend the seamless garment of our Lord, and in accordance with their vicious name, which means division, they would destroy the unity of that same indivisible faith. They would withdraw the sheep from Peter's guardianship, to which they were entrusted by the Good Shepherd. They are ravening wolves within, but feign a love for the flock, until they shall have crept into the Lord's fold. They are bad angels, sons of perversity, appointed by the father of lies and deception to mislead the simple minded. They are serpents who deceive the doves. Like serpents they creep stealthily abroad; with honeyed sweetness they vomit forth their virus. While they pretend to offer life-giving food, they strike with their tail, and prepare a deadly draught, as with some dire poison. These sects do not assume the old names, lest they should be recognized, but, what is perhaps more heinous, not content like the Arians, who took their name from Arius, or the Nestorians, from Nestorius, and others of the same class, they must imitate the example of the martyrs who suffered death for the catholic faith. They call themselves Patarins, as if they, too, were *sufferers*.[1] These same wretched Patarins, who refuse to accept the holy belief in the eternal Trinity, combine three offences in their wickedness. They offend God, their neighbor and themselves—God, since they refuse to place their faith in Him or recognize His Son; their fellow-men since they deceive them by offering them the seductions of a perverse heresy under the form of spiritual nurture. Against themselves they rage even more fiercely, for, prodigal of life and careless of death, in addition to the sacrifice of their souls, they involve their bodies in the toils of a horrible end, which they might avoid by acknowledging the truth and adhering to the true faith. What is worst of all, the survivors are not terrified by such examples.

Against these who offend alike against God, themselves and their fellow-men, we cannot restrain ourselves and must draw forth the sword of merited retribution. We pursue them the more closely, inasmuch as they are known, to the obvious prejudice of the Christian faith, to extend the crimes of their superstition toward the Roman Church, which is regarded as the head of all other churches. Thus from the confines of Italy, especially from parts of Lombardy, where we are convinced that their wickedness is widespread, we now find rivulets of their perfidy reaching even to our kingdom of Sicily. Feeling this most acutely, we decree, in the first place, that the crime of heresy and of reprehensible teaching of whatever kind, by whatever name its adherents may be known, shall, as provided by the older laws, be included among the recognized crimes. (For, should not what is recognized to be an offence against the Divine Majesty be judged more terrible than the crime of lese-majesty directed against ourself, although in the eyes of the law one is not graver than the other?) As the crime of treason deprives the guilty of life and property, and even blackens the memory of the dead, so in the aforesaid crimes of which the Patarins are guilty, we wish the same rules to be observed in all respects. And in order that the wickedness of

---

[1]The name, which seems here to be derived from *patior*, "to suffer," appears to have been given to the Milanese Cathari, because they lived among the rag-pickers or *Patari*. Compare with Lea's "History of the Inquisition," I., 114.

those who walk in darkness, since they do not follow God, should be thoroughly exterminated, we wish those who practice this class of crimes should, like other malefactors, be diligently sought for and hunted out by our officers. If such be discovered, even if there be only the slightest suspicion of their guilt, we command that they shall be examined by churchmen and prelates. If they shall be discovered by these to have deviated from the Catholic faith, even in a single respect, and if, when admonished by such churchmen in their function of pastors, they refuse, by leaving the wiles of the devil, to recognize the God of light, and stubbornly adhere to their error, we command, by this our present edict, that such condemned Patarins shall suffer the death they court; that, condemned to the sentence of the flames, they shall be burned alive in the sight of the people. Nor are we loath to satisfy their cravings in this respect, for they only suffer the penalty of their crime and reap no farther gain. No one shall dare to intercede with us for any such, and should any one presume to do this, we shall properly direct the darts of our indignation against him, too.

The emperor Frederick, concerning those who receive, adhere to or favor the Patarins, their accomplices or fautors.

All who shall receive, trust, aid or abet the Patarins in any way, seeking to shield others from a penalty which they rashly do not fear for themselves, shall be deprived of all their goods and banished forever. Their sons shall thereafter be excluded from all honors whatsoever and shall be branded with perpetual disgrace. They shall not be permitted to act as witnesses in any case, but shall be rejected as infamous. But if any one of the sons of such harborers or fautors shall point out a Patarin, whose guilt shall be thus proven, he shall, by the imperial clemency, be freed from the opprobrium and restored to his full rights in view of the good faith which he has shown.

Document 2: The Law Against Heretics in Southern Germany

The Schwabenspiegel *were the municipal laws used in southern Germany during the thirteenth century and they included provisions for dealing with heretics.*

Where persons are believed to be heretics, they shall be accused before the spiritual court, for they should in the first place be tried by ecclesiastics. When they are convicted they shall be taken in hand by the secular court, which shall sentence them as is right; that is to say, they shall be burned at the stake. If, however, the judge protects them, or makes any illegal concessions and does not sentence them, he shall be excommunicated, and that in the most severe form. This shall be done by a bishop. The delinquent judge shall, moreover, be judged by his superior temporal judge, if he have one, as he himself should have judged the heretic. In case a feudal prince does not bring heretics to judgment, but protects them, the ecclesiastical court shall excommunicate him. If such prince does not yield within the space of a year, his bishop, who excommunicated him, shall report his evil deeds to the pope and the length of time he has remained excommunicated for the same. Then shall he [the pope] with propriety deprive him of his princely office and of all his dignities. The pope shall bring his sentence to the notice of his king and his other judges. These shall substantiate the sentence of the pope with their sentence. The offender shall be deprived of all his goods, his fiefs and all his worldly honors. Thus shall lords and poor men be judged. The fitness of this is thus shown.

There was once a pope at Rome called Zacharias. In his time there was a king of France called Lescandus who protected the heretics unlawfully. He was king before King Pippin, King Charles' father. Him the pope deposed from his kingship and from all his

■■ *This allegorical picture shows the Church as a fortress of faith being defended by the pope, bishops, and clergy from the attacks of blind heretics.*

honors, and Pippin became king in his stead during his natural life. We read, too, that Pope Innocent deposed King Otto of the Roman Empire on account of his ill deeds. This the popes have a right to do, as God spake to Jeremiah, saying, "I have set thee over all the nations and over all the kingdoms to judge."

Document 3: Description of Two Heretics Working Miracles with the Help of the Devil

This account was written by Caesar of Heisterbach, a Cistercian monk, who wrote the book Dialogue on Miracles, *which was widely read during the Middle Ages.*

Two men simply clad, but not without guile, not birds but ravening wolves, came to Besançon, feigning the greatest piety. They were pale and thin. They went about barefooted and fasted daily. They did not miss a single night the early service in the cathedral, nor did they accept any alms from anyone except necessary food. When by such hypocrisy they had attracted the attention of everyone, they began to vomit forth their hidden poison and to preach to the ignorant new and unheard of heresies. In order, moreover, that the people might believe their teachings, they ordered meal to be sifted on the sidewalk and walked on it without leaving a trace of a footprint. Likewise walking upon the water, they could not be immersed. Also, they had little huts burnt over their heads, and after those had been burnt to ashes, they came out uninjured. After this they said to the people, "If you do not believe our words, believe our miracles."

The bishop and clergy hearing of this were greatly disturbed. And when they wished to resist those men, affirming that those were heretics and deceivers and ministers of the devil, they escaped with difficulty from being stoned by the people. Now that bishop was a good and learned man and a native of our province. Our aged monk, Conrad, who told me these facts and who was in that city at the time, knew him well.

The bishop seeing that his words were of no avail and that the people entrusted to his charge were being subverted by the devil's agents, summoned a certain clerk that he knew, who was very well versed in necromancy, and said, "Certain men in my city are doing so and so. I ask you to find out from the devil by your skill, who they are, whence they come, and by what means so many and so wonderful miracles are wrought by them. For it is impossible that they should do wonders through divine inspiration when their teaching is so contrary to God's." The clerk replied, "My lord, I have long renounced that art." The bishop replied, "You see clearly in what straits I am. I must either acquiesce in their teachings or be stoned by the people. Therefore I enjoin upon you for the remission of your sins, that you obey me in this matter."

The clerk, obeying the bishop, summoned the devil, and when asked, told why he had called him. "I am sorry that I have deserted you. And because I intend to be more obedient to you in the future than in the past, I ask you to tell me who these men are, what they teach, and by what means they work so great miracles." The devil replied, "They are mine and sent by me, and they preach what I have placed in their mouths." The clerk asked, "How is it that they cannot be injured, or sunk in the water, or burned by fire?" The demon replied again, "They have under their armpits, sewed between the skin and the flesh my compacts in which the homage done by them to me is written; and by virtue of these they work such miracles and can not be injured by anyone." Then the clerk, "Suppose those should be taken away?" The devil replied, "Then they would be weak just like other men." The clerk having heard this, thanked the demon, saying, "Now go, and when you are summoned by me, return."

He went to the bishop and recited these things to him in order. The latter filled with great joy, summoned all the people of the city to a suitable place and said, "I am your shepherd, ye are my sheep. If those men, as you say, confirm their teaching by signs, I will follow them with you. If, however, they deserve punishment, you shall penitently return to the faith of your fathers with me." The people replied, "We have seen many signs from them." The bishop, "But I have not seen them."

Why protract my words? The plan pleased the people. The heretics were summoned. The bishop was present. A fire was kindled in the midst of the city. Nevertheless, before the heretics entered it, they were secretly summoned to the bishop. He said to them, "I want to see if you have any evil about you." Hearing this they immediately stripped and said with great confidence, "Search our bodies and our garments carefully." The soldiers, truly, following the instructions of the bishop, raised their arms, and noticing under the armpits some scars that were healed up, broke them open with their knives and extracted from them the little scrolls which had been sewed in.

Having received these, the bishop went forth to the people with the heretics, and having commanded silence, cried out in a loud voice, "Now shall your prophets enter the fire, and if they are not injured I will believe in them." Then the wretched men, trembling said, "We are not able to enter now." Then the bishop told the people of the evil which had been detected, and showed the compacts. Then all furious hurled the devil's ministers, to be tortured with the devil in eternal flames, into the fire which had been prepared.

And thus through the grace of God and the action of the bishop the rising heresy was extinguished and the people who had been seduced and corrupted were cleansed by penance.

Document 4: Description of the Albigensians

This selection comes from the Conduct of the Inquisition *by Bernard of Gui, who from 1307–1323 served as the inquisitor for Toulouse in southern France, a center of the Albigensian heresy.*

It would take too long to describe in detail the manner in which these same Manichean heretics preach, and teach their followers, but it must be briefly considered here.

In the first place, they usually say of themselves that they are good Christians, who do not swear, or lie, or speak evil of others; that they do not kill any man or animal nor any thing having the breath of life, and that they hold the faith of the Lord Jesus Christ and His Gospel as Christ and His Apostles taught. They assert that they occupy the place of the apostles, and that on account of the above mentioned things those of the Roman Church, namely, the prelates, clerks and monks, persecute them, especially the Inquisitors of Heresy, and call them heretics, although they are good men and good Christians, and that they are persecuted just as Christ and his apostles were by the Pharisees.

They moreover talk to the laity of the evil lives of clerks and the prelates of the Roman Church, pointing out and setting forth their pride, cupidity, avarice and uncleanness of life and such other evils as they know. They invoke with their own interpretation and according to their abilities the authority of the Gospels and the Epistles against the condition of the prelates, churchmen and monks, whom they call Pharisees and false prophets, who say but do not.

Then they attack and vituperate, one after the other, all the sacraments of the church, especially the sacrament of the Eucharist, saying that it cannot contain the body of Christ, for had this been as great as the largest mountain Christians would have consumed it entirely before this. They assert that the host comes from straw, that it passes through the tails of horses, to wit, when the flour is cleaned by a sieve [of horse hair]. That moreover it passes through the body and comes to a vile end which, they say, could not happen if God were in it. Of baptism, they assert that water is material and corruptible, and is therefore the creation of the Evil Power and cannot sanctify the soul, but that the churchmen sell this water out of avarice, just as they sell earth for the burial of the dead, and oil to the sick when they anoint them, and as they sell the confession of sins as made to the priests. Hence, they claim that confession made to the priests of the Roman Church is useless, and that, since the priests may be sinners, they can not loose nor bind, and being unclean themselves, cannot make another clean. They assert, moreover, that the Cross of Christ should not be adored or venerated, because, as they urge, no one would venerate or adore the gallows upon which a father, relative or friend had been hung. They urge farther that they who adore the cross ought for similar reasons to worship all thorns and lances, because as Christ's body was on the cross during the passion so was the crown of thorns on his head and the soldier's lance in his side. They proclaim many other scandalous things in regard to the sacraments. They, moreover, read from the Gospels and the Epistles in the vulgar tongue, applying and expounding them in their favor and against the condition of the Roman Church in a manner which it would take too long to describe in detail, but all that relates to this subject may be read more fully in the books they have written and infected, and may be learned from the confessions of such of their followers as have been converted.

Document 5: A Heretic Healed by Confession Relapses and Is Burnt

This selection was also written by Caesar of Heisterbach.

In the same city, namely Argentina which is Strassburg, ten heretics were seized. When they denied their guilt, they were convicted by the ordeal of glowing iron and were condemned to be burnt. When on the appointed day they were being led to the fire, one of the attendants said to one of them, ''Wretched one, you are condemned. Now do penance and confess your sins, lest after the burning of the body, which is only momentary, hell-fire burns your soul eternally.'' When the man replied, "I certainly think that I have been mistaken, but I fear repentance in so great straits will be by no means acceptable to God." The former replied, "Only confess from your heart. God is merciful and will receive the penitent."

Wonderful fact! For as soon as the man confessed his perfidy, his hand was fully healed. While he delayed in confession, the judge summoned him to the punishment. His confessor replied to the judge, "It is not just that an innocent man should be condemned unjustly." Since no trace of a burn was found in his hand, he was dismissed.

The man had a wife living not far from the city and absolutely ignorant of these things which have been related. When he came to her rejoicing and said, "Blessed be God who has liberated me to-day from the loss of body and soul!" and explained to her the cause; she replied, "What have you done, most wretched man, what have you done? Why have you withdrawn from your holy and sacred faith from fear of momentary pain? You ought rather, if it were possible, to expose your body a hundred times to the flames than once to withdraw from a faith so well proven!"

Whom does not the voice of the serpent seduce? That man, unmindful of the favor divinely conferred upon him, unmindful of the so manifest miracle, followed his wife's advice and returned to his former error. God, not unmindful truly of the crime, in return for so great ingratitude, tortured the hand of each one. The burn was renewed in the hand of the heretic and, because his wife was the cause of his returning to his error, she was made his companion in the renewed pain. So vehement was the burn that it penetrated to the bones. And since they did not dare in the village to utter the cries which the violence of the pain extorted, they fled into the nearest woods, howling there like wolves. Why protract my words? They were betrayed, led back to the city, and together cast into the fire which was not yet fully extinguished and they were burnt to ashes.

Document 6: The Body of a Burnt Heretic Turns into Toads

Lucas of Tuy is the source of this story. While serving as bishop at Tuy in northwestern Spain during the early thirteenth century, he campaigned vigorously against both heretics and the clergy who were lax in opposing them.

From the lips of the same brother Elias, a venerable man, I learned that when certain heretics were scattering the virulent seeds of error in parts of Burgundy, both the Preaching Friars and the Minorites drew the two-edged sword of God's word against these same heretics, opposing them valiantly until they were finally taken by the magistrate of the district. He sent them to the fiery stake as they merited, in order that these workers of iniquity should perish with their wickedness as a wholesome lesson to others. Quantities of wood having been supplied in plenty to feed the flames, suddenly a toad of wonderful size, which is sometimes called *crapaldus,* appeared, and without being driven betook itself of its own accord into the midst of the flames. One of the heretics, who was reported to be their bishop, had fallen on his back in the fire. The toad took his place on this man's face and in the sight of all ate out the heretic's tongue. By the next day his whole body, except his bones, had been turned into disgusting toads, which could not be counted for their great number. The inhabitants, seeing the miracle, glorified God and praised Him in His servants, the preaching monks, because the Lord had, in His mercy, delivered them from the horror of such pollution. God omnipotent surely wished to show through the most unseemly and filthiest of animals, how foul and infamous are the teachings of heretics, so that all might thereafter carefully shun the heretic, as they would the poisonous toad. Just as among four-footed creatures the toad is held the foulest, so the teachings of the heretic are more debased and filthy than those of any other religious sect. The blindness of heresy justifies the perfidy of the Jews. Its pollution makes the madness of the Mohammedans a pure thing in contrast. The licentiousness of the heretics would leave Sodom and Gomorrah stainless. What is held most enormous in crime, becomes most holy, when compared with the shame and ignominy of heresy. Thus, Dear Christian, flee this unspeakable evil, in comparison with which all other crimes are as trifles.

■ ■ ■

STUDY QUESTIONS

1. Why did medieval people consider heresy to be so dangerous? What type of language do the law of Emperor Frederick II and the *Schwabenspiegel* (documents 1 and 2) use to describe heresy?

2. Heresy was a crime that was covered by the laws of the Church and the state. What type of legal steps were taken when a heretic was tried? Did the heretic appear to have any legal rights?

3. According to Caesar of Heisterbach and Bernard of Gui (documents 3 and 4), what beliefs did heretics espouse to attract converts? How did these beliefs directly threaten the medieval church?

4. How did supernatural occurrences figure in some cases of heresy? What do these supernatural occurrences tell about the popular images of the devil and God in medieval society?

5. In what different ways did the general population react to the appearance of heresy? Did they support it or oppose it?

BIBLIOGRAPHY

R. W. Southern, *Western Society and the Church in the Middle Ages* (1970), is an excellent, brief introduction to the topic of heresy. The best recent overviews of the history of medieval heresy are Malcolm D. Lambert, *Medieval Heresy: Popular Movements from Bogomil to Hus* (1977), and R. I. Moore, *The Origins of European Dissent* (1977). A good general survey is provided by David Christie-Murray, *A History of Heresy* (1989). Intellectual aspects of medieval heresy are emphasized in Gorden Leff, *Heresy in the Later Middle Ages: The Relation of Heterodoxy to Dissent, c.1250–c.1450* (1967). A bestselling history book that imaginatively studies the practice of the Albigensian heresy in one small Pyrennian village is Emmanuel Le Roy Ladurie, *Montaillou: The Promised Land of Error* (1978). For an up-to-date and brief introduction to the Inquisition, see Bernard Hamilton, *The Medieval Inquisition* (1981). Henry Charles Lea, *A History of the Inquisition in the Middle Ages* (3 vols., 1888), is a massive and classic study that, although dated and biased, is still worth consulting.

10. MARGARET OF CORTONA AND HOLY ANOREXIA

Rudolph M. Bell

Social historians will no doubt remember the 1980s in the United States—and to a lesser extent in Western Europe—as the "decade of fitness," a period of almost narcissistic obsession with body image, weight loss, physical fitness, and health. The dark side of this "cult of fitness" is eating disorders like anorexia nervosa and bulimia and the steroid scourge of athletes bent on enhancing strength, endurance, and muscle size. Psychologists and physicians have noticed an alarming increase of anorexia, which is a compulsive refusal to eat and to perceive one's true body image, among adolescent and young women in recent years. Those who treat anorexia patients note a fairly consistent personality type—an individual preoccupied with what others think of her, who wants to be perfect, and who ceases eating as a personal symbol of self-control. She often feels terribly inadequate in dealing with other people but sees in her anorexia total mastery of herself. Hilda Bruch, in *The Golden Cage* describes the typical anorectic as someone who struggles "against feeling enslaved, exploited, and not permitted to live a life of her own. They would rather starve than continue a life of accommodation . . . the main theme is a struggle for control, for a sense of identity, competence, and effectiveness."

But anorexia nervosa is not a new discovery or a new disease has afflicted people in western culture for centuries. In this essay, historian Rudolph Bell describes the case of anorexia nervosa that eventually killed Margaret of Cortona. Readers should understand, of course, that definitions of emotional illness have changed dramatically over the years; to conclude that Margaret was suffering from the same illness as many modern young women may be an ahistorical assumption. However, Christianity, along with many other religions, has a high regard for asceticism. To deny the body its physical wants was a discipline that helped a person resist sin and temptation. Margaret's anorexia was a religious passion, a conviction that in living an ascetic life she was pleasing God. Some psychologists might assume that it was a typical case of anorexia, but historians might sharply disagree.

The next thirteenth-century holy anorexic whose *vita* merits examination in some detail is Margaret of Cortona. Although she never married, Margaret shared her lover's bed for nine years and bore a son by him. That she had known the flesh, rather than the technicality of being an unwed mother, was but one of an interrelated set of forces that drove her to ever more severe levels of penitential asceticism. Her psyche, her humanity, are abundantly laid bare in her confessor's biography, much of which is a compilation of her spiritual experiences as she related them to him.

Margaret probably was born around 1247 in the hamlet of Laviano (in the present-day commune of Castiglione del Lago) near the shore of Lake Trasimeno on the Tuscany-Umbria border. Her father, presumably Tancredi di Bartolomeo, was a tenant farmer of modest means. We do not know her mother's name, only the likelihood that the apparently devout woman died when Margaret was still a child. Years later the Virgin Mary appeared to Margaret and reassured her that her prayers had been answered and that her mother, after having done penance in purgatory for ten years, was now in paradise. Her mother's piety was not extraordinary, however, at least to judge from what Christ said in a spiritual dialogue with Margaret after she had prayed in the way she had learned from childhood: "Daughter, your mother did not teach you well, because you must pray for everyone, and it is your general prayer that pleases me." Margaret's brother, Bartolo, who outlived her, was a Franciscan tertiary active in joining crusading missions to the Holy Land. Both children, and possibly a sister named Adriana, thus were faced at an early age with

the loss of their mother. Tancredi soon remarried, and legend has it that her stepmother was cold and hostile toward Margaret.

She was a stunningly attractive girl—and even years of harsh austerities could not mask entirely her natural beauty—with manners far more refined than her peasant origin would suggest. When she was fifteen she fell in love with a rich young nobleman from Montepulciano, by tradition Arsenio del Monte Santa Maria (or dei Pecora). The difference between them in social status caused his family to reject any possibility of marriage. Nevertheless, Margaret accepted his invitation to come live with him, and at the age of sixteen one night she left home by herself in a tiny boat to cross the marshes and take up residence as Arsenio's mistress. Although she was troubled by the irregularity of her position, and her beauty and enormous popularity among the Montepulciani only increased his family's hostility toward her, Margaret acted fully the part of the wealthy wife. She enjoyed being paid homage by the townsfolk, wearing dresses richer than anyone else's, the gold ringlets in her hair, facial makeup, and charging around the crowded streets on her adorned steed. Her fame would spread all the way back to the peasants of Laviano, who would envy and admire her as they remained stooped over their fields.

After a while Margaret tired of such ostentation, or perhaps the adulation she received became tinged with mockery, and she began to spend more time alone at Arsenio's country villa at Palazzi. There she conceived a son. After her conversion she recalled these years in a spiritual exchange with Jesus: "Remember also that when you still loved worldly things and lived in the darkness of sin, I your master and doctor of truth gave you such maternal compassion toward the poor and the afflicted and roused in you such delight in solitary and remote places that you went around saying in your fervor, 'Oh, how sweet it would be to pray here, and with what solemnity and devotion one could sing the praises of God and do redeeming penance, in tranquility and certainty.' ''

Whatever her yearnings and internal tribulations, they were not sufficient in themselves to jolt Margaret to a new path. Then one day, as she waited at home for Arsenio to return from a hunting expedition in the nearby woods of Petrignano, she was alarmed to see his dog return alone, baying and then pulling at her dress. Margaret followed the animal to an oak tree. Under its branches she came upon her lover's body, covered with blood. Arsenio's killing left Margaret with a practical problem: whether it was the work of unknown assassins or the just punishment of God, she herself was in danger. She could expect nothing from his family and so, suddenly reduced to the status of an impoverished unwed mother with a young son to care for, she returned home to Laviano, dressed in black, crying, and filled with shame.

Her stepmother had not forgiven Margaret's escape nine years earlier, and certainly not her ill-won prosperity with Arsenio, and at his new wife's instigation Tancredi refused to let his daughter and grandson set foot in the house. As she sat under a fig tree in the backyard Margaret felt tempted to accept her destiny. What alternative was there for a twenty-five-year-old mother with an illegitimate child, rejected by her father, yet still very attractive, except prostitution? The devil tried to trick her by reassuring her that she had nothing to feel guilty about since it was not she who had refused to marry and that given ''the beauty of your body you should be able to find love with important and carnal men.'' But Margaret resisted this temptation and instead determined to go with her little boy to the city of Cortona, there to place herself under the guiding mercy of the Franciscans. Dressed as a penitent and with her child in tow, Margaret appeared at the gates of Cortona, most likely some time in 1272, to seek refuge at the Moscari family's palace. There Donna

Marinaria and her daughter-in-law Raniera, who may have had advance word about the misfortunes of the deceased Arsenio's lover and who were active with the Franciscans in doing charitable work, took them in. In exchange for room and board, Margaret assisted the pious sisters by doing chores around the house and joined them in ministering to the poor people of Cortona. The Moscatis accompanied Margaret to the Convent of San Francesco, where she sought vestition as a penitential tertiary. Notwithstanding this noble introduction, however, the friars refused ''because at that time they doubted her perseverance, both because she was too pretty and because she was too young.'' Margaret then went to work as a midwife, and her services came to be much in demand among Cortona's patrician women, for many of whose children she stood as godmother. For a time, more as expiation than out of necessity, on her way to church she went from door to door as a beggar, but then she came to understand how ''inopportune'' such behavior was for a proper lady, and instead she went directly to mass or else stayed in her room at home with her son.

Throughout, she remained determined to overcome the hesitations of her spiritual advisers and to forge for herself a path of sanctity. When some of her noble friends jokingly reproached her—''What ever will become of you, they said, Margaret you are so vain!''— she replied: ''There will come a time when you will call me saint, because saint I will be; and you will come to visit me with pilgrim's staff and mendicant sacks hanging from your shoulders.'' It was not only a negative amending for sins past but also a positive drive for outstanding holiness (here innocently confessed by Margaret in a way so frankly heterodox that it is surprising that her biographer in his enthusiasm let it slip through) that carried this woman to the self-destruction of her body.

After three years and ''much insistence'' on her part the Franciscans finally accepted Margaret as a tertiary. In order to be free to devote

A sixteenth-century depiction of St. Margaret of Cortona.

friars around her, and let the teacher leave in a very agitated state, shouting and cursing as he made his exit. From her room in the Moscati palace she moved to a more isolated adjacent cell. There she remained for thirteen years, able to go about town regularly on charitable missions and yet free to engage in spiritual exercises in complete solitude. Her talents as a fundraiser and organizer soon became evident in her founding of a confraternity and establishment of a hospital in 1278, still functioning in Cortona as the Ospedale di S. Maria della Misericordia, dedicated especially to the care of poor mothers and their children.

It was among these people that Margaret became renowned for the exceptional humility with which she shouted out publicly her sins, moving her listeners to weep as she also discovered their defects and suffered with them for their misdeeds. Among her audience of penitents were not only humble people but also priests and even a visiting inquisitor. A story emerged, possibly a true one, that Dante Alighieri himself came before Margaret on February 2, 1289, to accuse himself of pusillanimity, and some scholars hold that he later represented Margaret as Lucia, the psychopomp who encouraged him to embark on his journey to Hell (*Inferno* 2.97). Whatever the factual basis of this matter, it symbolizes well the charismatic qualities of such a woman.

She determined to return once more to Laviano and there to seek public forgiveness during Sunday mass. With a cord tied around her neck in place of the jewelry she once had worn, she made peace with her father, and to a local gossip who charged her with false humility she gave her cloak, her shawl, and her meal; then, upon returning to Cortona, Margaret begged money to pay off all the gossip's debts. Had her confessor not refused to allow it, she also intended to go back to Montepulciano, but he worried that such self-abasement might in itself become an occasion for vainglory and that it would be imprudent to allow a young female of such fervid impulses to go

all her time to God she sent her son to a tutor in Arezzo and in due course he too joined the order as a friar. Occasionally she included the lad, whose religiosity was dutiful but not extraordinary, in her prayers, but from her earthly life Margaret cut him out completely. Rumors had spread among townspeople hostile to the penitent and her son that in desperation after she had abandoned him he had drowned himself in a well in Arezzo. Whether this evil gossip reached Margaret's ears we cannot be certain but for whatever reason, when her son's tutor came to bring news of him and to get paid, Margaret was so absorbed in prayer that she made no acknowledgment, even when asked repeatedly to do so by the on a long journey. Her wish was to be led around blindfolded by a woman who should cry out: " 'Here is Margaret, dear citizens! Here is she who once carried herself with such airs, and with her vanity and bad example did so much harm to the souls in this town!' Thus I will be deemed crazy by those before whom I boasted with my words and my looks."

Even her biography, according to a perceptive modern analysis, was constructed largely from autobiographical confessions written down by her Franciscan spiritual advisers and read to the faithful while Margaret was still alive and active among them. One Sunday, as Friar Giunta was preaching during mass, "as if beyond herself and out of her mind" Margaret "began to cry out in front of everyone, asking if I knew anything of Christ crucified and where had I put the Master." Because prayers should not be interrupted with such commotion, and to console his wailing penitent and the assembled worshipers who also had fallen into tears, the friar shouted out that God would not hide His presence from anyone who ardently sought Him, and that He would return shortly. At this Margaret became deadly pale and took a seat in front of all the people. Another time, on Good Friday, she emerged from her cell "with her head shaved, almost intoxicated, like a mother who has lost her son" and went around the streets of Cortona screaming in a loud voice. Inspired by compassion or curiosity, men left their work and women their children to come to the Oratory of the Convent of San Francesco to see Margaret meditate on the crucifixion. They were moved to tears as they found her suffering such atrocious internal pain that she seemed about to die. Her teeth chattered as she writhed like a worm or a snake and turned ashen in color, her pulse dropping and her body temperature falling as she became speechless, blind, and totally insensitive to the world.

At least one passage in which Jesus spoke to Margaret—words that may well have originated with her rather than her confessor—suggests a paranoid element in her thinking:

You must live in continuous fear because you find yourself among enemies, in full battle. Therefore, behave yourself as if you are alone and crossing a hostile and cruel land where you may be kidnapped, wounded, robbed, and killed; watch closely on all sides; never put down your weapons, nor abandon yourself in sleep, nor trust in anyone until you have reached the friendly land.

Spiritual dialogues of this sort also might be interpreted as colorful but hardly extraordinary variations on the timeless Christian exhortation to shut out the world and prepare for eternity, yet in the case of Margaret of Cortona I think there is more. Her desire to do public penance, to return to the earthly places of her sinfulness, her outbursts in church and on the streets, her autobiography, and then, possibly, her joining the audiences assembled to listen to its intimate details, suggest a form of *santa pazza* still very much linked to the living world. Margaret intended to be holy, indeed, predicted during the early years of her stay in Cortona that in the end she would be venerated as a saint. A saint necessarily lives both in the spirit and in the flesh. Her public behavior reveals a woman tormented by a world around her that was simultaneously an enemy of her soul and the theater in which her bodily self moved about on its missions of charity and her psyche bared itself in humiliating confession—the very actions to which people responded in ways that reassured Margaret, here in this world, that her path of holiness was true.

An analogous ambivalence characterizes Margaret's secluded life in her solitary cell. She would conquer her flesh as once she had indulged it, but to truly achieve complete victory over her bodily desires would have been to eradicate her link to the past, thus depriving her conversion from sinner to saint of its full unity and meaning. Even in the wicked days of her life with Arsenio, God had intervened with moments of light, just as now in the years of her holiness the devil plunged her into times of darkness, even when she was near death. The motif of inverted values, where the new makes little sense except in active contrast to the old, and where both the body and the spirit take on added meaning when their desires are in active conflict, is amply displayed in Margaret of Cortona's private austerities, especially her diet.

Upon her conversion Margaret had decided to offer her body to God as a sacrifice, and it was with this intent that she flagellated herself with a knotted rope and slapped and punched herself with such force that her naturally pale skin turned black and blue with bruises. At first she abstained from meat but continued to use animal fats in preparing her meals, and only later did she limit her condiments to a bit of olive oil. At that time, however, she was actively working as a midwife and, so as not to bother her patients' families with preparing special meals for her, she would eat whatever was served for everyone, including meat, but only sparingly. At the Moscati palace she was able to be more strict, and there she abstained from eggs or cheese except during Lent, when she ate these items but gave up fish. Often she would forget to cook anything at all. One day her son must have complained about this spartan regimen, to which his mother replied: "My son, when you come home if you find the food still uncooked, eat it as is, and in silence; because there is no point in my being bothered with you for such a small matter during time reserved for singing the praises of God."

About the time that she moved from her room in the palace to a more solitary adjacent cell she also increased the rigors of her fast, eating only vegetables with no condiments and shortly thereafter no cooked food except a little bread. Thus her regular diet for years consisted of bread, nuts, raw vegetables, and water—all in small quantities eaten at 3:00 P.M. and 6:00 P.M. At God's command, she never ate in the presence of others. "In order to be more light-headed and allow her soul more easily to be fervent," Margaret made no

exception for feast days, a rather clear indication that she realized and actively sought the obvious side effects of rigorous fasting. Not surprisingly, her diet weakened her so much that she had difficulty walking and had to spend more time in her cell. There she was tormented by demons in the forms of nude women and men, serpents, and beasts who paraded before her the worldly lust she once had enjoyed and tried to entice her with plates of delicate aromatic foods.

Margaret's confessors came to realize the dangers, spiritual as well as physical, of what she was doing and intervened. She was dismayed that her hard mortifications were not destroying her natural beauty as rapidly as she wished, and so she went to Friar Giunta and said, "have pity and allow me to redouble my rampage against this odious body, as I have wished for so long; not even your prohibition should impede the impulse of my free will. I assure you, that even though I would do so gladly, I will not wound myself mortally." The friar was very dubious about granting such a dangerous and unspecified penance to a woman well known to him for her extreme behavior, and he decided to question her further about exactly what she intended. Margaret then confessed that she secretly had bought a razor and meant to cut her nose and upper lip "because with the beauty of my face I did harm to many souls. Therefore, wishing to do justice upon myself, by myself, for this offense to God and to transform the beauty of my body into ugliness, I pray you to permit me without delay to offer to Christ the King this sacrifice which I propose." Friar Giunta absolutely refused, pointing out to Margaret that such an action might lead to hemorrhaging or other complications and then adding to this practical advice the warning that if she disobeyed him he would no longer hear her confessions and that none of his Franciscan brothers would care for her or guide her.

The ambience in which Margaret sought spiritual perfection through harsh austerity was one that offered considerable support for such a path. Under the influence of male ascetic mystics such as Jacopone da Todi, her contemporary, the Spiritual Franciscans actively lauded the virtues of extreme self-mortification, for men as well as for women. But Margaret's severity was too much even for these strict friars, who feared that she would bring about her own death, and in various ways they urged or ordered her to stop. Apparently she internalized their advice enough that in her dialogues with Jesus he too concurred, telling her that while he appreciated her efforts to macerate her body he did not want her so reduced by fasting and fever that she could not go to mass. For days Margaret had been unable to arise from the plank on the ground on which she rested, so weakened was she by her abstinence, but the divine consolation of her talk with Jesus greatly encouraged her, and the next morning she hurried off to church as if she had not been sick at all.

On another occasion we find Margaret confessing to an episode of binge eating, one that suggests as well significant tensions between male friars and the religious females of Cortona over this saint in their midst. Several pious townswomen had come to reprimand her for being too severe with her body and had brought along a plate of cooked figs which they insisted in God's name that she eat. Since she had promised Jesus to take at least a little food from time to time, while concentrating on meditation not on eating, there was nothing intrinsically wrong here. But instead of retiring to her cell with the plate to eat alone as she had vowed, Margaret went out and joined the women, apparently stuffing herself and not thinking very much about God. Quickly she felt the burden of this sin and wept inconsolably until Jesus appeared. At first he scolded her for "giving faith so easily to the words of women who told you that with such abstinence you would become crazy," and only then did he go on to encourage her to listen exclusively to him and to the good Franciscan friars. The women also must have told Mar-

garet to exchange her patched up veil for a new white one and to wash her filthy dress, because Jesus also explicitly countermanded this advice and assured Margaret that, whatever the opinions of townswomen, the friars who had put up with the stink of her sin years earlier would not be offended now by her smelly clothes.

Margaret's own doubts about what she was doing she expressed in the guise of diabolic visitations. Already the fame of her sanctity caused people to come to see her and try to touch her, Lucifer began, so did not her continued austerities now that surely she was among the saved reveal a strain of vainglory? Another time the devil calmly reasoned with her that it should be sufficient for her to follow the general rules on fasting observed by all Franciscans, because of course they were destined to go to heaven. "So what are you doing in this cell, where you are ruining your soul and your body?" But she resisted this sophistry, telling the devil that God had taught her a special penitential routine and had "promised me life eternal if I persevere." The pact was hard to keep, however, for at times Margaret, not unlike modern anorexics, was indeed weak and hungry. Once it was the cooked figs, another time a woman who brought her a dish of cauliflower that she ate only to find that it sat so heavily on her stomach that she was unable to pray all night—but always God forgave her, promising her that if her abstinence became so extreme that it truly debilitated her body excessively, he would allow her a richer diet, only however when she would come to lose all sense of taste. Her stomach in fact became so weak that wine and food tasted to her like earth. For days on end, as when she repeated her eight-day general confession, she was *unable* to eat.

Friar Giunta had pity and called in a physician, but Margaret refused to take any medicine and tearfully cried that "she wanted to see her body debilitated, infected, devoured by worms." She was sure her stomach was only pretending to be ill and she called it a "dark traitor." When the friar tried on his own to coax her to eat more he received this reply:

Dear Father, I have no intention of making a peace pact between my body and my soul, and neither do I intend to hold back. Therefore, allow me to tame my body by not altering my diet; I will not stop for the rest of my life, until there is no more life left. You should not think that [my body] is so mortified and weak as it seems; it acts this way so that I should not demand the debt it contracted in the world, when it liked pleasure. Let it be enough, my Father, let it be enough, that in these Easter holidays I condition vegetables with oil, to obey your orders, which I did not wish to do.

Then in a soliloquy Margaret goes on:

Oh my body, why do you not help me to serve my creator and redeemer? Why are you not as quick to obey as you were to disobey His commands? Do not lament, do not cry; do not pretend to be half dead. You will bear the weight that I place on your shoulders, all of it, just as at one time you bore it to displease our Creator . . . I not only wish to abstain from bodily food but I wish to die a thousand times a day, were it possible, in this mortal life of mine.

Worn out by years of active warfare against her body, Margaret longed for death and the seat in paradise which a vision had shown prepared for her. "I want to die of starvation to satiate the poor," she told her confessor. And to Jesus she expressed her readiness for even the most atrocious death because unlike him, who had died to atone for original sin, she had sinned by her willful action. Now by his grace her body had become a "vessel of purity," and

the time was appropriate to render it to him. But she was tormented by an apparition of a ferocious devil who told her, "God will never forgive you or show the mercy you expect because with your fasting you have committed suicide." Apparently many Cortonesi, and a few friars as well, had similar thoughts, because in a more reassuring vision Jesus advised Margaret to avoid any further conversation with secular people, and as she was near death he added that he was gravely offended by the busybody clerics who did not understand the real nature of her sickness and were trying to get her to eat.

Friar Giunta, seeing Margaret's body destroyed by fasting, tears, vigils, flagellation, hairshirts, and myriad illnesses, "feared that by her continued refusal to take nourishment" she was indeed shortening her life, and he ordered her to eat food appropriate for a sick person, with only the exception that the eating not damage her soul. This possible exception allowed Margaret a final chance to express God's will as she understood it through direct communication with Jesus, and against the men who claimed spiritual direction over her.

When you interrogate your confessor and ask him if he knows if you have offended me in any way, it is necessary that he not show instantly that he is so sure of himself, but that he consider carefully and examine attentively your acts and your words . . . Because you are my vessel and my bride and your purity must be watched over with perpetual integrity.

On February 22, 1297, Margaret of Cortona died, wasted in body but with joy beaming from her angelic face.

■■■

STUDY QUESTIONS

1. What is anorexia nervosa?

2. To what extent did Margaret's early life—her affair and birth of a child—affect her psychological stability?

3. Describe Margaret's religious experiences that helped to trigger her anorexia. Was her personality consistent with that of typical anorexia victims?

4. Margaret was apparently a beautiful woman. How did her beauty affect the way other people perceived her and the way she perceived herself?

5. Why was Margaret unwilling to end the anorectic behaviors that eventually killed her?

6. Why does anorexia nervosa usually strike women instead of men?

BIBLIOGRAPHY

The best account of the disease of anorexia nervosa is Hilde Bruch's *The Golden Cage: The Enigma of Anorexia Nervosa* (1978). Also see her earlier book *Eating Disorders: Obesity, Anorexia Nervosa, and the Person Within* (1973). Other general works include Salvador Minuchin, *Psychosomatic Families* (1978); Maria Selvini-Palazzoli, *Self-Starvation: From Individual to Family Therapy in the Treatment of Anorexia Nervosa* (1978); and Moses Kaufman and Marcel Heimann, eds., *Evolution of Psychosomatic Concepts: Anorexia Nervosa, A Paradigm* (1964). For the historical dimension, see Ilza Veith, *Hysteria: The History of a Disease* (1965), and Donald Weinstein and Rudolph M. Bell, *Saints and Society: The Two Worlds of Western Christendom, 1000–1700* (1982). For the most recent treatment of anorexia nervosa by a historian, see Joan Jacobs Brumberg, *Fasting Girls. The History of Anorexia Nervosa* (1989).

11. CRUSADING AS AN ACT OF LOVE

Jonathan Riley-Smith

Religious skeptics have often claimed that throughout human history "more people have been killed in the name of religion than for any other reason." A more accurate description of mass violence might be that "more people have been killed in the name of ideology than for any other cause." Certainly the twentieth century, a time in which religious sectarianism has actually declined, has not been free of ideological violence. Adolf Hitler's genocidal rage against European Jews, Josef Stalin's purge of millions of Russian peasants, and Pol Pot's annihilation of several million Cambodians are just a few examples.

Religion has certainly not been free of violent passion. There has been a militancy to Christianity, a warrior motif for missionaries bent on converting unbelievers. The traditional Protestant hymn "Onward Christian Soldiers" is one prime example. Today's religious passions do not match the intensity of medieval commitment. In the Middle Ages, religious fervor had few limits, especially when the Seljuk Turks expanded their territory into western Asia. During the 1050s and 1060s they conquered Syria, Palestine, and Egypt, threatened Constantinople, and struck fear into Roman Catholic Europe.

When Sultan Malik Shah died in 1092 and the Seljuk empire began to break up, Pope Urban II decided the time had come to strike back. In 1096 the first organized Crusade, composed largely of French and Norman crusaders, sought to liberate the Holy Land. On July 15, 1099, the crusaders marched into Jerusalem, and for more than a century European Christians carried out other crusades, trying to achieve a number of objectives, including serving the Church, fighting heathens, enjoying the smell of battle, and ensuring their own spiritual salvation. To justify much of this violence, they turned to the writings of the prominent early Christian theologian Augustine of Hippo (354–430). In this selection, Jonathan Riley-Smith treats medieval crusading as "an act of love"— the ultimate form of religious commitment.

In his encyclical *Quantum praedecessores* of December 1145, Pope Eugenius III wrote of those who had answered the call to the First Crusade that they had been "fired by the ardour of charity." In an *excitatorium* of the late 1180s Peter of Blois argued that Christians would gain merit if,

fired by the zeal of charity, they fight fiercely those who blaspheme against Christ, pollute the sanctuary of the Lord and in their pride and miscreance abase the glory of our Redeemer.

In the 1260s the French poet Rutebeuf, lamenting the failure of his countrymen to move themselves to recapture Jerusalem, exclaimed that "the fire of charity is cold in every Christian heart." These writers used the theological word *caritas, charitei* for Christian love, heightened it in a traditional Christian way with the words *fired, fire*, and linked it to the crusades. Because love has always been held to be fundamental to all Christian ethics, including the ethics of violence, it is worth asking how representative they were of the apologists for the crusading movement. I hope to show that the idea of the crusader expressing love through his participation in acts of armed force was an element in the thinking of senior churchmen in the central Middle Ages. An understanding of this can help us place the crusades in the context of the spiritual reawakening of western Europe that accompanied the eleventh-century reform movement. Christian love, however, was presented to the faithful in a way that they would understand, rather than in the form that would have reflected the complexities of the relationship between violence and charity as understood by theologians and canon lawyers. My discussion is limited to the justification of crusades to the East, although crusaders were not by any means only to be found in expeditions launched to recover or aid the Holy Land; they also campaigned in Spain, along the shores of the Baltic and even in the interior of western Europe.

Christian charity encompasses love of God and love of one's neighbour, and both these expressions of love were touched on by apologists for the crusades: in September 1096 Pope Urban II promised the indulgence to those Bolognese who joined the First Crusade, "seeing that they have committed their property and their persons out of love of God and their neighbour"; and St. Bernard, writing in the 1140s of news of Moslem victories in the East, asked

If we harden our hearts and pay little attention . . . where is our love for God, where is our love for our neighbour?

It was believed that crusaders particularly expressed their love of God in the way they became literally followers of Christ. From the first, they were treated as "soldiers of Christ," who had joined an expedition out of love for him. And the taking of the cross, the sewing of a cross on a man's garments as a symbol of his vow to crusade, was seen as a response to Christ's statement: "Whosoever doth not carry his cross and come after me cannot be my disciple" (Luke xiv, 27). It is notoriously difficult to establish exactly what occurred at the Council of Clermont in November 1095, but it is possible that Pope Urban II preached the First Crusade on the basis of this text: the author of one of the accounts of the council mentioned that he had done so when he ordered the crusaders to sew crosses on their clothes; and another witness also referred to it, in a narrative in which Urban was made to remind his audience of Christ's words,

He that loveth father or mother more than me is not worthy of me. And everyone that hath left house or father or mother or wife or children or lands for my name's sake shall receive an hundredfold and shall possess life everlasting (Matt. x, 37, xix, 29).

"Crusading as an Act of Love" by Jonathan Riley-Smith, *History*, Vol. 65, No. 214, June 1980. Copyright © 1980 The Historical Association. Reprinted by permission of Basil Blackwell, Oxford.

There is evidence that, whatever Urban actually said, a chord was struck in the hearts of those who responded to him. The anonymous author of the *Gesta Francorum*, who took part in the First Crusade, opened his narrative with a moving reference to the subject.

When already that time drew nigh, to which the Lord Jesus draws the attention of his people every day, especially in the Gospel in which he says, "If any man will come after me, let him deny himself and take up his cross and follow me" (Matt. xvi, 24), there was a great stirring throughout the whole region of Gaul, so that if anyone, with a pure heart and mind, seriously wanted to follow God and faithfully wished to bear the cross after him, he could make no delay in speedily taking the road to the Holy Sepulchre.

The German Ekkehard of Aura, who was himself in the East in 1101, compared the crusaders to Simon of Cyrene, and the French King's chaplain Odo of Deuil began his account of the Second Crusade with the words,

In the year of the Incarnation of the Word 1146, at Easter at Vezelay, the glorious Louis, . . . King of the Franks and Duke of the Aquitanians, . . . undertook to follow Christ by bearing his cross in order to be worthy of him.

An anonymous twelfth-century poet wrote:

You who love with true love
Awake! Do not sleep!
The lark brings us day
And tells us in this hideaway
That the day of peace has come
That God, by his very great kindness,
Will give to those who for love of him
Take the cross and on account of what they do
Suffer pain night and day
So that he will see who truly loves him.

This seam of devotion was richly worked by authority. In c.1144, in a bull that was often to be reissued, Pope Celestine II wrote that the Templars,

new Maccabees[1] *in this time of Grace, renouncing earthly desires and possessions, bearing his cross, are followers of Christ.*

And the image of the crusader denying himself and actually taking up Christ's cross was particularly strongly expressed at the turn of the twelfth and thirteenth centuries by Pope Innocent III, to whom God was a benefactor owed by all profound and unrepayable debts of gratitude.

Who would refuse to die for him, who was made for us obedient unto death, a death indeed on the cross?
    If God underwent death for man, ought man to question dying for God?

Innocent expatiated on the relationship between the crusader and the cross in his great encyclical *Quia maior*,[2] which launched the Fifth Crusade.

We summon on behalf of him who when dying cried in a great voice on the cross, made obedient to God his father unto death on the cross, crying so that he should save us from the eternal crucifixion of death; who, indeed, for his own sake summoned us and said, "If any man will come after me, let him deny himself and take up his cross and follow me" (Matt. xvi, 24). And in this clearly he said, "Whoever wishes to follow me to the crown should also follow me to the battle, which is now proposed to all as a test."

In a letter of 1208 to Leopold of Austria, Innocent had also stressed the insignificance of the crusader's action when compared to that of Christ.

You receive a soft and gentle cross; he bore one that was sharp and hard. You wear it superficially on your clothing; he endured it really in his flesh. You sew on yours with linen and silk

---

[1] A Jewish family that began a religious rebellion against the Seleucid Greeks in 168 B.C.

[2] What is great.

threads; he was nailed to his with iron and hard nails.

His pontificate marks a climax in the use of this imagery, but the love of God expressed by crusaders may still have been a popular theme in thirteenth-century sermons. The *Ordinacio de predicacione S. crucis in Anglia* of c. 1216, obviously following Innocent, referred to those entering the service of the cross as observing the commandment to love God with all one's heart, and Cardinal Odo of Châteauroux, who in 1245 was given the task of preaching and organizing a new crusade from France, devoted a homily to the subject. Preaching on the text, "Amen I say to you that . . . you who have followed me . . . shall also sit (alongside) . . . when the Son of Man shall sit on the seat of his majesty" (Matt. xix, 28), Odo enjoined his audience to forsake everything for the love of God: true conversion could only come about through love of God rather than of earthly things and a man could love his neighbour only as an expression of his love of God. He went on to tell his listeners that

It is a clear sign that a man burns with love of God and zeal for God when he leaves country, possessions, house, children and wife, going overseas in the service of Jesus Christ . . . Whoever wishes to take and have Christ ought to follow him; to follow him to death.

There can be little doubt that the audiences addressed by popes and preachers saw the expression of love for God in terms that were real to them, above all in the light of their relationship with and the loyalty they owed to secular rulers. And these rulers were also feudal lords. At the time the ties between vassals and their lords were regarded as being so close and were held in so emotional a way that feudal terminology was used by the poets of courtly love to describe the devotion of the perfect lover to his lady. To the crusaders, Christ was a king and lord who had lost his inheritance, his *haereditas* or *patrimonium*, to the pagans: indeed the image of the Holy Land as Christ's inheritance, which was an old one, was used in one of the accounts of Pope Urban II's speech at Clermont and often thereafter; even as late as 1274, Pope Gregory X wrote in his *Constitutiones pro zelo fidei* of the feelings of charity that should be aroused in Christian hearts at its loss. It was the duty of Christ's subjects to fight for the recovery or in the defence of Christ's heritage as they would for the domains of their own lords, and the anonymous twelfth-century poet, from whose crusade song I have already quoted, expressed a common opinion when he wrote that "he who abandons his lord in need deserves to be condemned."

Faced by a world that saw things in such concrete terms the popes tended to express themselves on this matter in a cloudy way, probably because theologians could not bring themselves to use too explicitly the feudal relationship, with its notions of contract and reciprocal obligations, as a means of describing man's relationship to God. Carl Erdmann has drawn attention to the ambiguous way in which, as he turned for help to the feudal knighthood in the 1070s and 1080s, Pope Gregory VII used the feudal terms *miles, fidelis,* and *servitium,* and the same was true of Gregory's successors. But popes could also on occasion specifically use the images of the everyday world to bring home to people what was meant by loving God. Innocent III, for instance, was fond of referring in this way to Christ as a king.

Consider most dear sons, consider carefully that if any temporal king was thrown out of his domain and perhaps captured, would he not, when he was restored to his pristine liberty and the time had come for dispensing justice, look on his vassals as unfaithful and traitors against the crown and guilty of lèse majesté *unless they had committed not only their property but also their persons to the task of freeing him? . . . And similarly will not Jesus Christ, the king of kings and lord of lords, whose servant you cannot deny being, who joined your soul to your body, who*

*redeemed you with his precious blood, who con-
ceded to you the kingdom, who enables you to
live and move and gave you all the good things
you have . . . condemn you for the vice of ingratitude and, as it were, the crime of infidelity if
you neglect to help him?*

At about the same time the great preacher
James of Vitry developed what Innocent was
saying in one of his sermons, although he was
careful to point out that man's relationship
with Christ was not a feudal one.

*When a lord is afflicted by the loss of his
patrimony he wishes to prove his friends and find
out if his vassals are faithful. Whoever holds a
fief of a liege lord is worthily deprived of it if he
deserts him when he is engaged in battle and loses
his inheritance. You hold your body and soul and
whatever you have from the Supreme Emperor
and today he has had you called upon to help
him in battle; and though you are not bound by
feudal law, he offers you so many and such good
things, the remission of all sins, whatever the
penalty or guilt, and above all eternal life, that
you ought at once to hurry to him.*

Later in the century, Odo of Châteauroux, in
the sermon to which I have already referred,
asked his audience a question coloured by the
aspirations and feelings of the world in which
they lived. "What is loving God if it is not
desiring his honour and glory?" Churchmen,
therefore, could portray the crusader's love of
God in terms that laymen could recognize as
being analogous to their regard for their earthly
superiors. But the presentation of theology in
everyday terms is revealed even more strikingly in the expression of the idea of love for
fellow-men.

The belief that crusading expressed love of
one's neighbour as well as love of God also
dated from the First Crusade. It has long been
accepted that an important element in Pope
Urban's thinking when he preached the cross
was the opportunity he saw of bringing fraternal aid to Christians in the East, oppressed by
or in danger from the Moslems. Baldric of Dol,

in his account of the sermon at Clermont, laid
emphasis on the supposed suffering of the Eastern Christians and made Urban make a typical distinction between the barbarisms of
internal strife in France and the virtues of helping the East.

*It is dreadful, brothers, dreadful, for you to raise
thieving hands against Christians. It is much less
evil to brandish the sword against the Moslems;
in a particular case it is good, because it is charity
to lay down lives for friends.*

The development of the idea of violence expressing fraternal love can be illustrated from
the sources for the history of the Military
Orders, which were linked closely to the crusades, even if the brothers in them were not
technically crusaders. The founding of the Order of Knights Templar[4] is a remarkable event
in the history of the religious life. One of the
chief attractions of the First Crusade, which followed closely on a change in the Church's
thinking on the rôle of laymen, was that now
at last the laity had a task to perform, pleasing to God, for which they were especially
equipped and which professed religious were
not permitted to undertake. In a well-known
passage in his history of the crusade, Guibert
of Nogent welcomed the fact that now laymen
could attain salvation through works without
entering a monastery; and the sudden realization that the leading crusader Tancred, torn between "the Gospel and the world," had of the
new rôle for Christian warriors, and his enthusiastic response to it, is evidence for the
force of this idea, as is the emphasis on the
"new knight" still to be found in the writings
of St. Bernard half a century later. But so dominant was the appeal of the religious life and
so superior was its status that, within 20 years
of the capture of Jerusalem, professed religious
were themselves taking on the rôle of warriors,
usurping the special function of the laity. All
contemporaries were struck by the fact that a

---

[3]Founded in 1119 to protect pilgrims.

new kind of religious life had come into being, in which the brothers could hardly have acted in a more secular way. The compilers of the Templar rule wrote that

We believe that by divine providence this new kind of religious order was founded by you in the holy places, so that you combine soldiering with the religious life and in this way the order can fight with arms and can without blame smite the enemy.

The association in the Templar life of both religious and military practices was a point also made in St. Bernard's treatise, the *De laude novae militiae*, and in the early thirteenth century, by which time the Hospitallers had also taken on military responsibilities and the Spanish and German Military Orders had been founded, James of Vitry wrote of the brothers

concerning whom the Lord says, "I will encompass my house with them that serve me in war, going and returning" (Zac. ix, 8). Going in time of war, returning in time of peace; going by means of action, returning by means of contemplation; going in war to fight, returning in peace to repose and devotion to prayer, so that they are like soldiers in battle and like monks in convent.

The appearance of religious dedicated to war was bound to lead to controversy. In the 1160s and 1170s Pope Alexander III was worried by the transformation of the Hospital of St. John into a Military Order, and as early as the 1120s someone, perhaps Hugh of St. Victor, had to answer on the Templars' behalf critics who maintained that a monastic profession to defend with arms the faith and Christendom was "illicit and pernicious" and that it would lead the Templars into sin because war was activated by hatred and greed.

I say to you that you do not hate, which is unjust, because you do not hate man but iniquity. Again I say, you are not greedy, which is unjust, because you acquire that which should justly be taken on account of sins and that which is justly yours because of the work that you do.

But the real reply was given in 1139 by Pope Innocent II in *Omne datum optimum*, the papal charter for the Templars, and it was a reply that drew attention to the love shown by the brothers.

As true Israelites and most instructed fighters in divine battle, filled with the flames of divine charity, you carry out in deeds the words of the Gospel, "Greater love than this no man hath, that a man lay down his life for his friends."

In 1155 this was reemphasized by Pope Adrian IV in *Sicut sacra evangelia*, in phrases that were often to be repeated in later papel letters.

The knights of the Temple . . . are especially called to the service of the omnipotent God and are numbered with the heavenly host. This is indicated by their reverend habit and is shown by the sign of the cross of Our Lord which they wear on their bodies. Indeed they have been founded for this purpose, that they do not fear to lay down their lives for their brothers.

The same attitude was to be found with regard to the Hospitallers[4] as they took on military duties. The first reference to a military wing in their statutes treated it as an extension of their charitable work.

These eleemosynary grants have properly been established in the holy Order of the Hospital, except for the brethren-at-arms, whom the holy Order keeps honourably, and many other bounties.

And in 1191 Pope Celestine III referred to the Hospitallers, fighting the infidel and looking after the poor, as "the children of peace and love . . . servants in Christ of the holy poor of Jerusalem and of all lands everywhere." In this respect the Military Orders sprang from the same stem as did the other new orders of the time, demonstrating in their own fashion the concern for charitable work and the care of one's neighbour that so many of them showed.

---

[4]Founded in 1048 to provide lodgings for poor pilgrims in Jerusalem.

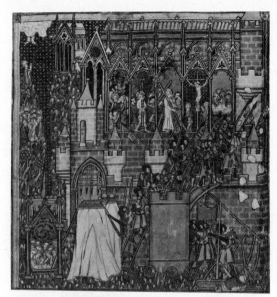

■ ■ *Crusading was an act of love, but it also involved hard fighting, including the bloody capture of Jerusalem in 1099 shown in this picture.*

The idea that crusading expressed fraternal love was, of course, also put forward in encyclicals directed chiefly at the laity. In 1169, Pope Alexander III, responding to a request for aid from the Kingdom of Jerusalem, published a major appeal with the widest possible circulation. He began it by stressing the rôle of love.

Among all the means that Divine Wisdom has provided for the exercise of charity in the midst of temporal affairs, it would be difficult to find a field of action in which this charity could be expressed with more glory with regard to virtue, and with better results with regard to rewards, than in aid to relieve the needs of the Church in the East and the faithful of Christ, by defending them against the onslaught of the pagans, so that both the cult of the Divine Name does not fail and the virtue of brotherhood shines forth praiseworthily.

In 1215 Innocent III returned to the theme of love in *Quia maior*, this time love for Christians in territories occupied by the Moslems.

How does a man love according to divine precept his neighbour as himself when, knowing that his Christian brothers in faith and in name are held by the perfidious Muslims in strict confinement and weighed down by the yoke of heaviest servitude, he cannot devote himself to the efficacious work of liberating them? In this he transgresses the command of that natural law which the Lord declared in the Gospel. "All things . . . whatsoever you would that men should do to you, do you also to them." (Matt. vii, 12). Is it by chance that you do not know that among them (the Muslims) many thousands of Christians are held in servitude and in jail, tortured with innumerable torments?

Now, the striking thing about these references to love is that they are one-dimensional and therefore not truly Christian. Love of neighbour was always treated in crusade propaganda in terms of fraternal love for fellow-Christians, never in terms of love shown for enemies as well as friends. And this one-sided view of love did not properly reflect Christian teaching in the past or at the time. One has only to read the *Sentences* of Peter Lombard to find a contemporary theologian putting before his readers a more fully rounded view. By neighbour, Peter stressed, one must mean all mankind. Certainly, he argued, fellow-Christians ought especially to be loved and, in that we cannot *show* equal love to all, they should come first, since they are members of the same body and recognize the same Father. It is, moreover, sufficient to love enemies straightforwardly and not to hate them; in this respect love of enemies comes last in a scale of expressions of love. But he emphasized that enemies must be included in our love for all men and he quoted St. Augustine to the effect that it is more virtuous to love enemies than friends.

The Christian tradition on violence, moreover, the foundations of which had been laid by the Fathers, naturally stressed the rôle of love, for enemies as well as friends, in the use of force. St. Augustine had treated the matter comprehensively. To him, just violence required right intention on the part of the imposers of force as an essential prerequisite. In his treatise on the Sermon on the Mount, containing one of his earliest essays on the subject, he stressed that the intention behind punishment designed for the purpose of correction had to be to make the offender happy; it had to be imposed out of love by those who had in this matter overcome hatred. Christ had denounced hatred seeking vengeance, not love desiring to correct the object of love. Further, many noble and saintly men had in the past inflicted death as a punishment for sins. Those put to death had suffered no injury from it; rather, they were already being injured by their sins and their state might have become far worse had they been allowed to live. Augustine referred here to the prophet Elijah killing on authority from God and he drew attention to St. Paul delivering a sinner over to Satan for the destruction of his flesh, so that his spirit might be saved (I Cor. v, 5). He admitted that he did not really understand the meaning of the words St. Paul had used, but he maintained that it was clear that, whatever St. Paul did mean, he intended to save a soul; in other words that this was a punishment imposed through love. To Augustine, the intentions of those who authorized violence and of those who participated in it had to be in favour of justice, a virtue which for him assigned to everyone his due, working through love of God and love of one's neighbour. It being often move loving to use force than indulgence, it followed that just violence had love for those on whom it was meted out as the mainspring of action; and this kind of motivation would mean that one would be careful to employ only such violence as was necessary. Augustine often wrote of the way parents could express their love for their children by correcting them, and he also referred to the violence sometimes needed in healing the sick or in rescuing men from physical danger against their wills. The scriptures were combed by him for references to acts or expressions of violence, motivated by love, perpetrated by Moses and Elijah, by St. Paul, by a loving God and even by a loving Christ, as when he scourged the stall-keepers out of the Temple and blinded St. Paul on the road to Damascus. All of this provided a basis for his justification of the repression of heresy. It was right, and a sign of love and mercy in imitation of Christ, for a loving Church, in collaboration with a loving state, to force heretics from the path of error for their own benefit, compelling them to goodness in the same way as the host at the wedding feast in Christ's parable had sent out his servant to force those in the high-ways to come to the banquet.

Augustine's thought was very influential in the central Middle Ages. On most of the criteria for Christian violence crusading ideas followed his. But they did not on love. One explanation might be that since Augustine devoted most of his writing on violence to justifying the suppression of heresy—and made little distinction between force associated with war against external foes and force used internally to repress heretics—his approach was one that could lead more naturally to an emphasis on love as a disciplinary force, for which parallels could be drawn with family life. But, in fact, writers at the time of the Crusades also treated violence against external and internal injurers under the same general heading. And since they did not distinguish the forms of violence, at least as far as the justification of force went, one would not expect crusade propagandists to have done so either.

It might also be pointed out that certain premises in Augustine's thought were alien to the theology of the central Middle Ages and that this might explain why the justifiers of crusading violence did not follow him on the issue of love of enemies as well as friends. In particular, he had a very negative attitude toward free will, and this led him to have a pessimistic view of the ability of most people truly to act through love. The fact was that those whom love restrained were less numerous in this world than those who had to be restrained by terror. Fear, instilled by the penal laws of the Roman emperors against heresy, forced people to truth, and many were brought to the true faith and to salvation who otherwise would not have known it. Moreover, fear gave the faint-hearted the excuse to break with heresy. Augustine could, therefore, compare just and unjust persecution: the Roman state, in alliance with the Church, imposed a just persecution, while the pagan emperors and the wicked persecuted unjustly. He argued that Christ had promised blessedness for those persecuted for justice's sake, but had said nothing about those persecuted for the sake of injustice. Nobody became a martyr merely by suffering for religion. "It is not the penalty that makes a martyr, but the cause." So the essential thing was the justice of the cause for which one suffered, and an image Augustine used was that of Christ, unjustly crucified, hanging on the cross between the two thieves, who had been justly condemned. Playing down free will it was, of course, fairly easy to justify violence in terms of love shown to those incapable of motivation to good except by fear. But it was far less easy to do so if one shared the highly developed notions of free will that were common in the central Middle Ages, since coercion potentially limited the operation of free will in the coerced. In a *dictum* in his important *Causa XXIII* on violence, the canonist Gratian, writing in c.1140, showed anxiety about this matter.

Augustine's approach to free will, moreover, resulted in an indifference to the salvific value of works. In fact he did not really believe that any special merit attached to the participants in his violence. He wrote that Abraham had shown "praiseworthy" compliance with God's order to sacrificed Isaac, but he seems to have regarded even acts of violence on God's specific command—a category of force to which he paid special attention—as

being merely blameless. One would be quite wrong to refuse such an order, but only doing one's duty if one obeyed it. In fact the man who owed obedience to the giver of a command, whether God himself or God's minister, did not himself kill: he was an instrument in the hand of the authorizer. To the apologists for the Crusades, on the other hand, merit, which of course stemmed from the dominant position held by the concept of free will, played so large a part that a recent historian of the crusades has defined holy war in terms of its meritoriousness.

But, apart from Gratian's *dictum* to which I have already referred, theologians of the time of the Crusades do not seem to have found it difficult to graft ideas of free will and merit onto Augustinian thought. Indeed, if there is one feature of their treatment of love and violence it is how Augustinian it is; and quotations from Augustine, including those which emphasized love of enemies, predominate in their writings. It was St. Anselm of Lucca, a supporter of Pope Gregory VII, who in books XII and XIII of his *Collectio canonum*, written in c.1083, collected the basic Augustinian texts on violence, including those on force and love, and passed them on to his successors as authorities for the arguments that the Church did not persecute but expressed love when she punished sin; that Moses, using force on orders from God, did nothing cruel; that punishment could be imposed not out of hatred but out of love; and that wars could be benevolent in intention. Anselm was followed by Ivo of Chartres who, in his *Decretum* and *Panormia*, written in France in c.1094 on the eve of the First Crusade, used his authorities to demonstrate that love of neighbour demanded that in normal circumstances one should not kill. One should not embark on punishment unless one had personally overcome hatred; indeed penalties could be imposed on those who killed out of hate and not out of zeal for justice. But Ivo stressed, in an Augustinian passage that was later to be used by Gratian, that the exercise of Christian forebearance *(patientia)* did not entirely rule out necessary fighting. Love, in fact, could involve physical correction, in the same way as a father punished a son or a master a servant. To coerce one's neighbour could be to love him and the man who punished evil did not persecute but loved. Indeed in the *Panormia*, which was a popular work, three chapters were devoted to the arguments, taken entirely from St. Augustine, that neighbourly love demanded that men prevent their neighbours from doing evil and that Christians could, in fact, sin if they did not persecute those engaged in evil works. Ivo maintained that wars fought by true Christians were in fact acts of pacification, since their aim was peace.

The works of Anselm of Lucca and Ivo of Chartres foreshadowed that of Gratian, but in no way approached the subtlety and honesty of Gratian's treatment of force in *Causa XXIII* of his *Decretum*, written in c.1140. He began by facing up squarely to the passages in the New Testament that appeared to forbid Christians to use violence of any kind, but he then took his readers through a mass of material that gradually revealed the Christian justification of violence. On the issue of love, including love of enemies, he was, like Anselm and Ivo, fundamentally Augustinian. The use of force was not entirely forbidden in the precepts of forebearance (*patientia*), for while they should be interpreted as meaning that clemency and tolerance should be shown, bad sins ought to be punished, as in the cases of Ananias and Sapphira on the condemnation of St. Peter— this was a favourite example of the Fathers and of those writing on violence in the central Middle Ages—of Elymas who was blinded on the word of St. Paul and of the sinner whom St. Paul handed over to Satan. Evil must not be rendered for evil and one should love, not persecute, enemies, but Augustine's analogies of the doctor prescribing for patients and the heads of households correcting sons and servants were drawn on. Out of maternal love the

Church could prescribe medicine for sinners, and anyway better the wounds of a friend than the kisses of an enemy. Men were bound to love their enemies, to pray for them and show mercy to them, but the demands of love should mean that they could not allow others to sin with impunity. Acts of mercy could themselves be unjust, and one such act could lead to universal harm. And so the restless were usefully corrected by the office of public power. It was better to love with severity: persecution was not always culpable for it could serve love. And the wicked could be forced to goodness: men had the example of Christ to follow here; nobody loved more than he did, yet he forced St. Paul onto the path of righteousness. Moses, too, punished the Israelites not out of cruelty but out of love. Correction was an attribute of mercy, as could be found by reading not only the Old Testament, but also the New, although the examples in it were more rare. Gratian believed that he had established from his authorities that punishment in itself was permitted and did not necessarily involve hatred.

As a final example of the treatment of love and violence at the time of the Crusades one might look at St. Thomas Aquinas's early polemical treatise *Contra impugnantes*, written in 1256. This again was Augustinian in its approach and it repeated the argument that Christ only gave the apostles, who were simple and uneducated men, power to authorize punishment by means of force after he had taught them to love their neighbours absolutely.

Reading these works one glimpses what seems to be a different world to that portrayed in crusading propaganda. Instead of the one-dimensional notion of fraternal love for fellow-Christians, violence is treated in the context of love for all mankind, enemies as well as friends. For all its obvious faults, one is bound to admire the subtlety and learning of the canonists' treatment of force and to recognize that it has an authentic place in the Christian ethical tradition. But it must be stressed that theologians and canonists and the popes and curial clerks who wrote the calls to crusade did not live in different worlds. Pope Alexander III, for instance, in whose name was issued one of the encyclicals from which I have quoted, was himself a canonist and the author of a commentary on Gratian's *Decretum*. It is not believable that the popes who proclaimed crusades and the more respectable preachers who whipped up enthusiasm for them did not grasp the complexity of the Christian position. They must have presented their one-sided version of love deliberately, with a view to the audience they were addressing.

It could be that they dared not do otherwise. A feature of the attitudes of twelfth-century lay society as revealed in its vernacular poetry was its blind, uncomprehending hatred of the infidel, expressed, for instance, in Charlemagne's famous declaration in the *Song of Roland* that "Never to paynims may I show love or peace." Through the epics runs the theme of an implacable war of conversion against non-Christians, a theme that expressed itself in the slaughters that accompanied the conquests of the First Crusade and the forced conversions that were perpetrated in the East and in Spain. Only toward the end of the twelfth century did the picture of the "noble heathen," the pagan who was capable of good actions, begin to take hold among ordinary laymen. Given this feeling, it was hardly possible for crusade propagandists to write in terms of love of enemy; on the contrary, crusading literature and propaganda played on the xenophobia by the use of emotive terms—enemies of God, servants of the Devil, servants of the Anti-Christ—to describe the Moslems.

But this negative explanation is not sufficient. The popes and their representatives must have brought up the subject of love because of the positive feelings they knew would be aroused in those who listened to their appeals. I believe that, as with love of God, we find here echoes of the secular world. It will have been noticed that in the sources from which I have quoted the words most commonly used to refer to fellow-Christians are brothers (*fratres*) and friends (*amici*). And at this time the word *amicus* as often as not meant kinsman, rather than simply friend, as in a French eleventh-century document that referred to

his friends, that is to say his mother, his brothers, his sisters and his other relatives by blood or by marriage.

People hearing these words would be encouraged to think of fellow-Christians as their relatives and the specific use of this kind of imagery is to be found in one of the reports of Pope Urban's sermon at Clermont, in which he was said to have referred to the Eastern Christians as

your full brothers, your comrades, your brothers born of the same mother, for you are sons of the same Christ and the same Church.

It is well-known that in the central Middle Ages kinship was regarded as creating the same sort of binding obligations as vassalage. The family was a source of strength to the individual, and ties of kinship took precedence, along with vassalage, over all others. It looks as though crusade propagandists decided to present crusading love to laymen in the same terms as love of family. And if one accepts Georges Duby's belief that in twelfth-century knightly families "the patrimony seemed indeed to have been the essential support for the recollection . . . of family consciousness," then the idea of Palestine as the hereditary patrimony of Christ takes on a new meaning. In an age obsessed by family land-holdings, Christ's children were being aroused by threats to their father's inheritance.

My suggestion that crusading charity was presented to the laity as an example of family love leads to a further point. Marc Bloch has written that "the Middle Ages, from beginning to end, and particularly in the feudal era, lived under the sign of private vengeance." The history of the eleventh, twelfth, and thirteenth centuries is punctuated by violent vendettas. The Church was naturally opposed to them, but it looks as though in its preaching of Crusades it was not averse to using the imagery of the family feud to attract knights. Vengeance on the infidel who had oppressed Christians' brothers and seized their father's patrimony was a theme in Crusade propaganda; and when in 1198 Pope Innocent III referred to crusaders being summoned

as sons to take vengeance on injury to their father and as brothers to avenge the destruction of their brothers

everyone must have known what he meant. The Crusade was in this sense a blood-feud waged against those who had harmed members of Christ's family.

But I would also argue that love, even in the debased form in which it was presented to potential crusaders, was theologically essential to the crusading movement, because for Christians in all ages sacred violence cannot be proposed on any grounds save that of love. And the idea of charity contributed to the Crusades' attraction in that, while all sorts of motives and feelings conditioned the response of Latin Christians to the popes' appeals to take the cross, contemporaries really did feel that they were engaging in something morally satisfying. In an age dominated by the theology of merit this explains why participation in Crusades was believed to be meritorious, why the expeditions were seen as penitential acts that could gain indulgences, and why death in battle was regarded as martyrdom. In the 1930s Carl Erdmann, in his influential book on the origins of the movement, linked it to the eleventh-century reformers who were, he explained, "the very men who stood for the idea of holy war and sought to put it into practice." His association of the reform movement with the development of the crusading idea was one of the most striking features of a brilliant study, but it can be argued that he did not take things far enough; that, although he gave evidence for a relationship between reform and sacred violence, he did not explain why such a relationship existed. In fact, as manifestations of Christian love, the crusades were as much the products of the renewed spirituality of the central Middle Ages, with its concern for living the *vita apostolica* and expressing Christian ideals in active works of charity, as were the new hospitals, the pastoral work of the Augustinians and Premonstratensians and the service of the friars. The charity of St. Francis may now appeal to us more than that of the crusaders, but both sprang from the same roots.

■■■

STUDY QUESTIONS

1. In what way did "crusading" constitute an act of love on behalf of God and on behalf of one's neighbor?

2. How often did Christian leaders use "analogues of war" or military metaphors to inspire commitment among Christians? Please cite some examples.

3. In what ways did Christian leaders create a relationship between the crusaders and Christ's death on the cross?

4. Were these people sincere? How did the context of social and political life in the eleventh and twelfth centuries make the crusades seem perfectly reasonable acts of love and devotion for God? Can you see any contemporary examples of similar forms of religious commitment?

5. Did the crusaders' sense of Christian love ever extend to nonbelievers? How did they justify the violence they committed against Moslems in the Middle East with Christ's teachings on love?

6. What did St. Augustine say about the relationship between Christian love and Christian violence? St. Thomas Aquinas?

BIBLIOGRAPHY

The literature of the Crusades is extensive. For a general survey see Jonathan Riley-Smith, *What Were the Crusades?* (1977). Carl Erdmann's *The Origin of the Idea of Crusade* (1977) deals with the background of the movement. For the ideas and role of particular individuals, see I. S. Robinson, "Gregory VI and the Soldiers of Christ," *History*, 58 (1973); J. S. C. Riley-Smith, *The Knights of St. John in Jerusalem and Cyprus* (1967); R. S. Hartigan, "St. Augustine on War and Killing: The Problem of the Innocent," *Journal of the History of Ideas*, 27 (1966); and Edward Gilson, *The Christian Philosophy of St. Augustine* (1961). Also see Steven Runciman, *A History of the Crusades*, 3 volumes (1951–1954).

12. LEPERS, JEWS, AND MOSLEMS: THE PLOT TO OVERTHROW CHRISTENDOM IN 1321

Malcolm Barber

Fears of unexplainable, deadly diseases, ethnic differences, and religious dissent have been at the heart of human conflict since the dawn of civilization. In the 1980s, for all of our technological sophistication, western society has faced a number of dilemmas with roots in those most primal of fears. The global epidemic of AIDS has inspired an extraordinary number of community disputes and public policy debates in the United States and Western Europe, whereas politicians in Africa, where the disease is rampant, are loath to even admit the existence of a public health hazard. Religious fundamentalism has become more intense among Israeli Jews, Middle Eastern Moslems, and American Protestants in the 1980s, spawning a host of social and political controversies that threaten domestic and international stability. And ethnic hatreds are creating ongoing hostility and violence in the Soviet Union, India, Pakistan, South Africa, Sri Lanka, Indonesia, and Southeast Asia.

In 1321 a similar combination of fears led to panic among Christians in France and Germany. Rumors of conspiracies to poison water supplies—wells, lakes, rivers, and streams—spread contagiously from village to village and town to town. A series of social and economic problems in the early fourteenth century had stimulated popular frustrations and fears, and people were anxious to find scapegoats for their problems. In 1321 French and German Christians found those scapegoats in Jews, Moslems, and lepers, whom they accused of plotting to overthrow established institutions. In this selection, Malcolm Barber describes the origins and the development of a widespread attack on Jews, Moslems, and lepers that took place in 1321.

In 1321," says Bernard Gui, Inquisitor at Toulouse between 1307 and 1324, "there was detected and prevented an evil plan of the lepers against the healthy persons in the kingdom of France. Indeed, plotting against the safety of the people, these persons, unhealthy in body and insane in mind, had arranged to infect the waters of the rivers and fountains and wells everywhere, by placing poison and infected matter in them and by mixing (into the water) prepared powders, so that healthy men drinking from them or using the water thus infected, would become lepers, or die, or almost die, and thus the numbers of the lepers would be increased and the healthy decreased. And what seems incredible to say, they aspired to the lordship of towns and castles, and had already divided among themselves the lordship of places, and given themselves the name of potentate, count or baron in various lands, if what they planned should come about." In this way, Bernard Gui begins his description of the hysteria that gripped a large part of France during the spring and summer of 1321 and that swelled into a tide of panic which engulfed the king and the court as well. For a short period, it was seen as the ultimate threat to the faith as conceived by the orthodox: a plan by subversive elements, both inside and outside society, to overthrow the whole structure of Christendom.

In June 1321, King Philip V was staying at Poitiers, where he intended to hold an assembly of representatives of the towns of southern and central France. According to the anonymous monk who continued the chronicle of Guillaume de Nangis, it was there that, about the time of the Feast of St. John the Baptist (24 June), rumour reached him that many lepers in Upper Aquitaine had been arrested and burnt to death because they had confessed to infecting the fountains and wells with poison, with the purpose of either killing or making leprous all the Christians of France and Germany. A French historian, G. Lavergne, has shown from a study of local archives that the lepers in and around Périgueux had been accused of this plot in the spring of 1321, and, on 16 April, a systematic arrest of the lepers of the neighbourhood had been ordered by the mayor of Périgueux. By May, many had been tortured into confession and condemned to death by burning. The news may therefore have been brought to the king by the representatives of Périgueux who had been sent to attend the meeting of the towns at Poitiers on 14 June.

The chroniclers Jean de Saint-Victor and the Nangis continuator report that "about this time," further details arrived from another source: that of the lord of Parthenay (just to the west of Poitiers), who is conveniently not named. "It is said," relates the continuator of Nangis with the customary caveat, that this lord sent the king a sealed letter containing the confession of an important leper who had been captured in his lands. The letter broadened the implications of the plot considerably, for the leper had confessed that he had been led to take part in the poisoning by "a certain rich Jew," who had given him the poisonous potions together with 10 *livres*, promising a large amount of money if he would corrupt the other lepers. The Jew had told him that the potion consisted of a mixture of human blood and urine, three unnamed herbs, and a consecrated host, all of which were mixed into a powder, placed in bags, tied with a weight, and thrown into the wells and fountains. The Nangis continuator claimed that he himself had seen at Poitiers the potions made by a certain female leper, which were intended for the town, but which she had thrown away in a panic, still in their bag, as she feared capture. "There was found in the bag the head of a snake, the feet of a toad and hairs as of a woman, having been mixed with a certain

"Lepers, Jews and Moslems: The Plot to Overthrow Christendom in 1321" by Malcolm Barber, *History*, Vol. 66, No. 216, February 1981. Copyright © 1981 The Historical Association. Reprinted by permission of Basil Blackwell, Oxford.

black and fetid liquid, so it was not only horrible to feel, but also to see." The strength of the poison was revealed when this bag was thrown on a fire, for the contents would not burn.

Philip V, himself a man of deeply superstitious nature, seems to have been prepared to believe the reports and, on 21 June, issued an ordinance from Poitiers to his *baillis* to effect a general arrest of the lepers. The ordinance states that "public knowledge and the course of experience" have shown that the lepers have attempted to kill Christians by throwing poisonous potions into the waters, not only in France, but "in all kingdoms subject to the faith of Christ." For this reason the king had caused them to be arrested and some had confessed and been burnt for the crime. However, others remained unpunished, so, with the advice of his council, the king had decided upon the following measures: (i) lepers who have confessed or who confess in the future are to be burnt alive; (ii) if they will not confess "spontaneously" then torture should be applied "so that the truth can be extracted"; (iii) female lepers should be treated in the same way, except those who were pregnant, who should be imprisoned until their infants are of sufficient age "to live and feed without their help," and then these women should be burnt; (iv) lepers who confess nothing, those who will be born in the future, and leper youths, both male and female, who were less than 14 years old, should be imprisoned in their places of origin; (v) lepers who have reached their majority, which was 14 years of age, and who confessed in the way set out above, were to be burnt. According to the ordinance, the crime of the lepers was one of *lèse-majesté* and therefore all the goods of the lepers "should be placed and held in our hand." The imprisoned lepers should be provided for from there, as should the brothers and sisters who had taken care of them and who had lived from the revenues of the leper property. The ordinance stressed that the nature of the crime meant that the administration of justice in this case appertained to the royal power only and not to any temporal lords.

However, unlike the arrest of the Templars in October 1307, which had been instituted by Philip IV and kept secret until a predetermined day, many lords had already executed lepers and confiscated their goods. The provisions of the ordinance notwithstanding, therefore, Philip V was unable to take advantage of the situation and reserve the goods entirely for himself. Although the *baillis* acted upon the royal orders, the king nevertheless found it politic to issue another ordinance on 16 August. This declared that, at the request of several prelates, barons, nobles, communities and others who said that from ancient times they possessed the right to administer the *léproseries* and to appoint their governors, he had restored the goods which he had seized, without prejudice to his own rights and without creating any new right. The king had already been forced to acknowledge local rights over *léproseries* in particular cases. In Narbonne the *sénéchal* had taken over the goods of the lepers in the king's name, but the *consuls* of Carcassonne had protested that they had been accustomed to administer the goods for pious ends, a protest accepted by the king who, on 4 August, ordered the *sénéchal* to release the goods. The king found it equally difficult to control local action against the lepers themselves. The Bishop of Albi and his justiciars, for instance, were among those who had taken the law into their own hands and arrested the lepers. Some had been condemned to death while the rest were imprisoned. Because the king had said that the crime was one of *lèse-majesté*, he had levied a fine on the bishop. However, by 18 August, he had been obliged to remit the fine and to order his *sénéchaux* at Carcassonne and Toulouse to accept the episcopal jurisdiction over the lepers' case on the grounds that there was some doubt whether the crime could be regarded as *lèse-majesté*. In a matter such as this, he said, which required immediate action, the delays caused while it was being resolved would be too great.

Local authorities were perhaps themselves carried along by popular fervour. According to the anonymous continuator of the chronicle of Rouen, the lepers were burnt "more by the people than by secular justice." Bernard Gui confirms this. "In many places, in detestation of the horrible act, the lepers, both men and women, were shut up in their homes with all their things, (and) fire having been applied, they were burnt by the people without any judgement." Flanders seems to have been an exception for, according to the *Genealogia Comitum Flandriae*, although they were arrested, they were afterwards freed, which "displeased not a few people."

The extent of popular involvement in the affair is shown by the pogrom against the Jews that accompanied the attacks upon the lepers. The royal ordinances make no mention of the involvement of the Jews, but their part in the well-poisoning was nevertheless readily believed, both by the chroniclers and by the populace. The anonymous *Chronique Parisienne*, for instance, asserted that "this devilry was done by the encouragement and the incitement of the Jews." According to the Nangis continuator, "the Jews in some parts were burnt indiscriminately and especially in Aquitaine." They seem to have received little protection from the authorities. At the royal castle of Chinon in the *bailliage* of Tours, for instance, the continuator of Nangis reports that 160 Jews were burnt to death in a large pit. Many women, widowed by the executions, were said to have thrown their own sons onto the fire to prevent them being baptized "by the Christians and the nobles present there." It seems unlikely that this could have taken place without the connivance of the *bailli* of Tours. Indeed, the chroniclers claim that attacks also took place against the Jews in Paris from

Medieval society required lepers to wear distinctive clothing and carry bells as a warning to the healthy.

which the king gained direct financial benefit. Those found guilty were burnt, whereas others were condemned to perpetual exile. Some of the richest were kept until their debts were known, and their incomes and goods were absorbed into the royal fisc. The king was said to have had 150,000 *livres* from them.

The chroniclers have one more dramatic example of the fate of the Jews. At Vitry 40 Jews held in the royal prison, despairing of survival, decided to commit suicide. Their most aged and venerable member was chosen to cut their throats, a task that he was not prepared to perform without the assistance of a younger man. The two men did as the community wished, but when they were the only ones left, they were faced with the problem of who should kill the other. At length the old man prevailed in his wish to be killed first, and the younger man was left the sole survivor. However, instead of killing himself, he took whatever could be found from the bodies in the way of gold and silver, made a rope from clothes and climbed down from the tower in which they had been imprisoned. Unfortunately, the rope was shorter than he needed and this fact, together with the weight of the gold and silver, caused him to fall and break his leg, thus making his recapture possible. He, too, was then executed. Lehugeur, in his study of the reign of Philip V, believes this to be merely a fable, "for the edification of the reader," and he is probably correct to be sceptical, because the story of the mass suicide among Jews in the face of adversity was well-established by 1321. Moreover, certain details, such as the possession of gold and silver by the imprisoned Jews, strike a false note. Nevertheless, because of the extent of popular fury not only in 1321, but also in the rising of the Pastoureaux of the previous year, the possibility of some further outrage at Vitry cannot be discounted.

Local jurisdictional claims and mob action therefore considerably diminished the control that the king sought through his ordinance of 21 June; nevertheless, he had ordered a general arrest and interrogation of the lepers. A number of depositions must undoubtedly have been produced by this action and, indeed, a royal order of 8 February 1322 commands that the *baillis* of Tours, Chaumont and Vitry send to *Parlement* "the confessions of the lepers and the Jews" relating to the poisoning of the waters and other crimes. Such depositions have not apparently survived, but they may well have been extensive, for the affair was widely known throughout France. Contemporary references to it occur in the provinces of Flanders, Vermandois, Anjou, Touraine and Aquitaine, and in the specific towns of Paris, Amiens, Rouen, Caen, Avranches, and Coutances in the north, Chaumont, Vitry and Mâcon in the east, Tours, Ouches, Limoges, Poitiers and Périgueux in the centre, and Toulouse, Carcassonne, Albi, Narbonne, Pamiers and Lyons in the south. However, the diligence of Jacques Fournier, Bishop of Pamiers between 1318 and 1325, makes it possible to examine a deposition of the kind which might have been produced by royal inquiries. The contents of this document suggest that it was through this and other depositions that tortured lepers greatly broadened the implications of the conspiracy to include not only lepers and Jews but also outside Moslem powers as well. The chroniclers, writing after the event, were then able to incorporate this additional strand within their narratives.

Guillaume Agasse, head of the leper colony at Estang in Pamiers, appeared before Marc Rivel, Fournier's deputy, on 2 June 1321, nearly three weeks before Philip V issued orders for the general arrest. In the story told by Agasse, two lepers from Estang, Guillaume Normand and Fertand Espanol, as long ago as the previous Feast of St. Catherine (25 November 1320) had gone to Toulouse to seek some poisons, staying overnight on the way back with a leper called Gaulaube, commander of the house of Auterive. On their return to Estang, they told the witness that they had done good work, for they had brought poisons that would be put into the waters of Pamiers and that would make everybody into lepers. They then proceeded to poison the water of the fountain of Tourong, among other watersources in Pamiers. Gaulaube at Auterive had been given poisons for the same purpose, while Etienne de Valès, a leper in Cahors, had poisoned the waters there too. At Estang the witness claimed that when the bank of the ditch of a local spring was opened up, he had seen a great ball of dung sunk into it, and that he had also seen, about a year ago, a certain leper coming away from that place. When asked if he had tried to prevent the poisoning, he replied that, on the contrary, it pleased him.

Guillaume Agasse appeared again on 9 June before Bernard Fassier, the official of Pamiers, and this time implicated himself more directly. In May 1320, a certain youth, whom he did not know, brought him some letters in which the preceptor of the lepers of Porte Arnaud Bernard of Toulouse asked him to come at once on the following Sunday to his house "to conduct and order certain things which would result to his advantage and honour." He set out, stopping overnight at the leper colony in Saverdun, where he discovered that Raimond, the commander of that house, had received a similar letter, and so, the next morning, they traveled to Toulouse together. On the Saturday night, they stayed at the house at Toulouse "with many other lepers, ministers, and preceptors." On Sunday, 11 May 1320, about 40 lepers assembled in the main hall (*aula*) of the house and were addressed by the commander: "You see and hear how other healthy Christians hold us who are ill in shame and disrespect, and how they throw us from their meetings and gatherings and that they hold us in derision and censure and disrespect." Because of this, it was decided that all healthy Christians in the world should be poisoned so that they too became lepers, and then the present lepers would take "their administration and governance." "And to obtain and cause this, the preceptor said and announced that it had been decided and ordained among the leaders that they would have the King of Granada in their aid and defence, which king, . . . had already announced to other leaders of the *malades* that he was prepared to give his advice, help and aid in the matter . . ." The plot would be achieved by placing powders in the waters, and to this end "with the advice of doctors" many powders had been made, a portion of which each of

those present would receive in a leather bag. The meeting broke up on the Tuesday, the witness and Raimond de Saverdun returning to their respective houses each with a full bag of powder. About a month after, Guillaume Agasse, "wishing to keep the oath which he had sworn at Toulouse," carefully distributed the powder in various fountains and wells in Pamiers, finally throwing what he had left into the River Ariège. Agasse knew that the commanders of the houses of Saverdun, Mazères, Unzent and Pujols had been present at the assembly at Toulouse, but had not recognized any of the others. They had done it because they had been promised the lordship of the various places where they lived. He repeated his story about the journey made to Toulouse by Guillaume Normand and Fertand Espanol, but this time confessed that he had helped Guillaume Normand place a bag of poison in the local fountain of Rive, which they had pegged down among the stones and tiles.

Guillaume Agasse made a third appearance on 6 July, before Jacques Fournier himself, stating that he had been tortured on the day that he had made his first confession, but not since. He still maintained, however, that his confessions were true. He then repeated his story of 9 June concerning the delivering of the letters and the journey to Toulouse, but appreciably enlarged his account of what had happened there. This time the number present had risen to 50 or 60 and he specified that they came from the Toulousain, the Quercy, the Limousin, and from Gascony and the Agenais. The commander of the house of Porte Arnaud Bernard was named as Jourdain, and he made them all swear an oath "on a certain book" from the chapel of the house not to reveal anything that occurred there, and to agree to do all the things which they were ordered to do. The assembly itself took place in the main hall of the house and there "on one side next to the door stood a certain man, tall and black, wearing a sword, having a helmet on his head, as it seemed, (and) holding a halberd in his hands." When one of the lepers asked what this man was doing there, Jourdain replied, that he was there "on account of those things which they ought to do there," adding that there were many others in the house who would come if it was necessary. Jourdain then explained that the plot to poison the Christians was supported by "the King of Granada and the Sultan of Babylon," who, in return for obedience to their orders, promised the leper commanders "great riches and honours" and the lordship of the places where they lived. The messenger from the two rulers was the commander of the leper house of Bordeaux. The Moslem rulers demanded that the lepers "deny the faith of Christ and his Law," and that they should receive the poison that the kings had ordered to be made. This was a mixture of the powdered remains of a consecrated host, "which the Christians call the body of Christ," and a concoction made from snakes, toads, lizards, and bats, together with human excrement. If any of the commanders resisted these orders, then the man with the halberd would at once decapitate him.

When the lepers present had denied Christ, Jourdain told them that in the near future there would be another chapter-meeting in which all the leper commanders of the Christian world would be present, where they would meet the King of Granada and the Sultan of Babylon. There, the commanders would again deny Christ and "spit on the cross of Christ and upon his body, and also that the body of the Lord and his cross should be trampled underfoot." This had been promised by the commander of Bordeaux and without this denial the two Moslem rulers "would not come to them nor confide in them." All the commanders present promised to do all this when the King and the Sultan came and to obey their orders. Indeed, there were said to be present at the time representatives of the two kings, who would report what had happened. Jour-

dain told them that these things "were done to the end that the Sultan of Babylon and the King of Granada would be lords of the whole land, which was now held by the Christians, the Christians having been killed or made lepers."

Jourdain and another commander, whom Guillaume Agasse thought was the commander of Bordeaux, then briefly left the room before returning with the deadly powders. Jourdain carried a large pot and the commander a large basin, which were placed in their midst. Jourdain told them that the pot contained the powdered host, and then proceeded to mix this with the powder in the basin, before distributing a portion contained in the leather bag to each of the commanders present. Guillaume Agasse received about half a pound. This was the powder that would infect the waters; care should be taken to put it in linen bags held under the water by a stone so that the poison did not dissipate too quickly, and should have the maximum effect. This was the end of the assembly and that day they ate together before returning to their homes. Ten or twelve days later (that is, 24 or 26 May), he began to put poison in the wells and fountains of Pamiers and into the Ariège, as he had explained before.

Finally, at the end of his deposition, Guillaume Agasse denied that the evidence that he had given against his fellow lepers, Guillaume Normand and Fertand Espanol, was true. It was he who had done these things and it was he who had remained for three months in the belief that the Christian faith was of no value. He had told no one nor given any poison to other lepers to place in the waters. He had also given false testimony against Raimond de Saverdun (who had already been burnt to death) and Pierre de Mazères. He confessed this "without any torture applied or threatened to him, freely and spontaneously, wishing to save his soul and repentant that he had committed the aforesaid." A year later, on 5 July

1322, Guillaume Agasse abjured his crime and received sentence of perpetual prison from Jacques Fournier. Bernard Gui was among those present.

Between Agasse's second and third depositions, two further pieces of evidence appeared that apparently lent support to stories such as those told by him involving Moslem powers in the plot. These are two letters allegedly written by the Moslem kings of Granada and Tunis, which suggest that they were actively providing financial support for the plot and indeed sending actual poison. The letter of the King of Granada is addressed to Sanson, son of Helias the Jew, and speaks of a plot already in being in which the king had provided money for the Jews, so that they could persuade the lepers to distribute poison in the cisterns, wells and fountains, poison sent by the king himself. One hundred and fifteen lepers had taken an oath that they would participate. The king was sending a special poison to be put into the water drunk by Philip V. No effort was to be spared to gain success. The letter of the King of Tunis is addressed generally "to his brethren and their children" and promises them sufficient money for their expenses. If they should wish to send their children to him he would guard them like his heart. The agreement among the king, the Jews, and the lepers had been made the previous Easter. An oath was sworn that involved 75 Jews and lepers. The letters are in French, having been translated from Arabic by Pierre d'Aura, a physician. The date given is 2 July. Unlike Agasse's deposition, however, they do not seem to have emanated from Languedoc, but from Mâcon, since Francon d'Avinières, the royal *bailli* of Mâcon, Pierre Maiorelli, a royal clerk, and two clerics, Bartholomew de Go, an archdeacon, and Guiot de l'Aubépin, a canon of Mâcon, together with 4 royal notaries and Pierre de Leugny, a leading citizen of the commune of Mâcon and keeper of its seal, attested their presence. The letters give no indication of the location of the originals or of how and where they entered France, but there seems little likelihood that they are genuine. Their content strongly suggests that whoever created them based his information upon confessions extorted from lepers similar to that made by Guillaume Agasse, following the ordinance of 21 June.

Some of the chroniclers also believed in Moslem perfidy. The Nangis continuator claimed "it was generally said" that the King of Granada, wishing to take revenge for his defeats at the hands of the Christians, especially by Peter, uncle of the King of Castile, had plotted this evil in concert with the lepers. He had promised the Jews "an infinite amount of money" if they would carry it out, but they refused to do so themselves because, "as they said, they were suspect to the Christians." The Jews, however, were "susceptible to evil" and, instead, arranged for the actual poisoning to be done by the lepers, "who continually mix with the Christians." The leaders of the lepers convoked four general councils, attended by representatives from all except for two English *léproseries*, and persuaded them that if everyone in the world became a leper then they would no longer be despised. As a further incentive, the offices of power were divided among the lepers in anticipation of their future victory. The Nangis continuator knew of a leper burnt at Tours who had called himself the Abbot of Marmoutier. Not all chroniclers, however, mention the Moslem connexion. The author of the *Chronique Parisienne* is apparently unaware of this dimension to the conspiracy, whereas Bernard Gui, who knew of the content of confessions such as that of Guillaume Agasse, nevertheless omits the accusation against the King of Granada, which suggests a certain scepticism on his part about this aspect of the affair.

Just like the Pastoureaux of the previous year, the disturbances seem to have spent themselves within a few months. The following summer, on 31 July 1322, at Paris, Charles IV issued an ordinance that permanently imprisoned the lepers within walls, their subsistence to be provided from their goods. In parishes where no proper endowments existed, the lepers were to be maintained at parish expense. Bernard Gui records this decision with approval, for although he believed in the existence of a plot, he clearly deplored action without due legal process as had characterized the pogroms of 1321. ''At length more mature advice and consultation having been taken, the rest, all and individually, who had remained alive and were not found guilty, circumspectly providing for the future, were enclosed in places from which they could never come out, but wither away and languish in perpetuity, so that they would not do harm or multiply, men being completely separated from women.'' As for the Jews, the accusations seem to have provided yet another excuse for monarchical financial extortion and, in 1322, for another ''expulsion in perpetuity.''

The delusion that a conspiracy between the lepers, the Jews, and the Moors actually existed in 1321, is a revealing instance of medieval mental attitudes under the strains created by the economic and social problems of the fourteenth century. Neither singly nor in combination did the elements in the supposed plot present any threat to society nor, as the anonymous chronicler of Tours admitted, did any Christian die or suffer ill from the poisoning of the water-supplies, yet the accusations were widely believed through the whole spectrum of the social order from the king downward. They were believed because the nature of the accusations accorded with the contemporary mental climate during a period of stress in which a scapegoat for society's ills seems to have been sought. The prosecutions of the previous twenty years had accustomed people to expect to find antisocial conspirators, ready to overturn society by whatever means came to hand. Most shocking of these plotters had been the Templars who, during their trial between 1307 and 1312, had confessed to the denial of Christ, spitting, trampling and urinating on a crucifix, the worship of monstrous idols, the encouragement of sodomy, and the abuse of the sacraments, especially by the omission of the words of consecration during the mass. These had been perpetrated in secret chapters and reception ceremonies which excluded outsiders. Other signs of stress had been present for some years. The famines between 1315 and 1317 in northern Europe had clearly been more prolonged and more serious in their impact than the frequent local shortages which were inseparable from the medieval agrarian system. However, local disasters also occurred, for in some regions affected by the leper conspiracy such events are recorded under the same year. In Flanders, for instance, extensive flooding from the sea is reported, destroying houses and drowning men and animals, while at the opposite end of the kingdom, at Lyons, there was a shortage of fruit, a lack of sun, famine and disease. At Tours, the chronicler was more cosmic in his observations. ''In this year, on the Feast of the Consecration of the Body of Christ (18 June), the halo (radius) of the sun was red in colour for the whole day, as if it were blood.'' This is not, however, to argue that there is a direct causal connexion between the famines of 1315–17 and the accusations against the lepers, or indeed to imply that the chroniclers make any link between the leper conspiracy and the natural and supernatural phenomena which they report, beyond the close juxtaposition of the events. It is rather to suggest that the existence of the widespread belief in such a plot is itself evidence of a society under stress and should be added to other such indications noted by historians.

These are, however, generalizations. Two specific questions arise from this affair: why did these particular groups become scapegoats and why were these particular allegations made? The Jews were of course the traditional victims of medieval prejudice, especially during the crusading era. They had suffered severely the previous year when the Pastoureaux or Shepherds' Crusade, frustrated in the attempt to reach Outremer, turned its fury upon the Jews more conveniently near at hand than the Moslems. The shepherds' movement had begun in the spring of 1320. Initially, they had concentrated upon Paris, but having failed to rouse the king to begin his long-awaited crusade, set off toward Languedoc. Here, during the summer, they attacked the Jews wherever they could find them: towns specifically named include Saintes, Verdun, Grenade, Castelsarrasin, Toulouse, Cahors, Lézat, Albi, Auch, Rabastens and Gaillac. Royal enquiries after the event stress the excesses committed against the Jews in the districts of Toulouse, Périgord and Carcassonne. Property was plundered, documentary evidence of debts burnt and whole communities of Jews massacred or forcibly baptized, usually with the complicity of the local inhabitants. The return of the Jews in 1315 after the expulsion of 1306 and the energetic pursuit of their debts by royal agents had made a major contribution to the diversion of these would-be crusaders against the Jews. Quite possibly, increased small-scale debts owed to the Jews incurred during the hardships of 1315–17 underlay some of the animosity. However, although the Pastoureaux had been crushed by royal military force, the fundamental reasons for anti-Semitism in medieval society—religious, cultural and economic—had been left untouched.

The association of the Jews with the lepers is more difficult to identify. It may have been the revival of an old prejudice which finds its written origins as long ago as the third century B.C., in which the Jews were chased out of Egypt as impure and leprous, a story which thereafter established itself in the mentality of the ancient Mediterranean world, or it may stem from a contrary idea based on the belief that the Jews rarely contracted leprosy, and could therefore have plotted with the lepers without fear of infection. Henri de Mondeville, physician to Philip the Fair and Louis X, listed as one of the causes of leprosy, sexual intercourse during menstruation, but explained that because Jews rarely have sexual intercourse during this time, few Jews are lepers.

The lepers themselves were new victims, but their circumstances made them vulnerable. Like the Jews, they formed distinctive and definable communities, and they could be recognized by their dress and sometimes by their disfigurement. The Church had contributed to their separation from society by applying the Levitical precepts of ritual defilement to leprosy, so that they were, in theory, to be regarded as unclean people to be kept apart from the rest of the community. A standard church service laid down detailed regulations for the separation of lepers and their conduct in relation to the rest of the community, and some of these are reiterated in the rules of leper houses. Ecclesiastical regulations, however, may simply have been formalizing an existing separation created by local communities rather than making new conditions. Canon 23 of the Third Lateran Council of 1179 established separate churches and cemeteries for lepers, but the reasoning behind the canon was that lepers had not been able to live with the healthy and attend their churches and therefore no proper religious provision was being made for them.

Perhaps most pertinent to the question of popular attitudes toward leprosy is the fact that it was the community that usually had to decide whether a person had contracted the disease, for medical advice was frequently unavailable. Leprosy, therefore, gained an accusatory aspect not dissimilar to heresy or witchcraft. Fear of infection, or simply repulsion at the appearance of those in the more advanced stages of the disease, must have powerfully reinforced the Church's precepts. The Nangis continuator portrays the leper leaders at their four great assemblies describing themselves and their fellow lepers as "the most vile and abject persons among the Christians," whereas the king demanded, in the ordinance of 18 August 1321, that the land be cleansed of the "putridity" of the "fetid lepers." Popular stories expressed this instinctive repulsion. The story from the *Gesta Romanorum*, for instance, "On the Evils of Leprosy," which must have had wide circulation in oral versions even though the stories were not collected together and written down until c.1340, taken literally, perpetuates the idea that leprosy could be sexually transmitted and this was in itself a means of ridding oneself of the disease and passing it on to another. At the same time, the moral interpretation of the story takes leprosy as a synonym for wickedness and describes the Fall as a process by which "man was spiritually made a leper." Even the Cathars, themselves outcasts and fugitives by 1321, viewed the lepers as the lowest among humanity. Guillaume Bélibaste, the last of the Cathar *perfecti*, is reported as describing the arrest of Christ in the following way: "And on these words the pharisees and their servants with them, sons of the devil, came, and they took him, and all the injuries and opprobrium which they could bring to him, the pharisees and ministers brought to the Son of God, to such an extent that a certain leper spat at him in the face . . ." Contemporary medical opinion did nothing to dispel this popular image. Henri de Mondeville apparently believed that the physical deterioration was accompanied by a disintegration of the leper's character, presumably because of a growing imbalance in the bodily humours. When the blood of a leper is washed through

a cloth, he said, black stains will remain, which are the evil elements. Perhaps this is what the chronicler Jean de Saint-Victor meant when he presents the Jews as saying that the lepers would consent to the plot, "having been easily debased (*dejecti*) by them (that is, the Jews)." Until this time, however, the lepers were less likely objects of antagonism than the Jews, because they were at least co-religionists and were seen as worthwhile objects of charity during the fashion for the endowment of hospitals in the twelfth and thirteenth centuries. Indeed, while both Biblical precepts and popular fears continued to influence the treatment of lepers throughout the High Middle Ages, the harsher effects of these attitudes had been mitigated by the greatly increased provision of leper hospitals. Ironically, in the long term, this contributed to the lepers' vulnerability, for it helped to make them an identifiable minority, collected in a distinct place, just like the Jews.

The second question that arises concerns the nature of the allegations. The essence of the allegations centres upon the magical use of poison that would either kill or make leprous. The ingredients of the poison have no apparent relationship to the alleged effects in the sense that they are not herbal or chemical poisons. The preference for a magical form of poison is further evidence of the panic which gripped society for, despite limited scientific knowledge, it is clear that more specific methods of poisoning, without the use of magic, were known even at a popular level. To take another contemporary example from the depositions of the Cathars: when the group of exiles in Catalonia centred upon Guillaume Bélibaste wished to poison a suspected traitress, an attempt was first made with "a herb called *vulaire*" placed in her food, and when this failed they tried to purchase *realgar* or red arsenic from the local apothecary for the same purpose, making the excuse that they wanted it to cure ailments among their animals. The necessity for making an excuse does itself suggest that the poisonous properties of the substance were well-known. The lepers' plot therefore was essentially based on magic in the sense that it is defined by Professor Thorndike: "Magic appears . . . as a way of looking at the world which is reflected in a human art or group of arts employing varied materials in varied rites, often fantastic, to work a great variety of marvelous results, which offer man a release from his physical, social and intellectual limitations. . . . The *sine qua non* seems to be a human operator, materials, rites, and an aim that borders on the impossible, either in itself or in relation to the apparently inadequate means employed."

The poison itself was a mixture, although the proportions of the elements included are not given and were indeed regarded as unknowable. According to the reported letter of the lord of Parthenay it included human blood and urine, three unnamed herbs and a consecrated host; in the continuator of Nangis it is made up of a head of a snake, the feet of a toad, and the hairs of a woman, all of which was mixed with a black and fetid liquid; and Guillaume Agasse claimed that it contained the powdered remains of a consecrated host mixed with a concoction made from snakes, toads, lizards, and bats together with human excrement. However, despite the irrelevance of the constituents to leprosy, they did at least have harmful associations. The reptiles named were those thought to be born in corruption or earth, like worms, rather than from seed, and they were believed in themselves to be poisonous. The popular view of these creatures was expressed by Guillaume Bélibaste, even though the Cathar outlook on the created world differed radically from that of the orthodox. He explained that Cathar *perfecti* could not kill anything that had blood, whether it walked on the ground or flew in the air, ex-

cept for a group which he called "impure," which included mice, snakes, toads, frogs and lizards. Human waste, which might be seen by some as the poisonous part of the elements being expelled from the body, was the corruption in which the "impure" beings flourished and was therefore associated with them, while the desecrated host linked the whole mixture with anti-Christian and heretical groups such as the Jews, who had been frequently accused of desecrating the host during the thirteenth century.

Finally, in the most detailed account of how the plot was supposedly organized—that of Guillaume Agasse—the "heretical" element emerges most markedly, which is not surprising in view of the inquisitorial nature of the hearing. In Agasse's deposition there are secret chapters, an oath sworn to preserve secrecy, the denial of Christ, spitting and trampling on the cross, and a sinister armed man or devil figure. Agasse's confession suggests not only that both he and his inquisitors had been directly influenced by the accusations made against the Templars in their recent trial, but also that their ideas could still pass muster as a means of establishing who were the enemies of society.

The attacks upon the lepers and the Jews were symptoms of pressures with which society could not cope. The previous year they had taken the form of a pseudo-crusade; in 1321 they expressed themselves as a belief in a phantom plot to overturn society. The need to protect society from enemies both external and internal had been a fundamental tenet of the twelfth and thirteenth centuries. But, despite massive efforts, it seemed that the threats remained, for the Mameluks had pushed the Christians into the sea in 1291, and the inquisitors continued to insist upon eternal vigilance against the enemy within. Even the idea that Moslem agents were sometimes sent to poison the Christian population had already had some currency, for Matthew Paris alleged that there had been found in the baggage of one of the leaders of the Pastoureaux movement of 1251 a large sum of money, some documents in Arabic and Chaldean and various poisonous powders. The documents were found to be letters from the Sultan, exhorting the leader to act in return for a promise of a great reward. Apparently, it was intended that innumerable Christians would be handed over to the Sultan. In 1321 this idea caught the imagination of a large section of the French population, although then the agents took the form of the lepers and the Jews. It can be seen as a prelude to the much more widespread pogroms that accompanied the Black Death, and perhaps helps to explain the nature of the society that was struck by the plague and therefore society's view of the causes of that disaster.

■■■

STUDY QUESTIONS

1. To what extent was there a genuine threat to Christendom in 1321?

2. Was the fear of a conspiracy confined to uneducated people, or did it affect Christians from all backgrounds?

3. When suspected conspirators were arrested, how were they treated? How were confessions extracted? Were their confessions valid?

4. Why were Jews, Moslems, and lepers the targets of the crusade?

5. What social and economic problems in the fourteenth century might have given rise to the panic and the attack on the lepers, Jews, and Moslems?

6. What did most people think the so-called poison was composed of? Why did people think that it had "magical" qualities?

BIBLIOGRAPHY

For popular attitudes toward Jews in medieval Europe, see R. B. Dobson, *The Jews of Medieval York and the Massacre of March 1190* (1974); Angus MacKay, "Popular Movements and Pogroms in Fifteenth Century Castile," *Past and Present*, 55 (1972); and Steven Haliczer, ed., *Inquisition and Society in Early Modern Europe* (1987). Also see John Parkes, *The Jew in the Medieval Community* (1938). Treatment of lepers in medieval Europe is described in Paul Richards, *The Medieval Leper and His Northern Heirs* (1977), and R. M. Clay, *The Medieval Hospitals of England* (1909). Also see S. C. Mesmin, ''The Leper Hospital of Saint Gilles de Pont-Audemer,'' unpublished Ph.D. dissertation, University of Reading (1978). N. J. Smelser's *Theory of Collective Behavior* (1962) and A. M. Meerloo's *Total War and the Mind* (1944) both deal with the relationship between social tensions and mass panic.

PART FOUR

LIFE IN THE MIDDLE AGES

A notion of order underlies any civilization. Since the earliest civilizations, humans have sought security, order, and an explanation for their world, often on the basis of religious authority. Without these elements, chaos and uncertainty hinder coordinated action, leading to the collapse of community values, rampant individualism, and a truly dark age. During the Middle Ages people organized themselves and their world economically, socially, politically, and religiously by means of the institutions of manorialism and feudalism. Seeking security in the comforting idea of a trinity, they divided society into three classes: the clergy, the nobility, and the artisans/farmers. People then explained how these classes fit into their religious scheme.

Each of the orders performed an important function. The clergy guided all people toward salvation. Each member, from the parish priest to the pope in Rome, instructed the living in God's ways and prayed for the dead. Because the clergy's efforts spread the Word and kept God alive in the hearts of the faithful, they formed the first order. Without the clergy, social order, humanity, and salvation were threatened. Without the clergy and the maintenance of the proper beliefs and behaviors, eternal damnation was as certain as the seasons.

The nobility filled the second order. They fought. They protected. They battled to keep the threats to society at bay. Vikings threatened Western Europe from the North, Moslems from the East. Bandits preyed upon travelers; rogue knights disturbed the peace of entire communities. Neighboring lands—Christian lands—threatened other Christian lands. To fulfill their appointed role, nobles needed enough leisure and luxury to maintain their prowess with arms. Instead of tilling the fields or spinning wool, they required time for jousting, sword practice, and hunting.

Farmers and artisans composed the third order. They fed the people of all three classes. These working people produced and sold the clothes people wore; they worked with metals and herbs and stones. They built and produced. Meager crop yields and harsh conditions plagued their lives.

Laws dictated distinctions among the orders, even as they worked for their mutual benefit. An urban artisan or trader, for example—no matter how rich— might be legally prohibited from wearing ermine or owning a carriage. Peasants might be forced to dress only in black or brown. The idea was that nobles should dress like nobles, clerics like clerics, and peasants like peasants. As one historian commented about medieval European society, "Florence allowed doctors and magistrates to share the nobles' privilege of ermine but ruled out for merchants' wives multicolored, striped or checked gowns, brocades, figured velvets, and fabrics embroidered in silver and gold. In France territorial lords and their ladies with incomes of 6000 livres or more could order four costumes a year; knights and bannerets with incomes of 3000 could have three a year . . . . Boys could have only one a year, and no *demoiselle* who was not the *chatelaine* of a castle or did not have an income of 2000 livres could order more than one costume a year.'' Some people could wear pointed shoes and hanging sleeves, and others could not. Prostitutes were expected to wear striped clothes or garments turned inside out. Efforts were also made to regulate food, music, and trousseaus. What one wore or ate or drank reflected God's natural order and the harmony of the universe and was thus a matter of some moment.

As can be seen, life was not equitable under the system of the three orders, and frequently the clergy and the nobility acted with even less justice than the system proscribed. Too often peasants were overtaxed and overworked. Their harvests were destroyed or stolen during times of war, and their homes and families were violated by the nobles who were supposed to protect them. Given these hard and unremitting circumstances, it is not surprising that some people rebelled against the system and the authorities who maintained it. Sometimes the acts of rebellion could be as simple as poaching game from the noble's forest to augment a wedding feast or to improve a child's diet. Far less frequently, despair fostered a rebellion that sought the restoration of a just social order, not the overturning of the three orders. Most serious of all was the spiritual rebellion of heresy, which rejected not only the social order of the temporal world but also the spiritual order of the universe. Such challenges were apocalyptic by their very nature, and authorities suppressed them with deadly finality. Despite the periodic injustices and discontent, the system of the three orders worked until economic and social change rendered it obsolete during the early modern period. And vestiges of it survived until the end of the eighteenth century in Western Europe, when the French Revolution swept them away.

It would be wrong, however, to view the system as static. Within the three orders were numerous gradations and subtle differences. A highly placed clergyman commanded more wealth, prestige, and power than most nobles. A lowly parish priest had more in common with the peasants. In addition, there were marked differences in the third order, especially between urban artisans and rural peasants or serfs.

Just as the three orders were not static, life in the Middle Ages was not motionless. The attempt to proscribe a costume for each order, for example, demonstrated that the orders were more fixed in theory than in practice. If one looks at life in the Middle Ages over a long period of time, changes become amply evident. The essays in this part examine the Middle Ages in theory and practice. Marc Bloch focuses on the nobility—its rights, obligations, and purpose. Witold Rybczynski's essay shows change by examining the evolving concept and function of the home. In the following reading, Norbert Elias emphasizes how manners have changed over the centuries.

13. THE LIFE OF THE NOBILITY

Marc Bloch

People in medieval Europe believed that God had ordained three estates—the clergy, the nobility, and the commoners. The clergy prayed for the salvation of all people; the commoners tilled the soil and fed the population; the nobility protected the clergy and the commoners. In theory, nobles protected society and maintained justice and order. Nobles were not supposed to fight for the sheer love of combat. In actuality, nobles trained to fight, reared on tales of noble struggle and valorous deeds. Noblemen were indoctrinated to love battle above all else, and they often fought simply because they found or manufactured an opportunity. As the troubadour writes at the start of Marc Bloch's essay, "I tell you, I find no such savour in food, or in wine, or in sleep, as in hearing the shout 'On! On!'" Or as Garin li Loherains, the hero of a *chanson de geste* (a "song of great deeds"), exclaimed, "If I had one foot already in Paradise, I would withdraw it to go and fight."

In return for protecting society, the nobleman exacted a high price. He was exempted from direct taxation. Because nobles exposed their "bodies and property in war," they felt that they were beyond taxation. Noblemen were also given land and authority over commoners. They could dispense justice with an iron fist or an open hand. Although their power was circumscribed by theory, in practice it often knew no check.

In this essay Marc Bloch discusses the activities of the nobility in battle and in times of peace. He examines the attitudes of the nobility and the rules that governed noblemen's lives. One of the leading figures of modern French history, Bloch was far more than an armchair academic who spent all his time in the classroom and the library. He knew war first hand. As a young man he had fought bravely in World War I. At the age of fifty-three, and a father of six minor children, he fought again in World War II. After Germany defeated France, Bloch joined the Resistance, an underground network that continued to oppose Germany. In 1944 the Gestapo captured, tortured, and executed Bloch. Thus, for Bloch, the "right of resistance" granted to the medieval warrior when his superior acted contrary to the law was more than an abstract principle; it was an article of faith. It governed Bloch's own life and is part of his most famous book, *Feudal Society.*

1 War

I love the gay Eastertide, which brings forth leaves and flowers; and I love the joyous songs of the birds, re-echoing through the copse. But also I love to see, amidst the meadows, tents and pavilions spread; and it gives me great joy to see, drawn up on the field, knights and horses in battle array; and it delights me when the scouts scatter people and herds in their path; and I love to see them followed by a great body of men-at-arms; and my heart is filled with gladness when I see strong castles besieged, and the stockades broken and overwhelmed, and the warriors on the bank, girt about by fosses, with a line of strong stakes, interlaced. . . . Maces, swords, helms of different hues, shields that will be riven and shattered as soon as the fight begins; and many vassals struck down together; and the horses of the dead and the wounded roving at random. And when battle is joined, let all men of good lineage think of naught but the breaking of heads and arms; for it is better to die than to be vanquished and live. I tell you, I find no such savour in food, or in wine, or in sleep, as in hearing the shout 'On! On!' from both sides, and the neighing of steeds that have lost their riders, and the cries of 'Help! Help!'; in seeing men great and small go down on the grass beyond the fosses; in seeing at last the dead, with the pennoned stumps of lances still in their sides."

Thus sang, in the second half of the twelfth century, a troubadour who is probably to be identified with the petty nobleman from Périgord, Bertrand de Born. The accurate observation and the fine verve, in contrast with the insipidity of what is usually a more conventional type of poetry, are the marks of an uncommon talent. The sentiment, on the other hand, is in no way extraordinary; as is shown in many another piece from the same social world, in which it is expressed, no doubt with less gusto, but with equal spontaneity. In war—"fresh and joyful war," as it has been called in our own day by someone who was not destined to see it at such close quarters—the noble loved first and foremost the display of physical strength, the strength of a splendid animal, deliberately maintained by constant exercises, begun in childhood. "He who has stayed at school till the age of twelve," says a German poet, repeating the old Carolingian proverb, "and never ridden a horse, is only fit to be a priest." The interminable accounts of single combats which fill the epics are eloquent psychological documents. The reader of today, bored by their monotony, finds it difficult to believe that they could have afforded so much pleasure—as clearly they did—to those who listened to them in days of old: theirs was the attitude of the sedentary enthusiast to reports of sporting events. In works of imagination as well as in the chronicles, the portrait of the good knight emphasizes above all his athletic build: he is "big-boned," "large of limb," the body "well-proportioned" and pitted with honourable scars; the shoulders are broad, and so is the "fork"—as becomes a horseman. And because this strength must be sustained, the valiant knight is known for his mighty appetite. In the old *Chanson de Guillaume*, so barbarous in its tone, listen to Dame Guibourc who, after having served at the great table of the castle the young Girart, her husband's nephew, remarks to her spouse:

Par Deu, bel sire, cist est de de vostre lin,
Et si mangue un grant braun porcin,
Et a dous traitz beit un cester de vin.
Ben dure guere deit il rendre a sun veisin.

By God! fair sire! he's of your line indeed,
Who thus devours a mighty haunch of boar
And drinks of wine a gallon at two gulps;
Pity the man on whom he wages war!

"The Life of the Nobility" from *Feudal Society: Social Classes and Political Organization* by Marc Bloch. Reprinted by permission of The University of Chicago.

A supple and muscular body, however, it is almost superfluous to say, was not enough to make the ideal knight. To these qualities he must add courage as well. And it was also because it gave scope for the exercise of this virtue that war created such joy in the hearts of men for whom daring and the contempt for death were, in a sense, professional assets. It is true that this valour did not always prevent mad panics (we have seen examples of them in face of the Vikings), nor was it above resorting to crude stratagems. Nevertheless the knightly class knew how to fight—on this point, history agrees with legend. Its unquestionable heroism was nurtured by many elements: the simple physical reaction of a healthy human being; the rage of despair—it is when he feels himself "wounded unto death" that the "cautious" Oliver strikes such terrible blows, in order "to avenge himself all he could"; the devotion to a chief or, in the case of the holy war, to a cause; the passionate desire for glory, personal or collective; the fatalistic acquiescence in face of ineluctable destiny, of which literature offers no more poignant examples than some of the last cantos of the *Nibelungenlied*; finally, the hope of reward in another world, promised not only to him who died for his God, but also to him who died for his master.

Accustomed to danger, the knight found in war yet another attraction: it offered a remedy for boredom. For these men whose culture long remained rudimentary and who—apart from a few great barons and their counsellors—were seldom occupied by very heavy administrative cares, everyday life easily slipped into a grey monotony. Thus was born an appetite for diversions that, when one's native soil failed to afford the means to gratify it, sought satisfaction in distant lands. William the Conqueror, bent on exacting due service from his vassals, said of one of them, whose fiefs he had just confiscated as a punishment for his having dared to depart for the crusade in Spain without permission: "I do not

believe it would be possible to find a better knight in arms; but he is unstable and extravagant, and he spends his time gadding about from place to place." Of how many others could the same have been said! The roving disposition was especially widespread among the French. The fact was that their own country did not offer them, as did half-Moslem Spain, or, to a less degree, Germany with its Slav frontier, an arena for conquests or swift forays; nor, like Germany again, the hardships and the pleasures of the great imperial expeditions. It is also probable that the knightly class was more numerous there than elsewhere, and therefore cramped for room. In France itself it has often been observed that Normandy was of all the provinces the richest in bold adventurers. Already the German Otto of Freising spoke of the "very restless race of the Normans." Could it have been the legacy of Viking blood? Possibly. But it was above all the effect of the state of relative peace which, in that remarkably centralized principality, the dukes established at an early date; so that those who craved the opportunity for fighting had to seek it abroad. Flanders, where political conditions were not very different, furnished an almost equally large contingent of roving warriors.

These knights-errant—the term is a contemporary one—helped the native Christians in Spain to reconquer the northern part of the peninsula from Islam; they set up the Norman states in southern Italy; even before the First Crusade they enlisted as mercenaries in the service of Byzantium and fought against its eastern foes; finally, they found in the conquest and defence of the Tomb of Christ their chosen field of action. Whether in Spain or in Syria, the holy war offered the dual attraction of an adventure and a work of piety. "No need is there now to endure the monk's hard life in the strictest of the orders . . ." sang one of the troubadours; "to accomplish honourable deeds and thereby at the same time to save oneself from hell—what more could one wish?'' These migrations helped to maintain relations between societies separated from each other by great distances and sharp contrasts; they disseminated Western and especially French culture beyond its own frontiers. A case to strike the imagination is that of one Hervé "the Francopol" who was taken prisoner by an emir in 1057 when in command on the shores of Lake Van. At the same time the bloodletting thus practised abroad by the most turbulent groups in the West saved its civilization from being extinguished by guerilla warfare. The chroniclers were well aware that at the start of a crusade the people at home in the old countries always breathed more freely, because now they could once more enjoy a little peace.

Fighting, which was sometimes a legal obligation and frequently a pleasure, might also be required of the knight as a matter of honour: In the twelfth century, Périgord ran with blood because a certain lord thought that one of his noble neighbours looked like a blacksmith and had the bad taste to say so. But fighting was also, and perhaps above all, a source of profit—in fact, the nobleman's chief industry. . . .

The baron, of course, out of regard for his prestige as well as his interest, could not afford to be niggardly in the matter of presents, even toward vassals summoned to his side by the strictest conventions of feudal duty. If it was desired to retain them beyond the stipulated time, to take them farther or call on them more often than an increasingly rigorous custom appeared to permit, it was necessary to give them more. Finally, in face of the growing inadequacy of the vassal contingents, there was soon no army that could dispense with the assistance of that wandering body of warriors to whom adventure made so strong an appeal, provided that there was a prospect of gain as well as of mighty combats. Thus cynically, our Bertrand offered his services to the count of Poitiers: "I can help you. I have already a shield at my neck and a helm on my

head . . . . Nevertheless, how can I put myself in the field without money?''

But it was undoubtedly considered that the finest gift the chief could bestow was the right to a share of the plunder. This was also the principal profit that the knight who fought on his own account in little local wars expected from his efforts. It was a double prize, moreover: men and things. It is true that the Christian code no longer allowed captives to be reduced to slavery and at most permitted a few peasants or artisans to be forcibly removed from one place to another. But the ransoming of prisoners was a general practice. A ruler as firm and prudent as William the Conqueror might indeed never release alive the enemies who fell into his hands; but most warriors were not so far-sighted. The ransoming of prisoners occasionally had more dreadful consequences than the ancient practice of enslavement. The author of the *chanson* of Girart de Roussillon, who certainly wrote from personal observation, tells us that in the evening after a battle Girart and his followers put to the sword all the humble prisoners and wounded, sparing only the "owners of castles," who alone were in a position to buy their freedom with hard cash. As to plunder, it was traditionally so regular a source of profit that in the ages accustomed to written documents the legal texts treat it as a matter of course—on this point, the barbarian codes, at the beginning of the Middle Ages, and the thirteenth-century contracts of enlistment at the end, speak with the same voice. Heavy wagons followed the armies, for the purpose of collecting the spoils of war. Most serious of all, by a series of transitions almost unnoticed by the rather simple minds of the time, forms of violent action that were sometimes legitimate—requisitions indispensable to armies without commissariat, reprisals exacted against the enemy or his subjects—degenerated into pure brigandage, brutal and mean. Merchants were robbed on the highway; sheep, cheeses, chickens were stolen from pens and farmsteads—as was done, typically, by a small Catalan landowner of the early thirteenth century bent on annoying his neighbours of the abbey of Canigou. The best of men contracted strange habits. William Marshal was certainly a valiant knight. Nevertheless when, as a young and landless man traveling through France from tourney to tourney, he encountered on the road a monk who was running away with a girl of noble family and who candidly avowed his intention of putting out to usury the money he was carrying, William did not scruple to rob the poor devil of his cash, under the pretext of punishing him for his evil designs. One of his companions even reproached him for not having seized the horse as well.

Such practices reveal a signal indifference to human life and suffering. War in the feudal age was in no sense war in kid gloves. It was accompanied by actions that seem to us today anything but chivalrous; as for instance—a frequent occurrence, sometimes even in disregard of a solemn oath—the massacre or mutilation of garrisons that had held out "too long." It involved, as a natural concomitant, the devastation of the enemy's estates. Here and there a poet, like the author of *Huon of Bordeaux* and later a pious king like St. Louis, protested in vain against this "wasting" of the countryside that brought such appalling miseries on the innocent. The epics, the German as well as the French, are faithful interpreters of real life, and they show us a whole succession of "smoking" villages. "There can be no real war without fire and blood," said the plain-spoken Bertrand de Born.

In two passages exhibiting striking parallels, the poet of *Girart de Roussillon* and the anonymous biographer of the Emperor Henry IV show us what the return of peace meant for the "poor knights": the disdainful indifference of the great, who would have no more need of them; the importunities of money-lenders; the heavy plough-horse instead of the mettlesome charger; iron spurs instead of gold—in short, an economic crisis as well as a disastrous

loss of prestige. For the merchant and the peasant, on the contrary, peace meant that it was possible once again to work, to gain a livelihood—in short, to live. Let us appeal once more to the evidence of the observant *trouvère* of *Girart de Roussillon*. Outlawed and repentant, Girart with his wife wanders through the countryside. They meet some merchants, and the duchess thinks it prudent to make them believe that the exile whose features they think they recognize is no more. "Girart is dead; I saw him buried." "God be praised," the merchants reply, "for he was always making war and through him we have suffered many ills." At these words, Girart's brow darkened; if he had had his sword "he would have smitten one of them." It is a story based on actual experience and illustrates the fundamental hostility that separated the classes. It cuts both ways. For the knight, proud of his courage and skill, despised the unwarlike *(imbellis)* people—the villeins who in face of the armies scampered away "like deer," and later on the townsmen, whose economic power seemed to him so much the more hateful in that it was obtained by means that were at once mysterious and directly opposed to his own activities. If the propensity to bloody deeds was prevalent everywhere—more than one abbot indeed met his death as the victim of a cloister feud—it was the conception of the necessity of war, as a source of honour and as a means of livelihood, that set apart the little group of "noble" folk from the rest of society.

2 The Noble at Home

Favourite sport though it was, war had its dead seasons; but at these times the knightly class was distinguished from its neighbours by a manner of life that was essentially that of a nobility.

We should not think of this mode of existence as having invariably a rural setting. Italy, Provence, and Languedoc still bore the age-old imprint of the Mediterranean civilizations whose structure had been systematized by Rome. In those regions, each small community was traditionally grouped round a town or large village that was at one and the same time an administrative centre, a market, and a place of refuge; and consequently the normal place of residence of the powerful. These people continued as much as ever to inhabit the old urban centres; and they took part in all their revolutions. In the thirteenth century, this civic character was regarded as one of the distinctive traits of the southern nobility. In contrast with Italy, said the Franciscan Salimbene, a native of Parma, who visited the kingdom of St. Louis, the towns of France are inhabited only by burgesses; the nobility live on their estates. But, though true in general of the period in which the good friar was writing, the contrast would not have been equally true of the first feudal age. Undoubtedly in the purely merchant cities that, especially in the Low Countries and trans-Rhenish Germany, came into being almost entirely from the tenth or the eleventh century onwards—Ghent, Bruges, Soest, Lübeck and so many others—the dominant caste was almost invariably composed of men grown rich through trade; though where there was a governor of princely rank a small body of vassals was sometimes maintained, consisting of unenfeoffed knights or those who came regularly to perform their turn of duty. In the old Roman cities such as Rheims or Tournai, on the other hand, groups of knights seem to have resided over a long period, many of them no doubt attached to the courts of bishops or abbots. It was only gradually and in consequence of a more pronounced differentiation of classes that knightly society, outside Italy and southern France, became almost entirely divorced from the urban populations properly so called. Although the noble certainly did not cease altogether to visit the town, he henceforth went there only occasionally, in pursuit of pleasure or for the exercise of certain functions.

Everything tended to induce him to live in the country. First, there was the habit, which was becoming more and more widespread, of remunerating vassals by means of fiefs, consisting in the vast majority of cases of rural manors; then there was the weakening of feudal obligations, which favoured the tendency among the retainers who had now been provided with fiefs to live each in his own home, far from the kings, the great barons, and the bishops, who controlled the towns; finally, a taste for the open air, natural to these sportsmen, played its part. There is a moving story, told by a German monk, of a count's son who had been dedicated by his family to the monastic life; on the day when he was first subjected to the harsh rule of claustration, he climbed up to the highest tower of the monastery, in order "at least to feast his vagrant soul on the spectacle of the hills and fields where he might no longer roam." The pressure of the burghers, who had very little desire to admit into their communities elements indifferent to their activities and their interests, accelerated the movement.

Thus whatever modifications it may be necessary to introduce into the picture of a nobility exclusively rural from the outset, it remains true that, ever since knights existed, a growing majority of them in the North and many even in the coastal regions of the Mediterranean ordinarily resided in a country mansion.

The manor-house usually stood in the midst of a cluster of dwellings, or nearby; sometimes there were several in the same village. The manor-house was sharply distinguished from the surrounding cottages, just as it was in the towns from the habitations of the poor—not only because it was better built, but above all because it was almost invariably designed for defence. The desire of the rich to protect their dwellings from attack was naturally as old as the social disorders themselves; witness those fortified *villae* whose appearance about the fourth century bears witness to the decline of the Roman peace. The tradition may have continued here and there in the Frankish period, but most of the "courts" inhabited by rich

■ ■ *Tournaments allowed medieval knights to showcase their martial skills.*

proprietors and even royal palaces themselves long remained almost without permanent means of defence. It was the invasions of the Northmen or the Hungarians which, from the Adriatic to the plains of northern England, led not only to the repair or rebuilding of town ramparts, but also to the erection on every hand of the rural strongholds *(fertés)* that were destined to cast a perpetual shadow over the fields of Europe. Internal wars soon added to their number. The rôle of the great potentates, kings or princes, in this prolific building of castles, and their efforts to control it, will be dealt with later; for the present they need not detain us. For the fortified houses of the petty lords, scattered over hill and dale, had almost always been constructed without any authorization from above. They answered elementary needs, spontaneously felt and satisfied. A hagiographer has given a very exact account of them, although in an unsympathetic spirit: "Their purpose was to enable these men, constantly occupied with quarrels and massacres, to protect themselves from their enemies, to triumph over their equals, to oppress their inferiors"; in short, to defend themselves and dominate others.

Their edifices were generally of a very simple type. For a long time the most common, at least outside the Mediterranean regions, was the wooden tower. A curious passage of the *Miracles of St. Benedict* describes, toward the end of the eleventh century, the extremely primitive arrangement of one of these castles. On the first floor there was a large room where the "powerful man . . . together with his household, lived, conversed, ate, slept"; on the ground floor there was a storeroom for provisions. Normally, a ditch was dug at the foot. Sometimes, at a little distance from the tower, there was a stockade or a rampart of beaten earth, surrounded in its turn by another ditch. This enclosure provided a place of safety for various domestic buildings and for the cookhouse, which it was considered wise to place away from the tower on account of the risk of fire; it served at need as a refuge for the dependants; it prevented an immediate assault on the main building and obstructed the most effective method of attack, which was to set fire to it. Tower and stockade frequently stood on a mound *(motte)*, sometimes natural, sometimes—at least in part—man-made. Its purpose was twofold: to confront the attackers with the obstacle of the slope and to gain a better view of the surrounding country. But to garrison even one of these primitive wooden castles required more armed retainers than the ordinary run of knights could maintain. It was the great men who first had recourse to stone as a building-material; those "rich men that build in stone," whom Bertrand de Born depicts amusing themselves by making "from lime, sand and freestone . . . gateways and turrets, vaults and spiral staircases." It was adopted only slowly, in the course of the twelfth century or even the thirteenth, for the houses of knights of lesser and middle rank. Before the completion of the great clearings, the forests seem to have been easier and less expensive to exploit than the quarries; and while masonry called for specialist workers, the tenants, a permanent source of compulsory labour, were almost all to some extent carpenters as well as wood-cutters. . . .

As is indicated by the very nature of his dwelling, the knight lived in a state of perpetual watchfulness. A lookout man, a familiar figure in the epic as well as in lyric poetry, kept his nightly watch on the summit of the tower. Lower down, in the two or three rooms of the cramped fortress, a whole little world of permanent residents, with an admixture of transient guests, lived together in conditions that admitted of no privacy. Partly, no doubt, this was due to lack of space, but it was also the result of habits that in that age seemed inseparable from the position of a chief. Day and night, the baron was surrounded by retainers—men-at-arms, menials, household vassals, young nobles committed to his care as "nurslings"—who served him, guarded him, conversed with him and who, when the hour of sleep at last arrived, continued to keep faithful watch over him even when he was in bed with his wife. "It is not seemly that a lord should eat alone" was an opinion still held in thirteenth-century England. In the great hall the tables were long and most of the seats were benches on which the diners sat side by side. Poor persons took up their lodging under the staircase—where two illustrious penitents died: St. Alexis, in legend, and Count Simon de Crépy, in fact. This way of living, incompatible with any sort of private meditation, was general at this time; the monks themselves slept in dormitories, not in cells. It explains why some people chose to take refuge in the only ways of life that at that time were compatible with the enjoyment of solitude—those of the hermit, the recluse, and the wanderer. On the cultural side, it meant that among the nobles knowledge was transmitted much less by books and study than by reading aloud, the reciting of verse, and personal contacts.

3 Occupations and Distractions

Though usually a countryman in the sense that his home was in the country, the noble was nevertheless no agriculturalist. To put his hand to the hoe or the plough would have been an indication that he had come down in the world—as happened to a poor knight whose history is known to us through a collection of anecdotes. And if he sometimes liked to contemplate the workers in the fields or the yellowing harvest on his estates, it does not appear that as a rule he took a very direct part in the management of the farm. The manuals of estate management, when they came to be written, were intended not for the master, but for his stewards; the "country gentleman" belongs to quite another age—after the economic revolution in the sixteenth century. Although the rights of jurisdiction that he possessed over his tenants constituted one of the essential sources of his power, the lord of the village as a rule exercised them much less frequently in person than through the agency of bailiffs, themselves of peasant extraction. Nevertheless the exercise of judicial functions was certainly one of the few peaceful occupations of the knight. As a rule he only concerned himself with judicial duties within the framework of his class, which meant that he either settled the law-suits of his own vassals or sat as judge of his peers in the court to which he had been summoned by his feudal lord; but where pub-

lic justice survived, as in England and Germany, he took his place in the court of the county or the hundred. There was enough of this activity to make the legal spirit one of the earliest cultural influences to be diffused in knightly circles.

The favourite amusements of the nobility bore the imprint of a warlike temper.

First, there was hunting. As has already been said, it was more than a sport. The people of western Europe were not yet living in surroundings from which the menace of wild beasts had been finally removed. Moreover, at a time when the flesh of cattle, inadequately fed and of poor stock, furnished only indifferent meat, much venison was eaten, especially in the homes of the rich. Because hunting thus remained an almost necessary activity, it was not altogether a class monopoly. The case of Bigorre, where it was forbidden to peasants as early as the beginning of the twelfth century, appears to be an exception. Nevertheless kings, princes, and lords, each within the limits of his own authority, everywhere tended to monopolize the pursuit of game in certain reserved areas: large animals in the "forests" (which term, originally, denoted every area thus reserved, whether wooded or not), rabbits and hares in the "warrens." The legal foundation of these claims is obscure; it seems as though they seldom had any save the decree of the master, and very naturally it was in a conquered country—the England of the Norman kings—that the creation of royal forests, too often at the expense of arable land, was most extensive, and their protection most stringent. Such abuses attest the strength of a taste that was very much a class characteristic; and so do the requisitions imposed on the tenants—the obligation to lodge and feed the lord's pack of hounds, and to construct hunting-boxes in the woods, at the season of the great meets. . . .

Then there were the tournaments. In the Middle Ages the tournament was generally thought to be of relatively recent origin, and the name of its supposed inventor was even mentioned—a certain Geoffroy de Preuilly, said to have died in 1066. In reality the practice of these make-believe combats undoubtedly dates back to the remotest times: witness the "pagan games," sometimes fatal, mentioned in 895 by the council of Tribur. The custom was continued, among the people, at certain feasts—Christianized rather than Christian—as for example those other "pagan games" (the recurrence of the word is significant) in 1077, during which the son of a cobbler of Vendôme, who was taking part in them with other young people, was mortally wounded. The contests of young men are an almost universal feature of folklore. In the armies, moreover, the imitation of war at all times provided a training for troops as well as a pastime. During the celebrated interview which the "Oaths of Strasbourg" made famous, Charles the Bald and Lewis the German diverted themselves with a spectacle of this kind, and did not disdain to participate actively. The distinctive contribution of the feudal age was to evolve from these contests, whether military or popular, a type of mock battle at which prizes were generally offered, confined to mounted combatants equipped with knightly arms; and hence to create a distinctive class amusement, which the nobility found more exciting than any other.

Because these meetings, which could not be organized without considerable expense, usually took place on the occasion of the great "courts" held from time to time by kings or barons, enthusiasts roamed the world from tournament to tournament. These were not only poor knights, sometimes grouped in "companies," but also very great lords, such as the count of Hainault, Baldwin IV, or among the English princes, Henry, the "Young King," who however scarcely distinguished himself in the lists. As in our present-day sporting events, the opponents were normally grouped by regions; a great scandal arose one day at a tournament near Gournay when the men of

Hainault took the side of the men of France proper, instead of joining the Flemings and the men of Vermandois, who were, in this sphere at least, their normal allies. There can be no doubt that these games helped to establish provincial solidarities. So much was this the case that it was not always a question of make-believe battle: far from it. Wounds were not uncommon, nor even mortal blows when—to borrow the words of the poet of *Raoul de Cambrai*—the jousting "took an ill turn." This explains why the wisest sovereigns frowned upon these frolics, in which the blood of vassals was drained away. The Plantagenet Henry II formally prohibited them in England. For the same reason—and also on account of their connection with the revels at popular feasts, which savoured of "paganism"—the Church rigorously forbade them, going to the length of refusing burial in consecrated ground to the knight who had met his death in this way, even if he had repented. The fact that, in spite of legislation by lay and ecclesiastical authorities, the practice could not be eradicated shows how deep was the need that it satisfied.

Nevertheless, the passion for tournaments, as for genuine warfare, was not always disinterested. Because the victor frequently took possession of the equipment and horses of the vanquished and sometimes even of his person, releasing him only on payment of a ransom, skill and strength were profitable assets. More than one jousting knight made a profession, and a very lucrative one, out of his skill in combat. Thus the love of arms inextricably combined the ingredients of "joy" and the appetite for gain.

4 Rules of Conduct

It was natural that a class so clearly defined by its mode of life and its social supremacy should eventually devise a code of conduct peculiar to itself. But it was only during the second feudal age, which was in every sense the age of awakening self-consciousness, that these rules assumed a precise form and, along with it, a more refined character.

The term that, from about the year *1100*, commonly served to describe the sum of noble qualities was the characteristic word *courtesy (courtoisie)*, which is derived from *cour* (at that time written and pronounced, as in English today, with a final *t*). It was in fact in the assemblies, temporary or permanent, that were formed round the principal barons and the kings, that these laws of conduct came to be evolved; the isolation of the knight in his "tower" would not have permitted their development. Emulation and social contacts were necessary, and that is why this advance in moral sensibility was bound up both with the consolidation of the great principalities or monarchies and with the restoration of a greater degree of intercommunication. Another term was *prudhomme*, and as *courteous (courtois)* gradually acquired a more commonplace meaning, this word was used more and more frequently to denote something higher: a name so great and so good that merely to pronounce it "fills the mouth," declared St. Louis, intending thereby to vindicate the secular virtues as against those of the monk. Here again the semantic evolution is extremely instructive. For *prudhomme* is in fact the same word as *preux* which, having departed from its first rather vague sense of "useful" or "excellent," was later applied above all to warlike valour. The two terms diverged—*preux* keeping its traditional meaning—when it began to be felt that strength and courage were not enough to make the perfect knight. "There is a great difference between the *homme preux* and the *prudhomme*," Philip Augustus is said to have remarked one day; he regarded the second as much the superior of the two. This might seem like hair-splitting; but if we go to the root of the matter it is a precious piece of evidence on the evolution of the knightly ideal.

Whether it was a question of ordinary usages of decorum or of moral precepts properly so called, of *courtoisie* in the strict sense, or of *prudhommie*, the new code was unquestionably born in the courts of France and in those of the Meuse region, which were completely French in language and manners. As early as the eleventh century French manners were being imitated in Italy. In the next two centuries, these influences became still more pronounced; witness the vocabulary of the German knightly class, full of "alien" words, which had come in as a rule via Hainault, Brabant or Flanders. *Höflich* itself is only an imitation of *courtois*, courteous. More than one young German-speaking noble came to learn the rules, as well as the language, of good taste at the courts of the French princes. Does not the poet Wolfram von Eschenbach call France "the land of well-conducted chivalry"? This dissemination of an aristocratic form of culture was only one feature of the influence exercised at that time throughout Europe—chiefly, it goes without saying, among the upper classes—by French culture as a whole; others were the propagation of artistic and literary ideals; the prestige of the schools of Chartres, and later of Paris; and the virtually international use of the French language. And doubtless it is not impossible to find reasons for this: the long expeditions through the West carried out by the most adventurous chivalry in Europe; the relative prosperity of a country affected much earlier than Germany (though not, indeed, than Italy) by the development of trade; the distinction, emphasized at a very early date, between the knightly class and the unwarlike rabble; the absence, despite so many local wars, of any internal conflicts comparable with those that resulted within the Empire from the great quarrels of emperors and popes. But this having been said, we may well ask ourselves if it is not futile to attempt to explain something that, in the present state of our knowledge of man, seems to be beyond our understanding—the ethos of a civilization and its power of attraction.

"We shall yet talk of this day in ladies' chambers," said the count of Soissons, at the battle of Mansurah. This remark, the equivalent of which it would be impossible to find in the *chansons de geste*, but which might have been heard on the lips of more than one hero of courtly romance as early as the twelfth century, is characteristic of a society in which sophistication has made its appearance and, with it, the influence of women. The noblewoman had never been confined within her own secluded quarters. Surrounded with servants, she ruled her household, and she might also rule the fief—perhaps with a rod of iron. It was nevertheless reserved for the twelfth century to create the type of the cultivated great lady who holds a salon. This marks a profound change, when we consider the extraordinary coarseness of the attitude usually ascribed by the old epic poets to their heroes in their relations with women, even with queens—not stopping at the grossest insults, which the lady requites with blows. One can hear the guffaws of the audience. The courtly public had not lost their taste for this heavy humour; but they now allowed it only—as in the *fabliaux*[1]—at the expense of the peasants or the bourgeoisie. For courtesy was essentially an affair of class. The boudoir of the high-born lady and, more generally, the court, was henceforth the place where the knight sought to outshine and to eclipse his rivals not only by his reputation for great deeds of valour, but also by his regard for good manners and by his literary talents.

As we have seen, the nobility had never been completely illiterate; still less had it been impervious to the influence of literature, though this was listened to rather than read. But a great step forward was taken when knights themselves became literary men. It is significant that the *genre* to which they devoted themselves almost exclusively up to the thirteenth century was lyric poetry. The earliest of the troubadours known to us—it should be added that he was certainly not the first—

ranked among the most powerful princes in France. This was William IX of Aquitaine (d. 1127). In the list of Provençal singers who followed him, as also a little later among their rivals, the lyric poets of the North, all ranks of the knighthood were abundantly represented—leaving aside, of course, the professional minstrels kept by the great. These short pieces, which were generally characterized by an intricate technique—sometimes amounting to deliberate hermeticism, the famous "close" style *(trobar clus)*—were admirably suited for recital in aristocratic gatherings. The fact that the nobility was thus able to savour and to find genuine enjoyment in pleasures too refined to be appreciated by villeins naturally reinforced its sense of superiority. As the poems were usually set off by singing and instrumental accompaniment the charm of music was wedded to the charm of words, and exercised an equally potent influence. . . .

Toward the pleasures of the flesh the attitude of the knightly class appears to have been frankly realistic. It was the attitude of the age as a whole. The Church imposed ascetic standards on its members and required laymen to restrict sexual intercourse to marriage and the purpose of procreation. But it did not practise its own precepts very effectively, and this was especially true of the secular clergy, among whom even the Gregorian reform purified the lives of few but the episcopate. Significantly, we are told with admiration of pious persons, parish priests, nay even abbots, of whom "it is said" that they died virgins. The example of the clergy proves how repugnant continence was to the majority of men: It was certainly not calculated to inspire it in the faithful. As a matter of fact—if we exclude such intentionally comic episodes as Oliver's boasting about his virility in the *Pèlerinage de Charlemagne*—the tone of the epics is fairly chaste. This was because their authors did not attach great importance to describing goings-on which had in fact no epic quality. Even in the less reticent narratives of the age of "courtesy," libertinism is commonly represented as something for which

---

[1] Humorous stories.

the womenfolk rather than the heroes are responsible. Here and there nevertheless a characteristic touch gives a hint of the truth— as in the old poem of *Girart de Roussillon* where we find a vassal, who is required to give hospitality to a messenger, providing him with a beautiful girl for the night. And doubtless those "delightsome" encounters were not wholly fictitious that, according to the romances, the castles so happily facilitated.

The evidence of history is clearer still. The noble's marriage, as we know, was often an ordinary business transaction, and the houses of the nobility swarmed with bastards. At first sight, the advent of "courtesy" does not seem to have effected any great change in these morals. Certain of the songs of William of Aquitaine sing the praises of sensual pleasure in barrackroom style and this attitude was to find more than one imitator among the poets who succeeded him. Nevertheless, with William, who was apparently the heir of a tradition whose origins elude us, another conception of love was already emerging—that "courtly" love, which was certainly one of the most curious products of the moral code of chivalry. Can we conceive of Don Quixote without Dulcinea?

The characteristic features of courtly love can be summarized fairly simply. It had nothing to do with marriage, or rather it was directly opposed to the legal state of marriage, since the beloved was as a rule a married woman and the lover was never her husband. This love was often bestowed upon a lady of higher rank, but in any case it always involved a strong emphasis on the man's adoration of the woman. It professed to be an all-engrossing passion, constantly frustrated, easily jealous, and nourished by its own difficulties; but its stereotyped development early acquired something of a ritual character. It was not averse to casuistry. Finally, as the troubadour Geoffrey Rudel said, in a poem which, wrongly interpreted, gave rise to the famous legend of Princess Far-away, it was, ideally, a "distant" love. It did not indeed reject carnal intercourse

on principle, nor according to Andrew the Chaplain, who discoursed on the subject, did it despise minor physical gratifications if obliged to renounce "the ultimate solace." But absence or obstacles, instead of destroying it, only enriched it with a poetic melancholy. If possession, always to be desired, was seen to be quite out of the question, the sentiment nonetheless endured as an exciting emotion and a poignant joy.

Such is the picture drawn for us by the poets. For courtly love is only known to us through literature and for that reason it is very difficult to determine to what extent it was merely a fashionable fiction. It is certain that, though tending in some measure to dissociate sentiment from sensuality, it by no means prevented the flesh from seeking satisfaction in a more direct way; for we know that with the majority of men emotional sincerity exists on several planes. In any case we may be sure that such an idea of amorous relationships, in which today we recognize many elements with which we have now become familiar, was at first a strikingly original conception. It owed little to the ancient arts of love, or even—although they were perhaps nearer to it—to the always rather equivocal treatises which Graeco-Roman civilization devoted to the analysis of masculine friendship. In particular the humble attitude of the lover was a new thing. We have seen that it was apt to express itself in terms borrowed from the vocabulary of vassal homage; and this was not merely a matter of words. The identification of the loved one and the lord corresponded to an aspect of social morality entirely characteristic of feudal society.

Still less, in spite of what has sometimes been said, was this code dependent on religious ideas. If we leave out of account a few superficial analogies, which are at the most only the result of environment, we must in fact recognize that it was directly opposed to them, although its adherents had no clear consciousness of this antithesis. It made the love of man and woman almost one of the cardinal virtues, and certainly the supreme form of pleasure. Above all, even when it renounced physical satisfaction, it sublimated—to the point of making it the be-all and end-all of existence—an emotional impulse derived essentially from those carnal appetites whose legitimacy Christianity only admits in order to curb them by marriage (profoundly despised by courtly love), in order to justify them by the propagation of the species (to which courtly love gave but little thought), and in order, finally, to confine them to a secondary plane of moral experience. It is not in the knightly lyrics that we can hope to find the authentic echo of the attitude of contemporary Christianity toward sexual relations. This is expressed, quite uncompromisingly, in that passage of the pious and clerical *Queste du Saint-Graal* where Adam and Eve, before they lie together under the Tree to beget "Abel the Just," beg the Lord to bring down upon them a great darkness to "comfort" their shame.

The contrast between the two moralities in their treatment of this subject perhaps provides us with the key to the problem of social geography presented by these new preoccupations with romantic love. Like the lyrical poetry that has preserved them for us, they arose as early as the end of the eleventh century in the courtly circles of southern France. It was only a reflection of them which appeared a little later in the North—still in the lyrical form or through the medium of the romances—and which subsequently passed into the German *Minnesang.*

Now, it would be absurd to attempt to explain this fact by attributing some indefinable superiority to the civilization of Languedoc. Whether relating to the artistic, the intellectual, or the economic sphere, the claim would be equally untenable. It would mean ignoring the French epic, Gothic art, the first efforts of philosophy in the schools between Loire and Meuse, the fairs of Champagne, and the teeming cities of Flanders. It is beyond dispute, on the other hand, that in the South the Church, especially during the first feudal age, was less

rich, less cultivated, less active than in the northern provinces. No great works of clerical literature, no great movements of monastic reform emanated from that region. This relative weakness of the religious centres alone can explain the extraordinary successes achieved, from Provence to the region of Toulouse, by heresies fundamentally international; and it was also no doubt the reason why the higher ranks of the laity, being less subject to clerical influence, were relatively free to develop their own secular morality. Moreover, the fact that these precepts of courtly love were subsequently so easily propagated shows how well they served the new requirements of a class. They helped it to become aware of itself. To love in a different way from the generality of men must inevitably make one feel different from them.

That a knight should carefully calculate his booty or his ransoms and, on returning home, impose a heavy "tallage" on his peasants provoked little or no criticism. Gain was legitimate; but on one condition—that it should be promptly and liberally expended. "I can assure you," said a troubadour when he was reproached for his brigandage, "if I robbed, it was to give, not to hoard." No doubt we are entitled to regard as a little suspect the insistence with which the minstrels, those professional parasites, extolled above all other duties that of generosity, *largesse*, "lady and queen in whose light all virtues shine." No doubt also, among the nobles of middle or lesser rank and still more perhaps among the great barons, there were always miserly or merely prudent individuals, more inclined to amass scarce coin or jewels in their coffers than to distribute them. It is nonetheless true that, in squandering a fortune that was easily gained and easily lost, the noble thought to affirm his superiority over classes less confident in the future or more careful in providing for it. This praiseworthy prodigality might not always stop at generosity or even luxury. A chronicler has preserved for us the record of the remarkable competition in wasteful expenditure witnessed one day at a great "court" held in Limousin. One knight had a plot of ground ploughed up and sown with small pieces of silver; another burned wax candles for his cooking; a third, "through boastfulness," ordered thirty of his horses to be burnt alive. What must a merchant have thought of this struggle for prestige through extravagance—which reminds us of the practices of certain primitive races? Here again different notions of honour marked the line of separation between the social groups.

Thus set apart by its power, by the nature of its wealth and its mode of life, by its very morals, the social class of nobles was toward the middle of the twelfth century quite ready to solidify into a legal and hereditary class. The ever more frequent use which from that time onwards seems to have been made of the word *gentilhomme*—man of good *gent* or lineage—to describe the members of this class is an indication of the growing importance attributed to qualities of birth. With the wide adoption of the ceremony of "dubbing" or formal arming of the knight, the legal class of nobility took definite shape.

■ ■ ■

STUDY QUESTIONS

1. Why did knights love war? How did their wartime activities contrast with their peacetime activities? What were the attractions of a holy war?

2. How did knights profit from war?

3. How did knights regard human suffering? What beliefs separated knights from the rest of society?

4. What common theme lay behind the construction of the knights' manors? What characteristics best describe life within the manors? Where could one go to find privacy?

5. What were the peaceful occupations of the knight? How did he amuse himself? What social and economic interests did tournaments serve?

6. What were the rules of conduct of knightly life? How did these rules affect relations between men and women?

BIBLIOGRAPHY

This selection is from Marc Bloch's *Feudal Society: Social Classes and Political Organization* (translated 1961), the second volume of his classic study on medieval society. The nature of feudalism is examined in F. L. Ganshof, *Feudalism* (translated 1964), and Carl Stephenson, *Medieval Feudalism* (1969). H. S. Bennett, *Life in the English Manor* (1960), discusses how the "other half" lived. Georges Duby, *The Chivalrous Society* (translated 1977), studies chivalry in theory and practice. On the beginning of the French nobility see Constance Bouchard, "The Origins of the French Nobility," *The American Historical Review* (1981). Finally, Emmanuel Le Roy Ladurie, *Montaillou* (translated 1978), is a beautiful re-creation of village life.

14. HOME

Witold Rybczynski

Modern homes are designed for comfort and privacy. We take this fact for granted unless those qualities happen to be missing. To achieve the goals of comfort and privacy, various rooms in a house are set aside for specific purposes: bedroom, dining room, family room, den, study, or living room. Sometimes when the circumstances of a family change but the house remains the same size, there is a need to change the purpose of certain rooms. A den might become a nursery for a newly arrived baby or an adult child's old bedroom might be converted to a sitting room or a study.

The problem, however, is of fairly recent origins. The idea that rooms should serve specific functions was rarely considered before the sixteenth century. It was uncommon for an adult, let alone an infant, to have his or her own room. Normally families and servants slept together in one large room—and that room was not just for sleeping. During the day, it might serve as a dining room, living room, study, or place of business. There were few tables or chairs, and what few there were served more than one function. A scholar would write on the same table at which his family ate. Perhaps more importantly, the home was not really a private place. It was a public place. Guests as well as business acquaintances came and went.

Nor were houses or furniture designed for comfort, but comfort was not expected. Before the eighteenth century, the word *comfortable*—as we know it today—did not exist. The Latin word *confortare* meant to strengthen or to console, and it was within that context that comfort was used for hundreds of years. One could comfort a friend who lost a spouse, or one could be a comfort to an elderly parent. A room could be comfortably—meaning sufficiently or tolerably—heated, or a person could have a comfortable income. But no one called a chair or a bed comfortable. When Sir Walter Scott wrote in the late eighteenth century, ''Let it freeze without, we are comfortable within,'' he was using the word in its newest sense.

Privacy and comfort, two aspects of a good home that we take for granted, were absent in the home of the Middle Ages. In this selection from the book *Home*, Witold Rybczynski discusses the medieval home. His discussion illustrates something of the evolving concept of the ideal home. As society and sensibilities changed, so too did the nature and design of the home.

The Middle Ages are an opaque period of history that is open to many interpretations. As a French scholar has written, "The Renaissance viewed medieval society as scholastic and static, the Reformation saw it as hierarchical and corrupt, and the Age of Enlightenment considered it to have been irrational and superstitious." The nineteenth-century Romantics, who idealized the Middle Ages, described them as the antithesis of the industrial revolution. Writers and artists like Thomas Carlyle and John Ruskin popularized the image of the Middle Ages as an unmechanical, rustic arcadia. This latest revision has greatly influenced our own view of the Middle Ages and has given rise to the idea that medieval society was both untechnological and uninterested in technology.

This notion is altogether mistaken. The Middle Ages not only produced illuminated books, but also eyeglasses, not only the cathedral, but also the coal mine. Revolutionary changes occurred in both primary industry and manufacturing. The first recorded instance of mass production—of horseshoes—occurred during the Middle Ages. Between the tenth and the thirteenth century, a technological boom produced the mechanical clock, the suction pump, the horizontal loom, the waterwheel, the windmill, and even, on both shores of the English Channel, the tidal mill. Agricultural innovations formed the economic foundation for all this technical activity. The deep plow and the idea of crop rotation increased productivity as much as fourfold, so that agricultural yields in the thirteenth century would not be surpassed for another five hundred years. Far from being a technological black hole, the Middle Ages marked the authentic beginning of industrialization in Europe. The period's

influence was felt until at least the eighteenth century in all aspects of everyday life, including attitudes toward the home.

Any discussion about domestic life during this period must include an important caveat: It cannot refer to most of the population, who were poor. Writing about the decline of the Middle Ages, the historian J. H. Huizinga described a world of sharp contrasts, where health, wealth, and good fortune (that old toast) were enjoyed as much for their rarity as for their advantages. "We, at the present day, can hardly understand the keenness with which a fur coat, a good fire on the hearth, a soft bed, a glass of wine, were formerly enjoyed." He also made the point that medieval popular art, which we appreciate for its simple beauty, was prized by its makers even more for its splendor and pomp. Its overdecorated sumptuousness, which we often overlook, is evidence of what was needed to make an impression on a public whose sensibilities were dulled by the wretched conditions under which they lived. The extravagant pageants and religious festivals that characterized that time can be understood not only as a celebration, but also as an antidote to the miseries of everyday life.

The poor were extremely badly housed. They were without water or sanitation, with almost no furniture and few possessions, a situation that, in Europe at least, continued until the beginning of the twentieth century. In the towns, their houses were so small that family life was compromised; these tiny one-room hovels were little more than shelters for sleeping. There was room only for the infants—the older children were separated from their parents and sent to work as apprentices or servants. The result of these deprivations, according to some historians, was that concepts such as "home" and "family" did not exist for these miserable souls. To speak of comfort and discomfort under such circumstances is absurd; this was bare existence.

If the poor did not share in medieval prosperity, there was a different class of persons who did: the town-dwellers. The free town was among the most important, and most original, of all the medieval innovations. Windmills and waterwheels could have been invented by other societies, and were, but the free town, which stood apart from the predominantly feudal countryside, was uniquely European. Its inhabitants—the *francs bourgeois*, the *burghers*, the *borghese*, and the burgesses—would create a new urban civilization. The word *bourgeois* first occurred in France in the early eleventh century. It described the merchants and tradesmen who lived in walled towns, governed themselves through elected councils, and in most cases owed allegiance directly to the king (who established the free town) instead of to a lord. These "cityzens" (the idea of national citizenship came much later) were distinct from the rest of society, which was either feudal, ecclesiastical, or agricultural. This meant that at the same time as the vassals were being dragged off to some local war, the bourgeois in the towns had a considerable measure of independence and were able to benefit from the economic prosperity. What places the bourgeois in the center of any discussion of domestic comfort is that unlike the aristocrat, who lived in a fortified castle, or the cleric, who lived in a monastery, or the serf, who lived in a hovel, the bourgeois lived in a house. Our examination of the home begins here.

The typical bourgeois townhouse of the fourteenth century combined living and work. Building plots had restricted street frontages, because the fortified medieval town was by necessity densely constructed. These long narrow buildings usually consisted of two floors over an undercroft, or basement, which was used for storage. The main floor of the house, or at least that part that faced the street, was a shop or—if the owner was an artisan—a work area. The living quarters were not, as we would expect, a series of rooms; instead, they consisted of a single large chamber—the hall—which was open up to the rafters. People cooked, ate, entertained, and slept in this space. Nevertheless, the interiors of restored medieval houses always look empty. The large rooms have only a few pieces of furniture, a tapestry on the wall, a stool beside the large fireplace. This minimalism is not a modern affectation; medieval homes were sparsely furnished. What furniture there was was uncomplicated. Chests served as both storage and seats. The less affluent sometimes used a chest *(truhe)* as a kind of bed—the clothes inside serving as a soft mattress. Benches, stools and demountable trestle tables were common. The beds were also collapsible, although by the end of the Middle Ages more important personages slept in large permanent beds, which usually stood in a corner. Beds also served as seats, for people sat, sprawled, and squatted wherever they could, on chests, stools, cushions, steps, and often the floor. If contemporary paintings are anything to judge by, medieval posture was a casual affair.

One place where people did not often sit was in chairs. The Pharaonic Egyptians had used chairs, and the ancient Greeks refined them to elegant and comfortable perfection in the fifth century B.C. The Romans introduced them to Europe, but after the collapse of their empire—during the so-called Dark Ages—the chair was forgotten. Its reappearance is difficult to pinpoint, but by the fifteenth century, chairs started to be used again. But what a different chair! The Greek *klismos* had had a low, concave backrest that was shaped to the human body, and splayed legs that allowed the sitter to lean back. The comfortable posture of a lounging Greek, with his arm bent casually over the low chair back and his legs crossed, is recognizably modern. No such position was possible in a medieval chair, which had a hard, flat seat and a tall, straight back whose function was more decorative than ergonomic. During the Middle Ages, chairs—even the boxlike armchairs—were not intended to be comfortable; they were symbols of authority. You had to be important to sit down in a chair—unimportant people sat on benches. As one historian put it, if you were

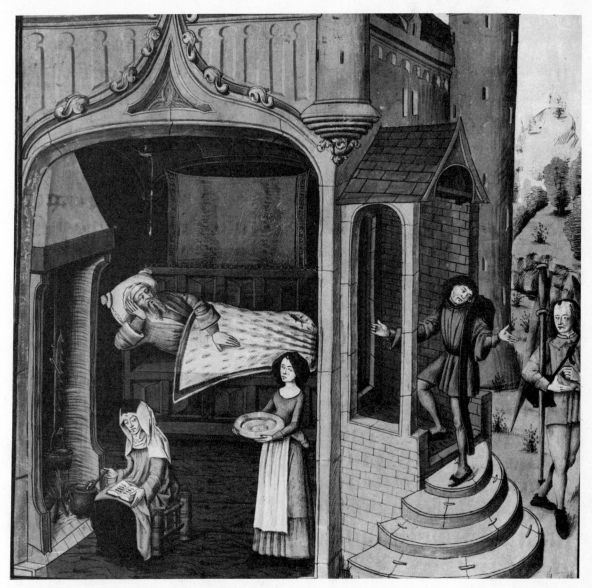

■ ■ *Medieval homes lacked privacy and specialized rooms. Here a man sleeps in the background while two women prepare a meal.*

entitled to a chair you sat up in it; nobody ever sat *back.*

One reason for the simplicity, and the scarcity, of medieval furniture was the way in which people used their homes. In the Middle Ages people didn't so much live in their houses as camp in them. The nobility owned many residences, and traveled frequently.

When they did so, they rolled up the tapestries, packed the chests, took apart the beds, and moved their household with them. This explains why so much medieval furniture is portable or demountable. The French and Italian words for furniture—*mobiliers* and *mobilia*—mean "the movables."

The town bourgeois were less mobile, but

they too needed movable furniture, although for a different reason. The medieval home was a public, not a private place. The hall was in constant use, for cooking, for eating, for entertaining guests, for transacting business, as well as nightly for sleeping. These different functions were accommodated by moving the furniture around as required. There was no "dining table," just a table which was used for preparing food, eating, counting money, and, in a pinch, for sleeping. Because the number of diners varied, the number of tables, and chairs, had to increase and decrease to accommodate them. At night, the tables were put away and the beds were brought out. As a result, there was no attempt to form permanent arrangements. Paintings of medieval interiors reflect an improvisation in the haphazard placement of the furniture, which was simply put around the edges of the room when not in use. Except for the armchair, and later the bed, one has the impression that little importance was attached to the individual pieces of furniture; they were treated more as equipment than as prized personal possessions.

Medieval interiors, with their stained-glass windows, pewlike benches, and Gothic tracery, always betray their ecclesiastical origins. The monastic orders were the multinational corporations of that time—they not only were the source of scientific and technological innovation but also influenced other aspects of medieval life, including music, writing, art, and medicine. Similarly, they affected the design of secular furniture, much of which originated in religious surroundings: the chest for storing vestments, the refectory table, the reading lectern, the stall. The first recorded drawers were used for filing church documents. However, because the life-style of the monks was to be ascetic, there was no reason for them to apply their prodigious inventive energy to making life more pleasurable, and most of their furniture was intentionally severe. Straight-backed pews focused the mind on higher matters (and kept the sitter awake), and hard benches

(which can still be found in Oxford colleges) discouraged dawdling at the refectory table.

What is unexpected about medieval houses, however, is not the lack of furniture (the emptiness of modern architecture has accustomed us to that) but the crush and hubbub of life within them. These houses were not necessarily large—except compared to the hovels of the poor—but they were full of people. This was partly because, in the absence of restaurants, bars, and hotels, they served as public meeting places for entertaining and transacting business, but also because the household itself was large. In addition to the immediate family it included employees, servants, apprentices, friends, and protégés—households of up to twenty-five persons were not uncommon. Because all these people lived in one or at most two rooms, privacy was unknown.[1] Anyone who has been in the military, or in a boarding school, can imagine what it must have been like. Only exceptional people—hermits or scholars (like St. Jerome)—could shut themselves up alone. Even sleeping was a communal business. Not only were there usually many beds in a room—the will of Richard Toky, a London grocer who died in 1391, indicates that he had four beds and a cradle in his hall—there were usually many people in each bed. This explains the size of medieval beds; ten feet square was normal. The Great Bed of Ware was so large that "Four couples might cosily lie side by side, And thus without touching each other abide." How did people achieve intimacy under such conditions? It appears that they did not. Medieval paintings frequently show a couple in bed or bath, and nearby in the same room friends or servants in untroubled, and apparently unembarrassed, conversation.

We should not, however, jump to the con-

---

[1]The concept of privacy is also absent in many non-Western cultures, notably Japan. Lacking an indigenous word to describe this quality, the Japanese have adopted an English one—*praibashii.*

clusion that medieval domestic life was primitive. Bathing, for instance, was fashionable. Here the monasteries also played a role, for not only were they centers of piety, they were also centers of cleanliness. Hygiene was important to the efficiency-minded Cistercian order; for example, St. Bernard, their founder, had spelled it all out in the Rule, an operating manual that dealt not only with religious matters, but also with the mundane. The purpose of the tonsure, for instance, was not symbolic; monks' heads were shaved to control lice. The Rule described work schedules in detail as well as the layout of the buildings, which followed a standardized plan, like businessmen's hotels today. It has been said that a blind monk could enter any of the more than seven hundred Cistercian monasteries and not get lost. Each complex included a *lavatorium*, or bathhouse, fitted with wooden tubs and with facilities for heating the water; small basins with constantly running cold water for hand-washing before and after meals were outside the refectory. The *misericord*, where dying monks were ritually bathed, was situated beside the infirmary, while the *reredorter*, a wing containing latrines, was built next to the dormitory (the *dorter*). The wastewaters from these facilities were carried away in covered-over streams, in effect underground sewers.

Most bourgeois houses in England were provided with household drainage and underground cesspits (although not with sewers). There are many examples of fifteenth-century houses (not only palaces and castles) which had so-called "garderobes" or privies on the upper floor, and chutes leading down to the basement. These were periodically cleaned out, and while the town slept, the "night soil" would be transported to the countryside, to be used as fertilizer. More often, garderobes and privies emptied directly into rivers and streams, which resulted in the contamination of well water and frequent outbreaks of cholera. It was the same type of scientific ignorance, not dirtiness, that accounted for the

inability of people in the fourteenth century to resist the Black Death—they did not understand that its principal carriers were rats and fleas.

Lacking the Rule, the laity were not as observant of hygiene as the monks, but there is evidence that they too paid attention to cleanliness. A fourteenth-century manual, *Ménagère de Paris*, counseled the housewife, "The entrance to your home, that is the parlor and the entrances whereby people come in to speak within the house, must be swept early in the morning and kept clean, and the stools, benches and cushions dusted and shaken." The floor of the hall was strewn with straw in winter, and with herbs and flowers in the summer. This charming practice had a practical purpose, both to keep the floor warm and to maintain an appearance, and an odor, of cleanliness. Washstands and tubs were widely used, although there were no bathrooms. Only in the monasteries, or in exceptional buildings such as Westminster Palace, was there a room devoted exclusively to bathing; most tubs, like the rest of the furnishings, were portable. The bathtubs, which were wooden, were often large, and communal bathing was common. Bathing was a social ritual in the Middle Ages, as it is in some oriental cultures today. It was often a part of festivities such as marriages and banquets, and it was accompanied by conversation, music, food, drink, and inevitably, lovemaking.

Medieval table manners were elaborate. Etiquette was taken seriously, and our custom of giving precedence to guests, or offering them second helpings, originated in the Middle Ages. Washing the hands before eating was another medieval politeness that has survived to the present day. Washing the hands before, after, and during the meal was necessary in the Middle Ages, because although soup spoons were used, forks were not, and people ate largely with their fingers; as in India or Saudi Arabia today, this did not imply indelicacy. Food was served on large platters, cut into smaller portions, and placed on trenchers, large slices of bread that—like Mexican tortillas or Indian chapatis—served as edible plates. The popular image of eating in the Middle Ages is one of homely meals where the food was plentiful but not very sophisticated; quite to the contrary, we would be struck by the diversity of medieval dishes. The growth of cities encouraged the exchange of commodities such as German beer, French and Italian wine, Spanish sugar, Polish salt, Russian honey, and, for the wealthy, spices from the East. Medieval food was far from bland; cinnamon, ginger, nutmeg, and pepper were combined with local herbs such as parsley, mint, garlic, and thyme. There is a good deal of documentation about court banquets, which were extravagant and consisted of many courses served in carefully orchestrated sequence. Much of the variety was the result of eating game as well as domestic animals, and regal menus sometimes sound like lists of an animal protection fund: peacocks, egrets, herons, bitterns, and eagles. Such exotica catch the eye, but even the humbler bourgeois ate well. Here are the ingredients for "farced chycken," a common dish described by Chaucer: a baked chicken stuffed with lentils, cherries, cheese, ale, and oats and garnished with a sauce of "pandemayne" (fine white bread) crumbs, herbs, and salt mixed with "Romeney" (a malmsey wine).

So what are we to make of the home in the Middle Ages? Walter Scott, after describing the interior of a twelfth-century castle in *Ivanhoe*, warned the reader, "Magnificence there was, with some rude attempt at taste; but of comfort there was little, and, being unknown, it was unmissed." According to the twentieth-century architectural historian Siegfried Giedion, "From today's point of view, the Middle Ages had no comfort at all." Even Lewis Mumford, who admired this period, concluded that "the medieval house had scarcely an inkling of . . . comfort." These judgments are true, but should not be misinterpreted. People in the Middle Ages did not altogether lack comfort, as I have tried to show. Their homes

were neither rustic nor crude, nor should we imagine that the persons inhabiting them did so without pleasure. But what comfort there was was never explicit. What our medieval ancestors did lack was the awareness of comfort as an objective *idea*.

If we were to sit down at a medieval meal we would complain about the hard bench. But the medieval diner was less concerned with how she or he sat than with *where* he or she sat. To be placed "above the salt" was an honor reserved only for a distinguished few. To sit in the wrong place, or next to the wrong person, was a serious gaffe. Manners dictated not only where and next to whom the members of the five social classes sat, but even what they could eat. We sometimes complain about our own regimented society, but order and ritual governed medieval life to an extent which we would find intolerable. People lived by the bell. The day was divided into eight periods, and the ringing of the matins or nones bells not only signified the time for prayers within the monastery but also regulated work and commerce in the town. There was no all-night shopping; markets opened and closed according to strict times. In the city of London, you could not buy foreign cheese before nones (midafternoon) or meat after vespers (sunset). When mechanical clocks were invented, these rules were refined, and fish could not be sold before ten o'clock in the morning, nor wine or ale before six o'clock. Disobedience was punished by imprisonment.

Rules also governed how people dressed. The prime function of medieval dress was to communicate status, and formal regulations described exactly how the different social classes should dress. An important baron was permitted to buy more new sets of clothes per year than a simple knight; a wealthy merchant was grudgingly allowed the same vanities as a nobleman of the lowest rank, although ermine was always reserved for the aristocracy. Some could wear brocade, others colored silk and embroidered fabrics. Even certain colors were privileged. Headgear was ubiquitous, and hats were rarely removed. Important people wore them while eating, sleeping, and even bathing. This was not necessarily uncomfortable, unless you were a bishop wearing a tall miter all through dinner, but it does indicate the importance that this obsessively ordered society placed on public expression and on formality, and the secondary role that it willingly assigned to personal comfort. This was especially so at the end of the Middle Ages, when conventions of dress became exaggerated to a ridiculous extent. Women wore the *hennin*, a tall conical headpiece with a trailing veil. Men wore *poulaines*—bizarre shoes with extremely long, pointed toes—and tunics with trailing sleeves and doublets resembling miniskirts. All who could afford it ornamented their clothes with tiny bells, colored ribbons, and precious stones. A well-dressed squire resembled Michael Jackson in a rhinestone-covered nightclub costume.

It is possible to describe how medieval people ate, dressed, and lived, but none of it makes much sense if we do not also make an effort to understand how they thought. That is difficult, for if ever the expression "a world of contrasts" applied, it was during the Middle Ages. Religiosity and avarice, delicacy and cruelty, luxury and squalor, asceticism and eroticism existed side by side. Our own more or less consistent world pales by comparison. Imagine a medieval scholar. After a morning of quiet devotion in a cathedral (which itself was a weird combination of sanctum sanctorum and bestiary), he could attend a public execution in which punishments of extreme cruelty would be carried out according to a pedantic etiquette. If he was like most people it would not be an occasion for ribaldry, but for shedding a tear as the condemned man or woman (before being dismembered) delivered a homily to the crowd. Life "bore the mixed smell of blood and of roses." Our idea of the Middle Ages is often based on music and religious art, which give a false impression of medieval sensibilities. Celebrations, for instance, were an astonishing mixture of good and bad

taste. The same scholar, invited to a court dinner, would wash his hands in perfumed water and exchange genteel courtesies with his neighbor or take part in a madrigal. At the same time he would guffaw at dwarfs jumping out of a huge baked *entremet* (pie), and have dishes brought to him by servitors mounted on horseback. In trying to explain the apparent incompatibility between the extreme indecency of certain customs and the modesty of behavior imposed by courtesy, Huizinga suggests that the Middle Ages consisted of two superimposed layers of civilization—one, primitive and pre-Christian, the other, more recent, courtly and religious. These two layers were frequently in conflict, and what seem to us to be inconsistent emotions are the not always successful attempts to reconcile a cruel reality with the ideal harmony that both chivalry and religion demanded. The excitable medieval mind was constantly oscillating between these opposite poles.

The combination of the primitive and the refined was reflected in the medieval home. Rooms hung with richly decorated tapestries were poorly heated, luxuriously dressed gentlemen and ladies sat on plain benches and stools, courtiers who might spend fifteen minutes in elaborate greeting slept three to a bed and were unmindful of personal intimacy. Why did they not simply improve their living conditions? Technical skill and ingenuity were not lacking. Part of the explanation is that people in the Middle Ages thought differently about the subject of function, especially when it came to their domestic surroundings. For us, the function of a thing has to do with its utility (the function of a chair is to be sat on, for example), and we separate this from its other attributes, such as beauty, age, or style; in medieval life there were no such distinctions. Every object had a meaning and a place in life that was as much a part of its function as its immediate purpose, and these two were inseparable. Because there was no such thing as "pure function" it was difficult for the medieval mind to consider functional improvements; that would have meant tampering with reality itself. Colors had meanings, events had meanings, names had meanings—nothing was accidental.[2] Partly this was superstition, and partly a belief in a divinely ordered universe. Utilitarian objects such as benches and stools, because they lacked meanings, were scarcely given any thought.

There was also little differentiation between utility and ceremony. Simple functions, like washing the hands, acquired ceremonial forms, and ceremonies like breaking bread were performed unself-consciously as a natural part of life. The emphasis that the Middle Ages placed on ceremony underlines what John Lukacs has called the external character of medieval civilization. What mattered then was the external world, and one's place in it. Life was a public affair, and just as one did not

have a strongly developed self-consciousness, one did not have a room of one's own. It was the medieval mind, not the absence of comfortable chairs or central heating, that explains the austerity of the medieval home. It is not so much that in the Middle Ages comfort was unknown, as Walter Scott would have it, but rather that it was not needed.

John Lukacs points out that words such as "self-confidence," "self-esteem," "melancholy," and "sentimental" appeared in English or French in their modern senses only two or three hundred years ago. Their use marked the emergence of something new in the human consciousness: the appearance of the internal world of the individual, of the self, and of the family. The significance of the evolution of domestic comfort can only be appreciated in this context. It is much more than a simple search for physical well-being; it begins in the appreciation of the house as a setting for an emerging interior life. In Lukacs's words, "as the self-consciousness of medieval people was spare, the interiors of their houses were bare, including the halls of nobles and of kings. The interior furniture of houses appeared together with the interior furniture of minds."

---

[2]Medieval houses, like church bells, swords, and cannons, were personified by being given proper names. This custom has continued up to the twentieth century—Adolf Hitler called his country house Eagle's Nest, Winston Churchill, with characteristic English self-depreciation, Cosy Pig—but as houses have become invested with economic rather than emotional value, names have given way to numbers.

■■■

STUDY QUESTIONS

1. How were the poor housed in the Middle Ages? What sort of homes did the bourgeois live in?

2. How did rooms and furniture serve different functions?

3. What rules of life governed dress, where one sat at the table, and daily relations between people?

4. How did the medieval home mirror the external world of the Middle Ages?

BIBLIOGRAPHY

This selection is taken from Witold Rybczynski, *Home: A Short History of an Idea* (1986). An architect and a historian, Rybczynski presents a fascinating overview of the evolution of the home as it reflects changing human values, beliefs, and social customs. For explanations of home furniture see Mario Praz, *An Illustrated History of Interior Decoration* (1982), and John Gloag, *A Social History of Furniture Design* (1966). For an overview of baths and toilets see Lawrence Wright, *Clean and Decent: The History of the Bath and the Loo* (1980). Changing social patterns are dealt with in J. H. Huizinga, *The Waning of the Middle Ages* (1954); Philippe Aries, *Centuries of Childhood* (1962); Barbara W. Tuchman, *A Distant Mirror* (1979); and Fernand Braudel, *The Structures of Everyday Life* (1981).

15. THE EVOLUTION OF MANNERS

Norbert Elias

What exactly constitutes good manners? We usually know it when we see it, but to define it is a different manner. The problem arises because good manners are relative, subject to a particular time and a particular place. Even a standard dictionary definition emphasizes this point: "The prevailing systems or modes of social conduct of a specific society, period, or group . . . . " What are good manners today may not be good manners in fifty years, and the manners of the past—which were quite acceptable in their time—might well strike us today as the height of bad manners. Take, for example, the simple task of blowing your nose. Modern books of etiquette seldom even mention the subject. It is just assumed that the proper way of blowing your nose will be taught to you before you learn to read or is simply too delicate a subject to be dealt with in a book on manners and etiquette. Emily Post's *Etiquette* has chapters on greetings, street behavior, conversation, formal dinners, engagements, funerals, clothes, letters, and much more, but not one word on how to properly blow your nose in public or private. Yet earlier books on etiquette and proper manners examined this subject in detail. In the 1609 edition of *Galateo*, Giovanni della Casa tells his readers never to offer a dirty handkerchief to a friend and never, after wiping their own nose, "to spread out your handkerchief and peer into it as if pearls and rubies might have fallen out of your head." And in *Civilité française* (1714), the anonymous social critic warns, "Take good care not to blow your nose with your fingers or on your sleeve *like children;* use your handkerchief and do not look at it afterward."

Although more than a hundred years separates the two guides to etiquette, both writers felt it necessary to touch upon the subject of the proper way to blow one's nose. Clearly manners were undergoing a transition. These writers worked to make what was once considered quite acceptable—the discharging of mucus without the aid of a handkerchief—become an offense to public standards—the standards of polite society. But why was this so? And more important what does a change in manners indicate about larger changes in society?

In 1939 Norbert Elias' book *Über den Prozess der Zivilisation* was published. Although it was ignored at that time, it was republished in 1969 and translated into English in 1978. *The History of Manners*, volume one of *The Civilizing Process,* considered why manners have changed over the years. The process, Elias notes, is enormously complex and moves with near glacial slowness. The key element in the process is the emergence of the modern state and "the lengthening chains of interdependence" it has fostered. The modern state demands many levels of social interaction. Thrown together in ever more complex societies and in ever larger cities, people have had to learn to mask their emotions, curb the expression of their desires, and live peacefully together. In the earlier periods of the modern state members of the aristocracy were largely responsible for cultivating "civilized" behavior. Courtly behavior was designed to maintain social tranquility among the elite of a nation. But it was not democratic. Thus Voltaire's mistress, the Marquise de Chatelet, who observed all the niceties of the Byzantine etiquette of the court of Louis XIV, bathed without shame in front of her male servants.

As the state grew in power and became more democratic the threshold of shame became narrower. Referring to exposure of the body, Elias comments, "First it becomes a distasteful offense to show oneself exposed in any way before those of higher or equal rank; with inferiors it can even be a sign of benevolence. Then, as all become socially more equal, it slowly becomes a general offense."

The formalization of etiquette indicates broad changes in society. Restraint, rather than a free expression of one's emotions and desires, became the dominant characteristic of human interaction. In Freudian terms, the superego gained ascendancy over the id. As a result, according to Elias, what was perfectly normal in adult behavior during the early medieval period is today considered a "misbehavior" and swiftly corrected at the childhood stage: "A child that does not attain the level of control of emotions demanded by society is regarded in varying gradations as 'ill,' 'abnormal,' 'criminal,' or just 'impossible' from the point of view of a particular caste or class, and is accordingly excluded from the life of that class." Elias also maintains that this systematized repression of certain behavior has rendered pleasure a "private" or "secret" emotion and fostered displeasure, revulsion, and distaste as "public" emotions.

The guidelines collected in this selection were collected by Elias to illustrate the changes in manners over the centuries. As you read them try to imagine or reconstruct the manners of people at a given time.

On Behavior at Table

(a) Examples representing upper-class behavior in a fairly pure form:

A

Thirteenth century
This is Tannhäuser's poem of courtly good manners:

1 I consider a well-bred man to be one who always recognizes good manners and is never ill-mannered.

2 There are many forms of good manners, and they serve many good purposes. The man who adopts them will never err.

25 When you eat do not forget the poor. God will reward you if you treat them kindly.

33 A man of refinement should not slurp with his spoon when in company; that is the way people at court behave who often indulge in unrefined conduct.

37 It is not polite to drink from the dish, although some who approve of this rude habit insolently pick up the dish and pour it down as if they were mad.

41 Those who fall upon the dishes like swine while eating, snorting disgustingly and smacking their lips. . . .

45 Some people bite a slice and then dunk it in the dish in a coarse way; refined people reject such bad manners.

49 A number of people gnaw a bone and then put it back in the dish—this is a serious offense.

53 Those who like mustard and salt should take care to avoid the filthy habit of putting their fingers into them.

57 A man who clears his throat when he eats and one who blows his nose in the tablecloth are both ill-bred, I assure you.

65 A man who wants to talk and eat at the same time, and talks in his sleep, will never rest peacefully.

69 Do not be noisy at table, as some people are. Remember, my friends, that nothing is so ill-mannered.

81 I find it very bad manners whenever I see someone with food in his mouth and drinking at the same time, like an animal.

85 You should not blow into your drink, as some are fond of doing; this is an ill-mannered habit that should be avoided.

94 Before drinking, wipe your mouth so that you do not dirty the drink; this act of courtesy should be observed at all times.

105 It is bad manners to lean against the table while eating, as it is to keep your helmet on when serving the ladies.

109 Do not scrape your throat with your bare hand while eating; but if you have to, do it politely with your coat.

113 And it is more fitting to scratch with that than to soil your hand; onlookers notice people who behave like this.

117 You should not poke your teeth with your knife, as some do; it is a bad habit.

125 If anyone is accustomed to loosening his belt at table, take it from me that he is not a true courtier.

129 If a man wipes his nose on his hand at table because he knows no better, then he is a fool, believe me.

141 I hear that some eat unwashed (if it is true, it is a bad sign). May their fingers be palsied!

From *The History of Manners* by Norbert Elias, translated by Edmund Jephcott. English Translation © 1978 by Urizen Books. Reprinted by permission of Pantheon Books, a division of Random House, Inc.

157 It is not decent to poke your fingers into your ears or eyes, as some people do, or to pick your nose while eating. These three habits are bad.

On v. 25, cf. the first rule of Bonvicino da Riva:

The first is this: when at table, think first of the poor and needy.

From *Ein spruch der ze tische kêrt* (A word to those at table):

313 You should not drink from the dish, but with a spoon as is proper.

315 Those who stand up and snort disgustingly over the dishes like swine belong with other farmyard beasts.

319 To snort like a salmon, gobble like a badger, and complain while eating—these three things are quite improper.

In the *Courtesies* of Bonvicino da Riva:

Do not slurp with your mouth when eating from a spoon. This is a bestial habit.

In *The Book of Nurture and School of Good Manners:*

201 And suppe not lowde of thy Pottage no tyme in all thy lyfe.

On v. 45, cf. *Ein spruch der ze tische kêrt:*

346 May refined people be preserved from those who gnaw their bones and put them back in the dish.

From *Quisquis es in mensa* (For those at table):

A morsel that has been tasted should not be returned to the dish.

On v. 65, cf. from *Stans puer in mensam* (The boy at table):

22 Numquam ridebis nec faberis ore repleto.
Never laugh or talk with a full mouth.

On v. 81, cf. from *Quisquis es in mensa:*

15 Qui vult potare debet prius os vacuare.
If you wish to drink, first empty your mouth.

From *The Babees Book:*

149 And withe fulle mouthe drinke in no wyse.

On v. 85, cf. *The Book of Curtesye:*

111 Ne blow not on thy drinke ne mete,
Nether for colde, nether for hete.

On v. 94, cf. *The Babees Book:*

155 Whanne ye shalle drynke,
your mouthe clence withe a clothe.

From a *Contenance de table* (Guide to behavior at table):

Do not slobber while you drink, for this is a shameful habit.

On v. 105, cf. *The Babees Book:*

Nor on the borde lenynge be yee nat sene.

On v. 117, cf. *Stans puer in mensam:*

30 Mensa cultello, dentes mundare caveto.
Avoid cleaning your teeth with a knife at table.

B

Fifteenth century?
From *S'ensuivent les contenances de la table* (These are good table manners):

I
Learn these rules.

II
Take care to cut and clean your nails; dirt under the nails is dangerous when scratching.

III
Wash your hands when you get up and before every meal.

XII
Do not be the first to take from the dish.

XIII
Do not put back on your plate what has been in your mouth.

XIV
Do not offer anyone a piece of food you have bitten into.

XV
Do not chew anything you have to spit out again.

XVII
It is bad manners to dip food into the saltcellar.

XXIV
Be peaceable, quiet, and courteous at table.

XXVI
If you have crumbled bread into your wineglass, drink up the wine or throw it away.

XXXI
Do not stuff too much into yourself, or you will be obliged to commit a breach of good manners.

XXXIV
Do not scratch at table, with your hands or with the tablecloth.

On v. 141, cf. *Stans puer in mensam:*

11 Illotis manibus escas ne sumpseris unquam.
Never pick up food with unwashed hands.

On v. 157, cf. *Quisquis es in mensa:*

9 Non tangas aures nudis digitis neque nares.
Touch neither your ears nor your nostrils with your bare fingers.

This small selection of passages was compiled from a brief perusal of various guides to behavior at table and court. It is very far from exhaustive. It is intended only to give an impression of how similar in tone and content were the rules in different traditions and in different centuries of the Middle Ages.

C

1530
From *De civilitate morum puerilium* (On civility in boys), by Erasmus of Rotterdam, ch. 4:

If a serviette[1] is given, lay it on your left shoulder or arm.

If you are seated with people of rank, take off your hat and see that your hair is well combed.

Your goblet and knife, duly cleansed, should be on the right, your bread on the left.

Some people put their hands in the dishes the moment they have sat down. Wolves do that. . . .

Do not be the first to touch the dish that has been brought in, not only because this shows you greedy, but also because it is dangerous. For someone who puts something hot into his mouth unawares must either spit it out or, if he swallows it, burn his throat. In either case he is as ridiculous as he is pitiable.

It is a good thing to wait a short while before eating, so that the boy grows accustomed to tempering his affects.

To dip the fingers in the sauce is rustic. You should take what you want with your knife and fork; you should not search through the whole dish as epicures are wont to do, but take what happens to be in front of you.

What you cannot take with your fingers should be taken with the *quadra.*

If you are offered a piece of cake or pie on a spoon, hold out your plate or take the spoon that is held out to you, put the food on your plate, and return the spoon.

If you are offered something liquid, taste it and return the spoon, but first wipe it on your serviette.

To lick greasy fingers or to wipe them on your coat is impolite. It is better to use the tablecloth or the serviette.

_____
[1]Table napkin.

D

1558

From *Galateo*, by Giovanni della Casa, Archbishop of Benevento, quoted from the five-language edition (Geneva, 1609), p. 68:

What do you think this Bishop and his noble company *(il Vescove e la sua nobile brigata)* would have said to those whom we sometimes see lying like swine with their snouts in the soup, not once lifting their heads and turning their eyes, still less their hands, from the food, puffing out both cheeks as if they were blowing a trumpet or trying to fan a fire, not eating but gorging themselves, dirtying their arms almost to the elbows and then reducing their serviettes to a state that would make a kitchen rag look clean.

Nonetheless, these hogs are not ashamed to use the serviettes thus sullied to wipe away their sweat (which, owing to their hasty and excessive feeding, often runs down their foreheads and faces to their necks), and even to blow their noses into them as often as they please.

E

1560

From a *Civilité* by C. Calviac (based heavily on Erasmus, but with some independent comments):

When the child is seated, if there is a serviette on the plate in front of him, he shall take it and place it on his left arm or shoulder; then he shall place his bread on the left and the knife on the right, like the glass, if he wishes to leave it on the table, and if it can be conveniently left there without annoying anyone. For it might happen that the glass could not be left on the table or on his right without being in someone's way.

The child must have the discretion to understand the needs of the situation he is in.

When eating . . . he should take the first piece that comes to his hand on his cutting board.

If there are sauces, the child may dip into them decently, without turning his food over after having dipped one side. . . .

It is very necessary for a child to learn at an early age how to carve a leg of mutton, a partridge, a rabbit, and such things.

It is a far too dirty thing for a child to offer others something he has gnawed, or something he disdains to eat himself, *unless it be to his servant.* [Author's emphasis]

Nor is it decent to take from the mouth something he has already chewed, and put it on the cutting board, unless it be a small bone from which he has sucked the marrow to pass time while awaiting the dessert; for after sucking it he should put it on his plate, where he should also place the stones of cherries, plums, and suchlike, as it is not good either to swallow them or to drop them on the floor.

The child should not gnaw bones indecently, as dogs do.

When the child would like salt, he shall take it with the point of his knife and not with three fingers.

The child must cut his meat into very small pieces on his cutting board . . . and he must not lift the meat to his mouth now with one hand and now with the other, like little children who are learning to eat; he should always do so with his right hand, taking the bread or meat decently with three fingers only.

As for the manner of chewing, it varies according to the country. The Germans chew with the mouth closed, and find it ugly to do otherwise. The French, on the other hand, half open the mouth, and find the procedure of the Germans rather dirty. The Italians proceed in a very slack manner and the French more roundly, finding the Italian way too delicate and precious.

And so each nation has something of its own, different to the others. So that the child will proceed in accordance with the customs of the place where he is.

Further, the Germans use spoons when eating soup and everything liquid, and the Italians forks. The French use either, as they think fit and as is most convenient. The Italians generally prefer to have a knife for each person. But the Germans place special importance on this, to the extent that they are greatly displeased if one asks for or takes the knife in front of them. The French way is quite different: A whole table full of people will use two or three knives, without making difficulties in asking for or taking a knife, or passing it if they have it. So that if someone asks the child for his knife, he should pass it after wiping it with his serviette, holding it by the point and offering the handle to the person requesting it: for it would not be polite to do otherwise.

F

Between 1640 and 1680

From a song by the Marquis de Coulanges:

In times past, people ate from the common dish and dipped their bread and fingers in the sauce.

Today everyone eats with spoon and fork from his own plate, and a valet washes the cutlery from time to time at the buffet.

G

1672

From Antoine de Courtin, *Nouveau traité de civilité*, pp. 127, 273:

If everyone is eating from the same dish, you should take care not to put your hand into it *before those of higher rank have done so,* and to take food only from the part of the dish opposite you. Still less should you take the best pieces, even though you might be the last to help yourself.

It must also be pointed out that you should always wipe your spoon when, after using it, you want to take something from another dish, *there being people so delicate that they would not wish to eat soup into which you had dipped it after putting it into your mouth.* [Author's emphasis]

And even, if you are at the table of very refined people, it is not enough to wipe your spoon; you should not use it but ask for an-

other. Also, in many places, spoons are brought in with the dishes, *and these serve only for taking soup and sauce.* [Author's emphasis]

You should not eat soup from the dish, but put it neatly on your plate; if it is too hot, it is impolite to blow on each spoonful; you should wait until it has cooled.

If you have the misfortune to burn your mouth, you should endure it patiently if you can, without showing it; but if the burn is unbearable, as sometimes happens, you should, before the others have noticed, take your plate promptly in one hand and lift it to your mouth and, while covering your mouth with the other hand, return to the plate what you have in your mouth, and quickly pass it to a footman behind you. Civility requires you to be polite, but it does not expect you to be homicidal toward yourself. It is very impolite to touch anything greasy, a sauce or syrup, etc., with your fingers, apart from the fact that it obliges you to commit two or three more improper acts. One is to wipe your hand frequently on your serviette and to soil it like a kitchen cloth, so that those who see you wipe your mouth with it feel nauseated. Another is to wipe your fingers on your bread, which again is very improper. The third is to lick them, which is the height of impropriety.

. . . As there are many [customs] which have already changed, I do not doubt that several of these will likewise change in the future.

Formerly one was permitted . . . to dip one's bread into the sauce, provided only that one had not already bitten it. Nowadays that would be a kind of rusticity.

Formerly one was allowed to take from one's mouth what one could not eat and drop it on the floor, provided it was done skillfully. Now that would be very disgusting. . . .

H

1717

From François de Callières, *De la science du monde et des connoissances utiles à la conduite de la vie*, pp. 97, 101:

This sixteenth-century picture of a family at meal-time shows a conspicuous lack of forks, spoons, and serving plates.

In Germany and the Northern Kingdoms it is civil and decent for a prince to drink first to the health of those he is entertaining, and then to offer them the same glass or goblet usually filled with the same wine; nor is it a lack of politeness in them to drink from the same glass, but a mark of candor and friendship. The women also drink first and then give their glass, or have it taken, to the person they are addressing, with the same wine from which they have drunk his health, *without this being taken as a special favor, as it is among us.* . . . [Author's emphasis]

"I cannot approve," a lady answers "— without offense to the gentlemen from the north—this manner of drinking from the same glass, and still less of drinking what the ladies have left; it has an air of impropriety that makes me wish they might show other marks of their candor."

(b) Examples from books which either, like La Salle's *Les Règles de la bienséance et de la civilité chrétienne*, represent the spreading of courtly manners and models to broader bourgeois strata, or, like Example I, reflect fairly purely the bourgeois and probably the provincial standard of their time.

In Example I, from about 1714, people still eat from a communal dish. Nothing is said against touching the meat on one's own plate with the hands. And the "bad manners" that are mentioned have largely disappeared from the upper class.

The *Civilité* of 1780 (Example L) is a little book of forty-eight pages in bad *civilité* type, printed in Caen but undated. The British Museum catalogue has a question mark after the date. In any case, this book is an example of the multitude of cheap books or pamphlets on *civilité* that were disseminated throughout France in the eighteenth century. This one, to judge from its general attitude, was clearly intended for provincial town-dwellers. In no other eighteenth-century work on *civilité* quoted here are bodily functions discussed so openly. The standard the book points to recalls in many respects the one that Erasmus's *De civilitate* had marked for the upper class. It is still a matter of course to take food in the hands. This example seemed useful here to complement the other quotations, and particularly to remind the reader that the movement ought to be seen in its full multilayered polyphony, not as a line but as a kind of fugue with a succession of related movement-motifs on different levels.

Example M from 1786 shows the dissemination from above to below very directly. It is particularly characteristic because it contains a large number of customs that have subsequently been adopted by "civilized society" as a whole, but are here clearly visible as specific customs of the courtly upper class which still seem relatively alien to the bourgeoisie. Many customs have been arrested, as "civilized customs," in exactly the form they have here as courtly manners.

The quotation from 1859 (Example N) is meant to remind the reader that in the nineteenth century, as today, the whole movement had already been entirely forgotten, that the standard of "civilization" which in reality had been attained only quite recently was taken for granted, what preceded it being seen as "barbaric."

I

1714
From an anonymous *Civilité française* (Liège, 1714?), p. 48:

It is not . . . polite to drink your soup from the bowl unless you are in your own family, and only then if you have drunk the most part with your spoon.

If the soup is in a communal dish, take some with your spoon in your turn, without precipitation.

Do not keep your knife always in your hand, as village people do, but take it only when you need it.

When you are being served meat, it is not seemly to take it in your hand. You should hold out your plate in your left hand while holding your fork or knife in your right.

It is against propriety to give people meat to smell, and you should under no circumstances put meat back into the common dish if you have smelled it yourself. If you take meat from a common dish, do not choose the best pieces. Cut with the knife, holding still the piece of meat in the dish with the fork, which you will use to put on your plate the piece you have cut off; do not, therefore, take the meat with your hand [nothing is said here against touching the meat on one's own plate with the hand].

You should not throw bones or eggshells or the skin of any fruit onto the floor.

The same is true of fruit stones. It is more polite to remove them from the mouth with two fingers than to spit them into one's hand.

J

1729
From La Salle, *Les Règles de la bienséance et de la civilité chrétienne* (Rouen, 1729), p. 87:

On Things to Be Used at Table
At table you should use a serviette, a plate, a knife, a spoon, and a fork. It would be entirely contrary to propriety to be without any of these things while eating.

It is for the person of highest rank in the company to unfold his serviette first, and the others should wait until he has done so before unfolding theirs. When the people are approximately equal, all should unfold it together without ceremony. [N.B. With the "democratization" of society and the family, this becomes the rule. The social structure, here still of the hierarchical-aristocratic type, is mirrored in the most elementary human relationships.]

It is improper to use the serviette to wipe your face; it is far more so to rub your teeth with it, and it would be one of the grossest offenses against civility to use it to blow your nose. . . . The use you may and must make of the serviette when at table is for wiping your mouth, lips, and fingers when they are greasy, wiping the knife before cutting bread, and cleaning the spoon and fork after using them. [N.B. This is one of many examples of the extraordinary control of behavior embedded in our eating habits. The use of each utensil is limited and defined by a multiplicity of very precise rules. None of them is simply self-evident, as they appear to later generations. Their use is formed very gradually in conjunction with the structure and changes of human relationships.]

When the fingers are very greasy, wipe them first on a piece of bread, which should then be left on the plate, before cleaning them on the serviette, in order not to soil it too much.

When the spoon, fork, and knife are dirty or greasy, it is very improper to lick them, and it is not at all decent to wipe them, or anything else, on the tablecloth. On these and similar occasions you should use the serviette, and regarding the tablecloth you should take care to keep it always very clean, and not to drop on it water, wine, or anything that might soil it.

When the plate is dirty, you should be sure not to scrape it with the spoon or fork to clean it, or to clean your plate or the bottom of any dish with your fingers: That is very impolite. Either they should not be touched or, if you have the opportunity of exchanging them, you should ask for another.

When at table you should not keep the knife always in your hand; it is sufficient to pick it up when you wish to use it.

It is also very impolite to put a piece of bread into your mouth while holding the knife in your hand; it is even more so to do this with the point of the knife. The same thing must be observed in eating apples, pears, or some other fruits. [N.B. Examples of taboos relating to knives.]

It is against propriety to hold the fork or spoon with the whole hand, like a stick; you should always hold them between your fingers.

You should not use your fork to lift liquids to the mouth . . . it is the spoon that is intended for such uses.

It is polite always to use the fork to put meat into your mouth, for *propriety does not permit the touching of anything greasy with the fingers* [Author's emphasis], neither sauces nor syrups; and if anyone did so, he could not escape subsequently committing several further incivilities, such as frequently wiping his fingers on his serviette, which would make it very dirty, or on his bread, which would be very impolite, or licking his fingers, which is not permitted to well-born, refined people.

This whole passage, like several others, is taken from A. de Courtin's *Nouveau traité* of 1672. It also reappears in other eighteenth-century works on *civilité*. The reason given for the prohibition on eating with the fingers is particularly instructive. In Courtin, too, it applies in the first place only to greasy foods, especially those in sauces, since this gives rise to actions that are "distasteful" to behold. In La Salle this is not entirely consistent with what he says in another place: "If your fingers are greasy . . ." and so on. The prohibition is not remotely so self-evident as today. We see how gradually it becomes an internalized habit, a piece of "self-control."

In the critical period at the end of the reign of Louis XV—in which, as shown earlier, the urge for reform is intensified as an outward sign of social changes, and in which the concept of "civilization" comes to the fore—La Salle's *Civilité*, which had previously passed through several editions largely unchanged, was revised. The changes in the standard are very instructive (Example K). They are in some respects very considerable. The difference is partly discernible in what no longer needs to be said. Many chapters are shorter. Many "bad manners" earlier discussed in detail are mentioned only briefly in passing. The same applies to many bodily functions originally dealt with at length and in great detail. The tone is generally less mild, and often incomparably harsher than in the first version.

K

1774

From La Salle, *Les Règles de la bienséance et de la civilité chrétienne* (1774 ed.), pp. 45ff.:

The serviette which is placed on the plate, being intended to preserve clothing from spots and other soiling inseparable from meals, should be spread over you so far that it covers the front of your body to the knees, going under the collar and not being passed inside it. The spoon, fork, and knife should always be placed on the right.

The spoon is intended for liquids, and the fork for solid meats.

When one or the other is dirty, they can be cleaned with the serviette, if another service cannot be procured. You should avoid wiping them with the tablecloth, which is an unpardonable impropriety.

When the plate is dirty you should ask for another; it would be revoltingly gross to clean spoon, fork, or knife with the fingers.

At good tables, attentive servants change plates without being called upon.

Nothing is more improper than to lick your fingers, to touch the meats and put them into your mouth with your hand, to stir sauce with your fingers, or to dip bread into it with your fork and then suck it.

You should never take salt with your fingers. It is very common for children to pile pieces one on top of the other, and even to take out of their mouths something they have chewed, and flick pieces with their fingers. [All these were mentioned earlier as general misdemeanors, but are here mentioned only as the "bad" manners of children. Grown-ups no longer do such things.] Nothing is more impolite [than] to lift meat to your nose to smell it; to let others smell it is a further impoliteness toward the master of the table; if you should happen to find dirt in the food, you should get rid of the food without showing it.

L

1780?
From an anonymous work, *La Civilité honete pour les enfants* (Caen, n.d.), p. 35:

Afterward, he shall place his serviette on him, his bread on the left and his knife on the right, to cut the meat without breaking it. [The sequence described here is found in many other documents. The most elementary procedure, earlier usual among the upper class as well, is to break up the meat with the hands. Here the next stage is described, when the meat is cut with the knife. The use of the fork is not mentioned. To break off pieces of meat is regarded here as a mark of the peasant, cutting it as clearly the manners of the town.] He will also take care not to put his knife into his mouth. He should not leave his hands on his plate . . . nor rest his elbow on it, for this is done only by the aged and infirm.

The well-behaved child will be the last to help himself if he is with his superiors.

. . . Next, if it is meat, he will cut it politely with his knife and eat it with his bread.

It is a rustic, dirty habit to take chewed meat from your mouth and put it on your plate. Nor should you ever put back into the dish something you have taken from it.

M

1786
From a conversation between the poet Delille and Abbé Cosson:

A short while ago Abbé Cosson, Professor of Belles Lettres at the Collège Mazarin, told me about a dinner he had attended a few days previously with some *court people* . . . at Versailles.

"I'll wager," I told him, "that you perpetrated a hundred incongruities."

"What do you mean?" Abbé Cosson asked quickly, greatly perturbed. "I believe I did everything in the same way as everyone else."

"What presumption! I'll bet you did nothing in the same way as anyone else. But I'll limit myself to the dinner. First, what did you do with your serviette when you sat down?"

"With my serviette? I did the same as everyone else. I unfolded it, spread it out, and fixed it by a corner to my buttonhole."

"Well, my dear fellow, you are the only one who did that. One does not spread out one's serviette, one keeps it on one's knees. And how did you eat your soup?"

"Like everyone else, I think. I took my spoon in one hand and my fork in the other. . . ."

"Your fork? Good heavens! No one uses his fork to eat soup. . . . But tell me how you ate your bread."

"Certainly, like everyone else: I cut it neatly with my knife."

"Oh dear, you break bread, you do not cut it. . . . Let's go on. The coffee—how did you drink it?"

"Like everyone, to be sure. It was boiling hot, so I poured it little by little from my cup into my saucer."

"Well, you certainly did not drink it like anyone else. Everyone drinks coffee from the cup, never from the saucer. . . ."

N

1859
From *The Habits of Good Society* (London, 1859; 2d ed., verbatim, 1889), p. 257:

Forks were undoubtedly a later invention than fingers, but as we are not *cannibals* I am inclined to think they were a good one.

On Blowing One's Nose

A

Thirteenth century
From Bonvesin de la Riva (Bonvicino da Riva), *De la zinquanta cortexie da tavola* (Fifty table courtesies):

(a) Precept for gentlemen:
When you blow your nose or cough, turn round so that nothing falls on the table.

(b) Precept for pages or servants:
Pox la trentena è questa:
   zaschun cortese donzello
Che se vore mondà lo naxo,
   con li drapi se faza bello;
Chi mangia, over chi menestra,
   no de'sofià con le die;
Con li drapi da pey se monda
   vostra cortexia.[1]

B

Fifteenth century
From *Ein spruch der ze tische kêrt*:

It is unseemly to blow your nose into the tablecloth.

C

From *S'ensuivent les contenances de la table*:

XXXIII

Do not blow your nose with the same hand that you use to hold the meat.[2]

D

From A. Cabanès, *Moeurs intimes du temps passé* (Paris, 1910), 1st series, p. 101:

In the fifteenth century people blew their noses into their fingers, and the sculptors of the age were not afraid to reproduce the gesture, in a passably realistic form, in their monuments.

Among the knights, the *plourans,* at the grave of Philip the Bold at Dijon, one is seen blowing his nose into his coat, another into his fingers.

E

Sixteenth century
From *De civilitate morum puerilium*, by Erasmus, ch. 1:

To blow your nose on your hat or clothing is rustic, and to do so with the arm or elbow befits a tradesman; nor is it much more polite to use the hand, if you immediately smear the snot on your garment. It is proper to wipe the nostrils with a handkerchief, and to do this while turning away, *if more honorable people are present.*

If anything falls to the ground when blowing the nose with two fingers, it should immediately be trodden away.

[From the scholia on this passage:]
Between snot and spit there is little difference, except that the former fluid is to be interpreted as coarser and the latter more unclean. The Latin writers constantly confuse a breastband, a napkin, or any piece of linen with a handkerchief.

---

[1]The meaning of passage (b) is not entirely clear. What is apparent is that it is addressed especially to people who serve at table. A commentator, Uguccione Pisano, says: "Those are called *donizelli* who are handsome, young, and the servants of great lords. . . ." These *donizelli* were not allowed to sit at the same table as the knights; or, if this was permitted, they had to sit on a lower chair. They, pages of a kind and at any rate social inferiors, are told: The thirty-first courtesy is this—every *courtois* "donzel" who wishes to blow his nose should beautify himself with a cloth. When he is eating or serving he should not blow (his nose?) through his fingers. It is *courtois* to use the foot bandage.

---

[2]According to an editor's note (*The Babees Book*, vol. 2, p. 14), courtesy consisted in blowing the nose with the fingers of the left hand if one ate and took meat from the common dish with the right.

F
1558
From *Galateo*, by Della Casa, quoted from the five-language edition (Geneva, 1609), pp. 72, 44, 618:

You should not offer your handkerchief to anyone unless it has been freshly washed. . . .

Nor is it seemly, after wiping your nose, to spread out your handkerchief and peer into it as if pearls and rubies might have fallen out of your head.

. . . What, then, shall I say of those . . . who carry their handkerchiefs about in their mouths? . . .

G
From Cabanès, *Moeurs intimes*, pp. 103, 168, 102:

[From Martial d'Auvergue, "Love decrees"] . . . in order that she might remember him, he decided to have one of the most beautiful and sumptuous handkerchiefs made for her, in which his name was in letters entwined in the prettiest fashion, for it was joined to a fine golden heart bordered with tiny heart's eases.[3]

[From Lestoil, *Journal d'Henri IV*] In 1594, Henri IV asked his valet how many shirts he had, and the latter replied: "A dozen, sire, and some torn ones." "And how many handkerchiefs?" asked the king. "Have I not eight?" "For the moment there are only five," he said.

In 1599, after her death, the inventory of Henri IV's mistress is found to contain "five handkerchiefs worked in gold, silver and silk, worth 100 crowns."

In the sixteenth century, Monteil tells us, in France as everywhere else, the common people blow their noses without a handkerchief, but among the bourgeoisie it is accepted practice to use the sleeve. As for the rich, they carry a handkerchief in their pockets; therefore, to say that a man has wealth, one says that he does not blow his nose on his sleeve.

H
Late seventeenth century

The Peak of Refinement
First Highpoint of Modeling and Restrictions

1672
From Courtin, *Nouveau traité de civilité:*

[At table] to blow your nose openly into your handkerchief, without concealing yourself with your serviette, and to wipe away your sweat with it . . . are filthy habits fit to make everyone's gorge rise. . . .

You should avoid yawning, blowing your nose, and spitting. If you are obliged to do so in places that are kept clean, do it in your handkerchief, while turning your face away and shielding yourself with your left hand, and do not look into your handkerchief afterward.

I
1694
From Ménage, *Dictionnaire étymologique de la langue française:*

Handkerchief for blowing the nose.

As this expression "blowing the nose" gives a very disagreeable impression, ladies ought to call this a pocket handkerchief, as one says neckerchief, rather than a handkerchief for blowing the nose. [N.B. *Mouchoir de poche, Taschentuch,* handkerchief as more polite expressions; the word for functions that have become distasteful is repressed.]

Eighteenth century
Note the increasing distance between adults and children. Only children are still allowed, at least in the middle classes, to behave as adults did in the Middle Ages.

---

[3]This cloth was intended to be hung from the lady's girdle, with her keys. Like the fork, night-commode, etc., the handerkerchief is first an expensive luxury article.

J

1714

From an anonymous *Civilité française* (Liège, 1714), p. 141:

Take good care not to blow your nose with your fingers or on your sleeve *like children;* use your handkerchief and do not look into it afterward.

K

1729

From La Salle, *Les Règles de la bienséance et de la civilité chrétienne* (Rouen, 1729), in a chapter called "On the Nose, and the Manner of Blowing the Nose and Sneezing," p. 23:

It is very impolite to keep poking your finger into your nostrils, and still more insupportable to put what you have pulled from your nose into your mouth. . . .

It is vile to wipe your nose with your bare hand, or to blow it on your sleeve or your clothes. It is very contrary to decency to blow your nose with two fingers and then to throw the filth onto the ground and wipe your fingers on your clothes. It is well known how improper it is to see such uncleanliness on clothes, which should always be very clean, no matter how poor they may be.

There are some who put a finger on one nostril and by blowing through their nose cast onto the ground the filth inside; those who act thus are people who do not know what decency is.

You should always use your handkerchief to blow your nose, and never anything else, and in doing so usually hide your face with your hat. [A particularly clear example of the dissemination of courtly customs through this work.]

You should avoid making a noise when blowing your nose. . . . Before blowing it, it is impolite to spend a long time taking out your handkerchief. *It shows a lack of respect toward the people you are with* to unfold it in different places to see where you are to use it. You should take your handkerchief from your pocket and use it quickly in such a way that you are scarcely noticed by others.

After blowing your nose you should take care not to look into your handkerchief. It is correct to fold it immediately and replace it in your pocket.

L

1774

From La Salle, *Les Règles de la bienséance et de la civilité chrétienne* (1774 ed.), pp. 14f. The chapter is now called only "On the Nose" and is shortened:

Every voluntary movement of the nose, whether caused by the hand or otherwise, is impolite and puerile. To put your fingers into your nose is a revolting impropriety, and from touching it too often *discomforts may arise which are felt for a long time.* Children are sufficiently in the habit of committing this lapse; *parents should correct them carefully.*

You should observe, in blowing your nose, all the rules of propriety and cleanliness.

All details are avoided. The "conspiracy of silence" is spreading. It is based on the presupposition—which evidently could not be made at the time of the earlier edition—that all the details are known to adults and can be controlled within the family.

M

1797

From La Mésangère, *Le voyageur de Paris* (1797), vol. 2, p. 95. This is probably seen, to a greater extent than the preceding eighteenth-century examples, from the point of view of the younger members of "good society":

Some years ago people made an art of blowing the nose. One imitated the sound of the trumpet, another the screech of a cat. Perfection lay in making neither too much noise nor too little.

On Behavior in the Bedroom

A

Fifteenth century
From *Stans puer in mensam*, an English book of table manners from the period 1463–1483:

215 And if that it forten so by
nyght or Any tyme
That you schall lye with Any man that is better than you
Spyre hym what syde of the bedd that most best will ples hym,
And lye you on thi tother syde,
for that is thi prow;
Ne go you not to bede before bot
thi better cause the,
For that is no curtasy, thus seys doctour paler.

223 And when you arte in thi bed,
this is curtasy,
Stryght downe that you lye with fote and hond.
When ze have talkyd what ze wyll,
byd hym gode nyght in hye
For that is gret curtasy so schall
thou understand.[4]

Let your better choose which side of the bed he'll lie on; don't go to bed first, till he asks you to (says Dr. Paler).

When you're both in bed, lie straight, and say "Good Night" when you've done your chat.

B

1530
From *De civilitate morum puerilium*, by Erasmus, ch. 12, "On the Bedchamber":

When you undress, when you get up, be mindful of modesty, and take care not to expose to the eyes of others anything that morality and nature require to be concealed.

If you share a bed with a comrade, lie quietly; do not toss with your body, for this can lay yourself bare or inconvenience your companion by pulling away the blankets.

C

1555
From *Des bonnes moeurs et honnestes contenances*, by Pierre Broë (Lyons, 1555):

If you share a bed with another man, keep still.

Take care not to annoy him or expose yourself by abrupt movements.

And if he is asleep, see that you do not wake him.

D

1729
From La Salle, *Les Règles de la bienséance et de la civilité chrétienne* (Rouen, 1729), p. 55:

You ought . . . neither to undress nor go to bed in the presence of any other person. Above all, unless you are married, you should not go to bed in the presence of anyone of the other sex.

It is still less permissible for people of different sexes to sleep in the same bed, unless they are very young children. . . .

If you are forced by unavoidable necessity to share a bed with another person of the same sex on a journey, it is not proper to lie so near him that you disturb or even touch him; and it is still less decent to put your legs between those of the other. . . .

It is also very improper and impolite to amuse yourself with talk and chatter. . . .

When you get up you should not leave the bed uncovered, nor put your nightcap on a chair or anywhere else where it can be seen.

E

1774
From La Salle, *Les Règles de la bienséance et de la civilité chrétienne* (1774 ed.), p. 31:

---

[4]To facilitate comprehension, the old spelling is not reproduced exactly. The philologically accurate text can be found in *A Booke of Precedence*, p. 63.

It is a strange abuse to make two people of different sex sleep in the same room. And if necessity demands it, you should make sure that the beds are apart, and that modesty does not suffer in any way from this commingling. Only extreme indigence can excuse this practice. . . .

If you are forced to share a bed with a person of the same sex, which seldom happens, you should maintain a strict and vigilant modesty. . . .

When you have awakened and had sufficient time to rest, you should get out of bed with fitting modesty and never stay in bed holding conversations or concerning yourself with other matters . . . nothing more clearly indicates indolence and frivolity; the bed is intended for bodily rest and for nothing else.

■ ■ ■

STUDY QUESTIONS

1. How have table manners changed over the centuries? Has there been any trend to the change? If so, what?

2. In blowing one's nose, what practices that were once considered acceptable would now be considered in poor taste?

3. How have standards of modesty changed over the centuries?

4. Social historians often study behavioral change over time. The changes in attitudes, manners, and habits indicate important social and cultural changes. How would you explain the changes in table manners, modesty, and blowing one's nose?

5. How does the attitude toward the body change over the centuries?

6. What examples can you find of a growing concern for restraint in public?

7. What century seems to mark the broadest changes in expectations for public behavior?

8. How do we separate "public" and "private" behavior today? What sanctions encourage conformity?

BIBLIOGRAPHY

The pioneering works in the study of manners are two studies by Norbert Elias: *The Civilizing Process* (volume I, *The History of Manners,* translated 1979, and volume II, *Power and Civility,* translated 1982); and *The Court Society* (translated 1983). Change in manners and behavior are also examined in Emmanuel Le Roy Ladurie, *Montaillou: The Promised Land of Error* (translated 1978); Witold Rybczynski, *Home: A Short History of an Idea* (1986); and Philippe Aries, *Centuries of Childhood* (1962). For issues about women and the family for the period see E. Power, *Medieval Women* (1976), and D. Herlihy, *Medieval Households* (1985). A good overview of medieval society is C. M. Cipolla, *Before the Industrial Revolution: European Society and Economy, 1000–1700* (1980).

Part Five

DEATH, SCHISM AND UNREST: LATE MEDIEVAL EUROPE, 1350–1500

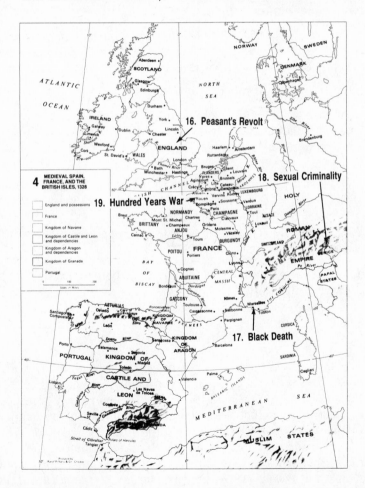

In the late fourteenth century a new dance became popular. Labeled the *Danse Macabre*—which loosely translates to the dance of the corpses—it probably developed during one of the recurring outbreaks of the plague, and street performers employed it to illustrate that death curried no favor. Rich and poor, high born and low—all were equal in the democratic kingdom of the dead. In murals, such as the one at the Church of the Innocents in Paris, the *Danse Macabre* is represented by healthy people dancing with decaying corpses and skeletons. In the same murals the dead dance with popes and kings, peasants and children, men and women. "Advance, see yourself in us," the skeletons say, "dead, naked, rotten and stinking. So will you be. . . . To live without thinking of this risks damnation. . . . Power, honor, riches are naught; at the hour of death only good works count." Stories about death fascinated society. As one historian notes, "Emphasis was on worms and putrefaction and gruesome physical details. Where formerly the dominant idea of death was the spiritual journey of the soul, now the rotting of the body seemed more significant. Effigies of earlier centuries were serene, with hands joined in prayer and eyes open, anticipating eternal life. Now . . . great prelates often had themselves shown as cadavers in realistic detail." The reality and the idea of death consumed many. Philosophers kept skulls on their desks. Artists showed a new interest in depicting the dead. The curious wandered through cemeteries and followed the endless funeral processions—until their turn arrived to entertain others.

This morbid fascination with death seemed natural by the end of the fourteenth century, for everywhere were signs of death, decay, suffering, and trouble. The end appeared so near. Like the victims of the plague, the Middle Ages was dying with halting, gasping, painful breaths. Strife ruled the land. Alienation followed strife and caused some people to turn to violence against their neighbors. As Guido Ruggiero shows, that violence was most often turned against women because they were less able to defend themselves. For many it seemed as if the Book of Revelation were coming true: that upon a pale horse sat Death and with him came war, famine, and disease. If priests dwelled upon the Four Horsemen and artists the *Danse Macabre*, they did so with good reason. Western Europe was enduring countless tribulations: Famine was real enough; so were disease, war, and religious and social turmoil.

Famine struck first. During the twelfth and thirteenth centuries, the population of Western Europe had gradually swelled, and an increased amount of land had been put under the plow. Then in the early fourteenth century bad weather and famine disrupted agrarian life. Rain washed away crops. Poor harvests left people undernourished. Many were weak, hungry, and sick. Some died as a result of a typhoid epidemic in 1316. But a far bigger killer hit Western Europe in 1347. Called the Black Death, it was a particularly virulent strain of the bubonic plague. The bacillus *Pasteurella pestis* lived in the stomachs of fleas, who in turn lived on rodents, especially the black rat. The bacillus came from Asia, but once in Europe it spread rapidly. The people bit by the infected fleas developed apple-size *buboes* on their necks, groins, or armpits. Black blotches appeared on their skin. The victims vomited blood, then within days they died. Physicians were dumb in the face of the disease. Crowded cities and abysmal health standards aided the spread of the disease. People in the cities suffered the most, but country dwellers did not escape the Black Death, as Barbara Tuchman notes in her selection. Perhaps one-third of the population of Western Europe died.

Governments were as useless to conquer the disease as the physicians. In fact, the leaders of the major countries were embroiled in political and religious conflicts. England and France were locked in the Hundred Years' War (1337–1453). It started over a dispute as to who should wear the French crown, but deep-seated economic and feudal conflicts also contributed to the outbreak of the war, as Anthony Tuck notes in his reading. Both countries suffered horribly. During the years of the Black Death, neither country could afford an additional population loss, but especially in France the fighting killed thousands of soldiers and civilians. Furthermore, the war disrupted the economies of both nations, and this was felt at all levels of society. Occasionally wartime frustrations created more violence and suffering. In 1358 the French peasantry, angered by the taxes that it had to pay in support of the Hundred Years' War, mounted a massive uprising. In Picardy and Champagne, peasants looted and burned castles, killed nobles and raped their wives and daughters, and terrorized the countryside. Called the *Jacquerie*, the peasants were often joined by equally frustrated townspeople—merchants, a few priests, artisans. The nobility violently defeated the ragtag peasant armies, but during the late fourteenth and early fifteenth centuries other peasant uprisings occurred. Most were in France, but the most serious revolt was the 1381 uprising in England, described by the chronicler in R. B. Dobson's account. Other factors contributed to the revolts, but in almost every case discontent over the war played at least some role in the outbreaks. It should be remembered, however, that the periodic peasant revolts also occurred in other parts of Western Europe.

Religious instability added to the general malaise. As a result of a complicated set of political circumstances, between 1309 and 1377 the popes lived in Avignon, a city in southeastern France. This blatant ascension of the political over the religious weakened the authority of the Church. When Pope Gregory XI returned the papal court to Rome, the troubles did not end. A new pope, Urban VI, so divided the religious establishment that a group of cardinals left

Rome and elected another pope, Clement VII. Now there were two popes—one in Rome and the other in Avignon. This Great Schism also undermined the authority of the Church or churches. Although in 1417 Martin V was chosen as the single pope, and he resided in Rome, the legacy of the Babylonian Captivity of the Papacy at Avignon and the Great Schism helped lead to the Reformation. On a more practical level, for over 100 years—during the years of the Black Death and the peasant revolts—the Church was something less than a stable religious institution. With all its talk of popes and antipopes, Christ and antichrists, the Church contributed to the notion that the world was close to the end.

16. THE PEASANT REVOLT OF 1381

R. B. Dobson

The fourteenth century was particularly traumatic for Europe. At the beginning of the century, land shortages bred discontent and increasingly poor harvests created the specter of hunger for millions of peasants. The specter became reality in 1315, when heavy rains throughout Europe ruined harvests and created an unprecedented famine. During the first half of the century, famine returned again and again to Western Europe. Those famines were followed by even greater suffering when the bubonic plague wiped out a third of the European population in the 1340s and 1350s. Like the famines of the early 1300s, the Black Death returned periodically to different regions of Europe in the last half of the fourteenth century. Europe entered a long period of population decline. Declining population created labor shortages, which altered traditional relationships between landlords and peasants. Landlords wanted to maintain the status quo, particularly their own incomes, whereas peasants wanted to enjoy the benefits of rising wages and the increasing availability of land. When landlords tried to maintain their own positions by raising taxes and rents and invoking discriminatory regulations to keep peasants servile, the lower classes grew restless and resentful. Major peasant uprisings occurred in Flanders (1323–1328), France (1358), Florence (1378), England (1381), Bohemia and Scandinavia (early 1400s), Italy (1420 and 1460), Spain (1462–1486), and Germany in the late 1400s and early 1500s.

The following document provides a contemporary account of the peasant rebellion that erupted in England in 1381. The fourteenth-century chronicler who described the rebellion was aware of the significance of the events that were taking place throughout England. Although historians do not know the name of the chronicler, they suspect he was an eyewitness to the events, probably as a member of the king's entourage.

On this same Wednesday and before the hour of Vespers, the commons of Kent, to the number of sixty thousand, arrived in Southwark where the Marshalsea was. They broke up and cast to the ground all the houses of the Marshalsea and removed all the prisoners imprisoned there for debt or felony. They then beat to the ground a fine place belonging to John de Imworth, then Marshal of the Marshalsea of the King's Bench and warden of the prisoners therein. All the houses of the jurors and professional informers (*questmongers*) belonging to the Marshalsea were also thrown to the ground during that night. At the same time the commons of Essex came to Lambeth, near London, a manor of the archbishop of Canterbury, entered into its buildings, destroyed a great number of the archbishop's goods and burnt all the register books and chancery remembrancers' rolls they found there.

On the next day, Thursday 13 June, which was the feast of Corpus Christi with the Dominical Letter F, the said commons of Essex went in the morning to Highbury, two leagues north of London and a very fine manor of the Master of the Hospital of St John of Clerkenwell. They set it on fire to the great damage and loss of the Hospitallers of St John. Some of these commons returned to London, but others stayed out in the open fields all night.

And on this same day of Corpus Christi, in the morning, the commons of Kent broke down a brothel (*une measone destwes*) near London Bridge, occupied by Flemish women who had farmed it from the mayor of London. And then they went on to the bridge so as to cross towards the city, but the mayor was ready before them and had the chain drawn up and the bridge lifted to prevent their passage. And the commons of Southwark rose with the others

and cried to the keepers of the said bridge to lower it and let them enter, or otherwise they would be undone. And for fear of their lives, the keepers let them enter, greatly against their will. At this time all the religious as well as the parsons and vicars devoutly went in procession to pray to God for peace.

At this same time the said commons took their way through London, doing no harm or injury until they came to Fleet Street. Meanwhile, so it was said, the commons of London had set fire to and burnt the fine manor of the Savoy, before the commons of the country arrived. In Fleet Street, the said commons of Kent broke open the Fleet prison, removed all the prisoners and let them go where they would. Then they stopped and cast to the ground and burnt a shop belonging to a chandler and another belonging to a marshal which stood in the middle of the said street. Men now suppose that there will never be another house there—to the destruction of the beauty of that street. Afterwards they went to the Temple to destroy the tenants of the said Temple; and they threw the houses to the ground and cast down the tiles so that the houses were left roofless and in a poor state. They also went into the church, seized all the books, rolls and remembrances kept in the cupboards of the apprentices of the law within the Temple, carried them into the high road and burnt them there.

And on their way to the Savoy they destroyed all the houses which belonged to the Master of the Hospital of St John. And then they went to the place of the bishop of Chester, near the church of St Mary-le-Strand, where lord John Fordham, bishop-elect of Durham and clerk of the Privy Seal, was staying; they rolled tuns of wine out of his cellar, drank their fill, and departed without doing further damage. Then they went towards the Savoy, and set fire to several houses belonging to various questmongers and others on the western side of the city; and at last they came before the Savoy, broke open the gates, entered the place

From *The Peasants' Revolt of 1381*, 2/E by R. B. Dobson. Reprinted by permission of Macmillan Publishers, Ltd., London and Basingstoke.

and came to the wardrobe. They took all the torches they could find, and lighted them, and burnt all the cloths, coverlets and beds, as well as all the very valuable head-boards (of which one, decorated with heraldic shields, was said to be worth a thousand marks). All the napery and other goods they could discover they carried into the hall and set on fire with their torches. They burnt the hall and the chambers as well as all the apartments within the gates of the said palace or manor, which the commons of London had left unguarded. It is said that they found three barrels of gunpowder, and thinking it was gold or silver, they threw them into the fire so that the powder exploded and set the hall in a greater blaze than before, to the great loss and damage of the duke of Lancaster. And the commons of Kent received the blame for this arson, but some said that the Londoners were really guilty of the deed, because of their hatred for the said duke.

Then one party of the rebels went towards Westminster and set on fire a place belonging to John of Butterwick, under-sheriff of Middlesex, and other houses of various people. They broke open Westminster prison, and let out all the prisoners condemned by the law. Afterwards they returned to London by way of Holborn, and in front of St Sepulchre's church they set on fire the houses of Simon Hosteler, and several others, and they broke open Newgate prison, and released all the prisoners, regardless of the reason for which they had been imprisoned. This same Thursday the said commons came to St Martin-le-Grand, and dragged out of the church from the high altar a certain Roger Legett, an important assizer (*cisour*); they took him into the Cheap where his head was cut off. On that same day eighteen persons were beheaded in various places of the town.

At this time a great body of the commons went to the Tower of London to speak with the king. As they could not get a hearing from him, they laid siege to the Tower from the side of St Katherine's, towards the south. Another group of the commons, who were within the city, went to the Hospital of St John, Clerkenwell, and on their way they burnt the place and houses of Roger Legett, questmonger, who had been beheaded in Cheapside, as well as all the rented property and tenements of the Hospital of St John they could find. Afterwards they came to the beautiful priory of the said hospital, and set on fire several fine and pleasant buildings within it—a great and horrible piece of damage to the priory for all time to come. They then returned to London to rest or to do more mischief.

At this time the king was in a turret of the great Tower of London, and saw the manor of the Savoy and the Hospital of Clerkenwell, and the houses of Simon Hosteler near Newgate, and John Butterwick's place, all in flames. He called all the lords about him into a chamber, and asked their counsel as to what should be done in such a crisis. But none of them could or would give him any counsel; and so the young king said that he would order the mayor of the city to command the sheriffs and aldermen to have it cried within their wards that everyone between the age of fifteen and sixty, on pain of life and limb, should go next morning (which was Friday) to Mile End, and meet him there at seven of the bell. He did this in order that all the commons who were stationed around the Tower would be persuaded to abandon the siege, and come to Mile End to see him and hear him, so that those who were in the Tower could leave safely at their will and save themselves as they wished. But it came to nothing, for some of them did not have the good fortune to be saved.

Later that Thursday, the said feast of Corpus Christi, the king, remaining anxiously and sadly in the Tower, climbed on to a little turret facing St Katherine's, where a large number of the commons were lying. He had it proclaimed to them that they should all go peaceably to their homes, and he would pardon them all their different offences. But all cried with one voice that they would not go before they had captured the traitors within the Tower, and obtained charters to free them from all manner of serfdom, and certain other points which they wished to demand. The king benevolently granted their requests and made a clerk write a bill in their presence in these terms: "Richard, king of England and France, gives great thanks to his good commons, for that they have so great a desire to see and maintain their king; and he grants them pardon for all manner of trespasses and misprisions and felonies done up to this hour, and wills and commands that every one should now quickly return to his own home: He wills and commands that everyone should put his grievances in writing, and have them sent to him; and he will provide, with the aid of his loyal lords and his good council, such remedy as shall be profitable both to him and to them, and to the kingdom." He put his signet seal to this document in their presence and then sent the said bill by the hands of two of his knights to the people around St Katherine's. And he caused it to be read to them, the man who read it standing up on an old chair above the others so that all could hear. All this time the king remained in the Tower in great distress of mind. And when the commons had heard the bill, they said that it was nothing but a trifle and mockery. Therefore they returned to London and had it cried around the city that all lawyers, all the men of the Chancery and the Exchequer and everyone who could write a writ or a letter should be beheaded, wherever they could be found. At this time they burnt several more houses within the city. The king himself ascended to a high garret of the Tower to watch the fires; then he came down again, and sent for the lords to have their counsel. But they did not know how to advise him, and were surprisingly abashed.

On the next day, Friday, the commons of the country and the commons of London assembled in fearful strength, to the number of a hundred thousand or more, besides some four score who remained on Tower Hill to watch those who were within the Tower. Some went to Mile End, on the way to Brentwood, to wait for the king's arrival, because of the proclamation that he had made. But others came to Tower Hill, and when the king knew that they were there, he sent them orders by a messenger to join their companions at Mile End, saying that he would come to them very soon. And at this time of the morning he advised the archbishop of Canterbury and the others who were in the Tower, to go down to the little water-gate, and take a boat and save themselves. And the archbishop proceeded to do this; but a wicked woman raised a cry against him, and he had to turn back to the Tower, to his own confusion.

And by seven of the bell the king himself came to Mile End, and with him his mother in a carriage (*whirlicole*), and also the earls of Buckingham, Kent, Warwick and Oxford, as well as Sir Thomas Percy, Sir Robert Knolles, the mayor of London and many knights and squires; and Sir Aubrey de Vere carried the royal sword. And when the king arrived and the commons saw him, they knelt down to him, saying "Welcome our Lord King Richard, if it pleases you, and we will not have any other king but you." And Wat Tyghler, their master and leader, prayed on behalf of the commons that the king would suffer them to take and deal with all the traitors against him and the law. The king granted that they should freely seize all who were traitors and could be proved to be such by process of law. The said Walter and the commons were carrying two banners as well as pennons and pennoncels while they made their petition to the king. And they required that henceforward no man should be a serf nor make homage or any type of service to any lord, but should give four pence for an acre of land. They asked also that no one should serve any man except at his own will and by means of regular covenant. And at this time the king had the commons arrayed in two lines, and had it proclaimed be-

■ ■ *After the mayor of London killed the peasant leader Wat Tyler (Tyghler) during negotiations, the young Richard II managed to calm the angry rebel army at Smithfield.*

fore them that he would confirm and grant that they should be free, and generally should have their will; and that they could go through all the realm of England and catch all traitors and bring them to him in safety, and then he would deal with them as the law demanded.

Because of this grant Wat Tyghler and the commons took their way to the Tower, to seize the archbishop and the others while the king remained at Mile End. Meanwhile the archbishop had sung his mass devoutly in the Tower, and confessed the prior of the Hospital of Clerkenwell and others; and then he heard two or three masses and chanted the *Commendatio*, and the *Placebo* and *Dirige*, and the Seven Psalms, and the Litany; and when he was at the words "Omnes sancti orate pro nobis," the commons entered and dragged him out of the chapel of the Tower, and struck and hustled him roughly, as they did also the others who were with him, and led them to Tower Hill. There they cut off the heads of Master Simon of Sudbury, archbishop of Canterbury, of Sir Robert Hales, High Prior of the Hospital of St John's of Clerkenwell, Treasurer of England, of Brother William of Appleton, a great physician and surgeon, and one who had much influence with the king and the duke of Lancaster. And some time after they beheaded John Legge, the king's serjeant-at-arms, and with him a certain juror. At the same time the commons had it proclaimed that whoever could catch any Fleming or other aliens of any nation, might cut off their heads; and so they did accordingly. Then they took the heads of the archbishop and of the others and put them on wooden poles, and carried them before them in procession through all the city as far as the shrine of Westminster Abbey, to the contempt of themselves, of God and of Holy Church: for which reason vengeance descended on them shortly afterwards. Then they returned to London Bridge and set the head of the archbishop above the gate, with the heads of eight others they had executed, so that all who passed over the bridge could see them. This done, they went to the church of St Martin's in the Vintry, and found therein thirty-five Flemings, whom they dragged outside and beheaded in the street. On that day there were beheaded 140 or 160 persons. Then they took their way to the places of Lombards and other aliens, and broke into their houses, and robbed them of all their goods that they could discover. So it went on for all that day and the night following, with hideous cries and horrible tumult.

At this time, because the Chancellor had been beheaded, the king made the earl of Arundel Chancellor for the day, and entrusted him with the Great Seal; and all that day he caused various clerks to write out charters, patents, and letters of protection, granted to the commons in consequence of the matters before mentioned, without taking any fines for the sealing or transcription.

On the next day, Saturday, great numbers of the commons came into Westminster Abbey at the hour of Tierce, and there they found John Imworth, Marshal of the Marshalsea and warden of the prisoners, a tormentor without pity; he was near the shrine of St Edward, embracing a marble pillar, hoping for aid and succour from the saint to preserve him from his enemies. But the commons wrenched his arms away from the pillar of the shrine, and dragged him into Cheap, and there beheaded him. And at the same time they took from Bread Street a valet named John of Greenfield, merely because he had spoken well of Brother William Appleton and the other murdered persons; and they brought him into Cheap and beheaded him. All this time the king was having it cried through the city that every one should go peaceably to his own country and his own house, without doing more mischief; but to this the commons would not agree.

And on this same day, at three hours after noon, the king came to Westminster Abbey and about 200 persons with him. The abbot and convent of the said abbey, and the canons and vicars of St Stephen's Chapel, came to meet him in procession, clothed in their copes and their feet bare, half-way to Charing Cross; and they brought him to the abbey, and then to the high altar of the church. The king made his prayers devoutly, and left an offering for the altar and the relics. Afterwards he spoke with the anchorite, and confessed to him, and remained with him some time. Then the king caused a proclamation to be made that all the commons of the country who were still within the city should come to Smithfield to meet him there; and so they did.

And when the king with his retinue arrived there, he turned to the east, in a place before St Bartholomew's, a house of canons: and the commons arrayed themselves in bands of great size on the west side. At this moment the mayor of London, William of Walworth, came up, and the king ordered him to approach the commons, and make their chieftain come to him. And when he was called by the mayor, this chieftain, Wat Tyghler of Maidstone by name, approached the king with great confidence, mounted on a little horse so that the commons might see him. And he dismounted, holding in his hand a dagger which he had taken from another man; and when he had dismounted he half bent his knee and took the king by the hand, shaking his arm forcefully and roughly, saying to him, "Brother, be of good comfort and joyful, for you shall have, in the fortnight that is to come, forty thousand more commons than you have at present, and we shall be good companions." And the king said to Walter, "Why will you not go back to your own country?" But the other answered, with a great oath, that neither he nor his fellows would leave until they had got their charter as they wished to have it with the inclusion of certain points which they wished to demand. Tyghler threatened that the lords of the realm would rue it bitterly if these points were not settled at the commons' will. Then the king asked him what were the points which he wished to have considered, and he should have them freely and without contradiction, written out and sealed. Thereupon the said Wat rehearsed the points which were to be demanded; and he asked that there should be no law except for the law of Winchester and that henceforward there should be no outlawry (*ughtelarie*) in any process of law, and that no lord should have lordship in future, but it should be divided among all men, except for the king's own lordship. He also asked that the goods of Holy Church should not remain in the hands of the religious, nor of parsons and vicars, and other churchmen; but that clergy already in possession should have a sufficient sustenance and the rest of their goods should be divided among the people of the parish. And he demanded that there should be only one bishop in England and only one prelate, and all the lands and tenements of the possessioners should be taken from them and divided among the commons, only reserving for them a reasonable sustenance. And he demanded that there should be no more villeins in England, and no serfdom nor villeinage (*ne nulle servage ne nayfte*) but that all men should be free and of one condition. To this the king gave an easy answer, and said that Wat should have all that he could fairly grant, reserving only for

himself the regality of his crown. And then he ordered him to go back to his own home, without causing further delay.

During all the time that the king was speaking, no lord or counselor dared or wished to give answer to the commons in any place except for the king himself. Presently Wat Tyghler, in the presence of the king, sent for a jug of water to rinse his mouth, because of the great heat that he felt; and as soon as the water was brought he rinsed out his mouth in a very rude and villainous manner before the king. And then he made them bring him a jug of ale, and drank a great draught, and then, in the presence of the king, climbed on his horse again. At that time a certain valet from Kent, who was among the king's retinue, asked to see the said Wat, chieftain of the commons. And when he saw him, he said aloud that he was the greatest thief and robber in all Kent. Wat heard these words, and commanded the valet to come out to him, shaking his head at him as a sign of malice; but Wat himself refused to go to him for fear that he had of the others there. But at last the lords made the valet go out to Wat, to see what the latter would do before the king. And when Wat saw him he ordered one of his followers, who was mounted on horseback and carrying a banner displayed, to dismount and behead the said valet. But the valet answered that he had done nothing worthy of death, for what he had said was true, and he would not deny it, although he could not lawfully debate the issue in the presence of his liege lord, without leave, except in his own defence: but that he could do without reproof, for whoever struck him would be struck in return. For these words Wat wanted to strike the valet with his dagger, and would have slain him in the king's presence; but because he tried to do so, the mayor of London, William of Walworth, reasoned with the said Wat for his violent behaviour and contempt, done in the king's presence, and arrested him. And because he arrested him, the said Wat stabbed the mayor with his dagger in the body in great anger. But, as it pleased God, the mayor was wearing armour and took no harm, but like a hardy and vigorous man drew his dagger (*baselarde*) and struck back at the said Wat, giving him a deep cut in the neck, and then a great blow on the head. And during this scuffle a valet of the king's household drew his sword, and ran Wat two or three times through the body, mortally wounding him. Wat spurred his horse, crying to the commons to avenge him, and the horse carried him some four score paces, and then he fell to the ground half dead. And when the commons saw him fall, and did not know for certain how it happened, they began to bend their bows and to shoot. Therefore the king himself spurred his horse, and rode out to them, commanding them that they should all come to him at the field of St John of Clerkenwell.

Meanwhile the mayor of London rode as hastily as he could back to the city, and commanded those who were in charge of the twenty-four wards to have it cried round their wards, that every man should arm himself as quickly as he could, and come to the king's aid in St John's Fields, where the commons were, for he was in great trouble and necessity. But at this time almost all of the knights and squires of the king's household, and many others, were so frightened of the affray that they left their liege lord and went each his own way.

Afterwards, when the king had reached the open fields, he made the commons array themselves on the west side. And presently the aldermen came to him in a body, bringing with them the keepers of the wards arrayed in several bands, a fine company of well-armed men in great strength. And they enveloped the commons like sheep within a pen. Meanwhile, after the mayor had sent the keepers of the town on their way to the king, he returned with a good company of lances to

Smithfield in order to make an end of the captain of the commons. And when he came to Smithfield he failed to find there the said captain Wat Tyghler, at which he marvelled much, and asked what had become of the traitor. And he was told that Wat had been carried by a group of the commons to the hospital for the poor near St Bartholomew's, and put to bed in the chamber of the master of the hospital. The mayor went there and found him, and had him carried out to the middle of Smithfield, in the presence of his companions, and had him beheaded. And so ended his wretched life. But the mayor had his head set on a pole and carried before him to the king, who still remained in the field. And when the king saw the head he had it brought near him to subdue the commons, and thanked the mayor greatly for what he had done. And when the commons saw that their chieftain, Wat Tyghler, was dead in such a manner, they fell to the ground there among the corn, like beaten men, imploring the king for mercy for their misdeeds. And the king benevolently granted them mercy, and most of them took to flight. But the king appointed two knights to lead the other men from Kent through London, and over London Bridge, without doing them harm, so that each of them could go peacefully to his own home. Then the king ordered Mayor Walworth to put a bascinet on his head because of what was to happen, and the mayor asked for what reason he was to do so; and the king told him that he was much beholden to him, and that for this reason he was to receive the order of knighthood. The mayor answered that he was not worthy nor able to have or maintain a knight's estate, for he was only a merchant and had to live by trade; but finally the king made him put on the bascinet, and took a sword in both his hands and strongly dubbed him knight with great good will. The same day he made three other citizens of London knights for the same reason and on that same spot: and these are their names—John Philipot, Nichol Brymber and (blank in the MS.); and the king gave Sir William Walworth £100 in land, and each of the others £40 in land, for them and their heirs.

And after this the king took his way to London to his Wardrobe to ease him of his great toils.

■ ■ ■

STUDY QUESTIONS

1. What appears to have precipitated the outbreak of violence among the peasants?

2. Were the peasants specific in the targets of their violence, or did the uprising assume the dimensions of a general, "shotgun" type of attack?

3. Who were the targets of peasant violence? Why?

4. Why did the peasants eventually move against the church?

5. What type of respect did the peasants show for the nobility, government officials, and the king?

6. After reading this selection, how do you evaluate the sympathies of the chronicler? With which side did he or she sympathize?

BIBLIOGRAPHY

For the background to the peasant rebellion, see James Bellamy, *Crime and Public Order in England in the Later Middle Ages* (1973), and J. O. Bolton, *the Medieval English Economy, 1150–1500* (1980). The best selection of documents concerning the revolt is R. B. Dobson, *The Peasants Revolt of 1381* (second edition, 1983). On the revolt itself, see Rodney Hilton, *Bond Men Made Free. Medieval Peasant Movements and the English Rising of 1381* (1973). Also see Charles Oman, *The Great Revolt of 1381* (1969); R. H. Hilton and H. Fagan, *The English Rising of 1381* (1950); and W. L. Warren, "The Peasants' Revolt of 1381," *History Today*, XII–XIII (1962–1963).

17. THE BLACK DEATH

Barbara W. Tuchman

As the Black Death swept across Western Europe in the late 1340s, chroniclers and social critics noticed a change in people. Abandonment and loss punctuated daily lives. Brothers abandoned brothers, parents abandoned children, husbands abandoned wives; and as close friends and relatives died horrible, painful deaths, people found themselves drained of sympathy and hope. A chronicler from Siena wrote, "And no bells tolled and nobody wept no matter what his loss because almost everyone expected death. . . . And people said and believed 'This is the end of the world.'"

The Black Death reached Western Europe in October 1347 when a Genoese fleet moored in the Messina harbor in northeast Sicily. The crew had "sickness clinging to their very bones." Many had died and others were dying from some strange disease contracted in the Orient. The dying crew could be and was quarantined, but death in the form of diseased rats and fleas scurried ashore on the ropes that secured the ships to the docks. Within six months half of the population of Messina was dead or had fled the city. From Messina the Black Death spread—north, south, east, and west. It spread to the great cities of fourteenth-century Europe: to Paris, Florence, Venice, and Genoa. It ravaged the countryside, claiming victims from all classes and all ages, though the poor and the young suffered a bit more. And before it had run its course the population had been reduced by perhaps one-third. Although there are no accurate figures, it seems clear that at least 20 million people died from the Black Death. Such devastation ranks the Black Death as one of the three worst catastrophes in the history of the world.

Plagues were not new to Europe in the fourteenth century. In 541 Justinian's plague killed millions of people. Like the Black Death, it was a form of the bubonic plague caused by the bacterial strain *Yersinia pestis*, which lives in the digestive tracts of fleas, particularly the rat fleas *Xenopsylla cheopis* and *Cortophylus fasciatus*. The Black Death, however, was even more severe than Justinian's plague because it was present in pneumonic and septicemic as well as bubonic forms. In this selection, Barbara W. Tuchman describes the impact of the plague on Europe. As she demonstrates, the Black Death touched society at every level.

In October 1347, two months after the fall of Calais, Genoese trading ships put into the harbor of Messina in Sicily with dead and dying men at the oars. The ships had come from the Black Sea port of Caffa (now Feodosiya) in the Crimea, where the Genoese maintained a trading post. The diseased sailors showed strange black swellings about the size of an egg or an apple in the armpits and groin. The swellings oozed blood and pus and were followed by spreading boils and black blotches on the skin from internal bleeding. The sick suffered severe pain and died quickly within five days of the first symptoms. As the disease spread, other symptoms of continuous fever and spitting of blood appeared instead of the swellings or buboes. These victims coughed and sweated heavily and died even more quickly, within three days or less, sometimes in 24 hours. In both types everything that issued from the body—breath, sweat, blood from the buboes and lungs, bloody urine, and blood-blackened excrement—smelled foul. Depression and despair accompanied the physical symptoms, and before the end "death is seen seated on the face."

The disease was bubonic plague, present in two forms: one that infected the bloodstream, causing the buboes and internal bleeding, and was spread by contact; and a second, more virulent pneumonic type that infected the lungs and was spread by respiratory infection. The presence of both at once cause the high mortality and speed of contagion. So lethal was the disease that cases were known of persons going to bed well and dying before they woke, of doctors catching the illness at a bedside and dying before the patient. So rapidly did it spread from one to another that to a French physician, Simon de Covino, it seemed as if one sick person "could infect the whole world." The malignity of the pestilence appeared more terrible because its victims knew no prevention and no remedy.

The physical suffering of the disease and its aspect of evil mystery were expressed in a strange Welsh lament which saw "death coming into our midst like black smoke, a plague which cuts off the young, a rootless phantom which has no mercy for fair countenance. Woe is me of the shilling in the armpit! It is seething, terrible . . . a head that gives pain and causes a loud cry . . . a painful angry knob . . . Great is its seething like a burning cinder . . . a grievous thing of ashy color." Its eruption is ugly like the "seeds of black peas, broken fragments of brittle sea-coal . . . the early ornaments of black death, cinders of the peelings of the cockle weed, a mixed multitude, a black plague like halfpence, like berries. . . ."

Rumors of a terrible plague supposedly arising in China and spreading through Tartary (Central Asia) to India and Persia, Mesopotamia, Syria, Egypt, and all of Asia Minor had reached Europe in 1346. They told of a death toll so devastating that all of India was said to be depopulated, whole territories covered by dead bodies, other areas with no one left alive. As added up by Pope Clement VI at Avignon, the total of reported dead reached 23,840,000. In the absence of a concept of contagion, no serious alarm was felt in Europe until the trading ships brought their black burden of pestilence into Messina while other infected ships from the Levant carried it to Genoa and Venice.

By January 1348 it penetrated France via Marseille, and North Africa via Tunis. Shipborne along coasts and navigable rivers, it spread westward from Marseille through the ports of Languedoc to Spain and northward up the Rhône to Avignon, where it arrived in March. It reached Narbonne, Montpellier, Carcassonne, and Toulouse between February and May, and at the same time in Italy spread to Rome and Florence and their hinterlands. Between June and August it reached Bordeaux, Lyon, and Paris, spread to Burgundy and Normandy, and crossed the Channel from Normandy into southern England. From Italy during the same summer it crossed the Alps into Switzerland and reached eastward to Hungary.

In a given area the plague accomplished its kill within four to six months and then faded, except in the larger cities, where, rooting into the close-quartered population, it abated during the winter, only to reappear in spring and rage for another six months.

In 1349 it resumed in Paris, spread to Picardy, Flanders, and the Low Countries, and from England to Scotland and Ireland as well as to Norway, where a ghost ship with a cargo of wool and a dead crew drifted offshore until it ran aground near Bergen. From there the plague passed into Sweden, Denmark, Prussia, Iceland, and as far as Greenland. Leaving a strange pocket of immunity in Bohemia, and Russia unattacked until 1351, it had passed from most of Europe by mid-1350. Although the mortality rate was erratic, ranging from one fifth in some places to nine tenths or almost total elimination in others, the overall estimate of modern demographers has settled—for the area extending from India to Iceland—around the same figure expressed in Froissart's casual words: "a third of the world died." His estimate, the common one at the time, was not an inspired guess but a borrowing of St. John's figure for mortality from plague in Revelation, the favorite guide to human affairs of the Middle Ages.

A third of Europe would have meant about 20 million deaths. No one knows in truth how many died. Contemporary reports were an awed impression, not an accurate count. In crowded Avignon, it was said, 400 died daily; 7000 houses emptied by death were shut up; a single graveyard received 11,000 corpses in six weeks; half the city's inhabitants reportedly died, including 9 cardinals or one third of the total, and 70 lesser prelates. Watching the endlessly passing death carts, chroniclers let normal exaggeration take wings and put the Avignon death toll at 62,000 and even at 120,000, although the city's total population was probably less than 50,000.

When graveyards filled up, bodies at Avignon were thrown into the Rhône until mass burial pits were dug for dumping the corpses. In London in such pits corpses piled up in layers until they overflowed. Everywhere reports speak of the sick dying too fast for the living to bury. Corpses were dragged out of homes and left in front of doorways. Morning light revealed new piles of bodies. In Florence the dead were gathered up by the Compagnia della Misericordia—founded in 1244 to care for the sick—whose members wore red robes and hoods masking the face except for the eyes. When their efforts failed, the dead lay putrid in the streets for days at a time. When no coffins were to be had, the bodies were laid on boards, two or three at once, to be carried to graveyards or common pits. Families dumped their own relatives into the pits, or buried them so hastily and thinly "that dogs dragged them forth and devoured their bodies."

Amid accumulating death and fear of contagion, people died without last rites and were buried without prayers, a prospect that terrified the last hours of the stricken. A bishop in England gave permission to laymen to make confession to each other as was done by the Apostles, "or if no man is present then even to a woman," and if no priest could be found to administer extreme unction, "then faith must suffice." Clement VI found it necessary to grant remissions of sin to all who died of the plague because so many were unattended by priests. "And no bells tolled," wrote a chronicler of Siena, "and nobody wept no matter what his loss because almost everyone expected death. . . . And people said and believed, 'This is the end of the world.' "

In Paris, where the plague lasted through 1349, the reported death rate was 800 a day, in Pisa 500, in Vienna 500 to 600. The total dead in Paris numbered 50,000 or half the population. Florence, weakened by the famine of 1347, lost three to four fifths of its citizens, Venice two thirds, Hamburg and Bremen, though smaller in size, about the same proportion. Cities, as centers of transportation, were more likely to be affected than villages, although once a village was infected, its death rate was equally high. At Givry, a prosperous village in Burgundy of 1200 to 1500 people, the parish register records 615 deaths in the space of fourteen weeks, compared to an average of thirty deaths a year in the previous decade. In three villages of Cambridgeshire, manorial records show a death rate of 47 percent, 57 percent, and in one case 70 percent. When the last survivors, too few to carry on, moved away, a deserted village sank back into the wilderness and disappeared from the map altogether, leaving only a grass-covered ghostly outline to show where mortals once had lived.

In enclosed places such as monasteries and prisons, the infection of one person usually meant that of all, as happened in the Franciscan convents of Carcassonne and Marseille, where every inmate without exception died. Of the 140 Dominicans at Montpellier only seven survived. Petrarch's brother Gherardo, member of a Carthusian monastery, buried the prior and 34 fellow monks one by one, sometimes three a day, until he was left alone with his dog and fled to look for a place that would take him in. Watching every comrade die, men in such places could not but wonder whether the strange peril that filled the air had not been sent to exterminate the human race. In Kilkenny, Ireland, Brother John Clyn of the Friars Minor, another monk left along among dead men, kept a record of what had happened lest "things which should be remembered perish with time and vanish from the memory of those who come after us." Sensing "the whole world, as it were, placed within the grasp of the Evil One," and waiting for death to visit him too, he wrote, "I leave parchment to continue this work, if perchance any man survive and any of the race of Adam escape this pestilence and carry on the work which I have begun." Brother John, as noted by another hand, died of the pestilence, but he foiled oblivion.

The largest cities of Europe, with populations of about 100,000, were Paris and Florence, Venice and Genoa. At the next level, with more than 50,000, were Ghent and Bruges in Flanders, Milan, Bologna, Rome, Naples, and Palermo, and Cologne. London hovered below 50,000, the only city in England except York with more than 10,000. At the level of 20,000 to 50,000 were Bordeaux, Toulouse, Montpellier, Marseille, and Lyon in France; Barcelona, Seville, and Toledo in Spain; Siena, Pisa, and other secondary cities in Italy; and the Hanseatic trading cities of the Empire. The plague raged through them all, killing anywhere from one third to two thirds of their inhabitants. Italy, with a total population of 10 to 11 million, probably suffered the heaviest toll. Following the Florentine bankruptcies, the crop failures and workers' riots of 1346–47, the revolt of Cola di Rienzi that plunged Rome into anarchy, the plague came as the peak of successive calamities. As if the world were indeed in the grasp of the Evil One, its first appearance on the European mainland in January 1348 coincided with a fearsome earthquake that carved a path of wreckage from Naples up to Venice. Houses collapsed, church towers toppled, villages were crushed, and the destruction reached as far as Germany and Greece. Emotional response, dulled by horrors, underwent a kind of atrophy epitomized by the chronicler who wrote, "And in these days was burying without sorrowe and wedding without friendschippe."

In Siena, where more than half the inhabitants died of the plague, work was abandoned on the great cathedral, planned to be the largest in the world, and never resumed, owing to loss of workers and master masons and "the melancholy and grief" of the survivors. The cathedral's truncated transept still stands in permanent witness to the sweep of death's scythe. Agnolo di Tura, a chronicler of Siena, recorded the fear of contagion that froze every other instinct. "Father abandoned child, wife husband, one brother another," he wrote, "for this plague seemed to strike through the breath and sight. And so they died. And no one could be found to bury the dead for money or friendship. . . . And I, Angolo di Tura, called the Fat, buried my five children with my own hands, and so did many others likewise."

There were many to echo his account of inhumanity and few to balance it, for the plague was not the kind of calamity that inspired mutual help. Its loathsomeness and deadliness did not herd people together in mutual distress, but only prompted their desire to escape each other. "Magistrates and notaries refused to come and make the wills of the dying," reported a Franciscan friar of Piazza in Sicily; what was worse, "even the priests did not come to hear their confessions." A clerk of the Archbishop of Canterbury reported the same of English priests who "turned away from the care of their benefices from fear of death." Cases of parents deserting children and children their parents were reported across Europe from Scotland to Russia. The calamity chilled the hearts of men, wrote Boccaccio in his famous account of the plague in Florence that serves as introduction to the *Decameron*. "One man shunned another . . . kinsfolk held aloof, brother was forsaken by brother, oftentimes husband by wife; nay, what is more, and scarcely to be believed, fathers and mothers were found to abandon their own children to their fate, untended, unvisited as if they had been strangers." Exaggeration and literary pessimism were common in the fourteenth century, but the Pope's physician, Guy de Chauliac, was a sober, careful observer who

reported the same phenomenon: "A father did not visit his son, nor the son his father. Charity was dead."

Yet not entirely. In Paris, according to the chronicler Jean de Venette, the nuns of the Hôtel Dieu or municipal hospital, "having no fear of death, tended the sick with all sweetness and humility." New nuns repeatedly took the places of those who died, until the majority "many times renewed by death now rest in peace with Christ as we may piously believe."

When the plague entered northern France in July 1348, it settled first in Normandy and, checked by winter, gave Picardy a deceptive interim until the next summer. Either in mourning or warning, black flags were flown from church towers of the worst-stricken villages of Normandy. "And in that time," wrote a monk of the abbey of Fourcarment, "the mortality was so great among the people of Normandy that those of Picardy mocked them." The same unneighborly reaction was reported of the Scots, separated by a winter's immunity from the English. Delighted to hear of the disease that was scourging the "southrons," they gathered forces for an invasion, "laughing at their enemies." Before they could move, the savage mortality fell upon them too, scattering some in death and the rest in panic to spread the infection as they fled. . . .

Flight was the chief recourse of those who could afford it or arrange it. The rich fled to their country places like Boccaccio's young patricians of Florence, who settled in a pastoral palace "removed on every side from the roads" with "wells of cool water and vaults of rare wines." The urban poor died in their burrows, "and only the stench of their bodies informed neighbors of their death." That the poor were more heavily afflicted than the rich was clearly remarked at the time, in the north as in the south. A Scottish chronicler, John of Fordun, stated flatly that the pest "attacked especially the meaner sort and common people—seldom the magnates." Simon de

Covino of Montpellier made the same observation. He ascribed it to the misery and want and hard lives that made the poor more susceptible, which was half the truth. Close contact and lack of sanitation was the unrecognized other half. It was noticed too that the young died in greater proportion than the old; Simon de Covino compared the disappearance of youth to the withering of flowers in the fields.

In the countryside peasants dropped dead on the roads, in the fields, in their houses. Survivors in growing helplessness fell into apathy, leaving ripe wheat uncut and livestock untended. Oxen and asses, sheep and goats, pigs and chickens ran wild and they too, according to local reports, succumbed to the pest. English sheep, bearers of the precious wool, died throughout the country. The chronicler Henry Knighton, canon of Leicester Abbey, reported 5000 dead in one field alone, "their bodies so corrupted by the plague that neither beast nor bird would touch them," and spreading an appalling stench. In the Austrian Alps wolves came down to prey upon sheep and then, "as if alarmed by some invisible warning, turned and fled back into the wilderness." In remote Dalmatia bolder wolves descended upon a plague-stricken city and attacked human survivors. For want of herdsmen, cattle strayed from place to place and died in hedgerows and ditches. Dogs and cats fell like the rest.

The dearth of labor held a fearful prospect because the fourteenth century lived close to the annual harvest both for food and for next year's seed. "So few servants and laborers were left," wrote Knighton, "that no one knew where to turn for help." The sense of a vanishing future created a kind of dementia of despair. A Bavarian chronicler of Neuberg on the Danube recorded that "Men and women . . . wandered around as if mad" and let their cattle stray "because no one had any inclination to concern themselves about the future." Fields went uncultivated, spring seed unsown. Second growth with nature's awful energy crept back over cleared land, dikes crumbled, salt water reinvaded and soured the lowlands. With so few hands remaining to restore the work of centuries, people felt, in Walsingham's words, that "the world could never again regain its former prosperity."

Though the death rate was higher among the anonymous poor, the known and the great died too. King Alfonso XI of Castile was the only reigning monarch killed by the pest, but his neighbor King Pedro of Aragon lost his wife, Queen Leonora, his daughter Marie, and a niece in the space of six months. John Cantacuzene, Emperor of Byzantium, lost his son. In France the lame Queen Jeanne and her daughter-in-law Bonne de Luxemburg, wife of the Dauphin, both died in 1349 in the same phase that took the life of Enguerrand's mother. Jeanne, Queen of Navarre, daughter of Louis X, was another victim. Edward III's second daughter, Joanna, who was on her way to marry Pedro, the heir of Castile, died in Bordeaux. Women appear to have been more vulnerable than men, perhaps because being more housebound, they were more exposed to fleas. Boccaccio's mistress Fiammetta, illegitimate daughter of the King of Naples, died, as did Laura, the beloved—whether real or fictional—of Petrarch. Reaching out to us in the future, Petrarch cried, "Oh happy posterity who will not experience such abysmal woe and will look upon our testimony as a fable."

In Florence Giovanni Villani, the great historian of his time, died at 68 in the midst of an unfinished sentence: " . . . *e dure questo pistolenza fino a* . . . (in the midst of this pestilence there came to an end. . .)." Siena's master painters, the brothers Ambrogio and Pietro Lorenzetti, whose names never appear after 1348, presumably perished in the plague, as did Andrea Pisano, architect and sculptor of Florence. William of Ockham and the English mystic Richard Rolle of Hampole both disappear from mention after 1349. Francisco Datini, merchant of Prato, lost both his parents and two siblings. Curious sweeps of mortality afflicted certain bodies of merchants in London. All eight wardens of the Company of Cutters, all six wardens of the Hatters, and four wardens of the Goldsmiths died before July 1350. Sir John Pulteney, master draper and four times Mayor of London, was a victim, likewise Sir John Montgomery, Governor of Calais.

Among the clergy and doctors the mortality was naturally high because of the nature of their professions. Out of 24 physicians in Venice, 20 were said to have lost their lives in the plague, although, according to another account, some were believed to have fled or to have shut themselves up in their houses. At Montpellier, site of the leading medieval medical school, the physician Simon de Covino reported that, despite the great number of doctors, "hardly one of them escaped." In Avignon, Guy de Chauliac confessed that he performed his medical visits only because he dared not stay away for fear of infamy, but "I was in continual fear." He claimed to have contracted the disease but to have cured himself by his own treatment; if so, he was one of the few who recovered.

Clerical mortality varied with rank. Although the one-third toll of cardinals reflects the same proportion as the whole, this was probably due to their concentration in Avignon. In England, in strange and almost sinister procession, the Archbishop of Canterbury, John Stratford, died in August 1348, his appointed successor died in May 1349, and the next appointee three months later, all three within a year. Despite such weird vagaries, prelates in general managed to sustain a higher survival rate than the lesser clergy. Among bishops the deaths have been estimated at about one in twenty. The loss of priests, even if many avoided their fearful duty of attending the dying, was about the same as among the population as a whole.

Government officials, whose loss contributed to the general chaos, found, on the whole, no special shelter. In Siena four of the nine members of the governing oligarchy died, in France one-third of the royal notaries, in Bristol 15 out of the 52 members of the Town Council or almost one third. Tax-collecting obviously suffered, with the result that Philip VI was unable to collect more than a fraction of the subsidy granted him by the Estates in the winter of 1347–48.

Lawlessness and debauchery accompanied the plague as they had during the great plague of Athens of 430 B.C., when according to Thucydides, men grew bold in the indulgence of pleasure: "For seeing how the rich died in a moment and those who had nothing immediately inherited their property, they reflected that life and riches were alike transitory and they resolved to enjoy themselves while they could." Human behavior is timeless. When St. John had his vision of plague in Revelation, he knew from some experience or race memory that those who survived "repented not of the work of their hands. . . . Neither repented they of their murders, nor of their sorceries, nor of their fornication, nor of their thefts."

■ ■ ■

Ignorance of the cause augmented the sense of horror. Of the real carriers, rats and fleas, the fourteenth century had no suspicion, perhaps because they were so familiar. Fleas, though a common household nuisance, are not once mentioned in contemporary plague writings, and rats only incidentally, although folklore commonly associated them with pestilence. The legend of the Pied Piper arose from an outbreak of 1284. The actual plague bacillus, *Pasteurella pestis,* remained undiscovered for another 500 years. Living alternately in the stomach of the flea and the bloodstream of the rat who was the flea's host, the bacillus in its bubonic form was transferred to humans and animals by the bite of either rat or flea. It traveled by virtue of *Rattus rattus,* the small medieval black rat that lived on ships, as well as by the heavier brown or sewer rat. What precipitated the turn of the bacillus from innocuous to virulent form is unknown, but the occurrence is now believed to have taken place not in China but somewhere in central Asia and to have spread along the caravan routes. Chinese origin was a mistaken notion of the fourteenth century based on real but belated reports of huge death tolls in China from drought, famine, and pestilence that have since been traced to the 1330s, too soon to be responsible for the plague that appeared in India in 1346.

The phantom enemy had no name. Called the Black Death only in later recurrences, it was known during the first epidemic simply as the Pestilence or Great Mortality. Reports from the East, swollen by fearful imaginings, told of strange tempests and "sheets of fire" mingled with huge hailstones that "slew almost all," or a "vast rain of fire" that burned up men, beasts, stones, trees, villages, and cities. In another version, "foul blasts of wind" from the fires carried the infection to Europe "and now as some suspect it cometh round the seacoast." Accurate observation in this case could not make the mental jump to ships and rats because no idea of animal- or insect-borne contagion existed.

The earthquake was blamed for releasing sulfurous and foul fumes from the earth's interior, or as evidence of a titanic struggle of planets and oceans causing waters to rise and vaporize until fish died in masses and corrupted the air. All these explanations had in common a factor of poisoned air, of miasmas and thick, stinking mists traced to every kind of natural or imagined agency from stagnant lakes to malign conjunction of the planets, from the hand of the Evil One to the wrath of God. Medical thinking, trapped in the theory of astral influences, stressed air as the communicator of disease, ignoring sanitation or visible carriers. The existence of two carriers confused the trail, the more so because the flea could live and travel independently of the rat for as long as a month and, if infected by the particularly virulent septicemic form of the bacillus, could infect humans without reinfecting itself from the rat. The simultaneous presence of the pneumonic form of the disease, which was indeed communicated through the air, blurred the problem further.

The mystery of the contagion was "the most terrible of all the terrors," as an anonymous Flemish cleric in Avignon wrote to a correspondent in Bruges. Plagues had been known before, from the plague of Athens (believed to have been typhus) to the prolonged epidemic of the sixth century A.D., to the recurrence of sporadic outbreaks in the twelfth and thirteenth centuries, but they had left no accumulated store of understanding. That the infection came from contact with the sick or with their houses, clothes, or corpses was quickly observed but not comprehended. Gentile da Foligno, renowned physician of Perugia and doctor of medicine at the universities of Bologna and Padua, came close to respiratory infection when he surmised that poisonous material was "communicated by means of air breathed out and in." Having no idea of microscopic carriers, he had to assume that the air was corrupted by planetary influences. Planets, however, could not explain the ongoing contagion. The agonized search for an answer gave rise to such theories as transference by sight. People fell ill, wrote Guy de Chauliac, not only by remaining with the sick but "even by looking at them." Three hundred years later Joshua Barnes, the seventeenth-century biographer of Edward III, could write that the power of infection had entered into beams of light and "darted death from the eyes."

Doctors struggling with the evidence could not break away from the terms of astrology, to which they believed all human physiology was subject. Medicine was the one aspect of medieval life, perhaps because of its links with the Arabs, not shaped by Christian doctrine. Clerics detested astrology, but could not dislodge its influence. Guy de Chauliac, physician to three popes in succession, practiced in obe-

■ ■ *The massive mortality caused by the Black Death traumatized European society and created a morbid fascination with death.*

dience to the zodiac. While his *Cirurgia* was the major treatise on surgery of its time, while he understood the use of anesthesia made from the juice of opium, mandrake, or hemlock, he nevertheless prescribed bleeding and purgatives by the planets and divided chronic from acute diseases on the basis of one being under the rule of the sun and the other of the moon.

In October 1348 Philip VI asked the medical faculty of the University of Paris for a report on the affliction that seemed to threaten human survival. With careful thesis, antithesis, and proofs, the doctors ascribed it to a triple conjunction of Saturn, Jupiter, and Mars in the 40th degree of Aquarius said to have oc-

curred on March 20, 1345. They acknowledged, however, effects "whose cause is hidden from even the most highly trained intellects." The verdict of the masters of Paris became the official version. Borrowed, copied by scribes, carried abroad, translated from Latin into various vernaculars, it was everywhere accepted, even by the Arab physicians of Cordova and Granada, as the scientific if not the popular answer. Because of the terrible interest of the subject, the translations of the plague tracts stimulated use of national languages. In that one respect, life came from death.

■ ■ ■

To the people at large there could be but one explanation—the wrath of God. Planets might satisfy the learned doctors, but God was closer to the average man. A scourge so sweeping and unsparing without any visible cause could only be seen as Divine punishment upon mankind for its sins. It might even be God's terminal disappointment in his creature. Matteo Villani compared the plague to the Flood in ultimate purpose and believed he was recording "the extermination of mankind." Efforts to appease Divine wrath took many forms, as when the city of Rouen ordered that everything that could anger God, such as gambling, cursing, and drinking, must be stopped. More general were the penitent processions authorized at first by the Pope, some lasting as long as three days, some attended by as many as 2000, which everywhere accompanied the plague and helped to spread it.

Barefoot in sackcloth, sprinkled with ashes, weeping, praying, tearing their hair, carrying candles and relics, sometimes with ropes around their necks or beating themselves with whips, the penitents wound through the streets, imploring the mercy of the Virgin and saints at their shrines. In a vivid illustration for the *Très Riches Heures* of the Duc de Berry, the Pope is shown in a penitent procession attended by four cardinals in scarlet from hat to hem. He raises both arms in supplication to the angel on top of the Castel Sant'Angelo, while white-robed priests bearing banners and relics in golden cases turn to look as one of their number, stricken by the plague, falls to the ground, his face contorted with anxiety. In the rear, a gray-clad monk falls beside another victim already on the ground as the townspeople gaze in horror. (Nominally the illustration represents a sixth-century plague in the time of Pope Gregory the Great, but as medieval artists made no distinction between past and present, the scene is shown as the artist would have seen it in the fourteenth century.) When it became evident that these processions were sources of infection, Clement VI had to prohibit them.

In Messina, where the plague first appeared, the people begged the Archbishop of neighboring Catania to lend them the relics of St. Agatha. When the Catanians refused to let the relics go, the Archbishop dipped them in holy water and took the water himself to Messina, where he carried it in a procession with prayers and litanies through the streets. The demonic, which shared the medieval cosmos with God, appeared as "demons in the shape of dogs" to terrify the people. "A black dog with a drawn sword in his paws appeared among them, gnashing his teeth and rushing upon them and breaking all the silver vessels and lamps and candlesticks on the altars and casting them hither and thither. . . . So the people of Messina, terrified by this prodigious vision, were all strangely overcome by fear."

The apparent absence of earthly cause gave the plague a supernatural and sinister quality. Scandinavians believed that a Pest Maiden emerged from the mouth of the dead in the form of a blue flame and flew through the air to infect the next house. In Lithuania the Maiden was said to wave a red scarf through the door or window to let in the pest. One brave man, according to legend, deliberately waited at his open window with drawn sword and, at the fluttering of the scarf, chopped off the hand. He died of his deed, but his village was spared and the scarf long preserved as a relic in the local church.

Beyond demons and superstition the final hand was God's. The Pope acknowledged it in a Bull of September 1348, speaking of the "pestilence with which God is afflicting the Christian people." To the Emperor John Cantacuzene it was manifest that a malady of such horrors, stenches, and agonies, and especially one bringing the dismal despair that settled upon its victims before they died, was not a plague "natural" to mankind but "a chastisement from Heaven." To Piers Plowman "these pestilences were for pure sin."

The general acceptance of this view created an expanded sense of guilt, for if the plague were punishment there had to be terrible sin to have occasioned it. What sins were on the fourteenth-century conscience? Primarily greed, the sin of avarice, followed by usury, worldliness, adultery, blasphemy, falsehood, luxury, irreligion. Giovanni Villani, attempting to account for the cascade of calamity that had fallen upon Florence, concluded that it was retribution for the sins of avarice and usury that oppressed the poor. Pity and anger about the condition of the poor, especially victimization of the peasantry in war, was often expressed by writers of the time and was certainly on the conscience of the century. Beneath it all was the daily condition of medieval life, in which hardly an act or thought, sexual, mercantile, or military, did not contravene the dictates of the Church. Mere failure to fast or attend mass was sin. The result was an underground lake of guilt in the soul that the plague now tapped.

That the mortality was accepted as God's punishment may explain in part the vacuum of comment that followed the Black Death. An investigator has noticed that in the archives of Périgord references to the war are innumerable, to the plague few. Froissart mentions the great death but once, Chaucer gives it barely a glance. Divine anger so great that it contemplated the extermination of man did not bear close examination.

Efforts to cope with the epidemic availed little, either in treatment or prevention. Helpless to alleviate the plague, the doctors' primary effort was to keep it at bay, chiefly by burning aromatic substances to purify the air. The leader of Christendom, Pope Clement VI, was preserved in health by this method, though for an unrecognized reason: Clement's doctor, Guy de Chauliac, ordered that two huge fires should burn in the papal apartments and required the Pope to sit between them in the heat of the Avignon summer. This drastic treatment worked, doubtless because it discouraged the attention of fleas and also because de Chauliac required the Pope to remain isolated in his chambers. Their lovely murals of gardens, hunting, and other secular joys, painted at Cle-

ment's command, perhaps gave him some refreshment. A Pope of prodigal splendor and "sensual vices," Clement was also a man of great learning and a patron of arts and science who now encouraged dissections of the dead "in order that the origins of this disease might be known." Many were performed in Avignon as well as in Florence, where the city authorities paid for corpses to be delivered to physicians for this purpose.

Doctors' remedies in the fourteenth century ranged from the empiric and sensible to the magical, with little distinction made between one and the other. Though medicine was barred by the Church from investigation of anatomy and physiology and from dissection of corpses, the classical anatomy of Galen, transferred through Arab treatises, was kept alive in private anatomy lessons. The need for knowledge was able sometimes to defy the Church: in 1340 Montpellier authorized an anatomy class every two years that lasted for several days and consisted of a surgeon dissecting a cadaver while a doctor of medicine lectured.

Otherwise, the theory of humors, along with astrology, governed practice. All human temperaments were considered to belong to one or another of the four humors—sanguine, phlegmatic, choleric, and melancholic. In various permutations with the signs of the zodiac, each of which governed a particular part of the body, the humors and constellations determined the degrees of bodily heat, moisture, and proportion of masculinity and femininity of each person.

Notwithstanding all their charts and stars, and medicaments barely short of witches' brews, doctors gave great attention to diet, bodily health, and mental attitude. Nor were they lacking in practical skills. They could set broken bones, extract teeth, remove bladder stones, remove cataracts of the eye with a silver needle, and restore a mutilated face by skin graft from the arm. They understood epilepsy and apoplexy as spasms of the brain. They used urinalysis and pulse beat for diagnosis, knew what substances served as laxatives and diuretics, applied a truss for hernia, a mixture of oil, vinegar, and sulfur for toothache, and ground peony root with oil of roses for headache.

For ills beyond their powers they fell back on the supernatural or on elaborate compounds of metallic, botanic, and animal substances. The offensive, like the expensive, had extra value. Ringworm was treated by washing the scalp with a boy's urine, gout by a plaster of goat dung mixed with rosemary and honey. Relief of the patient was their object—cure being left to God—and psychological suggestion often their means. To prevent pockmarks, a smallpox patient would be wrapped in red cloth in a bed hung with red hangings. When surgery was unavailing, recourse was had to the aid of the Virgin or the relics of saints.

In their purple or red gowns and furred hoods, doctors were persons of important status. Allowed extra luxury by the sumptuary laws, they wore belts of silver thread, embroidered gloves, and according to Petrarch's annoyed report, presumptuously donned golden spurs when they rode to their visits attended by a servant. Their wives were permitted greater expenditure on clothes than other women, perhaps in recognition of the large fees doctors could command. Not all were learned professors. Boccaccio's Doctor Simon was a proctologist who had a chamber pot painted over his door to indicate his specialty.

When it came to the plague, sufferers were treated by various measures designed to draw poison or infection from the body: by bleeding, purging with laxatives or enemas, lancing or cauterizing the buboes, or application of hot plasters. None of this was of much use. Medicines ranged from pills of powdered stag's horn or myrrh and saffron to potions of potable gold. Compounds of rare spices and powdered pearls or emeralds were prescribed, possibly on the theory, not unknown to modern medicine, that a patient's sense of therapeutic value is in proportion to the expense.

Doctors advised that floors should be sprinkled, and hands, mouth, and nostrils washed with vinegar and rosewater. Bland diets, avoidance of excitement and anger especially at bedtime, mild exercise, and removal wherever possible from swamps and other sources of dank air were all recommended. Pomanders made of exotic compounds were to be carried on going out, probably more as antidote to the plague's odors than to its contagion. Conversely, in the curious belief that latrine attendants were immune, many people visited the public latrines on the theory that foul odors were efficacious.

Sewage disposal was not unprovided for in the fourteenth century, though far from adequate. Privies, cesspools, drainage pipes, and public latrines existed, though they did not replace open street sewers. Castles and wealthy town houses had privies built into bays jutting from an outside wall with a hole in the bottom allowing the deposit to fall into a river or into a ditch for subsequent removal. Town houses away from the riverbank had cesspools in the backyard at a regulated distance from the neighbor's. Although supposedly constructed under town ordinances, they frequently seeped into wells and other water sources. Except for household urinals, the contents of privies were prohibited from draining into street sewers. Public flouting of ordinances was more to blame for unsanitary streets than inadequate technology.

Some abbeys and large castles, including Coucy, had separate buildings to serve as latrines for the monks or garrison. The *donjon* at Coucy had latrines at each of its three levels. Drainage was channeled into vaulted stone ditches with ventilating holes and openings for removal, or into underground pits later mistaken by investigators of a more romantic period for secret passages and oubliettes. Under the concept of "noble" architecture, the fifteenth and later centuries preferred to ignore human elimination. Coucy probably had better sanitation than Versailles.

During the plague, as street cleaners and

carters died, cities grew befouled, increasing the infection. Residents of a street might rent a cart in common to remove the waste, but energy and will were depressed. The breakdown in street-cleaning appears in a letter of Edward III to the Mayor of London in 1349, complaining that the streets and lanes of London were "foul with human faeces and the air of the city poisoned to the great danger of men passing, especially in this time of infectious disease." Removed as he probably was from the daily sight of corpses piling up, the King ordered that the streets be cleaned "as of old."

Stern measures of quarantine were ordered by many cities. As soon as Pisa and Lucca were afflicted, their neighbor Pistoia forbade any of its citizens who might be visiting or doing business in the stricken cities to return home, and likewise forbade the importation of wool and linen. The Doge and Council of Venice ordered burial on the islands to a depth of at least five feet and organized a barge service to transport the corpses. Poland established a quarantine at its frontiers which succeeded in giving it relative immunity. Draconian means were adopted by the despot of Milan, Archbishop Giovanni Visconti, head of the most uninhibited ruling family of the fourteenth century. He ordered that the first three houses in which the plague was discovered were to be walled up with their occupants inside, enclosing the well, the sick, and the dead in a common tomb. Whether or not owing to his promptitude, Milan escaped lightly in the roll of the dead. With something of the Visconti temperament, a manorial autocrat of Leicestershire burned and razed the village of Noseley when the plague appeared there, to prevent its spread to the manor house. He evidently succeeded, for his direct descendants still inhabit Noseley Hall.

■■■

St. Roch, credited with special healing powers, who had died in 1327, was the particular saint associated with the plague. Inheriting wealth as a young man, as had St. Francis, he had distributed it to the poor and to hospitals, and while returning from a pilgrimage to Rome had encountered an epidemic and stayed to help the sick. Catching the malady himself, he retreated to die alone in the woods, where a dog brought him bread each day. "In these sad times," says his legend, "when reality was so somber and men so hard, people ascribed pity to animals." St. Roch recovered and, on appearing in rags as a beggar, was thought to be a spy and thrown in jail, where he died, filling the cell with a strange light. As his story spread and sainthood was conferred, it was believed that God would cure of the plague anyone who invoked his name. When this failed to occur, it enhanced the belief that, men having grown too wicked, God indeed intended their end. As Langland wrote,

God is deaf now-a-days and deigneth not hear us,
And prayers have no power the Plague to stay.

In a terrible reversal, St. Roch and other saints now came to be considered a source of the plague, as instruments of God's wrath. "In the time of that great mortality in the year of our Lord 1348," wrote a professor of law named Bartolus of Sassoferrato, "the hostility of God was stronger than the hostility of man." But he was wrong.

The hostility of man proved itself against the Jews. On charges that they were poisoning the wells, with intent "to kill and destroy the whole of Christendom and have lordship over all the world," the lynchings began in the spring of 1348 on the heels of the first plague deaths. The first attacks occurred in Narbonne and Carcassonne, where Jews were dragged from their houses and thrown into bonfires. While Divine punishment was accepted as the plague's source, people in their misery still looked for a human agent upon whom to vent the hostility that could not be vented on God. The Jew, as the eternal stranger, was the most obvious target. He was the outsider who had separated himself by choice from the Christian world, whom Christians for centuries had been taught to hate, who was regarded as imbued with unsleeping malevolence against all Christians. Living in a distinct group of his own kind in a particular street or quarter, he was also the most feasible target, with property to loot as a further inducement. . . .

■■■

What was the human condition after the plague? Exhausted by deaths and sorrows and the morbid excesses of fear and hate, it ought to have shown some profound effects, but no radical change was immediately visible. The persistence of the normal is strong. While dying of the plague, the tenants of Bruton Priory in England continued to pay the heriot owed to the lord at death with such obedient regularity that fifty oxen and cattle were received by the priory within a few months. Social change was to come invisibly with time; immediate effects were many but not uniform. Simon de Covino believed the plague had a baneful effect upon morals, "lowering virtue throughout the world." Gilles li Muisis, on the other hand, thought there had been an improvement in public morals because many people formerly living on concubinage had now married (as a result of town ordinances), and swearing and gambling had so diminished that manufacturers of dice were turning their product into beads for telling paternosters.

The marriage rate undoubtedly rose, though not for love. So many adventurers took advantage of orphans to obtain rich dowries that the oligarchy of Siena forbade the marriage of female orphans without their kinsmen's consent. In England, Piers Plowman deplored the many pairs "since the pestilence" who had married "for greed of goods and against natural feeling," with result, according to him, in "guilt and grief . . . jealousy, joylessness and jangling in private"—and no children. It suited Piers as a moralist that such marriages should

be barren. Jean de Venette, on the other hand, says of the marriages that followed the plague that many twins, sometimes triplets, were born and that few women were barren. Perhaps he in turn reflected a desperate need to believe that nature would make up the loss, and in fact men and women married immediately afterward in unusual numbers.

Unlike the dice transformed into prayer beads, people did not improve, although it had been expected, according to Matteo Villani, that the experience of God's wrath would have left them "better men, humble, virtuous and Catholic." Instead, "They forgot the past as though it had never been and gave themselves up to a more disordered and shameful life than they had led before." With a glut of merchandise on the shelves for too few customers, prices at first plunged and survivors indulged in a wild orgy of spending. The poor moved into empty houses, slept on beds, and ate off silver. Peasants acquired unclaimed tools and livestock, even a wine press, forge, or mill left without owners, and other possessions they never had before. Commerce was depressed, but the amount of currency was in greater supply because there were fewer people to share it.

Behavior grew more reckless and callous, as it often does after a period of violence and suffering. It was blamed on parvenus and the newly rich who pushed up from below. Siena renewed its sumptuary laws in 1349 because many persons were pretending to higher position than belonged to them by birth or occupation. But, on the whole, local studies of tax rolls indicate that while the population may have been halved, its social proportions remained about the same.

Because of intestate deaths, property without heirs, and disputed title to land and houses, a fury of litigation arose, made chaotic by the shortage of notaries. Sometimes squatters, sometimes the Church, took over emptied property. Fraud and extortion practiced upon orphans by their appointed guardians became a scandal. In Orvieto brawls kept breaking out; bands of homeless and starving brigands roamed the countryside and pillaged up to the very gates of the city. People were arrested for carrying arms and for acts of vandalism, especially on vineyards. The commune had to enact new regulations against "certain rascals, sons of iniquity" who robbed and burned the premises of shopkeepers and craftsmen, and also against increased prostitution. On March 12, 1350, the commune reminded citizens of the severe penalty in store for sexual relations between Christian and Jew: the woman involved would be beheaded or burned alive.

Education suffered from losses among the clergy. In France, according to Jean de Venette, "Few were found in houses, villas and castles who were able and willing to instruct boys in grammar"—a situation that could have touched the life of Enguerrand VII. To fill vacant benefices the Church ordained priests in batches, many of them men who had lost their wives or families in the plague and flocked to holy orders as a refuge. Many were barely literate, "as it were mere lay folk" who might read a little but without understanding. Priests who survived the plague, declared the Archbishop of Canterbury in 1350, had become "infected by insatiable avarice," charging excessive fees and neglecting souls.

By a contrary trend, education was stimulated by concern for the survival of learning, which led to a spurt in the founding of universities. Notably the Emperor Charles IV, an intellectual, felt keenly the cause of "precious knowledge which the mad rage of pestilential death has stifled throughout the wide realms of the world." He founded the University of Prague in the plague year of 1348 and issued imperial accreditation to five other universities—Orange, Perugia, Siena, Pavia, and Lucca—in the next five years. In the same five years three new colleges were founded at Cambridge—Trinity, Corpus Christi, and

Clare—although love of learning, like love in marriage, was not always the motive. Corpus Christi was founded in 1352 because fees for celebrating masses for the dead were so inflated after the plague that two guilds of Cambridge decided to establish a college whose scholars, as clerics, would be required to pray for their deceased members. . . . .

The obvious and immediate result of the Black Death was, of course, a shrunken population, which, owing to wars, brigandage, and recurrence of the plague, declined even further by the end of the fourteenth century. The plague laid a curse on the century in the form of its own bacillus. Lodged in the vectors, it was to break out again six times over the next six decades in various localities at varying intervals of ten to fifteen years. After killing off most of those susceptible, with increasing mortality of children in the later phases, it eventually receded, leaving Europe with a population reduced by about 40 percent in 1380 and by nearly 50 percent at the end of the century. The city of Béziers in southern France, which had 14,000 inhabitants in 1304, numbered 4000 a century later. The fishing port of Jonquières near Marseille, which once had 354 taxable hearths, was reduced to 135. The flourishing cities of Carcassonne and Montpellier shrank to shadows of their former prosperity, as did Rouen, Arras, Laon, and Reims in the north. The vanishing of taxable material caused rulers to raise rates of taxation, arousing resentment that was to explode in repeated outbreaks in coming decades.

As between landowner and peasant, the balance of impoverishment and enrichment caused by the plague on the whole favored the peasant, although what was true in one place often had an equal and opposite reaction somewhere else. The relative values of land and labor were turned upside down. Peasants found their rents reduced and even relinquished for one or more years by landowners desperate to keep their fields in cultivation.

Better no revenue at all than that cleared land should be retaken by the wilderness. But with fewer hands to work, cultivated land necessarily shrank. The archives of the Abbey of Ramsay in England show that thirty years after the plague the acreage sowed in grain was less than half what it had been before. Five plows owned by the abbey in 1307 were reduced to one a century later, and twenty-eight oxen to five.

Hill farms and sections of poor soil were let go or turned to pasture for sheep, which required less labor. Villages weakened by depopulation and unable to resist the enclosure of land for sheep were deserted in increasing numbers. Property boundaries vanished when fields reverted to wasteland. If claimed by someone who was able to cultivate them, former owners or their heirs could not collect rent. Landowners impoverished by these factors sank out of sight or let castles and manors decay while they entered the military brigandage that was to be the curse of the following decades.

When death slowed production, goods became scarce and prices soared. In France the price of wheat increased fourfold by 1350. At the same time the shortage of labor bought the plague's greatest social disruption—a concerted demand for higher wages. Peasants as well as artisans, craftsmen, clerks, and priests discovered the lever of their own scarcity. Within a year after the plague had passed through northern France, the textile workers of St. Omer near Amiens had gained three successive wage increases. In many guilds artisans struck for higher pay and shorter hours. In an age when social conditions were regarded as fixed, such action was revolutionary.

The response of rulers was instant repression. In the effort to hold wages at pre-plague levels, the English issued an ordinance in 1349 requiring everyone to work for the same pay as in 1347. Penalties were established for refusal to work, for leaving a place of employment to seek higher pay, and for the offer of higher pay by employers. Proclaimed when Parliament was not sitting, the ordinance was reissued in 1351 as the Statute of Laborers. It denounced not only laborers who demanded higher wages but particularly those who chose "rather to beg in idleness than to earn their bread in labor." Idleness of the worker was a crime against society, for the medieval system rested on his obligation to work. The Statute of Laborers was not simply a reactionary dream but an effort to maintain the system. It provided that every able-bodied person under sixty with no means of subsistence must work for whoever required him, that no alms could be given to able-bodied beggars, that a vagrant serf could be forced to work for anyone who claimed him. Down to the twentieth century this statute was to serve as the basis for "conspiracy" laws against labor in the long struggle to prevent unionization.

A more realistic French statute of 1351, applying only to the region of Paris, allowed a rise in wages not to exceed one third of the former level. Prices were fixed and profits of middlemen were regulated. To increase production, guilds were required to loosen their restrictions on the number of apprentices and shorten the period before they could become masters.

In both countries, as shown by repeated renewals of the laws with rising penalties, the statutes were unenforceable. Violations cited by the English Parliament in 1352 show workers demanding and employers paying wages at double and treble the pre-plague rate. Stocks were ordered set up in every town for punishment of offenders. In 1360 imprisonment replaced fines as the penalty and fugitive laborers were declared outlaws. If caught, they were to be branded on the forehead with F for "fugitive" (or possibly for "falsity"). New laws were enacted twice more in the 1360s, breeding the resistance that was to come to a head in the great outbreak of 1381.

■ ■ ■

The sense of sin induced by the plague found surcease in the plenary indulgence offered by the Jubilee Year of 1350 to all who in that year made the pilgrimage to Rome. Originally established by Boniface VIII in 1300, the Jubilee was intended to make an indulgence available to all repentant and confessed sinners free of charge—that is, if they could afford the journey to Rome. Boniface intended the Jubilee Year as a centennial event, but the first one had been such an enormous success, attracting a reported 2 million visitors to Rome in the course of the year, that the city, impoverished by the loss of the papacy to Avignon, petitioned Clement VI to shorten the interval to fifty years. The Pope of the joyous murals operated on the amiable principle that "a pontiff should make his subjects happy." He complied with Rome's request in a bull of 1343.

Momentously for the Church, Clement formulated in the same Bull the theory of indulgences, and fixed its fatal equation with money. The sacrifice of Christ's blood, he stated, together with the merit added by the Virgin and saints, had established an inexhaustible treasury for the use of pardons. By contributing sums to the Church, anyone could buy a share in the Treasury of Merit. What the Church gained in revenue by this arrangement was matched in the end by loss in respect.

In 1350 pilgrims thronged the roads to Rome, camping around fires at night. Five thousand people were said to enter or leave the city every day, enriching the householders, who gave them lodging despite shortages of food and forage and the dismal state of the city's resources. Without its pontiff the Eternal City was destitute, the three chief basilicas in ruins, San Paolo toppled by the earthquake, the Lateran half-collapsed. Rubble and ruin filled the streets, the seven hills were silent and deserted, goats nibbled in the weed-grown cloisters of deserted convents. The sight of roofless churches exposed to wind and rain, lamented Petrarch, "would excite pity in a heart of stone." Nevertheless, famous saints' relics raked in lavish offerings, and Cardinal Anibaldo Ceccano, Legate for the Jubilee, administered an immense program of absolutions and indulgences to the crowds craving remission of sin. During Lent, according to Villani, who took a special interest in figures, as many as a million were in Rome at one time. The inpouring suggests either extraordinary recklessness and vigor so soon after the plague or a great need for salvation—or possibly that conditions did not seem as bad to participants as they seem in report.

The Church emerged from the plague richer if not more unpopular. When sudden death threatened everyone with the prospect of being carried off in a state of sin, the result was a flood of bequests to religious institutions. St. Germain l'Auxerrois in Paris received 49 legacies in nine months, compared to 78 in the previous eight years. As early as October 1348 the Council of Siena suspended its annual appropriations for religious charities for two years because these were so "immensely enriched and indeed fattened" by bequests. In Florence the Company of Or San Michele received 350,000 florins intended as alms for the poor, although in this case the directors of the company were accused of using the money for their own purposes on the grounds that the very poor and needy were dead.

While the Church garnered money, personal attacks on the clergy increased, stimulated partly by the flagellants, and partly by the failure of priests during the plague to live up to their responsibilities. That they died like other men was doubtless forgiven, but that they let Christians die without the sacraments or charged more for their services in the crisis, as many did, was violently resented. Even during the Jubilee the Roman populace, moved by some mysterious tremor of local hostility, jeered and harassed the Cardinal-Legate. On one occasion, as he was riding in a procession, he was shot at by a sniper and returned pale and trembling with an arrow through his red hat. Venturing out thereafter only with a helmet under his hat and a coat of mail under his gown, he departed for Naples as soon as he could, and died on the way—poisoned, it was said, by wine.

In England, where anticlericalism was endemic, citizens of Worcester in 1349 broke down the gates of the Priory of St. Mary attached to the cathedral, attacked the monks, "chased the Prior with bows and arrows and other offensive weapons," and tried to set fire to the buildings. At Yeovil in the same year, when the Bishop of Bath and Wells held a thanksgiving service to mark the passing of the plague, it was interrupted by "certain sons of perdition" who kept the Bishop and congregation besieged in the church all night until rescue came. . . .

The plague accelerated discontent with the Church at the very moment when people felt a greater need of spiritual reassurance. There had to be some meaning in the terrorizing experience God had inflicted. If the purpose had been to shake man from his sinful ways, it had failed. Human conduct was found to be "wickeder than before," more avaricious and grasping, more litigious, more bellicose, and this was nowhere more apparent than in the Church itself. Clement VI, though hardly a spiritual man, was sufficiently shaken by the plague to burst out against his prelates in a tirade of anger and shame when they petitioned him in 1351 to abolish the mendicant orders. And if he did, the Pope replied, "What can you preach to the people? If on humility, you yourselves are the proudest of the world, puffed up, pompous and sumptuous in luxuries. If on poverty, you are so covetous that all the benefices in the world are not enough for you. If on chastity—but we will be silent on this, for God knoweth what each man does and how many of you satisfy your lusts." In this sad view of his fellow clerics the head of the Church died a year later.

"When those who have the title of shepherd play the part of wolves," said Lothar of Sax-

ony, "heresy grows in the garden of the Church." While the majority of people doubtless plodded on as before, dissatisfaction with the Church gave impetus to heresy and dissent, to all those seeking God through the mystical sects, to all the movements for reform that were ultimately to break apart the empire of Catholic unity.

∎∎∎

Survivors of the plague, finding themselves neither destroyed nor improved, could discover no Divine purpose in the pain they had suffered. God's purposes were usually mysterious, but this scourge had been too terrible to be accepted without questioning. If a disaster of such magnitude, the most lethal ever known, was a mere wanton act of God or perhaps not God's work at all, then the absolutes of a fixed order were loosed from their moorings. Minds that opened to admit these questions could never again be shut. Once people envisioned the possibility of change in a fixed order, the end of an age of submission came in sight; the turn to individual conscience lay ahead. To that extent the Black Death may have been the unrecognized beginning of modern man.

Meantime it left apprehension, tension, and gloom. It accelerated the commutation of labor services on the land and in so doing unfastened old ties. It deepened antagonism between rich and poor and raised the level of human hostility. An event of great agony is bearable only in the belief that it will bring about a better world. When it does not, as in the aftermath of another vast calamity in 1914–18, disillusion is deep and moves on to self-doubt and self-disgust. In creating a climate for pessimism, the Black Death was the equivalent of the First World War, although it took fifty years for the psychological effects to develop. These were the fifty-odd years of the youth and adult life of Enguerrand de Coucy.

A strange personification of Death emerged

from the plague years on the painted walls of the Camposanto in Pisa. The figure is not the conventional skeleton, but a black-cloaked old woman with streaming hair and wild eyes, carrying a broad-blade murderous scythe. Her feet end in claws instead of toes. Depicting the Triumph of Death, the fresco was painted in or about 1350 by Francesco Traini as part of a series that included scenes of the Last Judgment and the Tortures of Hell. The same subject, painted at the same time by Traini's master, Andrea Orcagna, in the church of Santa Croce in Florence, has since been lost except for a fragment. Together the frescoes marked the start of a pervasive presence of Death in art, not yet the cult it was to become by the end of the century, but its beginning.

Usually Death was personified as a skeleton with hourglass and scythe, in a white shroud or bare-boned, grinning at the irony of man's fate reflected in his image: that all men, from beggar to emperor, from harlot to queen, from ragged clerk to Pope, must come to this. No matter what their poverty or power in life, all is vanity, equalized by death. The temporal is nothing; what matters is the after-life of the soul.

In Traini's fresco, Death swoops through the air toward a group of carefree, young, and beautiful noblemen and ladies who, like models for Boccaccio's storytellers, converse and flirt and entertain each other with books and music in a fragrant grove of orange trees. A scroll warns that "no shield of wisdom or riches, nobility or prowess" can protect them from the blows of the Approaching One. "They have taken more pleasure in the world than in things of God." In a heap of corpses nearby lie crowned rulers, a Pope in tiara, a knight, tumbled together with the bodies of the poor, while angels and devils in the sky contend for the miniature naked figures that represent their souls. A wretched group of lepers, cripples, and beggars (duplicated in the surviving fragment of Orcagna), one with nose eaten away, others legless or blind or holding out a cloth-covered stump instead of a hand, implore Death for deliverance. Above on a mountain, hermits leading a religious contemplative life await death peaceably.

Below in a scene of extraordinary verve a hunting party of princes and elegant ladies on horseback comes with sudden horror upon three open coffins containing corpses in different stages of decomposition, one still clothed, one half-rotted, one a skeleton. Vipers crawl over their bones. The scene illustrates "The Three Living and Three Dead," a thirteenth-century legend which tells of a meeting between three young nobles and three decomposing corpses who tell them, "What you are, we were. What we are, you will be." In Traini's fresco, a horse catching the stench of death stiffens in fright with outstretched neck and flaring nostrils; his rider clutches a handkerchief to his nose. The hunting dogs recoil, growling in repulsion. In their silks and curls and fashionable hats, the party of vital handsome men and women stare appalled at what they will become.

■■■

STUDY QUESTIONS

1. How did the Black Death affect the population of Europe? What impact did it have upon labor relations, productivity, and the economy?

2. How did individuals react to the massive catastrophe?

3. What was the cause of the plague, and how did it spread?

4. How did people explain the plague and how did they treat its victims? What roles did science and the church play?

5. What was the human condition after the plague? How did the plague affect the survivors?

BIBLIOGRAPHY

This selection was taken from Barbara W. Tuchman's *A Distant Mirror: The Calamitous 14th Century* (1978). A biography of Enguerrand de Coucy VII, Tuchman's book captures the feeling of the troubled age. Robert S. Gottfried, *The Black Death: Natural and Human Disaster in Medieval Europe* (1983), deals with the science and the impact of the plague. Two other fine studies of the event are G. G. Coultan, *The Black Death* (1930), and Philip Ziegler, *The Black Death* (1969). The impact of the plague on individual regions is explored in Michael Dols, *The Black Death in the Middle East* (1977), and J. F. D. Shrewsbury, *A History of the Bubonic Plague in the British Isles* (1971). An insightful look at the role of disease in history is William H. McNeill, *Plagues and Peoples* (1976). Finally, for a contemporary view of the plague see Giovanni Boccaccio, *The Decameron* and *The Corbaccio*.

18. SEXUAL CRIMINALITY IN THE EARLY RENAISSANCE: VENICE, 1338–1358

Guido Ruggiero

A popular theme in fourteenth-century painting, literature, and sermons was the Four Horsemen of the Apocalypse from the Book of Revelation. Famine, war, disease, and death seemed the natural order of things for people whose lives were disrupted by famine, war, disease, and death. Riding behind the Four Horsemen, however, was another scourge—crime. Of course, there were all forms of criminal activity, but a particular problem was the exploitation of the poor by the rich and titled. In England, for example, "fur-collar crime" exacted a heavy toll. So named because it was practiced by the nobility who were alone allowed to wear collars of miniver fur, this type of crime involved extortion, kidnapping, protection schemes, and other forms of robbing from the poor to further enrich the already wealthy. To escape punishment, fur-collar criminals bribed jurors, threatened witnesses, and used their connections to influence judges. Tales of Robin Hood gave expression to the hatred and deeply felt resentment of the common people for the abuses of the aristocracy.

Sexual criminality similarly demonstrated the abuses of power and acted as a bolt of lightning, illuminating the social landscape of this troubled time. In the case of rape, exploitation often worked on several levels. Foremost was the exploitation of females—young and old, married and single. That rape was treated as a relatively minor, almost victimless, crime indicates the status accorded to females by a male-dominated society. The crime of infanticide underscored this fact; girls were killed far more frequently than boys. Beyond the exploitation of females, rape often involved the exploitation of the poor and defenseless by the rich and powerful. The elite who controlled the legal definition, trial, and punishment of crime also committed rape the most frequently. In this essay, Guido Ruggiero examines the social, cultural, and political meanings of sexual criminality in fourteenth-century Venice. In so doing he casts light onto the mentality of the age.

It is certain, however, that rape, an act so very rare and so very difficult to prove, wrongs one's neighbor less than theft, since the latter is destructive to property, the former merely damaging to it. Beyond that, what objections have you to the ravisher? What will you say, when he replies to you that, as a matter of fact, the injury he has committed is trifling indeed, since he has done no more than place a little sooner the object he has abused in the very state in which she would soon have been put by marriage and love.

The Marquis de Sade

There is no question that the Marquis de Sade's perception of women and rape is distant from a modern one. Yet in early Renaissance Venice we find virtually the same perceptions of rape and sexual crime. Generally Renaissance sexual criminality has been studied in terms of rape, and though that society, like most past societies, defined sexual crime more broadly than is true in the present day, Renaissance historians have generally held that rape was a major crime very much in the context of modern values. What we are dealing with in other words is a problem in the historical perception of crime that is important to Renaissance historiography as well as to an understanding of the outlook of criminals and victims alike.

William Bowsky, for example, in an interesting article on violence in Siena maintains that rape was one of the ''so-called 'enormous crimes,''' similar to homicide, treason, arson, kidnapping, and poisoning. For Florence, Umberto Dorini, though citing laws which allowed milder penalties and wide judicial latitude, argues that in the fourteenth century penalties for rape varied between a minimum of £500 and a maximum of £2000—considerable sums of money. In Ferrara

From ''Sexual Criminality in the Early Renaissance: Venice 1338–1358'' by Guido Ruggiero, *Journal of Social History*, 1975, Vol. 8, pp. 18–37. Reprinted by permission of Carnegie-Mellon University and the author.

Werner Gundersheimer sees a similar severity: ''Under the law, thieves and murderers were hanged or like rapists, decapitated; counterfeiters were burned, sodomists hanged and then burned, traitors hanged and then quartered.'' Perhaps Venice was merely an exception, but it is significant that historians have not treated it as such. Stanley Chojnacki, in a pioneering article, presented the thesis that for rape in fourteenth-century Venice ''the penalty was very heavy.''

In fact it was not. Sexual criminality in general and rape in particular were viewed as minor offenses against victim and society in Venice. In his call to the republican sentiments of eighteenth-century Frenchmen, de Sade could have pointed with approval to the record of fourteenth-century republican Venice. The Venetian attitude towards sexual crime was in many ways similar to his own. But why? It seems to me the answer to this is closely tied to the obverse side of that urban elite mentality that makes the Italian renaissance unique—a darker side which de Sade compulsively articulated in his elite heroes of limitless power.

Venice in the fourteenth century was dominated by a merchant elite that had finally secured legal recognition as a nobility. Power, however, not land, law, or custom was their true source of noble status. Political power and economic power along with the exigencies of urban life caused them to evolve a distinct social mentality centering on order and control that was in many ways to change the way society as a whole perceived, indulged in, and reacted to criminal behavior. Sexual crime, though it has sometimes been maligned as a source of data for social history, provides unusual insights into the darker side of this elite mentality. This is especially true in a city such as Venice where, through its political and judicial monopoly of power in the offices of the Avogador di Comun, the Forty, the Signori di Notte, and the Giudici del Proprio, the elite controlled the legal definition, trial, and punishment of such crime.

The problem normally associated with sex-crime data is the variability of perception involved. But as this essay is primarily concerned with perception, what has been seen as a handicap is in reality an advantage. The data on sex crimes, because they revealed an elite's perceptions, can do more than define a set of crimes. They allow an examination of an elite's interaction with those crimes as perceivers, controllers, and participants: an elite's behavior, if you wish, studied in relation to an aberrant form of behavior.

The period 1338 to 1358 has been chosen for this essay because the documentation is unusually complete. Also, Venice in this period was finally stabilizing a social order that was legally new. At the end of the thirteenth century, perhaps in response to narrowing markets and economic possibilities, the Venetian elite made a legal move to define itself. Known as the Serrata or "Closing," it was designed, or over time in fact served, to limit political and economic power to the hands of a restricted hereditary group. Finally, after a series of trials and adjustments with the dogeship of Andrea Dandolo (1343–1353), this elite reached a position of political and social security. With an apparently firm control, it even began to pay lip service to a self-serving fantasy of Venetian history built upon cooperation of nobility and lower classes, a fantasy that was to become the myth of Venice. Immediately, the fantasy was to be challenged. The impact of the plague of 1347–1348 was reinforced by the drain of yet another economically devastating war with Genoa (1350–1355) and civic harmony gave way to a major conspiracy against the state led by its aged chief executive, the Doge Marin Falier, and supported by popular elements especially from the navy. Thus the period under consideration could be characterized as one of relative social stasis until 1347–1348 followed by relative turmoil, and therefore provides an excellent test for the continuity of the Venetian elite's perception of and relationship to sexual crime.

An elite's perceptions of crime can best be studied by examining the way it punished crime. Law traditionally has also provided a guide. But law in its social context is only as meaningful as its use, in this case its application to sexual crime. At least part of the problem with earlier pronouncements on renaissance sexual criminality is a reliance upon law, which though generally more accessible tends to be static, caught in an inertia that holds many forms of written value systems behind changing community or elite standards. Fortunately, in fourteenth-century Venice maximum leeway in imposing penalties was left to the judging body, which means that law interferes little with an examination of the immediate evaluation of sexual crime revealed by the penalties imposed.

Rape, successful or merely attempted, leads by far on the list of sexual crimes. Most commonly it is referred to as "cognovit carnaliter per vim" or some variation on that phrase. Other descriptions found occasionally are, "fornicationis per vim," "forcia," "violasse per vim." Force seems to be the constant element in such descriptions, as in the modern sense. But when we turn to the penalties for such crimes we see a very unmodern response. Rather, rape is treated as de Sade would have had his ideal republic treat it, as a petty crime. Because there was an even balance between money fines, jail sentences, and a combination of fines and jail sentences, to compare such penalties an equivalency scale is necessary (see Table 1).

Table 1. Point Scale for Fines and Imprisonment

Penalty		Points
£10p.	=	1
s.20 gr.	=	5
1 ducat	=	3.5
1 year jail	=	20

Using this table it becomes apparent that rape was not considered a serious crime in a class with murder, treason, or robbery. For the ninety-four clear rapes where penalties are listed, the average penalty came to a little over one year in jail or £216p. In an age where men were usually mutilated or executed for robbery or murder, this penalty is comparatively mild. And it becomes milder yet if we look more closely at the data. Breaking down these statistics further shows a different valuation of rape for women at various stages in life.

If we separate the penalties for rape of unmarried women from those for rape of married women, it appears that rape of an unmarried woman was perceived as more serious. The average penalty for the rape of a married woman (forty-seven cases) was 19.9 points as compared with 23.3 points for the average nonmarried woman (forty-seven cases). But these figures are misleading. The group of unmarried women should really be broken down into two groups: young girls not of marriageable age (*puellae*, about age twelve or below), and girls of marriageable age.

This division changes the picture of rape substantially. As might be expected the rape of young girls was severely punished, with the average penalty 34.6 points (fifteen clear cases). But when these exceptional cases are separated from the rank and file of single women above twelve, the average penalty for the latter drops to a low 14.0 points (thirty-two cases). Further, if we exclude two uncertain cases where the rapists were given large penalties, and the victims may have been *puellae*, the disparity is even more striking. For thirty rapes of girls of marriageable age, the penalty average was 8.7 points, that is, less than half a year in jail or about £87p. This is only slightly greater than the penalty for carrying a knife longer than the legal length at night, £50p. On a continuum, then, we have rape of single women valued at 8.7 points; rape of married women, 19.9 points; and rape of *puellae*, 34.6 points.

De Sade would have been pleased; indeed the damaged property of a rape victim was not taken too seriously. Rape was considered a minor crime. However, there were other considerations. Rape of an unmarried woman was and remains a hard crime to substantiate, especially in male-dominated societies. As there was wide leeway in the imposition of penalties, part of this leniency may be seen as a lack of certainty about culpability. From such a perspective married women and children were less likely, in descending order, to provoke or cooperate with sexual advances that might later be argued as rape. Still it is clear that the rape of a woman, especially a single nonnoble girl, was not viewed very seriously. Murderers or robbers were hanged or mutilated, poisoners were burned, as were forgers and sodomites, but rapists escaped with a comparative slap across the wrist that says much about the Venetian attitude towards women and sexuality.

Another sexual crime closely related to rape involved those who were accomplices. Women who aided, usually for pay, appear in the records as "rufiana," "mediatrix," or "lena." Men seem to have done without a title except in the case of Petrus de Lana who, along with his wife Zana, convinced a young girl named Marina to board the boat of Dardi Fontegarius where she was raped by Dardi. His wife is called a "rufiana" and he is given the masculine ending of the term, "rufianus." One problem caused by this lack of a name is that it is occasionally difficult to decide whether a male helped in a rape or actually participated. Normally, however, the records specify the assistance provided. For example, in January of 1345 Petrus and Scavolinus de Tarvisio were hired by the noble Luchas Corner to row a boat for him while he raped Beatrice de Feltre, a young servant of Marco Sanuto. Or there is the case of noble family solidarity where Simonetus Michael aided his uncle Anzeletus Michael in the rape of Lucia, wife of the boatman Marinus. Simonetus lured the woman to Anzeletus' house with the following words, "Si tu vis venire ad domum Anzeliti ego dabo tibi capuciam.''[1] When they arrived Simonetus took her into a room and tied her up. Then Anzeletus beat her with a ''bastone'' and raped her twice. Simonetus, for his ''relatively'' minor role, was fined £50p.

Thirty-one people were clearly convicted as accomplices, sixteen women and fifteen men. As might be expected, given the elite's attitude toward women, their penalties were generally more severe. They often received corporal punishment and banishment, while males were given generally short prison sentences and small fines. In fact, corporal punishment for sex crimes was virtually restricted to women and sodomites. Consciously or unconsciously, it seems that it was more outside the norm for women to aid in sex crimes than males and the penalties reflect this attitude.

Nobles, not surprisingly, employed thirteen of the thirty-one accomplices convicted, for they had the money to acquire such aid. This indicates a greater amount of planning on the nobles' part. Spontaneity there certainly was, but there was also a bit of the Marquis' rationality of pleasure and power in cases such as the already mentioned rape-beating perpetrated by Simonetus Michael and his uncle Anzeletus. A similar mentality is revealed in the rape of an eight-year-old girl by the noble Nicoletis Georgio, son of Pangratii Georgio. He paid a certain Blanca, who lived in the home of Benedicto Orbi in San Moise, to procure for him Ellena, the daughter of Francisci Grassi. Blanca brought the girl to her room, ''prepared her,'' and then aided in the rape.

In fact, no one was safe in the face of such power. Francischinus dalle Bochole, another Venetian noble, secured the help of his victim's mother in the rape of a *puella* in 1357. The mother, Francisca, brought the girl to him and helped as he raped the girl twice. Of course, her penalty was quite stiff for this act. She spent one day in a *berlina*, then was whipped from S. Marco to S. Croce with her crime being announced by a herald, and finally she spent a year in jail. Francischinus did not get off lightly either. He spent two years in jail and paid a fine of 200 ducats, one of the harshest penalties meted out to a noble in the period. An indication of the impact of fines on the nobility is revealed by the fact that Francischinus had no trouble raising the money and paid the fine the same day it was levied.

Where men of power and wealth are concerned, the records reveal just the surface of their criminality. Certainly many crimes of the type reported above went unrecorded. Money and power must have negated many a potential complaint. Despite the significant number of cases brought against the nobility (to be discussed later), we are dealing merely with the tip of a very large iceberg.

The most serious sex crime for early renaissance Venice was sodomy. It was a crime not frequently prosecuted, as it was seldom brought to light. In 1406–1407, however, a large group of homosexuals, including a considerable number of young nobles and clergymen, was discovered by the Signori di Notte. Because the crime was such a serious one and the penalty was burning, the Council of Ten stepped in, ostensibly because state security was involved in the burning of sixteen or seventeen Venetians of the highest family, but more realistically to suppress the evidence and reduce the number of those executed to a minimum.

In the theory the Signori di Notte were responsible for sodomy cases, but in our period three of the seven cases reported were handled by the Avogadori and tried before the Forty. This is unfortunate, for the archives of the Signori di Notte contain exceptional detail. There is, for example, the case of Rolandinus Ronchaia, who engaged in sodomy ''per multes et infinites homines.'' In this instance the records provide us with a biography of one homosexual's development. Rolandinus had always

---

[1] If you come to the house of Anzeletus I will give you a hat.

looked and acted like a woman. He had been married before the plague to a woman in Padua, but had had no interest in sexual intercourse with her. After her death he was introduced to homosexuality by a man who noticed his physical femininity. He then became a transvestite and at the time of his arrest he was working as a female prostitute in Venice.

One cannot generalize on the basis of seven cases, but it is interesting to note that in all the cases excepting that of Rolandinus, young boys or servants were involved. Normally, the younger partners were let off, the only exception being the case of Johannus Braganza. Johannus, a servant of Nicoletus Marmagna, was originally raped and beaten by Nicoletus. However, he did not report the crime even though the beatings and the sexual activity continued. Finally, it appears that Johannus came to accept and enjoy the relationship. Nicoletus even married this ex-servant to his niece Rubea, raising Johannus's status in life considerably and disguising their homosexual relationship. Everything crumbled rapidly, however, as they were arrested on 3 October 1357, tortured, convicted of sodomy by the Judices de Proprio, and both burned on 11 October 1357.

All the sodomy cases in our period were punished by burning, and over the century it was the most consistently applied criminal penalty. To a degree this represents the stiffness called for by morality and canon law, but it also represents a very strong psychological fear or aversion to "abnormal" sexuality in the early Renaissance. There is an interesting contrast here. On the one hand rape was handled relatively leniently, as we have seen, in part because it was perceived by the nobility in the context of normal admitted human passions. Homosexuality, however, was strictly punished because it represented passions that could not be admitted to exist even in the case of Rolandinus who sexually and perhaps hormonally was much closer to being a woman

■ ■ *Prostitution was a common aspect of city life in Renaissance Italy.*

than a man. Also, there is inherent in such a distinction in penalties an unconscious, higher valuation of the male and male morality.

Beyond rape and sodomy early renaissance Venice had a wide range of sex crimes that can be broken down into three general categories: fornication, adultery, and sexual activities that did not include actual intercourse. Interestingly, in the case of fornication and adultery the women were not regularly tried. Apparently discipline was left to the father or the spouse, though research revealed no law that stipulates this. Nonetheless, the records are quite clear on penalties for males involved in fornication and adultery, and a similar pattern emerges to that earlier noted for rape, though the sample is small. For eight cases of fornication with single women, the average penalty on the equivalency scale set up above was 5.9. Adulterers received considerably higher penalties; 10.8 points for sixteen cases. As marital status provides the primary distinction between the two crimes, again there emerges a higher valuation of the wife than the young girl of marriageable age. In both cases, however, the penalty is quite mild and considerably below the average for violent sexuality, such as rape, an indication that rape was not merely a property crime.

Sexual activities that did not include intercourse cover a wide range of sins—from threats to petty molestation to petty assault and major assault involving the drawing of blood. Women were invariably the object and sex was invariably the motive. This type of crime was much more general than the records of the Avogaria reveal, because most petty crime of this nature was handled immediately by the Cinque di Pace, whose records of petty crimes are now lost. Little can be done with such material except report the fact that some of it reached the Avogadori and eventually the Forty. Apparently when the case was clearly sexual it was brought to the Avogador.

Clearly the elite perceived sexual crimes, excluding sodomy, as minor crimes. But perceptions change and in the period covered by this essay there was a natural catastrophe—the plague of 1348, which surely should be a candidate for the type of jarring occurrence that challenges man's view of existence. The Lisbon earthquake of the eighteenth century apparently had this type of effect on the optimism of Enlightenment thinkers. Certainly the plague had a profound effect on chroniclers or writers like Boccaccio, but in fact there is little indication that it had an impact on Venetian attitudes towards sexual crime. This, of course, is just one more mark of a persistently low valuation of such crimes.

Moreover, the plague apparently had no immediate effect even on the level of sexual criminality. Sexual crime actually peaked several years after the plague, in 1351 and 1352. Even the plague year 1348 was virtually normal for sex crimes. Sixteen people were prosecuted in that year, whereas the average number prosecuted in preplague years was 15.5. Only in 1353–1354 does the level of crime drop off precipitously.

How does one account for this continuity? Surely when one-third of the population is lost, there must be some impact on sexual crime, or any type of interpersonal crime for that matter. A partial answer might be a change in the elite's perception of crime. If they felt the plague, as a punishment for society's sins, required a more strict handling of sexual crime, they might have increased the frequency of prosecution. Thus, though the general level of sexual criminality declined, a larger proportion of such crimes would have been prosecuted. As noted earlier, there was some increase in the strictness in penalties in the ten-year period following the plague. But clearly it was not an increase of the magnitude to warrant the assumption that society had suddenly decided to deal more harshly with its sinners.

A more valid answer to this problem might be found in the realization that sex crimes are unusual because they involve particular segments of a society. Although the documents do not allow us to confirm the hypothesis, it is a good working assumption that most sex crimes were committed by young men. Crucially, it is just this group of people that was least affected by the plague. The plague was devastating among the very young and the old, but had much less impact on those who were physically strong enough to make it through childhood. Those young criminals, though they may have called down God's wrath in the form of the plague for their sins, clearly felt that wrath much less than the general population.

A further explanation of these figures might be that Venice acted as a labor magnet throughout the fourteenth century and most intensively so following the plague. To replace its losses in sailors and workers, Venice drew from the mainland a new and young population unfamiliar with the city's ways, especially the higher level of discipline required by urban life in the predominantly merchant-oriented Venetian society. Thus whereas the total population may have remained considerably smaller than the preplague population, that portion likely to commit sexual crimes remained fairly constant. The precipitous drop in sexual crime came later, during the trying years of the war with Genoa, a period when a considerable portion of the potential criminal group was serving in the war effort. This and the disruption of the Falier conspiracy may also have decreased the efficiency with which records of such relatively minor crimes were kept, further deflating the statistics.

There is one final explanation for these statistics. It is the most complex, but it has considerable support in the documents. In the preceding analysis of sexual crime it was noted that crimes against young unmarried women were treated least strictly by Venetian authorities. If this was the most leniently viewed type of sex crime, it is reasonable to assume that it was the least reported type. In turn, this means that our largest source of error might be in unreported crimes committed against girls of marriageable age. Yet for girls of this age the plague had a most profound effect. Widowers sought new wives to care for children or procreate new ones, inheritors had the economic means to marry, and in general society felt a need for marriage as it felt a need for marriage's fruit—children. Thus, though the plague did not kill off as large a part of this group, its impact was to diminish the size of the group through marriage. A testimonial to this is the decrease in the number of sex crimes against unwed girls of marriageable age after the plague, both absolutely and in relation to said crimes against children and married women. The plague, then, by decreasing the size of the group of unwed girls of marriage-

able age, left for the victims of such crimes a relatively larger group of married women and those children too young to marry who had survived the plague. Crimes against both these groups were traditionally considered more serious and hence were more likely to be reported. Thus another factor in the continuity in sex crimes may have been an increase in reportage as groups of women gained a status that encouraged stricter prosecution at the expense of a group where penalties were less severe. This is an elaborate hypothesis, but it is clear that crimes against children and married women did increase after the plague and this suggests that the pool of unwed girls of marriageable age was depleted, presumably through marriage.

All these possible demographic explanations might be replaced by the psychological argument that people faced with the uncertainty of life decided to act as they pleased for a few years following the plague, adhering to no moral code. In fact there may have been some of this, but it is difficult to square such an interpretation with the small rise in penalties over that period and the absence of any contemporary Venetian reference to such a phenomenon. In the end these statistics remain a problem, for the Venetian data provide no definite answer. Hopefully, comparisons with sex-crime data from similar labor-magnet cities like Florence or Genoa will eventually clarify the interactions of these various factors—unless, of course, the Venetian case is a complete anomaly.

Though there was continuity in elite perceptions of criminal sexuality through the plague period, those perceptions did not exist in a vacuum, especially as that same class of men whose attitudes defined and punished sexual criminality were not loath to participate in such activity. The involvement of members of a society with crime, not as judges but as participants, provides the final context of perception. The key to this interaction is the place of such activity within society: first, quite literally, the location where such crimes occurred; second, more abstractly, the social position of those involved.

The records provide much locational information, as identifying the place where the crime occurred seems to have been a normal part of criminal reportage. And the Venetians were quite imaginative in the places they chose for their sex crimes. Boats were a popular location. Fourteen rapes were attempted or committed on boats in the lagoon alone. A typical case is that of Beneveneta de Ferrara, who was raped taking the traghetto from Mestre, on the mainland, to Venice, by the boatman Amadeus called Blancholinas. Apparently she was alone on the boat and Amadeus took advantage of the situation. Amadeus was sentenced to a year in jail. Significantly, his guilt and penalty were publicly announced at the Rialto and at the traghetto in Mestre as a warning to other boatmen against such activity. It seems, nonetheless, that the temptation of a woman alone was often too great for boatmen to resist, for, of the fourteen rapes on boats, ten were committed by boatmen.

The greatest number of sex crimes, however, were initiated at the home of the victim. Eighty-four out of 112 clearly located crimes began at home. This reflects the fact that Venetian women, once they reached marriageable age, spent a good part of their lives in the home. A woman's place, especially a woman of any standing, was in the home. The statistics of sex crime indicate that this was an ideal that even the lower classes sought to approximate as much as possible. In the end there was really no safe place for a woman. Rapes and abductions were successful in empty houses, by hosts against guests, in convents, in houses rented especially for the occasion, in the ducal palace, and even in jail by the head jailer.

Correlating with this lack of physical mobility for women is the fact that most sexual crimes were neighborhood affairs, increasing

in frequently as population density increased. The outlying districts of Venice accounted for very few crimes, while the areas immediately adjoining the Grand Canal and the Sestieri of San Marco and San Polo, areas of high population density, accounted for a majority of such crimes. Moreover, criminals rarely moved far from their own neighborhoods to commit a sexual crime. This reflects the intense localism of lower-class life in Venice, which is still observable in dialect variances between the six sestieri of Venice. The nobility appears to have been less marked by this characteristic localism and one assumes that this phenomenon probably correlates with social status.

The social basis of sexual crime is more difficult to analyze than the geographical, because the social geography of Venice in the fourteenth century is less well mapped than the physical. The gap between the nobility and the rest of society by 1338 was clear and legally defined. But distinctions within the mass below the nobility were less clear, though it is obvious that there were gradations of social place below the nobility. Basically, this mass, called in contemporary chronicles "il popolo" (the people), can be divided into three groups: men of some authority but not nobles (such as petty communal officials, shop owners, small merchants); laborers; and, finally, marginal members of society (such as vagabonds, wanderers, and slaves).

Unfortunately, to statistically assess responsibility by these broad groups for sex crimes is impossible, because we do not know what proportion of the population each constituted. Nonetheless, the figures are significant even as raw data. The nobility was brought to trial in sixty-two cases during the period 1338–1358, while important men below the nobility accounted for twenty-seven cases, workers accounted for eighty-six cases, and marginal people for nineteen cases. These data are shaky, however, because in ninety-one cases we cannot place criminals occupationally. This is too large a group to overlook, though it appears a sizable part probably belonged to the marginal group at the bottom of the social continuum or were newcomers to the Venetian scene without a clearly defined place.

In the end comments on lower-class sex crimes must be primarily subjective. On the whole these crimes seem less planned, less organized, and as noted earlier, more likely to be strictly local. The penalties more often involved jail sentences, and because fines that could not be paid required a stay in jail until the money could be raised or a commutation worked out on the basis of time in jail, the likelihood of prison time made conviction more serious at this level of society. Still, the penalties for sexual crimes against single women remained generally nominal and reportage at the lower levels of society may well have been minimal. Such crimes may have been regularly committed without much fear of punishment or much thought.

Significantly for lower-class perceptions of sexual criminality, sex crime did not have upward social mobility; members of the lower classes did not rape noble girls. To a degree this must have been because noble girls were better watched and protected. But this cannot entirely explain the situation, for this presumed superior guard did not successfully protect noble girls from noble rape. A second element in the lack of upward mobility in sex crime must be the other side of the coin of an elite world view: a lower-class perception that sexual crimes against the nobility were much more serious than a normal sex crime, in fact, almost inconceivable. Such a crime was not a petty crime like rape, but a crime with political and social overtones too large to be merely a matter of passion.

Turning to the nobility, however, it is apparent that they were responsible for much more than their share of sexual crimes. Of the 285 people accused of committing sexual crimes, 62 were nobles. Thus the nobility, who constituted roughly between 3 and 7 percent of the population, were brought to trial for more than 21 percent of such crimes. As noted earlier, this was clearly only a fraction of their criminality. Less clear are the reasons why the nobility were accused of committing more than three times their share of such crimes, especially when they controlled the judicial process. One seemingly significant reason is that noble males married at a late age, generally in their late twenties or beyond, and thus lacked sexual outlets in their most virile years. However, the reality of a later marriage age must be tempered by the fact that prostitution in Venice, monitored by the Commune, provided a legal outlet for sexual desires which could not be expressed in marriage. Young nobles thus were not forced to commit rape by a lack of sexual opportunity.

A second probable factor in the high level of accusations against the nobility may have been the hope of economic gain from fines. But in the sixty-two cases involving the nobility only three convicted nobles paid fines that went to the victim, hardly a rate of return worthy of the effort. This should not seem strange. What would be strange is a system of justice controlled by an elite that would work unjustly to their disadvantage, allowing them to be robbed by young girls seeking dowries. In the end the bringing to trial of such a large group of the nobility must reflect a high level of noble criminal activity in the sexual area.

Also, it reflects a willingness to prosecute the nobility for such crimes. Some historians have seen this as proof of the remarkable evenhandedness of Venice's nobility—the proverbial justice of the Venetian system vindicated. Such a rosy view of the Venetian myth, which these days needs all the shoring up it can get, must be qualified by the minor importance attributed to sexual crimes. The penalties imposed upon the nobility even for the most reprehensible sexual crimes were relative slaps on the wrist, especially as most were fines. Prosecution for rape again provides a good example. Of a total of thirty-three successfully prosecuted clear cases of rape committed by nobles, only twelve involved jail sentences. Furthermore, among these twelve, four jail sentences were given for rape of noble women, two for rapes of girls under twelve, and one for the rape of a nun from a noble family. The remaining five jail sentences handed out for rape of single girls of marriageable age were all negligible, three being jail terms of a month or less. Thus, jail terms were either minimal or used for the most serious noble offenses. The norm was a fine, and obviously a fine's burden on the nobility was much lighter than on most of the rest of society.

Moreover, when we examine the penalties given the nobility for rape using the point equivalency set up in Table 1, they actually fall below the average for rape. The average penalty for all rapes was 21.6 points, whereas for thirty-three noble rapes the average is 18.5 points. Thus not only did the nobility tend to pay for their crimes in relatively painless fines; they actually paid less money as well. In the end then we cannot make too much of the nobility's willingness to penalize their fellows for sexual crimes. The penalties were mild and the crime not at all serious; thus, it was an ideal place to make a show of justice.

There is another important factor in the high level of illegal noble sexual activity. Rape, attempted rape, and abduction for sexual purposes were not serious crimes, especially when they were directed against lower-class women. If we eliminate from the statistics the cases of nobles raping nobles, the average penalty for rape by a noble was 11.1 points or £111p. Clearly this was perceived as a minor crime, a kind of youthful excess for the nobility, a crime, in sum, that could be committed without much fear of the consequences.

A final factor is that elite mentality itself supported less the control of rape than the commitment of rape. Again, here, the Venetian nobility come close to the values of de Sade. Such values are difficult to demonstrate with the limited literary output of Venetian society in the fourteenth century, but the criminal records give a clue. For example, the disparity between penalties for noble rape of noble women, 35.6 points, and noble rape of lower-class women, 11.1 points, is a strong indicator of such a mentality. Where such an attitude prevails, sex crimes downward across class lines tend to be viewed as less serious and thus are that much more possible, especially for a young nobility without real responsibility or place in society. Thus, although prostitution was available for a sexual outlet for the nobility, their view of their own position in society and their attitude towards sex crimes made the latter for many a viable alternative.

The career of the noble rapist Paulus de Canali demonstrates this well. In May of 1351 he was accused of raping the wife of a carpenter named Marcus. According to witnesses, he broke into her house and raped her, but the Forty acquitted him. Six months later he was back before the Forty, this time with a crime his noble brothers were less likely to overlook. Again it was breaking and entering and rape, but the victim was the wife of Marcus Corner, a noble of rich connections socially, politically, and economically. Paulus and two young friends, the noble Moretus Vituri and Moretus de Buora, were found guilty. Youthful excess had become excessive, and all three were fined 20 ducats each, jailed for three years, and then banned for three years. For Paulus and his friends it appears rape was a minor crime until they overstepped the line that their society chose to draw—a line that reveals very clearly a Venetian elite mentality already well formed.

To a degree, then, de Sade's ideal did exist once. Sex crimes in the fourteenth-century Venetian Republic were relatively minor crimes—damaging but not destructive to property. There were gradations in penalties for status and position and fluctuations in criminality, but still the Venetian approach to sexual criminality was surprisingly similar to de Sade's vision. Yet perhaps that closeness is not so strange when we consider for a moment that de Sade's vision was based upon the use of rationality to maximize personal power and pleasure for a new elite, a vision that had been, to a degree, already realized in the urban environment of the early Italian renaissance. The changes of perception spawned by this new elite were certainly essential in the intellectual and artistic triumphs of the Renaissance, but de Sade in theory and the history of Venetian sexual criminality in fact reveal a darker side as well.

■ ■ ■

STUDY QUESTIONS

1. How were the rapes of young girls, women of marriageable age, and unmarried women treated differently by the courts? What accounts for this difference?

2. How did the Black Death affect the incidence of rape in Venice? Did it seem to have any effect on private or public morality?

3. Why were noble men more prone to commit rape? How did the courts regard nobles charged with the crime of rape?

4. What does the history of rape in fourteenth-century Venice say about the status of women at that time?

BIBLIOGRAPHY

Guido Ruggiero, who wrote this essay, has developed his ideas further in *Violence in Early Renaissance Venice* (1980) and *The Boundaries of Eros: Sex Crime and Sexuality in Renaissance Venice* (1985). Lauro Martines, ed., *Violence and Civil Disorder in Italian Cities: 1200–1500* (1972), provides an important collection of essays. On the history of sexuality see especially Michel Foucault, *The History of Sexuality* (translated 1978); Vern L. Bullough, *Sex, Society and History* (1976); Lawrence Stone, *The Family, Sex and Marriage in England: 1500–1800* (1977); and several of the essays in Natalie Zemon Davis, *Society and Culture in Early Modern France* (1965). Infanticide is dealt with in R. C. Trexler, "Infanticide in Florence: New Sources and First Results," *History of Childhood Quarterly* (Summer 1973). Fur-collar crime is discussed in Barbara A. Hanawalt, "Fur Collar Crime: The Pattern of Crime Among the Fourteenth-Century English Nobility," *Journal of Social History* (Spring 1975).

19. WHY MEN FOUGHT IN THE HUNDRED YEARS' WAR

Anthony Tuck

After the Great War—World War I—had ended, after the millions who died were counted and the financial cost of the war was tabulated, people began to wonder what caused the war and why so many were so willing to die for so little. In the United States this search for answers became particularly intense. Newspaper and magazine articles, books, and Congressional investigations sought to answer the same question: Why was a nation that was not attacked drawn into the most bloody war in the history of the world? Many diverse answers were advanced. It was British propaganda, some said. In the age of the mass man, when public opinion became important, psychologists teamed with advertisers to sell America a product: war. Others said that bankers and arm dealers—the "merchants of death"—pushed the United States into the war for their own greedy motives. Still others asserted that men went to battle with dreams of glory and heroism clouding their vision.

The quest for why people fight and die in battle is not of recent origin. The same questions—and many of the same arguments—can be found swirling around the Hundred Years' War. Here, too, some people fought for dynastic rights—to put King Edward III of England on the throne of France; or, conversely, to prevent Edward from usurping the French crown. Here, too, some fought because of propaganda. Both sides sent out royal decrees that exaggerated the wickedness of their enemy. And here, too, combatants went to war with mouths full of vainglory and eyes wide to the chance to loot and plunder. The Hundred Years' War exhibited medieval and modern traits. There were moments of great chivalry, of knight fighting knight surrounded by color and pomp. But there were also times when commoners killed knights with crudely fashioned weapons. Indeed, the English owed their victories at Crécy, Poitiers, and Agincourt more to their yeoman archers than to their mounted knights. In the Hundred Years' War a very modern greed pushed people into battle, but Joan of Arc fought out of a medieval sense of religious inspiration.

In this essay Anthony Tuck examines some of the reasons why Englishmen and Frenchmen wanted to kill each other in their battles between 1337 and 1453. Often their motives were not much different than those of the soldiers who fought in the trenches of Europe from 1914 to 1918.

In the middle decades of the fourteenth century, the English attitude to war underwent a profound change. In the century that followed the loss of most of the French territories of the Angevin kings, the English nobles and knights showed little enthusiasm for campaigning overseas: indeed, it was said at the time that the English knights did not give a bean for the whole of France. The refusal of the Earl of Norfolk to serve in Flanders in 1297 provoked the famous retort from Edward I: *"Aut ibis aut pendebis"* (You will go or you will hang), to which the Earl replied that he would neither go nor hang. The wars in France and Scotland in the reign of Edward I and Edward II gave rise to financial and constitutional strains and to conflict in parliament between the King and both nobility and commons. In terms of military success there was little to show for the expenditure of so much blood and treasure, and in Scotland the English were compelled by 1328 to abandon everything that Edward I and his son had fought for.

Thus at the accession of Edward III England enjoyed no very high reputation as a military power, and there was no sign of a will to war that might induce men to accept the financial and political problems that lengthy campaigning engendered. Indeed, the military campaigns of Edward III's early years were not notably successful or popular. His first campaign against the Scots, in the summer of 1327, almost ended in disaster and was followed by the humiliating Treaty of Edinburgh. The renewal of war in Scotland in 1332 produced some initial success, but by 1335 the pro-English forces had been dislodged and French mobilisation on behalf of the Scots presented a serious threat to English security. The raising of money, supplies, and men for the Scottish wars provoked the same sort of discontent that had been voiced in Edward I's and Edward II's reigns. Even with the shift of empha-

sis in campaigning from Scotland to France after 1337, attitudes did not change immediately. Although there is some evidence that men were more ready to volunteer for service in France than in Scotland, the diplomacy and the military preparations of the opening phase of the Hundred Years' War imposed unprecedented financial strains on England, and underlay the political crisis of 1340–41. Indeed, it has been suggested that the weight of taxation between 1336 and 1341 was greater than at any other time in the Middle Ages, and serious unrest was perhaps only narrowly averted.

Yet six years later, the English victory over the French at Crécy generated an atmosphere of euphoria. The Commons thanked God for the great victory He had given their King, and they declared that all the money they had voted had been well spent. Henceforward, there could be little doubt about the popularity of the war with France. The victory of the Black Prince at Poitiers in 1356 and the capture of the French King himself raised enthusiasm to new heights, though it also created expectations about the fruits of victory that soon appeared unrealistic. Even the stalemate of the 1370s led to demands that the war should be properly, efficiently, and economically conducted rather than abandoned. The frustration of English aims in France brought the government political unpopularity, but no widespread desire for peace. Indeed, Richard II's attempt to negotiate peace with France in the 1390s was regarded with suspicion, if not downright hostility, by important sections of opinion in England. Henry V found little difficulty in renewing and orchestrating popular enthusiasm for the war, and the victory at Agincourt in 1415 produced an atmosphere of euphoria and a loosening of the purse strings reminiscent of the aftermath of Crécy. Within a generation of Edward III's accession, England had become the foremost, and perhaps the most feared, military power in Europe; her reputation for military success outlived her final collapse in France between 1449 and 1453,

"Why Men Fought in the 100 Years War" by Anthony Tuck, *History Today*, Vol. 33, April 1983, pp. 35–40. Reprinted by permission.

and helps to explain the wariness with which the French kings of the latter part of the fifteenth century approached their dealings with the English.

For most of the period between 1337 and 1453, therefore, popular enthusiasm for the war with France can scarcely be doubted; but it requires explanation. To some extent, enthusiasm for the war was generated by royal propaganda, stressing the rightness of the King's cause, the danger to England and the English language from the aggressive ambitions of the French, and—in the Lancastrian phase of the war—the duty of the King and his subjects to maintain their lawfully acquired inheritance in France. Royal propaganda was accompanied by ceremonial which reinforced the military ethos of Edward III's court. In 1344, for instance,

The lord king . . . took a corporal oath that he himself . . . would begin a Round Table in the same manner and estate as the lord Arthur, formerly king of England, maintained it, namely to the number of 300 knights, a number always to be maintained, and he would support and cherish it according to his power. . . . The Earls of Derby, Salisbury, Warwick, Arundel, Pembroke and Suffolk, and many other barons and knights, whom uprightness and fame put forward to be worthy of praise, made a like oath.

The following year the building of a "round house" at Windsor was begun. The Order of the Garter, founded in 1349, united chivalric idealism to religious devotion, and was open even to "simple knights" who by their "proven worth" were fit to associate with the King and the great earls.

But propaganda and court ceremonial alone could not whip up and sustain support for war, persuade the Commons to finance military campaigns, and induce men of all social ranks to take up arms. The excitement and glory of war, especially successful war, was for many a justification in itself. The upbringing and education of young men of the noble and knightly classes stressed the importance of

military values and prowess in battle, whereas the literature that such men read presented a chivalric ideal that, however far from being realised in practice, made the profession of arms appear a noble calling. To young men in particular the glamour, idealism, and patriotism of the king's wars had a strong appeal, and it is as well to remember the extent to which war in the fourteenth and fifteenth centuries was a young man's business. The Black Prince was sixteen when he "won his spurs" at Crécy; Edward III's companions in arms, chief amongst whom was Henry of Grosmont, Earl of Lancaster, were mostly in their twenties when the war began, and Henry V was twenty-eight when he won his victory at Agincourt. A recent study of the Gloucestershire gentry has suggested that for most men of the knightly class war was an occupation of youth, and those who survived assumed careers as administrators in the county in middle life when war no longer held the same appeal.

Throughout the war, however, part of the attraction and glamour of campaigning was the opportunity it offered for profit, and there can be little doubt that the profit motive was of even greater importance than propaganda and patriotism in persuading men to serve and in sustaining enthusiasm for war. In 1391, according to Froissart, the Duke of Gloucester argued that the prosperity of "the poor knights and esquires of England" depended upon war, and in 1414 the Chancellor, Bishop Beaufort, used the prospect of profit as an inducement to persuade the Commons to grant a tax for the forthcoming campaign in Normandy. To a freebooter such as the Bascot de Mauleon, portrayed by Froissart, profit was the principal purpose of war. The Battle of Brignais, Froissart records the Bascot as saying, "was a godsend to (his) companions, for they were very hard up. They all grew rich on the good prisoners and the towns and fortresses they took in the Archbishopric of Lyons and down the Rhone." It has even been suggested that Henry V's order to kill the French prisoners at Agincourt was resisted or ignored because of

■ ■ ■ *A town under siege during the Hundred Years' War. Note the use of cannons by the besieging army.*

the profits that the English expected to win from ransoming their captives.

Although the armies that Edward III and his successors put into the field were paid, wages were not the main financial attraction and source of wealth for those who enlisted. Rates of pay—6d per day for a mounted archer, 3d for an infantryman in Edward III's reign— were not generous, and they did not increase to keep pace with the rise in agricultural labourers' wages in the years after the Black Death. Wages were commonly supplemented by a *regardum*, a "reward" or bonus that most captains of retinues agreed to pay. Yet even when supplemented by the "reward," wages in themselves could hardly be a reason for serving, especially when men might often have to wait weeks or months to receive what was due to them. The real source of profit was exploitation of the enemy, in the form of ransoms of prisoners, loot from captured towns, booty seized on the battlefield, and, especially in the fifteenth century, the systematic and long-term exploitation of land captured and settled by Englishmen in France.

Because the war took place, of course, on French territory, and because, until the last four years, the English won most of the major battles, there was little in the way of loss to off-set the profits from warfare in France. Casualties in battle were probably not as low as has sometimes been supposed, and disease claimed as many, if not more, victims than enemy action; but in comparison with the other hazards that faced young men in the fourteenth and fifteenth centuries war was not an especially risky activity. Some English soldiers of all ranks were captured, imprisoned, and ransomed: the Earl of Pembroke, for example, was captured by the Castilians at the battle of La Rochelle in 1372 and ransomed for 120,000 francs. More pathetically, one Walter Ferrefort wrote, probably in 1375 or 1376, to his lord Sir John Strother from prison in St. Brieuc where he was being held "with iron fetters on his feet and hands," beseeching him to arrange for his release, presumably by ransom. On balance, however, the traffic in ransoms was heavily in favour of the English. At Poitiers the English gained the biggest prize of all when they captured the French King, John II. His ransom was fixed at 3 million gold crowns, the equivalent of £500,000 sterling, though rather less than half was eventually paid. In all, 1,974 captives were said to have been taken at Poitiers, including thirteen counts, five viscounts, and twenty-one bannerets. At Agincourt, where French casualties seem to have been substantially higher than at Poitiers, one chronicler estimated the number of prisoners at 700, excluding those killed by Henry V's order, and heading the list of captives were two dukes, Orleans and Bourbon, three counts, and the veteran Marshal of France the Sire de Boucicaut.

It is scarcely surprising, therefore, that the traffic in ransoms acquired all the characteristics of a business, and gave rise to disputes, litigation, and sometimes violence. The Black Prince sold three French lords taken at Poitiers to his father for £20,000; Richard II granted the proceeds of the ransom of Jean de Bretagne, Count of Penthièvre, to Robert de Vere, Duke of Ireland, with the intention that the money should contribute towards the cost of de Vere's expedition to Ireland; and a dispute about the ransom of the Count of Denia led to the famous episode in 1378 when Robert Hanley, one of the Count's captors, was murdered on the steps of the altar of Westminster Abbey.

It is much less easy to quantify the profits from loot and booty, though there can be little doubt about their importance. The chronicler Thomas Walsingham wrote that in 1348 there was no woman in England who did not have some booty from Caen, Calais, and other overseas towns. After Poitiers the English ransacked the French camp, and according to Froissart "they found plate and gold and silver belts and precious jewels in chests crammed full of them, as well as excellent cloaks, so that they took no notice of armour, arms or equipment." Lancaster's army returned from a raid into Poitou in 1346 "so laden with riches that they made no account of cloths unless they were of gold or silver, or trimmed with furs." Walsingham probably exaggerated the extent to which booty from

the war was distributed amongst the people of England. Even for the combatants, there could be no certainty of profit: the attraction was the possibility—the chance that the revolution of Fortune's wheel might bring riches—even though only a small number of those who enlisted enjoyed big winnings and a permanent improvement in their wealth and status.

With the profit motive so important a reason for enlistment, it is scarcely surprising that during Edward III's reign rules were established governing the sharing out of ransoms and booty. Each company had an official known as a *butiner* whose duty it was to control the division of the loot taken on campaign; and in the fifteenth century each garrison in Normandy had a controller attached to it who was responsible to the receiver-general of Normandy for ensuring that the share of ransoms and booty due to the king was handed over. By the 1360s a series of conventions governing the sharing out of profits had been evolved which, with a few exceptions, held good for the rest of the war. In the early stages of the war, some commanders, such as the Black Prince, expected one half of the gains of their subordinates; but by the 1360s the so-called rule of thirds had evolved, under which the soldier making the gain could expect to retain one third of its value, with a third going to the captain of his company and one third to the king. These rules for the division of plunder were sometimes written into the indentures under which men agreed to serve in a lord's retinue, an indication of the importance ordinary soldiers attached to the possibility of profit and of the need to ensure that the rules for the division of the spoils of war were clearly understood.

The principal sources of profit from the campaigns of the fourteenth century, therefore, were ransoms and booty; but in the fifteenth century the opportunity for profit from the war was greatly increased by the English occupation and settlement of Normandy and Maine. The conquest and systematic long-term exploitation of French territory had formed no part of Edward III's war aims. Englishmen had been encouraged to settle in Calais after the capture, and English garrisons in strongholds such as Cherbourg and Brest had created "ransom districts" in the surrounding countryside, from which food, materials, and labour services were exacted to sustain the garrisons. But Edward III did not grant lands to Englishmen in those parts of France which recognised him as king: to grant lands in Normandy or Brittany to Englishmen would in all probability have jeopardised the diplomatic relationships with the Duke of Brittany and those Breton and Norman nobles who, for whatever reason, supported Edward III's claim to the French throne.

Henry V's approach to the question of land grants was quite different, however. In his propaganda at the start of his campaign in Normandy he stressed the ancient connection between England and Normandy: as one of the best contemporary narratives put it, Henry

prepared to cross to Normandy in order first to recover his duchy of Normandy, which belongs to him entirely by a right dating from the time of William the first, the Conqueror, even though now, as for a long time past, it is thus withheld, against God and all justice, by the violence of the French.

However, Henry's real motives in conquering Normandy were to secure the strategically placed Duchy as a base for further conquest in France, to create a vested interest in the English conquest by land grants to Englishmen, and to place in English hands the substantial resources of the Duchy, resources that might be used to pay for the war elsewhere in France and thus reduce the financial burden on the English taxpayer. Thus the grants of land in Normandy to English settlers had a military and a fiscal purpose, but they also proved a source of substantial profit to the English settlers, and much of this profit was repatriated. The late K. B. McFarlane showed how one captain and recipient of lands in Normandy, Sir John Fastolf, derived substantial wealth from the English occupation of Normandy and

Maine, and set up an administrative system to handle the repatriation of his gains. The fifteenth-century writer William of Worcester, who resided in Fastolf's household from 1422 to 1435, said that at the battle of Verneuil (August 17th, 1424) Fastolf "won by the fortune of war about 20,000 marks." From Henry V and Bedford he received the barony of Silly-Guillaume near Le Mans; lands in the Pays de Caux, ten castles, and other property in Normandy. Even in 1445, when English control over Normandy and Maine was weakening, he was still able to derive an income of £401 a year from his French lands.

It is impossible to say how typical Fastolf's career of service and profit in Normandy and Maine was. The sixteenth-century antiquarian John Leland believed that many castles and houses in England had been built out of the profits of the French war. Sir William Bowes, for example, was in France with the Duke of Bedford for seventeen years and "waxid riche," rich enough to build "*a fundamentis* the manor place of Streatlam, Co. Durham." Some lords on the other hand were absentees, drawing revenue from Normandy without contributing to its defence. Sir John Grey of Heton in Northumberland, for instance, was granted the *conté* of Tancarville in 1419 but was killed at Baugé two years later; his young son's guardians in England drew the profits from the *conté* but even when he came to manhood Henry played no part in the defence of Normandy. Conversely, other settlers, particularly men of lower social status, had no resources other than their Norman lands, and lost everything when Normandy fell in 1449–50: Oliver Kathersby esquire, lieutenant of the Captain of Domfront, was captured by the French when they retook the town in August 1450, eventually returned to England where "he died of grief of heart at Westminster . . . in very great poverty."

The impact on English society of the wealth won from war has never been fully analysed, and indeed perhaps it cannot be. For it was essentially the lucky individual who gained; for each soldier who made money on the scale of Sir John Fastolf there were many who made nothing at all, and a few who lost everything by being captured themselves or, like Sir John Grey, did not live long enough to enjoy their profits. Some of the wealth won from war was invested in land: the Earl of Arundel's systematic purchase of manors in Surrey and Sussex in the 1370s probably represented the investment of the profits of war. Some money, as Leland realised, was spent on that most conspicious of all forms of consumption, building. Sir John de la Mare thought to have financed the building of Nunney Castle in Somerset out of wealth gained in France, and there is little doubt that Fastolf used his income from France in building his castle at Caistor-by-Yarmouth. Most conspicuously of all, Edward III spent some of the ransom of John II on building

works at Windsor Castle, where the remodeled royal apartments represent one of the most enduring monuments to the wealth the English won from war in France. Some individuals greatly enhanced their social status by means of their gains in war and their rewards from a grateful king for their deeds of valour on the battlefield. The prospect of gain was a powerful incentive to serve in the king's wars, and did perhaps more than anything else to sustain popular support for the war; but when set beside the long-term effects of demographic decline and economic contraction it would be hard to show that the wealth won from war, however powerful a motivating force on individuals, had more than a marginal impact on English society in the fourteenth and fifteenth centuries.

■ ■ ■

STUDY QUESTIONS

1. What role did propaganda play in spreading enthusiasm for war with France? How did the propaganda appeal to England's mythical past?

2. How was the idealism of the young used to generate support for the war? What other appeals did war have for young—and old—nobles?

3. What were the financial attractions of war? How were the booty and loot of war divided?

4. How did war gains affect English society?

BIBLIOGRAPHY

A very good one-volume treatment of the Hundred Years' War is Edoiard Perroy, *The Hundred Years War* (1965). Wallace K. Ferguson, *Europe in Transition, 1300–1520* (1962), is a well-balanced and insightful overview of the period. John Keegan, *The Face of Battle* (1977), has a long chapter on Agincourt in which he discusses how the battle was fought and what warfare meant for the common soldier. The war is also treated in C. T. Allman, *Society at War: The Experiences of England and France during the Hundred Years War* (1973), and H. J. Hewitt, *The Organization of War Under Edward III* (1966). Barbara Tuchman, in *A Distant Mirror* (1980), similarly paints a colorful picture of the war. Edward A. Lucie-Smith, in *Joan of Arc* (1977), discusses the end of the war and the life and death of France's greatest heroine.

Part Six

NEW FAITHS, NEW WORLDS, NEW WEALTH: SIXTEENTH-CENTURY EUROPE

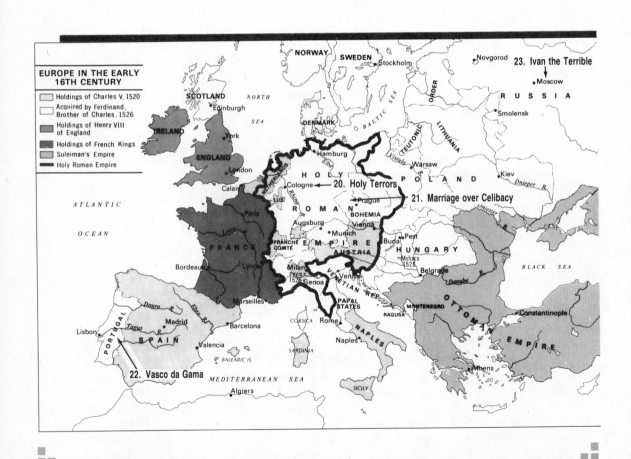

During the sixteenth century Europe experienced three changes that made it a very different society from the medieval culture that preceded it. The first change was the invention of the printing press, which created an intellectual revolution by making possible the mass production of books. This intellectual revolution merged with the second great change of the sixteenth century: the Protestant Reformation. Although the Church had faced serious challenges to its authority in the past, the printing press helped make the challenges of the sixteenth century far less easy to control. Erasmus' criticisms of the Church paved the way for Martin Luther's Reformation, and printing spread both men's words farther and faster than ever before. Many reformers considered the printing press to be a gift of God, sent for the purpose of furthering the Reformation.

As Edmund Stillman's selection explains, the Protestant Reformation split Christianity deeply and permanently. Profound differences quickly developed in the attitudes of Catholics and Protestants toward such basic human activities as sex and marriage. Steven Ozment describes some of the new Protestant values in his article. This religious division in society also opened the way for challenges to traditional authority. Groups like the Anabaptists made religious belief a primarily personal rather than a social matter and so threatened the traditional church and the traditional social hierarchy. Savage but ultimately unsuccessful repression followed.

The Great Age of Discovery also occurred at the beginning of the sixteenth century. In 1492, Christopher Columbus discovered the New World, although he actually thought it was a far eastern portion of Asia. A few years later in 1497, Vasco da Gama reached India by sailing around Africa. Both voyages opened vast new lands to Europe's potential exploitation, as the excerpts from the explorer's journal describe. Thanks to their superior sailing ships, which were larger and armed with more and better cannon, the Europeans were able to dominate the populous and sophisticated Asian states. The less technologically advanced tribes and kingdoms of the Americas and Africa were even easier prey. For the Europeans, these contacts brought vast new wealth in the form of American gold and silver and Asian spices and other trade goods.

New wealth brought its own great changes. More than ever before, the European economy became based on money. This change began to undermine the traditional social hierarchy based on feudalism's three orders of society. As Maureen Perrie describes for Ivan the Terrible, the new riches made monarchs more powerful even while it tempted them to seriously overextend themselves and the resources of their realms. Henry VIII of England, Henry IV of France, and Ivan the Terrible of Russia were quick to use their new power, making the sixteenth century an era of growth in monarchical control.

20. THE HOLY TERRORS OF MÜNSTER

Edmund Stillman

When Martin Luther (1483–1546) wrote his 95 Theses in 1517, he was seeking to purify the late medieval church by returning it to its apostolic origins. He never intended to divide the Church or challenge the existing social order. But Luther's Reformation did open up the entire existing social order to challenge when it upset the religious establishment. Various religious splinter groups appeared, including the Anabaptists.

Early Anabaptism's most obvious characteristic was its belief in the rebaptism of adults. Rebaptism symbolized the Anabaptist teaching that membership in the invisible church of true believers was a voluntary and conscious action. Another important aspect of Anabaptist theology was a belief in social equality and the essential brotherhood of all true Christians. At the same time, these true Christians needed to withdraw as much as possible from participation in the affairs of the surrounding society such as public office-holding, oaths, and wars. As a result, Anabaptism possessed great appeal for the poor and the uprooted, who were relatively more numerous in the sixteenth century than they are in modern industrial societies. Unfortunately for the Anabaptists, their egalitarian teachings threatened the existing European religious and social structure, which was based on an individual's membership and participation in a hierarchy of various ranks or orders that were unequal in the status and privileges they possessed. Everywhere the authorities and the social elites, both Catholics and Protestants, opposed the Anabaptists and persecuted them. Moderate Anabaptists accepted these tribulations stoically and pacifically. Some radical Anabaptists, however, questioned pacifism. Why should they, the true Christians, passively submit to the outrages of the wicked and ungodly? Simmering in self-righteous anger and resentment, they looked for an opportunity to take charge and establish their Kingdom of God on earth. They got their chance at Münster, an important city in Germany, but, as Edmund Stillman's essay shows, the result was a bloody tragedy.

In the long record of man's savagery to man, there can be no more brutal episode than the drama of the Anabaptist revolution played out in the small city of Münster in northwest Germany in 1534–35. There, as the medieval world was dying and the modern age dawning, as an ancient social order disintegrated and a new proletariat was born, starving and desperate men conceived a utopian kingdom of eternal goodness and eternal peace—and ended by creating a forerunner of the modern totalitarian state. . . .

Within the walls of the city, Jan of Leyden had proclaimed himself the Anabaptist king and messiah. Determined to destroy the institutions of private property and marriage, he presided over a mounting orgy of political terror and sexual license. Sitting in the marketplace, surrounded by two hundred courtiers and fifteen wives, he passed judgment on traitors, appeasers, and the merely weak-willed, whom he beheaded with his own sword.

Outside the city gathered all the forces of the Holy Roman Empire, Catholic and Protestant alike. Acting to protect privilege and what they conceived to be God's true order, they buried their doctrinal differences in a counterrevolutionary alliance and pledged to extirpate the Holy City of the Anabaptists by death and fire. In the end they succeeded, but not until they had matched atrocity for atrocity in the sixteen-month siege of Münster.

In some sense Martin Luther had started it all, though the Anabaptist heresy—as all rebellion—was repugnant to him. "Rebellion brings with it a land full of murder," he wrote in 1525, condemning those who undermined the secular order. "Let everyone who can, smite, slay, and stab . . . remembering that nothing can be more poisonous, hurtful, or devilish than a rebel."

Luther had dreamed of a *spiritual* freedom. In his view the earthly order was trivial, a mere anteroom to Paradise and Hell. It was also sacrosanct, because disorder was the Devil's work. What Luther could not see was that the medieval structure of belief he helped to bring tumbling down was a marvelously intricate web of social relations in which lord, priest, artisan, and peasant had, for something like a thousand years, functioned in close interrelationship. Medieval man shivered in the cold and was lucky if he died peacefully of the fever, in his bed; but unlike today's rootless and alienated men, medieval man did not doubt his place in the scheme of things. To question the medieval dogmas was tantamount to questioning everything, and so to open the floodgates of doubt.

Lutherans might care only for the question of man's relationship to God. But men could not question that relationship without questioning the secular law as well—simply because few men had learned to distinguish between the two. In the process of revolutionary questioning, the Anabaptists were a phenomenon that has become familiar in our own time. They were the lunatic fringe or, perhaps more fairly, they were the radical left wing of those many others who sought a new Godly dispensation in the world.

That the old social order was corrupt, few serious men denied. Rome, where a few years earlier a Borgia had managed to attain the throne of Saint Peter, was a scandal. In 1490, according to the great historian Henri Pirenne, there were at least 6,800 courtesans in the Holy City. The pope and his cardinals "consorted publicly with their mistresses, acknowledged their bastards," Pirenne says, and endowed them with riches stolen from the coffers of the Church. The conduct of the clergy outside Rome was hardly better, as Erasmus and Sir Thomas More, men who died faithful to their church, repeatedly pointed out.

From "The Holy Terrors of Münster" by Edmund Stillman, *Horizon*, Summer 1967, Vol. IX, No. 3, pp. 90–95. Copyright © 1967 Horizon, a division of the American Heritage Publishing Co., Inc. Reprinted by permission.

But the state of the Church alone does not account for the turmoil that convulsed the sixteenth century. As the century began, an old way of life was passing in the northwest of Europe: put simply, it was the death of the old, static, agrarian, traditional culture and the birth of a new, urban, commercial, capitalist, and protoindustrial civilization that has led down, in an unbroken line since then, to our own.

Lewis Mumford has called the sixteenth century the dawn age of technology—the "Eotechnic Age." Vast technological improvements were either invented or put into widespread operation in that century—among them the blast furnace, artillery, the printing press, the power loom, the domestic clock, and cheap paper for books. The initial effect of such devices was not simply to improve life but to contort it: the new inventions spurred the growth of factories and created a new, rootless industrial proletariat siphoned off from the once stable peasant communities of the countryside.

The capitalism of sixteenth-century Europe was naked, entrepreneurial capitalism, unchecked by social conscience or the intervention of governments—which, in any case, were too weak to govern the burgeoning new industries. And as industrialism grew and the old order died, the whole peasant world was shaken. Inflation, overpopulation, and repeated bad harvests and plagues reduced the peasants of Germany and The Netherlands to a misery they had rarely known.

In such circumstances the old tradition of the last days revived. Men began to see in their afflictions the coming of the Biblical "Apocalypse"—the reign of Antichrist to be succeeded by a perfect peace on earth wherein men would dwell in harmony with one another. Thus, the men who followed Jan of Leyden in his brutal effort to take the millennium by frontal assault were not comfortable burghers, artisans, and peasants secure in their place in society. They were not men tightly integrated into the old system of city guilds and manorial farms. They were landless peasants, or peasants with too little land; they were beggars and unskilled workmen, on the fringes of society. They were the abandoned, the desperate, and the afraid—in short, the stuff of which every fanatic movement of modern times has been made.

Dangerous social unrest in Germany dated back to the early years of the century. The early sporadic peasant risings against the feudal lords had been largely conservative in character. Even the Great Peasants' War of 1524–25, which aroused Luther's fury and in which one hundred thousand died, impresses us today with the reasonableness of its demands. But when the peasant uprising was crushed, the vision of God's kingdom on earth went underground, ready to burst forth with greater violence once again.

■■■

Anabaptism began, at about this time, as a purely religious movement in opposition to conservative Lutheranism. Its name means, in Greek, "to baptize again," and its basic doctrine was that infant baptism did not suffice to make a man a Christian. As Anabaptism developed, however, it was transformed into a genuine revolutionary movement of the poor and disinherited who broke with Lutheranism because they saw in it a bulwark of the authority of the princes.

Caring little for theological speculation, the followers of Anabaptism read their Bibles literally and with total commitment, and riveted their attention on the social doctrines of the Gospels: to the poor belonged the earth and eternal life. Private property was at best a hindrance to salvation; and the extremists among the Anabaptists believed that communal ownership was God's order for the world.

The princes hunted down the Anabaptists by the thousands, but in doing so, only intensified the Anabaptists' fanatical belief in the

■■ *Anabaptist Münster under siege by Catholic and Protestant forces during 1534 and 1535.*

imminent coming of the Earthly Kingdom. Like revolutionaries before and since, the Anabaptists were divided into pacifist and militant wings, and from the princes' point of view, the worst feature of the persecutions was that they tended to kill off the peaceful Anabaptists and drive the movement more and more into the hands of those who wanted to take the Earthly Kingdom by blood and fire.

Münster in the sixteenth century was that anomaly of the jerry-built Holy Roman Empire, a petty ecclesiastical state ruled by a bishop who was at the same time a prince. In the state of Münster the privileged clergy were everything, and there were many of them: the tiny prince-bishopric boasted four monasteries, seven convents, ten churches, and a cathedral, each with its vast bureaucracy. Throughout the principality, monks carried on a thriving commerce outside the jurisdiction of the guild. Virtually all the clergy were exempt from taxation. Thus the real public burden was carried by a struggling merchant middle class,

by artisans who bitterly resented the competition of the monks (who, they charged, supported no families, paid no taxes, and did no military service), and by the wretched Münster proletariat, who had three times between 1498 and 1522 been forced to contribute a sizable donation to the Roman Curia when a new Bishop was elected. By 1534, to make matters worse, the prince-bishop was not even a true priest but a secular lord who had not taken the trouble to be ordained.

■■■

Against this background of general misery and discontent, as Norman Cohn has pointed out in his excellent study *The Pursuit of the Millennium*, one disaster followed another: in 1529 an outbreak of the Black Death ravaged Westphalia; the crops failed; warfare in the Baltic closed the ports and prevented the importation of grain. Between 1529 and 1530 the price of rye, the poor man's staple, rose by 300 percent. In 1530 the prince-bishop sought to *sell* his bishopric to the Bishop of Paderborn. Two years later, the town opted for Lutheranism and drove out its priests.

But Münster would not remain Lutheran, and conservative, for long. When, in 1532, the nearby Duchy of Cleves expelled its Anabaptists, many of them migrated to Münster, carrying with them their doctrinal contagion. From then on the movement grew within the walls of the city. In 1533 new recruits, the first of many, arrived from The Netherlands, among then Jan Bockelson of Leyden, a young man of twenty-four who had been baptized into the movement only a few months before. "And so they came," records a chronicle, "the Dutch and the Frisians and the scoundrels from all parts who had never settled anywhere: they flocked to Münster and collected there." And these new arrivals called attention to a startling fact: the year 1533, in their eschatology, was the fifteenth centenary of the Passion of Christ. The last days of the world, the Anabaptists declared, were now at hand.

About the same time, as Cohn says, an elderly baker from Haarlem named Matthys had succeeded to the mantle of the Anabaptist prophets; but unlike his peaceful predecessors, Matthys preached that the millennium demanded blood. From Haarlem he sent out his "apostles" to preach the doctrine of the imminent Coming and of rebellion against the princes of this world. He watched the rising fever in Münster. In February 1534, he followed his young disciple, Jan of Leyden, to the city and proceeded to take control.

In its feverish state the city was helpless before him. Street crowds ruled the town, their numbers increased by the immigrants. A further cause of hysteria came from the hundreds of nuns who had broken their vows, put on secular dress, and accepted baptism in the new faith preached by Matthys.

The Anabaptists seized the town hall and the market place. The town council, Protestant in its sympathies, hesitated to use force, and the result was a compromise. The Anabaptists won legal recognition, but in the uncertain atmosphere of the town the conservative elements began to flee. By early 1534 the fanatical sectarians made up the majority of the population. In leaflets exhorting neighboring towns they warned that the earth was doomed; by Easter it would be destroyed. But Münster, that New Jerusalem, that new Ark, would be saved. All who desired salvation were to come to the city. They were to come bringing arms.

The result of these hysterical appeals was a new influx of believers, from parts as distant as Brabant in southern Holland. On February 23, 1534, in a new election of the town council, the Anabaptists won a decisive victory. The first official move of the once-persecuted sect was to expel the remaining Catholics and Lutherans—all of them destitute, many of them half-naked in the dead of the German winter. Those who remained underwent mass baptisms in the marketplace. By March there were no "disciples of the Devil" left in Münster. Addressing one another as "Brother" and "Sister," preaching perfect communal love, the Anabaptists made both Catholicism and Lutheranism capital offenses.

From his residence outside the town, the reigning prince-bishop, Franz von Waldeck, had uneasily watched the progress of the doctrinal revolution within his city. He had tolerated the conservative Lutheran burghers; but now as the social revolution began, he determined to crush it. Anticipating a war, the Anabaptists in their turn established a regular army, appointed officers of the watch, manned the walls, emplaced cannon, and dug earthworks to strengthen the town's defenses. Every man and woman within the walls was conscripted. The property of the exiles was confiscated; and each Anabaptist family was assigned, according to its need, a patch of communal land. All account books and promissory notes found among the effects of the exiles were burned. What was wearable or edible was taken into a central storehouse to be distributed by seven "deacons." "The poorest amongst us, who used to be despised as beggars, now go about dressed as finely as the highest and most distinguished," boasted an Anabaptist leaflet. "By God's grace they [the despised] have become as rich as the burgomasters . . . "

When at last the prince-bishop's forces moved in to begin the siege of Münster, the Dutch extremists instituted a reign of "justice and virtue." For two months there was unremitting propaganda against private ownership and capital. The surrender of private wealth to the public stores was made a test of Christian faith. Once the money was seized, it was used only for public purposes—for the hiring of mercenaries to bolster the town's defenses and for the purchase of needed stores. Workers within the town received their wages in kind. "Amongst us," an Anabaptist wrote, "God . . . has restored community as it was in the beginning and as befits the Saints of God. . . . And accordingly, everything which has served the purposes of self seeking and private property, such as buying and selling, working for money, taking interest and practicing usury . . . or eating and drinking the sweat of the poor . . . all such things are abolished amongst us by the power of love. . . . "

In the meantime the authorities of the bishopric and neighboring principalities of Cleves and Cologne cordoned off the city. Cavalry patrolled the roads into Münster and all traffic to and fro was halted. In April 1534, Matthys made a sortie against the prince-bishop's forces. He moved against the great army with only a dozen men, acting, he alleged, on a vision sent him by God, and believing himself to be invincible. He was instantly captured and butchered by the prince-bishop's men.

The movement might have collapsed with the death of the prophet, but his disciple, Jan of Leyden, now came forward, revealing new qualities of leadership. Haranguing the crowds, he restored their faith in victory, and military operations continued. In May, running naked through the streets, Jan fell into a trance. When he awoke, he proclaimed *his* great vision: Jan of Leyden was to reign as king in God's new Israel, assisted by a council of Twelve Elders.

The messianic kingdom was now established, and a new legal code eliminated nearly every vestige of private property. But it was in the realm of sexual behavior that Jan of Leyden now moved to legislate. God, he asserted, had required of men that they increase and multiply. Like the patriarchs of Israel, the Anabaptists of Münster were to take many wives: there was a surplus of women in the town—spoiled nuns and the widows of the slain. Once again, those who demurred were executed. (There is no record in any case that the new legislation caused much grief to these derelict and desperate women, though under the system of strict sexual subordination they had little opportunity to speak.) For a woman to complain of plural marriage became, like so much else in this new kingdom, a capital offense.

■■■

Jan of Leyden himself took fifteen wives—the most beautiful of them Divara, the widow of the old prophet Matthys. The king set up his court in the old palace of the bishops and dressed himself—as a symbol of God's magnificence—in silks and gold.

At the same time he did not entirely neglect the war. By summer two hundred of the prince-bishop's mercenaries had gone over to the Anabaptists. In an attack on the walls at the end of August 1534, the bishop's forces were repulsed—and disintegrated. For the moment it seemed that Münster was reprieved.

Alas for Münster, the victory went to the head of the Anabaptist king. Perhaps he really believed that God had already sent salvation to the faithful and that new victories were in store. In any event, rather than flee the besieged city, Jan of Leyden maintained his profligate court, played at theatricals, and legislated a new social order that grew more and more bizarre.

Jan proclaimed himself king of all the world. His elite troops wore emblems of a globe pierced by two swords—the sword of Faith and the sword of secular Power. His throne was draped with cloth of gold. Beside him stood two pages—one bearing a copy of the Old Testament and the other a sword. The court played and feasted through the night. Meanwhile, the common people were worked in a regimen of tireless austerity, as the king's councilor suddenly announced that God hated all excess of dress. Eighty-three wagonloads of clothing and bedding were collected for the central stores.

■■■

The town grew more and more debauched; the defenses were neglected—and the prince-bishop returned to the attack. The town was doomed when, in April 1535, at an Imperial Diet at Worms all the states of the Holy Roman Empire voted to contribute money and forces to the siege. Münster was completely isolated from aid by an elaborate ring of "trenches and blockhouses, and by a double line of infantry and cavalry," so that even the expected Anabaptist relief forces from Holland and north Germany could not hope to break through. As the people of Münster starved, the king ordered dances in the market square. He first promised military deliverance by foreign allies, and when that was seen to be futile, he promised a divine salvation. God the Father, he proclaimed, would change the cobblestones to bread. Men wept when the cobblestones remained stone. By late spring every animal in the town had been killed and eaten. Men gnawed at pieces of leather, and at "the bodies of the dead."

Soon the only relief from horror was sexual. Having abolished monogamy and proclaimed plural marriage early in his divine reign, Jan presided over a protracted orgy. All notions of family broke down. Men and women coupled freely, joining and parting each day, not caring any longer even for the forms of authorized communal marriage. Even that, it seemed to the populace, presupposed permanence in a world of terrifying impermanency. In this, too, the king was an example to his people: he could not sin, he proclaimed, because he was "wholly dead to the world."

"At last, in May [1535], when most of the inhabitants had tasted no bread for eight weeks," writes Cohn, "the king agreed that those who wished should leave the town. Even then he cursed the fugitives, promising them that the reward for their infidelity would be everlasting damnation. Their earthly fate was indeed fearful enough. The able-bodied men were at once put to the sword; as for the women and old men and children, the Bishop feared—not unreasonably—that if they passed through his lines they would stir up trouble in the rear and accordingly refused to allow them past the blockhouses. These people therefore lingered on for five long weeks in the no man's land before the town walls, begging the mercenaries to kill them, crawling about and eating grass like animals and dying in such numbers that the ground was littered with corpses."

Within the city the Anabaptists watched from the walls and jeered, acting out the belief so dear to medieval man that the greatest delight of the saved in Paradise was watching the sufferings of the damned in Hell.

In the end it was the king's brutality in driving the misbelievers from the city that destroyed him. On the night of June 24, 1535, one of the starving expellees crawling about between the siege works and the town walls offered to show the prince-bishop's troops a secret entry into the city. An assault breached the town's defenses. By morning the town had fallen. About three hundred Anabaptist troops surrendered on promise of their lives, only to be slaughtered almost to a man.

■ ■ ■

The end of Jan of Leyden was grimmer still. Captured by the bishop, he was led about the Empire for a time, exhibited on a chain. In January 1536, he was returned to Münster, branded and clawed by pincers, and forced to sit on a blazing iron throne.

The bishop's power and the Catholic faith were restored in Münster. Everything was as before. Until this century, the bones of Jan of Leyden swung in their cage from the tower of the Church of St. Lambert's in Münster. The Anabaptist movement, in its militant wing, was stamped out. The direct survivors of the Anabaptists today are the peaceful Mennonites and Amish of the Pennsylvania countryside.

But the impulse that drove the Anabaptists to rebellion did not die. The vision of the Earthly Kingdom of justice, and the tradition of taking the millennium by assault, survived underground—among the poor, desperate, and degraded, wherever one social order died and a new one struggled for birth. Indeed the story of the Anabaptists of Münster is an antecedent of what Carl Jung has called the "psychic epidemics of our time."

■ ■ ■

STUDY QUESTIONS

1. Although Luther opposed the Anabaptists, Stillman here credits him with making their tumultuous movement possible. In what ways is that assertion true?

2. The people of the early sixteenth century experienced much turmoil. Some of it was caused by religious conflicts, but economic changes also contributed to the problem. What were these changes and why did they cause problems?

3. How did the Anabaptist movement begin, and what were its basic ideas?

4. What were the political, social, and religious situations of Münster before the Anabaptist takeover? Why was it so vulnerable to social revolution?

5. What were the characteristics of the Anabaptist kingdom that Matthys and Jan of Leyden set up in Münster?

6. Which groups in Germany opposed the Anabaptist takeover of Münster? What did they do to try to stop it?

Bibliography

The recent and readable survey of early sixteenth-century Europe is Lewis W. Spitz, *The Protestant Reformation, 1517–1559* (1985). More concerned with the medieval background of the Reformation and the explanation of theological matters is Steven Ozment's excellent *The Age of Reform, 1250–1550: An Intellectual and Religious History of Late Medieval and Reformation Europe* (1980). Anabaptism in all its aspects is exhaustively studied in George H. Williams, *The Radical Reformation* (1962), but also see James Stayer, *Anabaptists and the Sword* (1972). The classic study of radical religious movements, including Münster, is Norman Cohn, *The Pursuit of the Millennium: Revolutionary Millenarians and Mystical Anarchists of the Middle Ages* (1970). Hans J. Hillerbrand has edited a collection of short studies in *Radical Tendencies in the Reformation: Divergent Perspectives* (1988). A more recent study covering a smaller period of time is Michael Mullet, *Radical Religious Movements in Early Modern Europe* (1980). For a study of Münster covering mostly the years after the tragic Anabaptist episode, see R. Po-chia Hsia, *Society and Religion in Münster, 1535–1618* (1984).

21. MARRIAGE OVER CELIBACY IN EARLY SIXTEENTH-CENTURY GERMANY

Steven Ozment

Early in the German Reformation, on April 4, 1523 (the day before Easter), nine well-born Cistercian nuns escaped from their cloister at Nimbschen. With the help of Leonard Kopp, a solid citizen of Torgau and a supplier of foodstuffs to the monastery, they made their way to Wittenberg by 7 April. There they sought the protection of Martin Luther, the leader of the Reform movement in Germany. He agreed to help them even though the penalty for aiding runaway nuns was death under both Canon and Civil Law. Soon, some of the women rejoined their families, some became governesses, and some married.

One nun, however, proved to be a problem. At twenty-four years of age, Katherine von Bora was past the normal age for marriage. Being vivacious, she still managed to attract a suitor, whom she also loved. But the match never came to pass because the man's family objected to his marriage to a renegade nun. Late in 1524 efforts began to find Katherine von Bora another suitor, which she firmly resisted. Suddenly she stated her willingness to marry either Luther or his associate, Nicholas von Amsdorf. A hitherto confirmed bachelor, Luther agreed that at the age of forty-two, the time was right for him to wed. So on June 13, 1525, the ex-monk and the ex-nun were wed.

Married life agreed with Luther, who grew to love his "Katie" dearly and had six children with her. His action was also stunning testimonial to the Reformation's position concerning marriage and celibacy of religious leaders. As this excerpt shows, Luther—along with many of his predecessors and contemporaries—considered the state of matrimony to be far more pleasing to God than celibacy, in spite of the long-standing teachings of the Roman Catholic Church.

Three years before his own marriage, Martin Luther wrote a treatise, *Vom ehelichen Leben* (On the estate of marriage, 1522), his first lengthy discussion of the subject, in which he complained that "marriage has universally fallen into awful disrepute," that peddlers everywhere are selling "pagan books which treat of nothing but the depravity of womankind and the unhappiness of the estate of marriage"—a reference to classical misogynist and antimarriage sentiments and to the bawdy antifeminist stories that were popular among Luther's contemporaries. The connection between the celibate ideal and misogyny was revealed in Sebastian Franck's collection of popular German proverbs (1541), which preserved a proverb used by St. Jerome to defend the single life: "If you find things going too well, take a wife"—a proverb Franck paired with another: "If you take a wife, you get a devil on your back." Parents, said Luther, were buffeted by such sentiments and by the religious propaganda in praise of celibacy; in response they turned their children away from marriage and encouraged them to enter the cloister.

Luther was not alone in making such complaints. An observer in Augsburg reported in 1534 that marriage there had become a "weak, despised, and rejected estate," which the young, especially men, fled in fear; everywhere women were said to make fools of men (the biblical stories of the downfall of Adam, Samson, and David at the hand of a woman were current), and both sexes looked on the birth and rearing of children with "superstitious dread." Caspar Gütell, Protestant pastor in Eisleben (Saxony), commented on his contemporaries in a sermon published in the same year: "Having seen how much effort, anxiety,

pain, need, care, and work are involved in marriage, they would not recommend it to a dog, and to save their children from it, they give them over to the Devil by forcing them into the cloister. Thereby they gain for them an easy life on earth, but they dispatch their souls to hell."

Although contemporary Catholic parents did not consider the cloister a danger to the souls of their children, they did tend to view it as a place for the weak, or in some way failed, child who needed special protection. Although Hermann von Weinsberg was later very proud of his illegitimate daughter Anna when she became mother superior in the family convent in Cologne, he originally viewed her entrance into the cloister as fitting for one with her social handicap. He also was not surprised when a frail niece who had left the cloister to live with her mother found life in the world so stressful that she sought to enter another cloister. And he recommended the religious life to a sickly nephew who, he was convinced, would not be able to lead a "more vigorous" life in the world. In his old age Martin Luther explained his own entrance into the cloister at Erfurt in 1505 as an act of weakness occasioned by his then "pusillanimous temperament," which his parent's very strict discipline had unintentionally brought about.

Protestant pamphleteers accused the secular and clerical critics of marriage of desiring personal and sexual freedom in the single life and of conjuring false fears and excuses to escape the responsibility and self-discipline imposed by monogamous marriage. "Because they prefer whoring and Sodomy, not a few want to avoid holy matrimony," argued the Eisleben pastor Gütell.

For this reason they say: "It would be nice to get married but how will I live? I have nothing; if I take a wife things will really get tight. And marriage brings with it many new troubles and cares and requires much effort and work. The wife complains or gets sick; the children wail and

Reprinted by permission of the publishers from *When Fathers Ruled* by Steven Ozment, Cambridge, Mass.: Harvard University Press, Copyright © 1983 by the President and Fellows of Harvard College.

scream, this one demanding something to drink, another something to eat. . . .'' Here [in having to assume these new responsibilities] is truly the greatest obstacle to marriage.

Concern for the estate of marriage was not confined to the ranks of Protestants and humanists. An anonymous tract, written in 1545 by self-critical Catholic clergy to urge the newly convened Council of Trent to allow the clergy to marry, accused the Catholic clergy themselves of undermining marriage and family life by their lax and hypocritical sexual lives and confessional practice. The authors pointed out that the clergy openly had sexual amours and that many lived publicly in concubinage, a widespread practice in the fifteenth and sixteenth centuries. According to the authors, the sight of celibate priests whoring and committing other sexual sins, yet receiving only small fines and continuing to perform their clerical offices, only encouraged weak and immoral laity to take their own seductions and adultery lightly, especially when they, too, for the penance of a few groschen, could obtain absolution from a priest for such acts.

Protestant pamphleteers were quick to condemn clerical sexual hypocrisy and a penitential system by which the church profited from the irrepressible desires of human nature (bishops regularly fined priests for whoring and forced those living in concubinage to pay annual penitential fees and ''cradle taxes'' when children arrived). According to Eberlin von Günzburg, a Franciscan convert to the Reformation and after Luther the most prolific Protestant pamphleteer, many priests felt torn apart by this contradiction. He recorded a fictitious assembly of ''seven pious but disconsolate priests whom no one can comfort,'' who were said to have met secretly to discuss the most burdensome aspect of their vocation. The first to speak declared it to be without question celibacy, and he recounted in graphic detail his own unsuccessful struggle to maintain it—his sensuous dreams, nocturnal emissions,

masturbation, and lechery. He told of an affair with a married woman that became doubly grievous to his conscience because he continued to befriend her cuckolded husband. Guilt-ridden, he ended this relationship and took a concubine, an arrangement that continued to burden his conscience not only because of its illegality but also because he forced her to practice birth control. After her death he took another concubine through whom he claims to have fathered seventeen children. Although church authority officially disapproved of such arrangements, he pointed out that it also tolerated them so long as priests paid the prescribed penitential fee (*hurenzinss*). The laity had awkwardly adjusted to such clerical whoring, ''like stableboys become accustomed to dung.'' The priest was convinced that by his own example he had taught his parishioners that whoring is no sin, and he lamented the hardships imposed on his children by the stigma of illegitimacy. His was a true dilemma:

Thus am I entangled: on the one hand, I cannot live without a wife; on the other, I am not permitted a wife. Hence, I am forced to live a publicly disgraceful life, to the shame of my soul and honor and to the damnation of many who have taken offense at me [that is, by refusing to receive the sacraments from his hands]. How shall I preach about chasteness and against promiscuity, adultery, and knavish behavior, when my own whore goes to church and about the streets and my own bastards sit before my eyes?

Protestants apologists for marriage concerned themselves also with the burdens these contradictions led priests to impose upon the laity, especially upon married women and adolescent girls. Heinrich of Kettenbach, another Franciscan convert to the Reformation and a Lutheran pamphleteer, accused confessors of impregnating sexually aggressive women who could not be satisfied by their husbands, alleging that a single confessor

■■ *Luther's Roman Catholic opponents liked to make fun of his marriage. Note that Katherine von Bora is shown dressed in a nun's habit.*

might service as many as twenty such women—wives, daughters, and maids, "like a steer a herd of cows." Kettenbach further accused confessors of impregnating young girls who had been forced by parents or circumstance into nunneries, proof of which, he claimed, was visible in moated cloisters where the drains ran free (infanticide was here alleged). He accused confessors further of "debasing respectable women and girls who are simple and pious" by their interrogations during confession, causing them "often to leave confession without hope of salvation, godless, dishonored, soulless, having become whores in their own minds, because there, in confes-

sion, their hearts have been secretly and subtly stolen, betrayed, and sold." Kettenbach also alleged that confessors were not above passing the names of adulterers on to the Fiscal, the powerful administrative office of the bishop, whose agents privately extorted from them a gulden or two on threat of exposure.

Protestants were faced with what they considered to be a crisis in domestic relations, one that could be traced to the institutions of medieval religion. To correct the situation, they exalted the patriarchal nuclear family as the liberation of men, women, and children from religious, sexual, and vocational bondage. Humanists and Protestants were not the first to

defend the estate of marriage; medieval theologians and preachers had earlier done so
when confronted by extreme ascetical sects
like the Cathars, who questioned the propriety even of procreation. The Protestant
reformers were, however, the first to set the
family unequivocally above the celibate ideal
and to praise the husband and the housewife
over the monk and the nun in principle.
Repeatedly one reads that God respects marriage as much as virginity, that an unhappy
marriage is preferable to unhappy chastity,
that celibacy, while more desirable than marriage for those few who can freely and happily maintain it, is a supernatural gift God
rarely bestows. Commenting on his own experience under vows, Eberlin von Günzburg
described the celibate life as a daily nagging of
conscience and unrest of mind, a state in
which all joy became a suffering, all consolation saddening, all sweetness bitter, a condition that dulled and deadened the senses,
hardened the heart, restrained natural honesty, made one uncivil, inhumane, and frequently susceptible to feelings of remorse, at
times so twisting one's judgment that one
came to hate salvation and the good in one's
life and to long for misfortune. Erasmus
deemed vows of celibacy "blind superstition"
arising from inadequate knowledge of human
nature. Well before the Protestants made it
their issue, Erasmus had ridiculed the church's
condemning of clerical marriage, while it tolerated and profited from clerical concubinage,
and he praised family life over the cloister.
Erasmus was also concerned that celibacy in-
hibited the growth of population in the west
at a time of Turkish expansion; not only was
celibacy a contradictory ideal in light of God's
command to procreate, it also threatened to
become self-destructive if large segments of society embraced it.

No tribute to the estate of marriage was
more eloquent than that of the fifteenth-
century Bamberg humanist and canon Al-
brecht von Eyb:

*What could be happier and sweeter than the
name of father, mother, and children [that is, a
family], where the children hang on their parents'
arms and exchange many sweet kisses with them,
and where husband and wife are so drawn to one
another by love and choice, and experience such
friendship between themselves that what one
wants, the other also chooses, and what one says,
the other maintains in silence as if he had said it
himself; where all good and evil is held in common, the good all the happier, the adversity all
the lighter, because shared by two.*

Not only did the creation of woman and the
blessing of marriage make it possible for humankind to know, love, obey, and enjoy God
into eternity, but marriage also controlled the
sins of concupiscence and fornication by giving each person a handy, regular, and legitimate sexual partner. Men and women have
been so created for marriage that they resist it
at their peril (*muss dran*), declared the Thurin-
gian Lutheran Justus Menius; it is both the rule
of nature and the command of God; to ask
whether one should marry is like asking
whether one should breathe, eat, drink, or attend to other natural needs and functions: "Every man should and must have his wife and
every woman her husband." One who truly
understands marriage, still another reformer
maintained, does not fret over how much must
go into it, as do its critics, but rather marvels
at how much comes out of it. Boomed Luther,
still unmarried: "When a father washes di-
apers or performs some other mean task for his
child, and someone ridicules him as an ef-
feminate fool . . . God with all his angels and
creatures is smiling."

According to its defenders, marriage stabi-
lized both individuals and society as a whole.
By creating families, von Eyb pointed out,
marriage filled a land with homes and communities, instruments of civil peace, and by
turning strangers into relatives and friends, it
reduced enmity, war, and hostility. Marriage
not only created sound bodies, good con-

science, property, honor, and families, Luther insisted, it also helped pacify entire cities and lands by bringing order and purpose to sexual commerce. As marriage laid the foundation of household government (*Oeconomia, Haushaltung*), family life in turn imparted to a new generation the values by which society at large was governed.

The profound social significance that Protestants attached to marriage was illustrated by the marriage services of newly reformed Wittenberg (1524) and Nuremberg (1526), both of which elaborated the second chapter of Genesis. The new service in Wittenberg stressed that marriage was "a far different thing than what the world presently jokes about and insults"; on the one hand, it is the end of a man's loneliness, as he and his bride become "one thing, like a cake"; on the other, it is a penitential institution in which the wife freely accepts the pain of childbirth and subjection to her husband, and the husband the pain of daily labor and worry over his family's well-being. Before the prospective bride and bridegroom formalized their vows in Nuremberg, they were read the story of the first marriage, the subsequent fall of Adam and Eve, and mankind's consequent guilt and need for penance and redemption. The couple's assumption of the responsibility, self-discipline, and suffering of marriage—the husband's "toil" and the wife's "labor"—was presented as part of the process by which mankind recovers from its fallen condition. Although this was not the most cheery of nuptial messages, both services exalted marriage as the foundation and nucleus of society and the divine instrument for its stability and reform. Little wonder that Lutherans described parents as "priests" and "bishops."

The home, then, was no introspective, private sphere, unmindful of society, but the cradle of citizenship, extending its values and example into the world around it. The habits and character developed within families became the virtues that shaped entire lands.

Where today children were raised to be god-fearing, obedient, and virtuous, the reformers expected tomorrow to find a citizenry capable of self-sacrifice and altruism, as well. In the great housefather books of the seventeenth century, written as comprehensive guides to the management of home and manor, direction of a household was presented as the highest human art. A father not only provided for the present and future needs of his immediate family but also extended his household throughout the fatherland, as its members assisted church and school, friends and neighbors, the poor and the needy.

■ ■ ■

STUDY QUESTIONS

1. Contrast the attitudes of Protestants and Catholics toward life in the cloisters of monasteries and nunneries.

2. Why did Protestants and some Catholics condemn the practice of clerical celibacy?

3. What did pre-Reformation and Protestant thinkers feel was the role of the patriarchal nuclear family in human society, and how did Protestant attitudes differ from medieval defenses of family life?

BIBLIOGRAPHY

Attitudes toward marriage in the Middle Ages are surveyed by Christopher Brooke, *The Medieval Idea of Marriage* (1989), and Georges Duby, *The Knight, the Lady, and the Priest: The Making of Modern Marriage in Medieval France* (1983). For a classic overview of the history of clerical celibacy, see Henry Charles Lea, *History of Sacerdotal Celibacy in the Christian Church* (1867, reprinted 1966). Family life in early modern France and England are described, sometimes controversially, by Jean-Louis Flandrin, *Families in Former Times: Kinship, Household and Sexuality* (1979); Lawrence Stone, *Family, Sex, and Marriage in England 1500–1800* (1977); and Alan MacFarlane, *Marriage and Love in England: Modes of Reproduction 1300–1800* (1987). A useful short study is John Yost, "The Value of Married Life for the Social Order in the Early English Renaissance," *Societas* 6 (1976): 29–31. Directly related to the above reading is Lyndal Roper, "Luther: Sex, Marriage and Motherhood," *History Today* 33 (December 1983): 33–38. For an interesting study of early modern European attitudes toward women, see Ian Mclean, *The Renaissance Notion of Woman: Study in the Fortunes of Scholasticism and Medical Science in European Intellectual Life* (1980). An excellent new biography of Martin Luther is Heiko Oberman's *Luther: Man Between God and the Devil* (1989).

22. VASCO da GAMA WIDENS EUROPE'S HORIZONS

True understanding of another culture is difficult to achieve, despite all our modern resources of information. For the people of the Great Age of Discovery (1450–1550), such understanding was almost impossible. Ethnocentricity, xenophobia, and religious bigotry dominated people's approach to the new peoples and cultures that they came across during their explorations. Vasco da Gama and his men were no exception to this bigoted view when they first visited India.

Vasco da Gama's voyage to India in 1497–1498 was the culmination of decades of Portuguese exploration along the west coast of Africa. Beginning in 1415 under the sponsorship of Prince Henry the Navigator, the Portuguese ranged down the African coast seeking a way to attack the Moslems in North Africa from behind. They also hoped to take over the lucrative gold trade and quickly realized the slave trade's potential for profits. As the Portuguese sailors moved farther down the coast, about 1470, it occurred to them that a sea route to Asia might be a possibility. At first their efforts to find that sea route were frustrated, because Africa turned out to be much bigger than the explorers expected. But voyages by Diogo Cao in 1482–1484 and 1485 and Bartolomeu Dias in 1487–1488 at last showed them the true way.

The honor of finally completing the sea route to India was given to Vasco da Gama, a minor nobleman and a trusted soldier of the Portuguese kings John II and Manuel. As a typical Portuguese of his day, he hated any Moslem (or Moor as they were then commonly called) and looked down on the black Africans as uncivilized heathens. In addition, the Prester John legends strongly influenced his geographical thinking. These legends told of a great Christian empire that had been cut off from European Christendom by the rise of Islam. Its extent and exact nature were unknown, but Prester John, its ruler, would be a ready and able ally against the Moors whenever he was reunited with the rest of Christendom.

When Vasco da Gama departed from Portugal in 1497, that tiny nation consisted of less than a million people scattered throughout a rocky coastline and a mountainous interior located on Europe's southwestern periphery. Although the Portuguese were neither a rich nor a powerful people, thanks to the aggressive leadership of their kings and some bold seafaring, during the fifteenth century the Portuguese blazed an oceanic trail to Asian riches. Arriving in the Indian Ocean, they found a flourishing spice trade that was largely carried by the Moslem merchants of that region.

Long before the Portuguese appeared, the Indian Ocean had been an important part of East–West commerce. Ancient Romans had visited it and the Chinese under their admiral Cheng Ho had temporarily made an appearance there with a large force in the early fifteenth century. No state, however, dominated these waters militarily. Instead, large Moslem trading companies associated with various coastal cities controlled the important trade of the region. Oceanic commerce was free as long as the individual merchant was connected with one of the Moslem trading groups that virtually monopolized it.

The late-fifteenth-century India Vasco da Gama saw was fragmented politically and religiously. Although Moslems and Hindus harmoniously coexisted to a large degree, there were numerous competing and sometimes aggressive subgroups within both religions that made that state of relative religious calm somewhat precarious. So when the Portuguese introduced their anti-Moslem crusading mentality, they upset a long-standing but delicate peace. Fortunately for them, the political disunity of India meant that no effective resistance could be mounted against the Portuguese incursions. Furthermore, India's greatest powers at that time were land-based. Vijayanagar, the great Hindu state of southern India, had its attention fixed on its Moslem neighbors to the north. Beyond those states of Bijapur, Bidar, and Golconda lay the declining Sultanate of Delhi. It would swiftly fall in 1525 to the army of Babur, the creator of the land-based Mughal Empire.

Therefore, at the time of Vasco da Gama's first voyage, the attention of the entire Indian subcontinent was nervously focused on the precarious situation in the north. This confused state of affairs was ultimately what helped make it possible for the Portuguese to take over the spice trade in the Indian Ocean.

The Portuguese faced some stiff competition for control of the spice trade despite the relative power vacuum that existed in the area. At the time of Vasco da Gama's first voyage, the major powers involved in the spice trade of the Indian Ocean were the once powerful Mameluke Sultans of Egypt, the Moslems of Gujarat, and the locally powerful Zamorin (king) of Calicut, the dominant city of the Malabar Coast. Fortunately for Portuguese ambitions, when they made their grab for control of the Indian Ocean's trade, their superior sailing ships and cannon, their courage, and a fair amount of luck combined to make them the victors.

Thanks to the reports of Pedro de Covilha, a Portuguese traveler in the Middle East, and other sources of intelligence, a rudimentary knowledge of the political and economic organization of the Indian Ocean existed in Portugal. This information rightly prompted Vasco da Gama to make Calicut his destination. Apart from that, when he arrived at Calicut on May 20, 1498, Vasco da Gama was ignorant about the peoples and customs of India. Oddly enough, the first people to meet the Portuguese in Calicut harbor turned out to be Tunisian Moslems who exclaimed in Spanish, "May the Devil take you! What brought you here?" A taken-aback Portuguese replied, "We seek Christians and spices." It was just the beginning of many misunderstandings and surprises.

During his entire visit, Vasco da Gama remained convinced that the Hindus were actually Christians of a heretical type. The fact that the name of the Hindu god Krishna sounded like *Cristo* and that a local goddess was named Mari fostered this confusion. Countless retellings of the Prester John tales had conditioned the Portuguese to expect to find other Christians. This mistake also made the quite apparent friendliness and cooperation between the Hindus and the Moslems seem inexplicable and even sinister to the Portuguese. Furthermore, they completely underestimated the political importance of the Zamorin of Calicut. Accustomed to dealing with the chieftains of the less-advanced societies of Africa, the Portuguese gifts to the Zamorin were ridiculously poor by Asian standards. Misunderstanding led to suspicion and suspicion led to mutual hostility.

The original narrative that follows is part of a Portuguese eyewitness's account of Vasco da Gama's first voyage. It preserves the first impressions that contact with a new world made on the Portuguese. Preconceptions and ethnocentricity directed how the Portuguese interpreted what they saw. What the Indians thought of their Portuguese visitors is not recorded, but from the events that ensued, it seems doubtful that the Indians were positively impressed. This encounter was a fateful foreshadowing of Europe's stormy relationship with Asia.

Arrival

That night [May 20] we anchored two leagues from the city of Calecut, and we did so because our pilot mistook *Capua*, a town at that place, for Calecut. Still further there is another town called *Pandarani*. We anchored about a league and a half from the shore. After we were at anchor, four boats (*almadias*) approached us from the land, who asked of what nation we were. We told them, and they then pointed out Calecut to us.

On the following day [May 21] these same boats came again alongside, when the captain-major sent one of the convicts to Calecut, and those with whom he went took him to two Moors from Tunis, who could speak Castilian and Genoese. The first greeting that he received was in these words: "May the Devil take thee! What brought you hither?" they asked what he sought so far away from home, and he told them that we came in search of Christians and of spices. They said: "Why does not the King of Castile, the King of France, or the Signoria of Venice send hither?" He said that the King of Portugal would not consent to their doing so, and they said he did the right thing. After this conversation they took him to their lodgings and gave him wheaten bread and honey. When he had eaten he returned to the ships, accompanied by one of the Moors, who was no sooner on board, than he said these words: "A lucky venture, a lucky venture! Plenty of rubies, plenty of emeralds! You owe great thanks to God, for having brought you to a country holding such riches!" We were greatly astonished to hear his talk, for we never expected to hear our language spoken so far away from Portugal.

A Description of Calecut

The city of Calecut is inhabited by Christians. They are of a tawny complexion. Some of them have big beards and long hair, whilst others clip their hair short or shave the head, merely allowing a tuft to remain on the crown as a sign that they are Christians. They also wear moustaches. They pierce the ears and wear much gold in them. They go naked down to the waist, covering their lower extremities with very fine cotton stuffs. But it is only the most respectable who do this, for the others manage as best they are able.

The women of this country, as a rule, are ugly and of small stature. They wear many jewels of gold round the neck, numerous bracelets on their arms, and rings set with precious stones on their toes. All these people are well disposed and apparently of mild temper. At first sight they seem covetous and ignorant. . . .

At Anchor at Pandarani, May 27

A pilot accompanied our two men, with orders to take us to a place called Pandarani, below the place [Capua] where we anchored at first. At this time we were actually in front of the city of Calecut. We were told that the anchorage at the place to which we were to go was good, whilst at the place we were then it was bad, with a stony bottom, which was quite true; and, moreover, that it was customary for the ships which came to this country to anchor there for the sake of safety. We ourselves did not feel comfortable, and the captain-major had no sooner received this royal message than he ordered the sails to be set, and we departed. We did not, however, anchor as near the shore as the king's pilot desired.

When we were at anchor, a message arrived informing the captain-major that the king was already in the city. At the same time the king sent a *bale*,[1] with other men of distinction, to Pandarani, to conduct the captain-major to

_____
[1] Governor.

where the king awaited him. This *bale* is like an *alcaide*, and is always attended by two hundred men armed with swords and bucklers. As it was late when this message arrived, the captain-major deferred going.

Gama Goes to Calecut

On the following morning, which was Monday, May 28th, the captain-major set out to speak to the king, and took with him thirteen men, of whom I was one. We put on our best attire, placed bombards in our boats, and took with us trumpets and many flags. On landing, the captain-major was received by the *alcaide*, with whom were many men, armed and unarmed. The reception was friendly, as if the people were pleased to see us, though at first appearances looked threatening, for they carried naked swords in their hands. A palanquin was provided for the captain-major, such as is used by men of distinction in that country, as also by some of the merchants, who pay something to the king for this privilege. The captain-major entered the palanquin, which was carried by six men by turns. Attended by all these people we took the road of Qualecut, and came first to another town, called Capua. The captain-major was there deposited at the house of a man of rank, whilst we others were provided with food, consisting of rice, with much butter, and excellent boiled fish. The captain-major did not wish to eat, and when we had done so, we embarked on a river close by, which flows between the sea and the mainland, close to the coast. The two boats in which we embarked were lashed together, so that we were not separated. There were numerous other boats, all crowded with people. As to those who were on the banks I say nothing; their number was infinite, and they had all come to see us. We went up that river for about a league, and saw many large ships drawn up high and dry on its banks, for there is no port here.

When we disembarked, the captain-major

■ ■ *A portrait of Vasco da Gama from 1524.*

once more entered his palanquin. The road was crowded with a countless multitude anxious to see us. Even the women came out of their houses with children in their arms and followed us.

A Christian Church

When we arrived [at Calecut] they took us to a large church, and this is what we saw:

The body of the church is as large as a monastery, all built of hewn stone and covered with tiles. At the main entrance rises a pillar of bronze as high as a mast, on the top of which was perched a bird, apparently a cock. In addition to this, there was another pillar as high as a man, and very stout. In the centre of the body of the church rose a chapel, all built of hewn stone, with a bronze door sufficiently wide for a man to pass, and stone steps leading up to it. Within this sanctuary stood a small image which they said represented Our Lady. Along the walls, by the main entrance, hung seven small bells. In this church the captain-major said his prayers, and we with him.

We did not go within the chapel, for it is the custom that only certain servants of the church, called *quafees*, should enter. These *quafees* wore some threads passing over the left shoulder and under the right arm, in the same manner as our deacons wear the stole. They threw holy water over us, and gave us some white earth, which the Christians of this country are in the habit of putting on their foreheads, breasts, around the neck, and on the forearms. They threw holy water upon the captain-major and gave him some of the earth, which he gave in charge of someone, giving them to understand that he would put it on later.

Many other saints were painted on the walls of the church, wearing crowns. They were painted variously, with teeth protruding an inch from the mouth, and four or five arms.

Below this church there was a large masonry tank, similar to many others which we had seen along the road. . . .

The king sent a brother of the *bale*, who was a lord of this country, to accompany the captain, and he was attended by men beating drums, blowing *anafils* and bagpipes, and firing off matchlocks. In conducting the captain they showed us much respect, more than is shown in Spain to a king. The number of people was countless, for in addition to those who surrounded us, and among whom there were two thousand armed men, they crowded the roofs and houses.

The King's Palace

The further we advanced in the direction of the king's palace, the more did they increase in number. And when we arrived there, men of much distinction and great lords came out to meet the captain, and joined those who were already in attendance upon him. It was then an hour before sunset. When we reached the palace we passed through a gate into a courtyard of great size, and before we arrived at where the king was, we passed four doors, through which we had to force our way, giving many blows to the people. When, at last, we reached the door where the king was, there came forth from it a little old man, who holds a position resembling that of a bishop, and whose advice the king acts upon in all affairs of the church. This man embraced the captain when he entered the door. Several men were wounded at this door, and we only got in by the use of much force.

A Royal Audience, May 28

The king was in a small court, reclining upon a couch covered with a cloth of green velvet, above which was a good mattress, and upon this again a sheet of cotton stuff, very white and fine, more so than any linen. The cushions were after the same fashion. In his left hand the king held a very large golden cup [spittoon], having a capacity of half an almude [8 pints]. At its mouth this cup was two palmas [16 inches] wide, and apparently it was massive. Into this cup the king threw the husks of a certain herb which is chewed by the people of this country because of its soothing effects, and which they call *atambor*. On the right side of the king stood a basin of gold, so large that a man might just encircle it with his arms: this contained the herbs. There were likewise many silver jugs. The canopy above the couch was all gilt.

The captain, on entering, saluted in the manner of the country: by putting the hands together, then raising them towards Heaven, as is done by Christians when addressing God, and immediately afterwards opening them and shutting the fists quickly. The king beckoned to the captain with his right hand to come nearer, but the captain did not approach him, for it is the custom of the country for no man to approach the king except only the servant who hands him the herbs, and when anyone addresses the king he holds his hand before the mouth, and remains at a distance. When the king beckoned to the captain he looked at us others, and ordered us to be seated on a stone bench near him, where he could see us. He ordered that water for our hands should be given us, as also some fruit, one kind of which resembled a melon, except that its outside was rough and the inside sweet, whilst another kind of fruit resembled a fig, and tasted very nice. There were men who prepared these fruits for us; and the king looked at us eating, and smiled; and talked to the servant who stood near him supplying him with the herbs referred to.

Then, throwing his eyes on the captain, who sat facing him, he invited him to address himself to the courtiers present, saying they were men of much distinction, that he could tell them whatever he desired to say, and they would repeat it to him (the king). The captain-major replied that he was the ambassador of the King of Portugal, and the bearer of a message which he could only deliver to him personally. The king said this was good, and immediately asked him to be conducted to a chamber. When the captain-major had entered, the king, too, rose and joined him, whilst we remained where we were. All this happened about sunset. An old man who was in the court took away the couch as soon as the king rose, but allowed the plate to remain. The king, when he joined the captain, threw himself upon another couch, covered with various stuffs embroidered in gold, and asked the captain what he wanted.

And the captain told him he was the ambassador of a King of Portugal, who was Lord of many countries and the possessor of great wealth of every description, exceeding that of any king of these parts; that for a period of sixty years his ancestors had annually sent out vessels to make discoveries in the direction of India, as they knew that there were Christian kings there like themselves. This, he said, was the reason which induced them to order this country to be discovered, not because they sought for gold or silver, for of this they had such abundance that they needed not what was to be found in this country. He further stated that the captains sent out travelled for a year or two, until their provisions were exhausted, and then returned to Portugal, without having succeeded in making the desired discovery. There reigned a king now whose name was Dom Manuel, who had ordered him to build three vessels, of which he had been appointed captain-major, and who had ordered him not to return to Portugal until he should have discovered this King of the Christians, on pain of having his head cut off. That two letters had been intrusted to him to be presented in case he succeeded in discovering him, and that he would do so on the ensuing day; and, finally, he had been instructed to say by word of mouth that he [the King of Portugal] desired to be his friend and brother.

In reply to this the king said that he was welcome; that, on his part, he held him as a friend and brother, and would send ambassadors with him to Portugal. This latter had been asked as a favour, the captain pretending that he would not dare to present himself before his king and master unless he was able to present, at the same time, some men of this country.

These and many other things passed between the two in this chamber, and as it was already late in the night, the king asked the captain with whom he desired to lodge, with Christians or with Moors? And the captain replied, neither with Christians nor with Moors, and begged as a favour that he be given a lodging by himself. The king said he would order it thus, upon which the captain took leave of the king and came to where we were, that is, to a veranda lit up by a huge candlestick. By that time four hours of the night had already gone. . . .

Presents for the King

On Tuesday [May 29] the captain got ready the following things to be sent to the king, viz., twelve pieces of *lambel*, four scarlet hoods, six hats, four strings of coral, a case containing six wash-hand basins, a case of sugar, two casks of oil, and two of honey. And as it is the custom not to send anything to the king without the knowledge of the Moor, his factor, and of the *bale*, the captain informed them of his intention. They came, and when they saw the present they laughed at it, saying that it was not a thing to offer to a king, that the poorest merchant from Mecca, or any other part of India, gave more, and that if he wanted to make a present it should be in gold, as the king would not accept such things. When the captain heard this he grew sad, and said that he had brought no gold, that, moreover, he was no merchant, but an ambassador; that he gave of that which he had, which was his own [private gift] and not the king's; that if the King of Portugal ordered him to return he would intrust him with far richer presents; and that if King Camolim would not accept these things he would send them back to the ships. Upon this they declared that they would not forward his presents, nor consent to his forwarding them himself. When they had gone there came certain Moorish merchants, and they all depreciated the present which the captain desired to be sent to the king.

When the captain saw that they were determined not to forward his present, he said, that as they would not allow him to send his present to the palace he would go to speak to the king, and would then return to the ships. They approved of this, and told him that if he would wait a short time they would return and accompany him to the palace. And the captain waited all day, but they never came back. The captain was very wroth at being among so phlegmatic and unreliable a people, and intended, at first, to go to the palace without them. On further consideration, however, he thought it best to wait until the following day. As to us others, we diverted ourselves, singing and dancing to the sound of trumpets, and enjoyed ourselves much.

A Second Audience, May 30

On Wednesday morning the Moors returned, and took the captain to the palace, and us others with him. The palace was crowded with armed men. Our captain was kept waiting with his conductors for fully four long hours, outside a door, which was only opened when the king sent word to admit him, attended by two men only, whom he might select. The captain said that he desired to have Fernnão Martins with him, who could interpret, and his secretary. It seemed to him, as it did to us, that this separation portended no good.

When he had entered, the king said that he had expected him on Tuesday. The captain said that the long road had tired him, and that for this reason he had not come to see him. The king then said that he had told him that he came from a very rich kingdom, and yet had brought him nothing; that he had also told him that he was the bearer of a letter, which had not yet been delivered. To this the captain rejoined that he had brought nothing, because the object of his voyage was merely to make discoveries, but that when other ships came he would then see what they brought him; as to the letter, it was true that he had brought one, and would deliver it immediately.

The king then asked what it was he had come to discover: stones or men? If he came to discover men, as he said, why had he brought nothing? Moreover, he had been told that he carried with him the golden image of a Santa Maria. The captain said that the Santa Maria was not of gold, and that even if she were he would not part with her, as she had guided him across the ocean, and would guide him back to his own country. The king then asked for the letter. The captain said that he begged as a favour, that as the Moors wished him ill and might misinterpret him, a Christian able to speak Arabic should be sent for. The king said this was well, and at once sent for a young man, of small stature, whose name was Quaram. The captain then said that he had two letters, one written in his own language and the other in that of the Moors; that he was able to read the former, and knew that it contained nothing but what would prove acceptable; but that as to the other he was unable to read it, and it might be good, or contain something that was erroneous. As the Christian was unable to *read* Moorish, four Moors took the letter and read it between them, after which they translated it to the king, who was well satisfied with its contents.

The king then asked what kind of merchandise was to be found in his country. The captain said there was much corn, cloth, iron, bronze, and many other things. The king asked whether he had any merchandise with him. The captain replied that he had a little of each sort, as samples, and that if permitted to return to the ships he would order it to be landed, and that meantime four or five men would remain at the lodgings assigned them. The king said no! He might take all his people with him, securely moor his ships, land his merchandise, and sell it to the best advantage. Having taken leave of the king the captain returned to his lodgings, and we with him. As it was already late no attempt was made to depart that night.

■ ■ ■

STUDY QUESTIONS

1. What type of attitudes did the late fifteenth-century Portuguese have toward foreigners and people of different religions?

2. What was the political and religious situation of the Indian subcontinent at the time of the first voyage of Vasco da Gama, especially those states involved in the spice trade?

3. How did the Portuguese perceive Hindu religion, and what specific misconceptions did they have concerning it?

4. Describe the meetings between Vasco da Gama and the Zamorin (king) of Calecut. How did they react toward each other? What was the tone of their meetings? Was the Zamorin hospitable?

5. How did the local government officials and populace of Calecut react to the Portuguese? Did the Hindus and the Moslems react differently?

BIBLIOGRAPHY

The story of Portugal's great age of discovery is given an up-to-date scholarly narrative by Bailey W. Diffie and George D. Winius, *Foundations of the Portuguese Empire, 1415–1580* (1977). Also see the classic C. R. Boxer, *The Portuguese Seaborne Empire: 1415–1825* (1963). Portuguese activities in India are studied in a volume of *The New Cambridge History of India*, M. N. Pearson's *The Portuguese in India* (1987). More information on the historical background of India can be found in the one-volume survey by Stanley A. Wolpert, *A New History of India* (1977). Donald F. Lach, *Asia in the Making of Europe*, 2 vols. (1965), is a detailed and fascinating study of the impact of increased Asian contacts on European society during and after the sixteenth century. The influence of the Prester John tales is studied in L. N. Gumilev, *Searches for an Imaginary Kingdom: The Legend of Prester John* (1988). A detailed narrative of Vasco da Gama's first voyage is provided by Elaine Sanceau, *Good Hope, the Voyage of Vasco da Gama* (1967). Armando Cortesao, *The Mystery of Vasco da Gama* (1972) is a controversial interpretation of Portuguese explorations that postulates the existence of secret voyages to the South Atlantic and Indian Ocean.

23. THE POPULAR IMAGE OF IVAN THE TERRIBLE

Maureen Perrie

Ivan IV, known as the Terrible (1530–1584) is one of the most notorious rulers in history. For English speakers, even his nickname, "Terrible," demands attention. The Russian word *Groznyi* from which it is derived is actually more accurately translated as "dread" or "awesome." Be that as it may, the English merchants trading and living in Moscow during Ivan Groznyi's reign would not have objected to the label of "Terrible."

Russia was a vast and potentially powerful realm, but it was also prone to anarchy and surrounded by dangerous enemies. Ivan the Terrible's troubled reign began when he, as a very young child, became Grand Prince of Muscovy in 1533. During his teens, he assumed the title of Tsar of Russia in 1547. *Boyars* (noblemen) and *voyevods* (princes) throughout Russia wanted a weak ruler. Instead, Ivan IV proved to be strong. From 1547 to 1563, he continued to build up the powers of the centralized Russian state in the same manner as had his father Vasily III (1505–1533) and his grandfather Ivan III (1462–1505). This process included setting limitations on or abolishing various *boyar* prerogatives such as the abolition of the *kormleniye*. This traditional practice gave *boyar* administrators the right to assess the territories under their control for their living expenses. It was a much abused privilege that the peasantry deeply resented.

Policies of this sort soon aroused resistance from the *boyars* in the form of plots and foreign intrigues. In reaction, Ivan IV became increasingly frustrated, bitter, and angry. Eventually, this short-tempered man became truly terrible. From 1564 to 1584, he assumed increasingly despotic powers. Creating the *Oprichnina*, a state separate from the rest of Russia and under his unlimited control, Ivan also became irresistible in his power. All Russia suffered from his wrath and the plunderings of his *oprichniky*, Ivan IV's personal guard and police. But despite these actions, the common people loved him and thought he was a good tsar. With Ivan arose the peasants' long tradition—which indeed endured until 1905—of viewing their tsar as a protector and loving father-figure, despite evidence to the contrary. Maureen Perrie argues in her essay that this virtually unshakable faith in the goodness of their tsars did not develop by chance. Rather, Ivan tailored his actions and justified his policies in ways designed to please his common subjects. This sixteenth-century autocrat courted public opinion in a most modern way.

It is a curious paradox that Ivan the Terrible, whose name in written history is synonymous with arbitrary cruelty and despotism, should be the first historical figure to feature as a "good" tsar in Russian folklore. The folklore tradition that identified certain tsars as popular heroes, the champions of the people against their social oppressors, the landowners and officials, was an aspect of the "monarchist" political outlook of the Russian people, which survived, in one form or another, at least until the revolution of 1905. The object of this article is to explore the origins of the popular image of the tsar and to put forward an explanation for its emergence.

Interesting evidence of a positive popular image of Ivan IV in the seventeenth century is provided by the tales that were collected and published in 1671 by Dr Samuel Collins, the Englishman who was court physician to Tsar Aleksey Mikhaylovich in the 1660s. Chapter 12 of Collins's book is devoted entirely to Ivan IV, and contains a number of tales about the tsar that were evidently current in Moscow in the mid-seventeenth century. Some of these are simply anecdotes with little more than curiosity value, but others are designed to illustrate his general statement that "The people loved him [Ivan] very well, for he treated them kingly, but chastised his boyars." These tales, which I shall number (1) to (5) for ease of reference, are as follows:

(1) He had a staff with a very sharp spike in the end thereof, which in the discourse he would strike through his boyars' feet, and if they could bear it without any flinching, he would highly prefer them.

(2) Another vayod [voyevoda][1] Prince had taken a goose for a bribe stuffed full of ducats,

and being complained of, he took no notice of him, till one day passing through the Poshiarr [Pozhar] (an open place like Smithfield, where execution was used to be done) he commanded the hangman to cut off his arms and his legs; and at every blow the hangman asked him whether goose was good meat.

(3) When Ivan went his progress, many of the commons as well as gentry presented him with fine presents. A good honest bast-shoemaker, who made shoes of bast for a copeak [kopeyka] a pair, consults with his wife what to present his Majesty. Says she, a pair of fine lopkyes [lapotki], or shoes of bast. That is no rarity, quoth he; but we have a huge great turnip in the garden, we'll give him that, and a pair of lopkyes also. Thus they did; and the Emperor took the present so kindly, that he made all his nobility buy lopkyes of the fellow at five shillings a pair, and he wore one pair himself. This put the man in stock, whereby he began to drive a trade, and in time grew so considerable, that he left a great estate behind him. . . . A gentleman seeing him so well paid for his turnip, made account by the rule of proportion to get a great reward for a brave horse; but the Emperor, suspecting his design, gave him nothing but the great turnip, for which he was both abashed and laughed at.

(4) Ivan in a disguise sought a lodging in a village nigh the city. None would let him in but a poor man whose wife was then in travail, and delivered whilst he was there. Away he went before day, and told the man he would bring him some godfathers next day. Accordingly he and many of his nobility came and gave the poor fellow a good largess, and burned all the houses in the village but his, exhorting them to charity, and telling them, because they refused to admit strangers into their houses, they should be forced so seek their fortunes, and try how good it was to lie out of doors in the winter.

(5) Sometimes he would associate with thieves in a disguise, and once he advised them to rob the Exchequer; for (says he) I know the way to it,

The Popular Image of Ivan the Terrible" by Maureen Perrie, *Slavonic and East European Review*, pp. 275–286. Copyright © 1978 University of London (School of Slavonic and East European Studies). Reprinted by permission.

___
[1]Prince.

but one of the fellows up with his fist, and struck him a hearty good blow on the face, saying, Thou rogue, wilt thou offer to rob his Majesty who is so good to us; let us go rob such a rich boyar who has cozened his Majesty of vast sums. At this Ivan was well pleased, and at parting changed caps with the fellow, and bid him meet him next morning in the dvaretz [dvorets] (a place in the court where the Emperor used often to pass by) and there (said he) I will bring thee to a good cup of aqua-vitae and mead. The thief came accordingly, and being discovered by his Majesty, was called up, admonished to steal no more, preferred in court, and served for a discoverer of thieves.

In these tales, Ivan appears as the dispenser of rough justice to his subjects. The villains are the boyars and *voyevody*—they are acquisitive, take bribes, and cheat the treasury; the representatives of the common people, on the other hand, are good, honest, generous, and charitable. The tsar deals with these groups according to their deserts: the popular heroes (the bast-shoemaker, the poor father, the loyal thief) are rewarded by the tsar with ''preferment,'' whereas the villains are cruelly punished. The sociopolitical content of Collins's tales, with their depiction of the interrelationships of the tsar, the boyars and the common people, is very similar to that of the folklore which we know from the later Russian records. It is clear, therefore, that the image of Ivan as a ''good'' tsar had developed within a century of his death, and that his image had already attracted some universal folklore themes associated with popular monarchy (such as numbers 3, 4, and 5).

These tales collected by Collins are the earliest recorded evidence of the image of Ivan IV as a just, ''popular'' tsar that appears in the numerous cycles of historical songs and legends of which the earliest recorded Russian versions date only from the late eighteenth century. But Collins's tales are evidence only of the existence of such an image in the seventeenth century. The question of the popular image of the tsar in the sixteenth century is a separate issue that must be examined separately.

There is considerable debate among folklorists as to how far the historical songs and legends about Ivan IV can be considered to reflect popular sixteenth-century attitudes towards the tsar, rather than a retrospective idealization. We know that some songs about the Time of Troubles are of contemporary composition, and we know that songs about Ivan IV existed in his lifetime; but we cannot be sure that the songs relating to the capture of Kazan' and Astrakhan' which we know in versions dating from the eighteenth century were those that the tsar sang at the wedding of Mariya Vladimirovna to the Danish Prince Magnus in 1573. Stief in fact considers it inherently improbable that the eighteenth-century versions of these songs, in which the hero is not the tsar but a young gunner, and the image presented of the tsar is rather an unflattering one, could have been the eulogies and paeans to which writers such as Olearius referred.

A major obstacle to our acceptance of the positive folklore image of Ivan as that of contemporaries is its sharp contrast with the negative image of Ivan as a cruel and bloodthirsty tyrant that is presented by Western and Russian contemporaries. These, admittedly, were not ''popular'' images, although they can be found in some regional versions of the folklore. But they also tally with what we know from independent historical evidence of the plight of the lower classes in Russian society during Ivan's reign. if the contemporary popular image of Ivan was indeed a positive one, it can hardly have been a true reflection of reality. It is probably for this reason that some scholars are reluctant to accept the ''just tsar'' image of Ivan as that of contemporaries but consider it to be a retrospective view, perhaps from the standpoint of the political and social chaos that followed the end of the dynasty with the death of Tsar Feodor Ivanovich in

■■ *Ivan the Terrible at worship with his boyars.*

1598. Thus the Soviet scholar Chistov argues that it was necessary for two or three decades to have elapsed since the horrors of the *oprichnina* before a positive image could have been created of Dimitry as Ivan's son and hence the natural continuer of his struggle against the boyars. A similar view was put forward by the Englishman Samuel Purchas. Writing in a work first published in 1625, with a knowledge of the Time of Troubles, Purchas put forward three explanations for the existence of a positive image of Ivan, in spite of his cruelties:

Yea, his memory is savoury still to the Russians, which (either of their servile disposition needing such a bridle and whip, or for his long and prosperous reign, or out of distaste for later tragedies) hold him in little less reputation (as some have out of their experience instructed me) than a saint.

Of the Soviet scholars who believe that the later folklore image does accurately reflect contemporary sixteenth-century attitudes towards Ivan, V. K. Sokolova has put forward the most persuasive case. She argues that Ivan's struggle against the boyars created his popular image as a just and ideal tsar:

For the broad masses the boyars were their fundamental class enemies, their direct oppressors, and therefore the Tsar, who restricted the arbitrary powers of the feudal lords and cruelly punished them, was perceived as the ally and defender of the people.

Elsewhere Sokolova cites as evidence of a contemporary popular image of Ivan the chronicle account of the introduction of the *oprichnina*, in which the merchants and citizens of Moscow responded to Ivan's threatened abdication by begging him "not to leave the country and abandon them to be ravened by the wolves, but to deliver them from the hands of the mighty." Sokolova notes, however, that this popular image of Ivan was essentially illusory, because his policies were directed at least as much against the interests of the masses as against those of the boyars. While I am basically in agreement with Sokolova's approach to the problem, I believe that there is also another element, previously unremarked by historians, which may have contributed to the formation of a positive popular image of Ivan IV. There is some evidence to suggest that Ivan himself sought to project an image of the tsar as the ally of the people against their social oppressors, the "traitor-boyars."

The first piece of evidence comes from the chronicle passage previously cited, concerning the introduction of the *oprichnina*. In December 1564 Ivan, together with his family and courtiers and a vast hoard of the royal treasure, left Moscow, providing no explanation of his unprecedented departure. A month later, on 3 January 1565, he sent two messages from Aleksandrova Sloboda to the Metropolitan Afanasy in Moscow, announcing his decision to abdicate because of the treason of the boyars, *voyevody*, and officials. The significance of these messages lies not only in the fact that the first accused the boyars, all the upper military and civil service classes and the ecclesiastical hierarchy, of treason, whereas the second message specifically excluded the "*gosti* and merchants and all the Orthodox Christians of the city of Moscow" from his anger and dis-

favour, but also in the definitions of treason that the first message provides. Ivan accused his boyars of both "external" and "internal" treason. The external treason consisted in their intrigues with the tsar's enemies, the Tatars, Lithuanians and Germans; the internal treason, significantly, consisted not only in their expropriation of state revenue and lands during Ivan's minority, but also in offences against the people: they "caused much harm to the people, . . . they did not care for all the Orthodox Christians, . . . but they subjected the people to violence. . . . " Ivan was here clearly bidding for the support of the citizens against the boyars, and in their reply the Muscovites not only called upon the tsar to defend them against "the wolves" and "the mighty," but also offered to help him to destroy their common enemies: "and as for the evil-doers and traitors to the tsar, we will not support them, and will ourselves destroy them."

Nor, despite the exceptional circumstances of the abdication crisis, was this a unique instance of Ivan's use of demagogic appeals to the populace to gain support for his campaign against the boyars. In this context, it is instructive to note that Ivan's message of January 1565 includes a reference to the *kormleniye* system as an example of the abuses of the people perpetrated by the boyars. Ivan's *gramoty*[2] of 1555 that abolished the *kormleniye* system had referred specifically to such abuses as a major motive for the reform: the many complaints of the people against the arbitrary rule of the *kormlenshchiki*, Ivan said, had led him to abolish the system, "since we had pity on the peasants for the great damages and losses they had suffered." Even the vocabulary of the 1565 message is an echo of the *gramoty* of 1555 (*lyudem mnogiye ubytki delali; chinyat im prodazhi i ubytki velikiye*). The reference to *kormleniye* in his message of January 1565 may be seen as evidence that Ivan was seeking to present the introduction of the *oprichnina* as a continuation

---

[2] Decree.

of the policy of curtailing the power of the boyars which had begun in the earlier reform period. Whatever the real aim of his policies, he was at least trying to win the support of the common people for his reforms, by claiming that he had their interests at heart. And the response of the citizens of Moscow to Ivan's threatened abdication suggests that he was on the whole successful in his projection of this image.

Another piece of evidence concerning Ivan's use of demagogic devices to gain popular support for his policies can be found in Giles Fletcher's *Of the Russe Commonwealth*. In this account, Fletcher describes how the tsars increased their revenues:

To prevent no extortions, exactions, or briberies whatsoever, done upon the commons by their dukes, diacks [d'yaki] or other officers in their provinces: but to suffer them to go on until their time be expired, and to suck themselves full. Then to call them to the pravevsh [pravezh] (or whip) for their behaviour, and to beat out of them all, or the most part of the booty (as the honey from the bee), which they have wrung from the commons, and to turn it into the Emperor's treasury, but never anything back again to the right owners, how great or evident soever the injury be.

Fletcher continues his list of the ''means used to draw the wealth of the land into the Emperor's treasury'':

To make of these officers (that have robbed their people) sometimes a public example, if any be more notorious than the rest: that the Emperor may seem to mislike the oppression done to his people and transfer the fault to his ill officers.

As among divers others, was done by the late Emperor Ivan Vasilowich [Vasil'yevich] to a diack in one of his provinces: that (besides many other extortions and briberies) had taken a goose ready dressed full of money. The man was brought to the market place in Moscow. The Emperor himself present made an oration. These good people are they that would eat you up like bread, etc.

Then asked he his polachies [palachi] or executioners, who could cut up a goose, and commanded one of them first to cut off his legs about the midst of the shin, then his arms above his elbows (asking him still if goose flesh were good meat), in the end to chop off his head: that he might have the right fashion of a goose ready dressed. This might seem to have been a tolerable piece of justice (as justice goeth in Russia) except his subtle end to cover his own oppressions.

This anecdote is of interest for several reasons. Firstly, Fletcher's view of Ivan's cynical use of ''demagogic'' or ''populist'' devices to gain popular support for measures that were ultimately in the interests of the state rather than the common people corresponds closely to the most recent interpretations of Ivan's reforms by Soviet historians. Secondly, the tale of the ''golden goose,'' which Fletcher uses to illustrate his view, is identical to the anecdote related by Collins (no. 2 above) nearly a century later, as part of his collection of tales about Ivan IV as a ''just tsar.'' Thus Fletcher's recording of this tale provides a link between the seventeenth-century source and the sixteenth-century reality it purports to depict. And finally, it is interesting to note that the earliest manuscript version of Fletcher's work identifies the ''diack'' in the tale of the ''golden goose'' as I. M. Viskovaty; and indeed, even without this evidence, the peculiarly gruesome method of execution—even by Ivan's standards—recalls the accounts of Viskovaty's execution in 1570 provided by foreign contemporaries such as Schlichting. However, it is equally clear from these sources that Viskovaty was executed, not for extortion and bribetaking, as Fletcher suggests, but on charges of treasonous links with foreign monarchs. If we can take Fletcher's tale as the reflection of a belief current in Moscow in the late 1580s that Viskovaty (and possibly also other high-ranking victims of the *oprichnina* terror) had been executed not for external treason, but for their exploitation of the people, this would be further evidence of the success of Ivan's attempt to present his campaign against the boyars as a crusade against oppression in which the tsar was the defender of the interests of the common people.

It may be objected at this point that such evidence as has been adduced so far relates mainly to the formation of the "just tsar" image among the townspeople, and even there among the upper and middle strata—the merchants and craftsmen—whereas by the Time of Troubles "popular monarchism," in the form of support for pretenders, was most evident among the lower orders—the slaves (*kholopy*), peasants, and Cossacks. It is of course possible that these middle strata acted as intermediaries between the tsar and the lower classes, and thus channeled their view of the monarchy downward. But there was a common practice in late sixteenth-century Russia which may have encouraged even the humblest classes to view the tsar as their ally against their social enemies. This was the practice of political denunciations of superiors by inferiors, a practice which was officially encouraged by successive tsars. Indeed, the offer by the citizens of Moscow in January 1565 to destroy traitors to the tsar may have been an oblique reference to denunciations.

Both Horsey and Fletcher mention denunciations for treason as a device employed by Ivan in his campaign against the boyars. Horsey states that Ivan

still did discover their plots and treasons, by ennobling and countenancing all the rascalliest and desperate soldiers he could pick out, to affront the chief nobility.

And Fletcher tells us that in his attempts to weaken the old aristocracy, Ivan

used to set on the inferiors, to prefer or equal themselves to those that were accounted to be of the nobler houses. Where he made his advantage of their malice and contentions, the one against the other, by receiving devised matter, and accusations of secret practice and conspiracies to be intended against his person, and state.

The practice of slaves making political denunciations against their masters, presumably in the hope of personal gain, was apparently quite widespread in Ivan's reign. It was abolished only in 1582, in response to a petition to the tsar from two of his boyars, by an act that the Soviet historian Skrynnikov interprets as a symptom of a tempering of the terror, and the partial rehabilitation of the victims of the *oprichnina* in the period of remorse in Ivan's last years, following his murder of his heir, the Tsarevich Ivan Ivanovich.

The practice of encouraging slaves to denounce their masters for treason was revived by Boris Godunov in the early years of Feodor's reign, as a device to aid him in the power struggle against the rival aristocratic families. The chronicle tells us that in 1586 Boris incited the slaves (*lyudi*) of the Shuysky family to denounce their masters. Boris resorted to this device again in the opening years of his own reign, the objects of political denunciations by their slaves at this time including the Romanovs. The slaves who made such denunciations were generously rewarded by the tsar for their loyalty. One Voika, the slave (*chelovek*) of Prince Fyodor Sherstunov, was granted a *pomest'ye* for his services, and promoted to the rank of an urban *syn boyarskiy*. The promise of similar rewards, according to the chronicle, inspired whole groups of five or six men to conspire together to accuse their masters of treason and to bear false witness against them. Slaves who refused to denounce their masters were tortured and punished, whereas the accusers were, like Voika, rewarded, some with *pomest'ya*, and some with money payments.

Thus we have clear evidence that in the second half of the sixteenth century it was already well established practice that the tsar should seek to exploit in his own political interest conflicts between individual slaves and their masters. Such campaigns of denunciation probably reinforced in the minds of the lower classes the identification of their social enemies as the political enemies of the tsar. Of course, it was dangerous and ultimately counter-productive for the tsars to create such an idea, as the Time of Troubles was to demonstrate. It was only a short step from the idea of the "traitor-boyars" to the idea of the "false tsar"; and Boris Godunov's rewarding of Voika with an estate for denouncing his master as a traitor was equally close to Bolotnikov's promises of *boyarstvo* to the slaves in Moscow who rose against their masters who had betrayed "Tsar Dimitry."

But if popular monarchism could be such an ambivalent phenomenon, why should Ivan IV have sought to promote this ideology? The short answer may be that he simply did not realize the dangers. But, at a deeper level, his policy of centralization of the power of the state obliged him to seek political support from social groups other than the traditional ruling class. Although the absolutist state that was the eventual outcome of policies initiated by Ivan was if anything more oppressive of the masses than the older Muscovite state, its relative independence from the class of serf-owners enabled subsequent tsars to continue to pose as defenders of the people against exploitation, and thus to reinforce the "tsarist illusions" of the Russian peasantry.

The folklore image of Ivan IV as a good tsar is part of the broader phenomenon of "popular monarchism" in Russian history. "Popular monarchism," of course, was not an exclusively Russian phenomenon, but has many parallels in other countries. Insofar as it is a universal phenomenon, popular monarchism may be based in part upon the patriarchalism of precapitalist society, and of the peasantry in particular, and reinforced by religious ideas, such as those of medieval Christianity, which stress the quasi-sacerdotal nature of the ruler and his secular role as a supra-class arbiter and dispenser of justice. Yet it seems that certain concrete historical situations are more conducive than others to manifestations of popular monarchism. One such situation may be the formation in the late medieval period of a centralized state with a degree of autonomy from the upper classes. In the reign of Ivan IV, the consolidation of the centralized state was accompanied by the tsar's savage persecution of those of his boyars whom he accused, apparently arbitrarily, of treason. This article has attempted to demonstrate that the popular image of Ivan as a "just tsar" was not only formed on the basis of a passive interpretation by the people of Ivan's struggle with the boyars, but that Ivan himself sought to create such an image by populist devices and appeals to the people for support. To use the terminology of the Soviet historians, the "tsarist illusions" of the people corresponded to the "social demagogy" of the tsar. The two were mutually reinforcing, and their interaction may help to explain the peculiar strength of popular monarchist ideas in Russian history.

■ ■ ■

STUDY QUESTIONS

1. What was the "popular image" of Ivan the Terrible that was already well established in Russian peasant folklore by the middle of the seventeenth century?

2. Was the "popular image" of Ivan the Terrible an accurate reflection of his policies as tsar? Why or why not?

3. What sorts of actions and policies did Ivan the Terrible use to secure the good will of the common people of Russia?

4. How did the system of denunciations by inferiors against their superiors operate in sixteenth-century Russia? Was it an important tool of Ivan the Terrible's government and did any other Russian rulers use it?

5. What was the phenomenon of "popular monarchism"? How did it function in tsarist Russia and was it unique to that society?

BIBLIOGRAPHY

A good overview of the events leading up to Ivan the Terrible's reign and those immediately following it is provided by Robert O. Crummey, *The Formation of Muscovy: 1304–1613* (1987). Benson Bobrick, *Fearful Majesty: The Life and Reign of Ivan the Terrible* (1987), is a recent and very readable biography. For a short study that sets Ivan the Terrible in a European context, see Michael Cherniavsky, "Ivan the Terrible as Renaissance Prince," *Slavic Review* 27 (1968): 195–211. The reaction of the English merchants to the policies of Ivan the Terrible is studied in Samuel H. Baron, "Ivan the Terrible, Giles Fletcher, and the Muscovite Merchants," *Slavonic and East European Review* 56 (1978): 563–585. *Rude and Barbarous Kingdom*, edited by Lloyd E. Berry and Robert O. Crummey (1958), prints the relevant firsthand accounts of the English community. Ivan the Terrible's popular image as a "good tsar" is given detailed study in Maureen Perrie, *The Image of Ivan the Terrible in Russian Folklore* (1987). The history of Russian "popular monarchism" after Ivan the Terrible is traced by Daniel Field, *Rebels in the Name of the Tsar* (1976).